Capitalism at War
Industrial Policy and Bureaucracy in France 1914–1918

Capitalism at War
Industrial Policy and Bureaucracy in France
1914–1918

JOHN F. GODFREY

With a Foreword by JAY WINTER

BERG
Leamington Spa/Hamburg/New York
Distributed exclusively in the US and Canada by
St. Martin's Press, New York

Published in 1987 by
Berg Publishers Limited
24 Binswood Avenue, Leamington Spa, CV32 5SQ, UK
Schenefelder Landstr. 14K, 2000 Hamburg 55, W.-Germany
175 Fifth Avenue/Room 400, New York, NY 10010, USA

© John F. Godfrey 1987

British Library Cataloguing in Publication Data

Godfrey, John F.
Capitalism at War:
Industrial policy and bureaucracy in France
1914–1918.
1. Industry and state—France—History—
20th century 2. World War, 1914–1918—
Economic aspects—France
I. Title
338.944   HD3616.F83

ISBN 0–85496–519–X

Library of Congress Cataloging-in-Publication Data

Godfrey, John F.
Capitalism at war.

Bibliograpy: p.
Includes index.
1. Industry and state—France—History.
2. Bureaucracy—France—History. 3. France—Economic
conditions—20th century. 4. France—Politics and
government—1914–1940. 5. Government business
enterprises—France—History. I. Title.
HD3616.F82G63 1987   338.944   86–32708
ISBN 0–85496–519–X

Printed in Great Britain by Billings of Worcester

Contents

Foreword

The political economy of war in the twentieth century is a central theme in European history. It is surprising, therefore, that relatively few studies have appeared which reconstruct the unique and unplanned experiment in state capitalism which took place during the 1914–1918 conflict. The only full treatment of this theme available until now has been Gerald Feldman's magisterial *Army, Industry and Labour in Germany 1914–1918*. This essential work has stood in majestic isolation in the two decades since its appearance. No similar guide to the political economy of any other major combatant country exists.

The gap filled by John Godfrey's book is, therefore, a yawning one, even if, as he explains in his Preface, there are a few other recent studies which try to tackle the relationship between state and society under the impact of total war. However, most of these are concerned either with the European experience as a whole or they focus primarily on the post-war period. Godfrey's contribution is to have provided both a new interpretation of the working of the French war economy, based on previously unexploited archives, and material out of which a comparative history of the economy of total war can now be fashioned.

The story he tells is that at the heart of any explanation of the Allied victory in the 1914–1918 war. There are those who see the American entry into the war as decisive, both in terms of manpower and *matériel*. But the capacity of the Allies to defend the living standards of their populations and to equip mass armies was based as much on internal as on international factors.

Germany's war effort was flawed decisively by the absence of effective political controls over her war economy. As Feldman showed, the imperial bureaucracy was too cumbersome and inefficient to run the war economy, and the Reichstag was too weak and unprepared to act in its place. Consequently, industrialists and the Army ran the show by default.

The results were disastrous. War production was maintained and profits soared; but the costs were passed on to the consumer and to the state, thereby ensuring the worst inflationary spiral in European history, and a subsistence crisis which undermined the regime itself.

The German war economy of the First World War presents one of the earliest and least successful examples of a 'military-industrial complex' in action. What made it so weak was its failure to balance the claims of competing sectors of the economy. Instead a vast free-for-all ensued, in which a supposedly authoritarian state dissolved into a field of force in which competing interest groups grabbed what they could.

The strength of John Godfrey's study is that it helps to explain why this did not happen on the other side. In Britain and France, the history of war administration is largely one of the restriction of the power of employers to take advantage of their unusual market position. It is not that they abjured in principle the idea of making weapons of war at the expense of the state and the consumer alike. It is rather that the political economy of war prevented them from doing so.

How this was achieved is the central theme of this book. It examines critically the development of the consortium system in France under the control of the Minister of Commerce, Etienne Clémentel, as a function of the international character of the Allied war effort. Given the disastrous loss of men, *matériel* and industrial potential suffered by France in the first months of the war, there was no alternative to a growing reliance on British economic support. The British insisted upon the co-ordination of Allied supply policy, and set up international commissions to oversee wheat, coal, credit, and shipping. In effect this structure gave Britain virtual control of the essential supplies required by French industry.

What the Allies were forced to do on the international level, Clémentel succeeded in doing within the French economy. He used the fact of French dependence on Britain to justify his control of supply to individual firms, thereby undermining their autonomy and room for manoeuvre.

This was no mean achievement. The businessmen with whom Clémentel dealt were well-versed in the techniques of political influence, and on occasion their concern over the position of rivals or competitors seemed to eclipse their anxiety over the outcome of the war. As Godfrey shows, the risks Clémentel faced were substantial. But through the consortium system, the essential balance was maintained: production and profits were secured, without undue pressure on prices and thereby on wages. Herein lies one crucial source of the maintenance of living standards in wartime France which, together with similar developments in Britain, were the material foundation of Allied victory in the 1914–1918 war.

J.M. WINTER
Pembroke College
Cambridge

Preface

The argument of this book is structured around a series of power struggles: ministers and bureaucrats against industrialists, ministers against parliament, one industrial firm against another, and politicians against politicians. There is an assumption that the players were rational and aware: they were all consciously playing a game whose rules they knew, even as they were attempting to bend or break them. It is further assumed that most of the players had short-term, definable goals and that they were, with one or two notable exceptions, neither motivated by long-term strategies, nor unconsciously reflecting in their actions vast psychological sea-changes — transformations of 'mentalities'. They were simply playing the game.

Since the text of the book was completed over a decade ago, a number of works have appeared which touch directly or indirectly on the question of state intervention in the French economy during the First World War. It is a relief to report that no one seems either to have filled the gap the book was intended to fill nor substantially refuted its major premises. What has been altered is the historiographical context into which the book must now be fitted. Recent scholarship on the subject can be divided into three categories: (1) comparative studies of other nations; (2) studies of the evolution of economic management in France; (3) studies of European society which emphasise the continuity of capitalism and of bourgeois dominance in modern Europe.

When the book was written, it owed a great deal conceptually to Gerald Feldman's *Army, Industry, and Labour in Germany 1914–1918* and Arthur Marwick's *The Deluge: British Society and the First World War*. Since then, further work by Gerald Feldman[1]

---

1. G. Feldman, *Iron and Steel in the German Inflation, 1916–1923* (Princeton,

and the writings of Kathleen Burk and her associates, particularly in *War and the State: The Transformation of British Government, 1914–1919* (1982) have added considerably to our understanding of the period.

The second new emphasis in recent scholarship has been on the development of economic management in France. Richard Kuisel's valuable *Capitalism and the State in Modern France* (1981) attributes the renovation of the French economy in the first half of the twentieth century to two changes: 'a shift in goals from stability to modernity and the development of economic management'. He sees the First World War as one of the 'catastrophic economic, political, and military events that undermined traditional ways and beliefs'.

Painting on a much larger canvas, William H. McNeill, in his *The Pursuit of Power: Technology, Armed Force and Society Since A.D.1000* (1982) speaks of the First World War as a 'managerial metamorphosis'. This metamorphosis was aided partly by the discipline of war: 'Time-tested customs and institutions became soft and malleable in the hands of rival technocratic elites who made millions into soldiers and other millions into war workers'.[2] Another reason for the completeness of the transformation was that it appeared unplanned. 'Part of the secret of war mobilization was that when it was launched every one thought it would last for only a few months. . . . This disarmed conservatives time and again.'[3] A final factor in the metamorphosis was that it represented not so much a break with the past as the intensification of a trend which had been developing since the end of the nineteenth century.

> Preexisting bureaucracies from private industry, from civil government, and from the armed forces came together to make [supplying the armed forces] possible; but the principles of management — an unobstructed flow-through of appropriately assorted factors of destruction — were the same as those which had evolved since the 1880's by big business firms for managing the production and distribution of goods for private consumption.[4]

The third development in the historiography of the period has been a re-examination of capitalism and the role of the bourgeoisie in twentieth-century Europe. Here, the critical work has been by Charles S. Maier, *Recasting Bourgeois Europe: Stabilization in*

1977)
2. McNeill, *Pursuit*, 317
3. Ibid., 337
4. Ibid., 345

France, Germany, and Italy in the Decade after World War I (1975), although the debate had been broadly joined earlier by a number of European historians.[5] The broad theme of this school of historians can perhaps best be summarised as follows:

> The conception of 'organized capitalism' as developed by the social democratic theorist Rudolf Hilferding (1877–1941), served as a model for comparative analysis of developments which seem to be distinctive of capitalist societies in the period between the economic crash of 1873 and the end of World War I. The general traits . . . are a growing degree of economic concentration and interest group organization, the gradual replacement of individual entrepreneurs by large-scale corporations, and the steadily increasing economic and social activities of government authorities.[6]

Building on this base, Charles Maier carries the story through to the 1920s. Maier stresses the theme of 'middle-class commonality' — the shared characteristics of Western Europe's bourgeoisie, their stability and continuity despite the travails of the Great War.[7] He concentrates on the period after the war and the way in which Europe's middle classes retained power by reorganising the way in which they held it: 'What began to evolve was a political economy that I have chosen to call corporatist. This involved the displacement of power from elected representatives or a career bureaucracy to the major organized forces of European society and economy. . . . In each case corporatism meant the growth of private power and the twilight of sovereignty'.[8]

Since Maier's story really begins at the end of the war, it may be instructive to read this present study of the war itself in the light of his argument. Was the behaviour of industrialists, bureaucrats, and politicians in France during the 1914–1918 War the true origin of this process or was it a temporary aberration, to be corrected by a return to 'normalcy' at the end of the war?

1914 has become a cardinal date in the history of Western Europe. As 1789 ushered in the nineteenth century, so it was the 1914–1918 War which truly ended it. The Great War was a system break, creating or intensifying those conditions which have formed the contemporary world.

Traditionally, European historians have ascribed to the 1914–18

---

5. H. Winckler (ed.), *Organisierter Kapitalismus: Voraussetzungen und Anfänge* (Göttingen, 1974)
6. *Journal of Modern History*, vol. 46, no. 4, December 1974, Abstract 741
7. Maier, *Recasting*, ix
8. Ibid., 9

War a vast range of changes: political, social, economic, psychological, literary, artistic and philosophical, to name the most obvious. Economic historians in particular have written of the great impact of the First World War on the growth of the power of the state over the economy in modern Europe. The modest goal of this book is to explore one aspect of the effect of the 1914–1918 War on one country, France: the unprecedented involvement of the state in the industrial sector of the economy. I hope that future historians may thus better understand the nature of at least one aspect of the vast changes brought about in Europe by the First World War.

John Godfrey
King's College Halifax
Nova Scotia
Canada

CHAPTER 1

Bureaucracy, Industry, and Politics in France Before the First World War

Standard texts on French government in the twentieth century usually make some broad generalisation about the economic consequences of the First World War for the French state: 'The World War of 1914–18 and its economic aftermath gave to this emerging *étatisme* a tremendous impetus which it has not ceased to feel to this present day'.[1] The purpose of this study is to examine one aspect of this process in detail: the intervention of the French state in industry during the First World War. The main body of the book will outline the various forms government interference took in France and how far the process went.

The particular character of the French experiment with state industrial controls can be understood only by examining the activities of three groups of men — bureaucrats, industrialists, and politicians — who were forced to interact with each other under the pressure of war. The story must begin with a description of the three groups of men as they were before 1914. A survey of the pre-war situation of bureaucrats, industrialists, and politicians will give some indication of how prepared or unprepared they were to deal with each other when the war broke out. It is an assumption of this study that the pre-war attitudes, aptitudes, and experiences of each group explain in some measure their actions during the First World War. There must also be a careful definition of which bureaucrats, which industrialists, and which politicians are being talked about, since, in the final analysis, key decisions concerning state control of industry were made by a relatively small number of men.

1. W. Sharp, *The Government of the Third Republic* (New York, 1938), 207.

1

Bureaucrats: the State and Industry

What experience had French civil servants had with industrial matters on the eve of the First World War? Which of these bureaucrats were to be directly concerned with industrial questions during the war, and what sort of qualifications would they bring to the task?

The direct intervention of the French state in industry is by no means a recent phenomenon. The tradition of state ownership of industry dates back to the reign of Louis XIV, on whose behalf Colbert created the workshops of Gobelins, Sèvres, and Beauvais for the manufacture of fine tapestries, porcelain and cabinet work. In addition to these directly-owned *manufactures du roi*, Colbert also created a system of *manufactures royales*, workshops which remained in private hands but were given monopoly status, fiscal privileges, favourable rates for work, and guaranteed government contracts in exchange for being subject to strict government control over the quantity and quality of finished articles.

Several of the state-owned workshops survived the Revolution of 1789, and in the nineteenth century the state added the exclusive manufacture of tobacco in 1811 and matches in 1872 to its industrial portfolio, principally as a means of raising money. As in most countries, the state acquired a postal service, a public mint, a government printing office, and a telegraph and telephone system during the same period.[2]

Another traditional field of industrial activity for the state was the manufacture of weapons, a right first sanctioned by royal edict in 1572. By 1914, a considerable amount of French armament production was carried out in arsenals belonging to the state. Privately owned armament factories employed 12,500 workers, while those of the state employed 38,000.[3] State arsenals had little to do before the war and were often rented out to private industrialists who required temporary factory space. The administration of these institutions was quaint, book-keeping methods were haphazard, and production statistics were kept in such a way that it was frequently impossible to tell what the annual production of shells

---

2. W. Baum, *The French Economy and the State* (Princeton, 1958), 169–72. B. Chenot, *Les Entreprises nationalisées* (Paris, 1956), 9–12. A. Delemer, *Le Bilan de l'étatisme* (Paris, 1922), 3–6. A. Piettre, *Economie dirigée d'hier et d'aujourd'hui du colbertisme a notre temps* (Paris, 1947), 9–55. M. Ventenat, *L'Expérience des nationalisations* (Paris, 1947), 63–6.
3. W. Oualid, C. Picquenard, *La Guerre et le travail* (Paris, 1928), 45.

had been.[4] The administration of these arsenals came under the jurisdiction of the Ministry of War.

Such, then, with the exception of railways, was the sum total of the French state's direct ownership of industry before 1914. A few observations are in order. First, it should be stressed that this traditional industrial activity of the state was restricted to artistic workshops, fiscal monopolies, and certain public and military services, none of which was intended to compete with private enterprise. This *de facto* state control should not be confused with the theories of state control of industry and state socialism which sprang up in the nineteenth century.[5] The former was simply an unconnected series of practical solutions to particular problems, the latter an ideology of interference. Proposals for the state to take over existing private industries such as railways, alcohol, and petrol provoked sharp political controversies, unlike the continuation of the old monopolies, which were accepted as part of the traditional order of things. The purchase by the state of a railway company, the Western, in 1908, is an example of the state taking over an industry for reasons of doctrine as much as practicality. The political controversy surrounding that decision will be discussed later in this chapter. Secondly, it is apparent from the kinds of traditional industrial activity in which the state engaged that the bureaucrats who were connected with these enterprises (with the exception of the arsenals) would have little to contribute to the creation of a wartime industry. In short, the civil servants who administered the Gobelins workshop or the match factories were not those who would be extending the control of the state over private industry during the war.

Apart from such direct participation in industry, the state also had some regulatory authority over private industry before the war. The most obvious agent of this limited involvement was the Ministry of Commerce and Industry. The Ministry of Commerce and Industry was one of the economic ministries which, along with the Ministries of Public Works and Agriculture, had been shed by the Ministry of the Interior during the nineteenth century.[6] The Ministry was concerned to a large degree with exports and imports: the

4. C.J. Gignoux, *L'Arsenal de Roanne et l'état industriel de guerre* (Roanne, 1920), 16.
5. P. Naville, *L'Etat entrepreneur. Le cas de Renault* (Paris, 1971), 10–11.
6. W. Sharp, *The French Civil Service: Bureaucracy in Transition* (New York, 1931), 10. B. Chenot, *Organisation économique de l'état* (Paris, 1951), 45–6. F. Ridley, J. Blondel, *Public Administration in France* (London 1964), 214–15.

promotion of French exports abroad and the protection of domestic industries from foreign imports. Its interests were for the most part concentrated outside France; commercial attachés on its behalf negotiated trade agreements and provided information services in foreign lands. Generally these officials were attached not to the Ministry of Commerce but to the Ministry of Foreign Affairs, to whom they reported first on subjects as diverse as maritime movement in the Republic of Salvador, or the commercial prospects of trade with the island of Andros.[7] The Ministry's authority within France hardly extended inwards from the customs posts on the frontiers: it supervised chambers of commerce, provided a weights and measures service, was responsible for technical education, distributed decorations to deserving businessmen, and organised trade fairs. In no way did the Ministry assume any direct economic role or control economic activity within France before 1914. Nor was it considered that the Ministry might be called upon to direct French industrial activity in wartime, unlike Germany, where a study was prepared in 1913 by the Ministry of Commerce about the industrial implications for the German state of a future European war.[8]

One other area in which the Ministry of Commerce was indirectly involved with private industry before the First World War was in the formulation of social legislation. Laws regulating the use of women and children in factories in 1892, health and security legislation for workers in 1893, compulsory insurance for miners, accident insurance for workers in 1899, and limitations of hours of work and minimum wage scales for workers working on government contracts in 1899 generally came under the aegis of the Ministry of Commerce, until the creation of the Ministry of Labour in 1906.[9] Social reforms such as these represented a new form of state intervention and challenged traditional ideas about the sanctity of private property and the rights of individual industrialists to govern their own affairs. This form of intervention was of little significance during the war, however, since social legislation in general and factory legislation in particular took a decided step backwards as industrialists were encouraged by the government to ignore safety regulations and produce more war materials in any way possible.

To complete this survey of points of contact between ministries

---

7. Ministère du Commerce, *Bulletin consulaire français* (Paris, 1886).
8. P. Renouvin, *La Crise européenne et la Première Guerre Mondiale* (5th edn., Paris, 1969), 283.
9. C. Pipkin, *Social Politics and Modern Democracies* (New York, 1931), ii.

of the state and private industry in France before 1914, the Ministry of Public Works should be mentioned since it was responsible for enforcing the mining code and the laws relating to electricity and petroleum.[10] As well, reference should be made to the Ministry of Justice, since it was responsible for the enforcement of a series of laws relating to the incorporation and organisation of industries and businesses in France, such as the law of 1864 governing professional organisations, the law of association of 1884, and the prohibition of monopolistic activities under Article 419 of the Penal Code.

Hence, by 1914 the French state had become both directly and indirectly involved with industry. The state owned and operated a number of industries, ranging from tapestries to matches, and arsenals to railways. In addition, bureaucrats of the Ministry of Commerce, Justice, Public Works, and Labour all had some experience in dealing with private industry in 1914, whether it was in the field of trade promotion, mining regulations, the restriction of monopolies, or factory legislation.

Having answered the broad question about the general experience of French civil servants with industrial matters before the First World War, the field of enquiry must now be narrowed down to those bureaucrats who were to be specifically concerned with formulating and administering government industrial policy during the war. These are the 'bureaucrats' of the title of this volume. How many of them were there, who were they, and what is known about them?

These bureaucrats may be defined by a process of elimination. Estimates of the total number of civil servants in France in 1914 vary between 621,000 and 1 million, depending on how one counts the army and part-time employees. Clearly, postmen, school teachers, and minor clerks have no bearing on this study, and a distinction between *employés* and *fonctionnaires* should be drawn. As one contemporary commentator put it:

The economists call anybody who works for the State and receives a salary for doing so a State "employé". The common people reserve the name of employé to certain officials, and know the others by their title in the hierarchy. They say a "president", a "professor", or a "chief clerk", but a "postal employé", a "customs employé", a "ministry employé". The notion of employé seems to be made up of the following factors: he is a subordinate, he has no decision-making powers, and only differs from a domestic servant or a workman because his labour is not physical. He is always hard up: his choice of a career has not been decided by

10. Ridley, *Public Administration*, 214–15.

wealth, vocation, or patronage. He works for his living and is a poor
devil, and the name of clerk (*commis*) sometimes given him seems to have
lost all prestige since it has been applied to decent people.[11]

It was the *employés* who attracted most of the attention in France
before the First World War by going on strike and attempting to
form unions, but the concern of this study is with those civil
servants who held positions of authority: the leading *fonctionnaires*.
From contemporary accounts, this group numbered about one thousand.[12] From them must be further subtracted prefects, army com-
manders, university rectors and, indeed, all of the top civil servants
of all French ministries except two: the Ministry of Commerce and
the Ministry of War. It was the senior bureaucrats of these two
ministries which were required to make the first industrial decisions
of the war on behalf of the state in 1914.

What is known about these men? To begin with, these two
ministries shared a common plan of organisation of their central
offices with all French ministries:

> Each is divided into a number of divisions, called *directions*, or *services*,
> and these in turn are subdivided into bureaus. There are certain services,
> moreover, that are common to all ministerial departments. These are
> (1) the minister's personal secretariat (*cabinet*), (2) the purchasing divi-
> sion (*matériel*), (3) the accounting division and (4) the personnel bureau.
> The grade of assistant bureau chief marks everywhere the dividing line
> between the directing and executing personnel.[13]

Thus the bureaucrats who made the decisions were the directors
and assistant directors, the bureau chiefs and the assistant bureau
chiefs.

In 1913, the Ministry of Commerce had only twenty-three such
bureaucrats. The minister's personal secretariat consisted of three
men, a publicist, a lawyer, and a university graduate. There was an
inspector of finance who controlled the finances of the Ministry of
Labour as well as those of the Ministry of Commerce. Personnel,
weights and measures, fishing, the merchant marine, expositions,
industrial relations, and bookkeeping were administered by six
men. Six others were responsible for overseeing technical and

11. Guimbaud, 'L'Employé de l'Etat en France' (thesis, Caen, 1898), quoted in R.
    Gregoire, *The French Civil Service* (Brussels, 1964), 25.
12. M. le vicomte G. d'Avenel, 'Les Riches depuis sept cents ans. — Fonctionnaires
    de l'Etat et des administrations privées', *La Revue des Deux Mondes*, 15 July
    1906, 409.
13. Sharp, *French Civil Service*, 39.

commercial schools in France, while the remaining seven bureaucrats dealt with customs legislation, commercial agreements, reports on foreign commerce, chambers of commerce, and industrial legislation.[14]

The Ministry of War in 1913 was a much larger affair with a total complement of 174 bureaucrats, including the general staff of the army and military inspectors. Of these, however, only ten could be said to have any direct involvement with industrial matters. The artillery and military equipment section of the Ministry consisted of five men who between them supervised all artillery establishments and schools, as well as arsenals, forges, foundries, small arms factories, cartridge works, flag workshops, harness shops for cavalry, and a good deal else besides. Three bureaucrats were in charge of the powder and saltpeter section, and administered state powderworks and research laboratories, as well as dealing with private dynamite manufacturers. Finally, there was one permanent inspector of artillery production and one inspector of artillery experiments and trials.[15]

Before 1914 these leading bureaucrats were recruited in two ways. The first was by competitive examination which stressed a literary facility combined with a legal, historical, or scientific background. Traditionally, the top candidates gravitated towards the Ministry of Foreign Affairs, the Council of State, the General Inspectorate of the Ministry of Finance, and the 'political' ministries, such as the Interior, and not to such ministries as Commerce or War.[16] The second method of recruitment was more irregular, but widespread nevertheless. This was selection by political patronage. During every ministerial crisis, potential ministers were bombarded with the names of young men thought worthy of the post of director or assistant bureau chief by their various sponsors. Once in office, these recruits tended to become part of the permanent civil service after the departure of the minister who had brought them in. Some observers of the day went so far as to claim that the upper echelons of entire ministries were completely staffed with such people, who, for all their youth and willingness, often had no particular training or aptitude for the task.[17] Naturally, the morale of career civil servants was not improved by their presence.

14. *Almanach national. Annuaire officiel de la République française pour 1913* (Paris, 1913), 435–51.
15. Ibid., 200–26.
16. Sharp, *French Civil Service*, 102–16, 150–6.
17. H. Chardon, *L'Administration de France. Les Fonctionnaires* (Paris, 1908), 123–5.

Traditionally, the French civil service had attracted candidates of a very high calibre, but by 1914 the pattern had changed. Commerce, industry, and the private professions were drawing away the brightest young men, and government personnel offices noted a considerable decline of suitable candidates for top posts.[18] Partially, this was explicable by the fact that the civil service could not compete with the salaries offered by industry and commerce. Another reason suggested at the time was that it was no longer as important and prestigious to work for the state as it once was:

> The State has no longer the same importance; it no longer plays the same role in our lives. Certainly it has grown, but "private France" has grown even more than the State, than "public France"; and it is still easier for a man of talent — excluding the field of politics — to become something today *despite the people* than it formerly was *despite the king*.[19]

What conclusions are to be drawn about these bureaucrats? First, that a very small group of men were directly involved with industrial questions before the war. Secondly, that the functions they exercised before 1914 hardly prepared them for the sorts of industrial decisions they would be required to make in wartime. Thirdly, the civil service was not attracting the best talent in France by 1914, what talent it did attract tended to go to ministries other than Commerce and War, and even the best people were liable to be displaced by inexperienced ministerial *protégés*. Finally, it should be remembered that after 1914 these men would ultimately constitute only a minority of France's wartime bureaucrats. The Ministry of Commerce and Industry created a special group of Extra-ordinary War Services which were staffed by men who had not been bureaucrats before the war. Similarly, the Under-Secretariat of State for Artillery and Munitions, the body responsible for war industries, was created as a separate branch of the Ministry of War in 1915 and eventually became the Ministry of Armament. It too was filled with men of non-bureaucratic backgrounds.

Industrialists and the State

Turning from pre-war French bureaucrats to pre-war French industrialists, the same questions must be asked: which industrialists

18. Sharp, *French Civil Service*, 85–6.
19. d'Avenel, 'Les fonctionnaires', 413.

are being discussed? what were their chief characteristics? and finally, what were their relations with their fellow industrialists and, above all, with the state, before 1914?

Before these questions can be answered, a number of generalisations commonly made about French industrialists must briefly be considered. It is almost mandatory, for example, to begin any discussion of the French rich in general and French industrialists in particular with some reference to the theory that France was controlled during the Third Republic by 200 families of financiers and industrialists.[20] This conspiratorial view of a French society dominated by a network of personal relationships linking industry, business, banks, insurance companies, press, and parliament has been bruited about for over a century. It achieved the zenith of its popularity during the 1930s and has enjoyed a certain vogue in more recent times.[21] Undoubtedly there has always been some truth behind the theory, though in the period under consideration commentators were inclined to label the phenomenon with less mathematical precision and more joviality as *camaraderie*.[22] For present purposes, however, the theory is of marginal interest since it was not an important factor in the extension of state power over industry during the war.

Another way of looking at industrialists in France both before and after the First World War has been to measure their performance in terms of economic growth. Since 1945 there has been a great and continuing controversy among economic historians about the causes of French economic retardation in the nineteenth and twentieth centuries. Recently the debate has concentrated on the primary issue of whether France actually *was* economically retarded during this period. Not only are historians divided among themselves on this issue, there is at least one who is divided within himself: having offered in 1957 a compelling description of French economic stagnation and its causes, by 1970 he had come round to the view that France by certain standards of measurement had done rather better economically than England and even Germany.[23] Generally, however, France's relatively slow rate of growth over the

20. See, for example, T. Zeldin, *France 1848–1945* (Oxford, 1973), i. Chapter 5.
21. A. Hamon, *Les Maîtres de France* (Paris, 1936–7), 2 vols. H. Coston, *Le Retour des "200 familles"* (Paris 1960).
22. R. de Jouvenal, *La République des camarades* (Paris, 1914, reprinted 1934), 529.
23. R. Cameron, 'Profit, croissance et stagnation en France au XIXe siècle', *Economie appliquée*, vol.10, no.1, 1957. R. Cameron, 'L'Economie française: passé, present, avenir', *Annales*, September–October 1970.

past century has been accepted as a given, and the debate has been over the explanation of this phenomenon. The quarrel has, on the whole, been dominated until recently by two groups of historians. One school has stressed economic and material factors, and have been jocularly labelled the 'coal men', taking their lead to some degree from J.H. Clapham's classic account of the shortage of French coal as a major retardative economic element in industrial development.[24] The leading exponents of this theory have been Alexander Gerschenkron, Rondo Cameron and, in a very sophisticated and qualified way, Charles Kindleberger.[25] The opposing school, the 'role men', have put forward a sociological and cultural explanation for the failure of French industrialists to display greater entrepreneurship. Here, the leading lights have been David Landes, John Sawyer, and Jesse Pitts.[26] Fortunately, however, it is not the purpose of this book to resolve the great debate about French economic growth. Rather, its task is to describe the chief features of certain French industrialists before the war so that there may be a better understanding of how and why these men and the industries they ran functioned as they did during the war. The aim is not to establish behavioural models, or what sociologists call 'the analysis of ideal types', or to search for deeper value systems, it is simply to extract from the entrepreneurial argument certain useful observations regarding financing, relations with consumers and competitors, and relations with the state.

The treatment of industrialists in this chapter varies in one critical respect from the approach taken towards bureaucrats: whereas it is of limited interest to know a great deal about the composition and behaviour of pre-war French civil servants, since these men were

24. J. Clapham, *The Economic Development of France & Germany* (4th edn., Cambridge 1951), 234.
25. P. Bell, 'The Direction of Entrepreneurial Explorations', *Explorations in Entrepreneurial History/ Second Series*, vol.5, no.1, 1967. A. Gerschenkron, *Economic Backwardness in Historical Perspective* (Cambridge, Mass., 1962), Chapter 3. A. Gerschenkron, *Continuity in History & Other Essays* (Cambridge, Mass., 1968), Chapter 6. C. Kindleberger, *Economic Growth in France & Britain 1851–1950* (Cambridge, Mass., 1964), Chapter 6.
26. D. Landes, 'French Entrepreneurship & Industrial Growth in the Nineteenth Century', *The Journal of Economic History*, no.1, 1949. D. Landes, 'Observations on France: Economy, Society, & Polity', *World Politics* ix. 1959. D. Landes, 'French Business & the Businessman', in *Modern France*, ed. E.M. Earle (New York, 1964). J. Pitts, 'The French Bourgeois Family & French Economic Retardation' (Harvard University, Ph.D. thesis 1957). J. Sawyer, 'The Entrepreneur & the Social Order, France & the United States', in *Men in Business*, ed. W. Miller (Cambridge, Mass., 1952).

soon to be replaced in key positions by men who had not been bureaucrats before the war and whose approach was accordingly non-bureaucratic, it is of greater importance to have some notion of what French industrialists were like before the war, since wartime industrialists were not only the same men but continued to behave in the same way as before it.

The case-studies in this volume concentrate on a few key heavy industries: iron and steel, chemicals, and petroleum. In addition, two other industries appear briefly: the vegetable oil industry and the shoe industry. The former were among the more dynamic industrial sectors of the French economy before 1914, the latter among the more conservative, small-scale, and traditional industries. Thus this study by no means constitutes a complete survey of all French industrial activity before and during the First World War; rather, representative industries have been selected which will allow some conclusions to be drawn about the more general question of French industrial mobilisation during the war. The method employed will be to describe briefly the chief technical and administrative characteristics of each industry, making reference where appropriate to the more general theories of French industry outlined above. As will soon become apparent, these generalisations tend to break down when tested by the reality of specific French industries.

One might begin by asking how representative these representative industries were, and what the relative importance of each was within the overall structure of the economy in 1914. Recent studies by French economic historians have shown that from 1810 to 1914 the contribution of industry (as opposed to food, public works, and construction) to the total of French production rose from one-quarter to one-half.[27] Lévy-Leboyer's research reveals that, excluding textiles, the iron and steel industry constituted 40.3 per cent of the basic industry sector, while chemicals represented 16.5 per cent.[28] The petroleum industry was still relatively small. Markovitch and Crouzet show that all three industries attained dynamic growth rates during this period, unlike the vegetable oil and shoe industries, which at best stagnated and at worst declined in the period from 1895 to 1913. What these five industries share in common is that

27. F. Crouzet, 'Essai de construction d'un indice annuel de la production industrielle française au XIXe siècle', *Annales*, 1970, 56–99. T. Markovitch, 'L'Industrie française de 1789 à 1964', *Cahiers de l'Institut de Science économique appliquée*, AF, 4, July 1965.
28. M. Lévy-Leboyer, 'La Croissance économique au XIXe siècle', *Annales*, 1968, 788–807.

they were all vital to a war economy, and hence all susceptible to state interference.

Vegetable Oil and Shoes

Of the vegetable oil and shoe industries, little need be said, since they perform but minor roles in the story. The essential characteristic of the French vegetable oil industry is that it depended heavily on the importation of oil-yielding seeds — cotton, flax, rape-seed, peanuts — from French colonies or from foreign countries. Vegetable oils were used to produce shortening and butter substitutes, soap, paint, varnish, grease, fuel, pharmaceuticals, and dyes. Once the oil had been extracted from the seeds, the remnants were converted to oil-cake, which in turn was used for animal food or fertiliser.[29] The industry was dominated by three regional syndicates of manufacturers representing Marseilles, Bordeaux, and the North and East. The chief contact between these industrialists and the state before the war was over the question of tariffs on oil-seeds; industrialists were generally successful in preventing them from being applied.[30] Any attempt by the state to impose control over the vegetable oil industry would come up against the hurdle of the enormous technical and commercial complexities of the industry, with the great variety of oil-seeds, the multitude of foreign ports from which they were shipped, and the range of products derived from oil-seeds.[31]

The French shoe industry in 1914 was in serious straits. Whereas in 1891 France had exported shoes worth 63.895 million francs and imported only 2.183 million francs worth, by 1913 exports had declined to 12.268 million while imports increased to 27.095 million.[32] The reason was simple: most French shoes were still handmade by individual shoemakers while Germans and Americans had developed techniques of mass production. Any French industrialist who wished to mass produce shoes was obliged to rent his equipment from either the United Shoe Company of Boston, or the Maschinenfabrik Venus of Frankfurt, and the rental charges were so high that they virtually doubled the price of a pair of shoes. Thus the French shoe industry remained generally labour-intensive and low in productivity, which meant that when labour was scarce there

---

29. Ministère du Commerce, *Rapport général sur l'industrie française* (Paris, 1919), ii. 369–93.
30. Clapham, *Economic Development*, 263.
31. See Chapter 4.
32. Ministère du Commerce, *Rapport général*, ii. 517–19.

was no easy way of greatly increasing production to meet special demands, as in the case of army boots during the war, while still maintaining regular production. As well, the fact that the industry was essentially small-scale — perhaps it would be more accurate to classify it as a trade rather than an industry — and consisted of thousands of individual shoemakers made any form of government regulation difficult to administer.[33]

Iron and Steel

The French iron and steel industry in 1914 presents a far more complex picture. As has been indicated, the industry was dynamic: in the period from 1890 to 1913, for example, while German steel production increased 2.62 times, American 2.32 times, and British 1.52 times, French steel production increased 3.10 times.[34] In itself, this phenomenon would seem to contradict the basic premise of the 'role men' that French business was inherently undynamic, though it has been argued that the growth of the industry during this period was artificial and took place only because the preceding period of depression had postponed investment.[35] Economists have also pointed to a paradoxical weakness in the four-fold growth of French iron ore production from 1900 to 1913, since the percentage of ore exported to foreign competitors rose from 8 per cent to 45 per cent during the same period, indicating an inability on the part of French industry to utilise national resources to the fullest.

Despite these qualifications, however, there was real growth in the iron and steel industry during this period. The growth can be explained in terms of both 'coal' and 'role', that is, natural resources and entrepreneurship. The outstanding factor was undoubtedly the discovery of the Thomas method of steelmaking in the 1870s, which allowed France to utilise her vast supplies of phosphoric iron ore in Lorraine, ore which had previously been considered worthless. When one considers that France had the second greatest reserves of this kind of ore in the world, and that by 1913, of the 21.918 million tons of iron ore produced in France that year, 20.059 million were phosphoric, the significance of the discovery becomes apparent.[36] But it was the way in which French ironmasters responded to the challenge of applying this new technology which led to the growth

---

33. See Chapter 5.
34. Ministère du Commerce, *Rapport général*, i. 87.
35. G. Palmade, *French Capitalism in the Nineteenth Century (1961)* (Newton Abbot, 1972), 209.
36. Ministère du Commerce, *Rapport général*, i. 63.

of the industry. Far from resisting innovation, far from clinging fiercely to their independence, French ironmasters combined almost immediately to exploit the Thomas process to maximum advantage. In 1880, la Société de Wendel et Cie. was formed, a joint partnership of the de Wendel family and the Schneider family to build a steelworks at Joeuf in Lorraine.[37] In the same year, the de Wendels joined with other traditional ironmasters to create another steelworks at Longwy, which became one of the largest, most efficient, and most integrated metallurgical operations in the world, with a large mining field, seven blast-furnaces, several Thomas converters, a Martin steelworks for special steel, rolling mills which produced rails, rods, and section steel, and wire and sheet metal works. By the turn of the century, Longwy was producing 12,000 tons of steel a month.[38]

Not only were French ironmasters quick to exploit the new technology of steelmaking, they showed great enterprise in adjusting to the new dominance of the Lorraine area. The ironmasters from the Centre of France, such as the Schneiders of le Creusot, abandoned rail and sheet-metal production in favour of finer work, notably armaments. Firms in the north of France responded to the discovery of the Thomas method either by installing their own Thomas converters and importing ore from the east by rail or canal, or by switching the bulk of their operations to Lorraine and retaining only their workshops for finished products in such northern towns as Valenciennes or Lille.

One of the basic contentions of the Landes–Pitts school is that family firms have a curious 'guild ideology' which makes them reluctant to take each other over or wipe each other out. Since the honour and independence of the family was supposed to be coextensive with that of the firm, the amalgamation of firms in the name of efficiency was to be eschewed. The history of the French iron and steel industry hardly sustains this theory. Even in the mid-nineteenth century, there were examples of firms combining in the interests of economic rationality, such as the forges of Fourchambault with the coal fields of Commentry in 1854 to form Chatillon-Commentry.[39] But it was the Thomas process which forced the pace of concentration in the industry. The economic advantages of vertical integration from iron ore to finished product proved irresistible. In 1903, for example, the Société des Aciéries de la Marine

---

37. Palmade, *Capitalism*, 201–2.
38. J. Boudet, *Le Monde des affaires en France de 1850 à nos jours* (Paris, 1952), 92–4.
39. B. Gille, *La Sidérurgie française au XIXe siècle* (Paris, 1968), 71.

et des Chemins de fer (Saint-Chamond) took over a number of mines, factories, forges, and rolling mills and became the Société des Forges et Aciéries de la Marine et d'Homécourt. In short, industrialists placed economic efficiency above absolute independence; technology dictated the shape of corporate structures.

Building new integrated factories to exploit the new technology of metallurgy, or acquiring other companies took a great deal of money. The source of this money was the huge reserves which individual companies built up over the years. Critics of French industry point to this *auto-financement* as a sign of the reluctance of French industrialists to endanger their independence by using outside finance and risk capital. The iron and steel industry certainly offers conspicuous examples of the tendency. Between 1854 and 1914, the firm of Commentry, Fourchambault, and Decazeville never paid a yearly dividend above 60 francs a share despite the fact that net profits exceeded 200 francs a share in twenty-four of those years. In 1914, the capital plant of the Longwy steelworks was listed as 30 million francs, while liquid assets amounted to 35 million.[40] There are several ways of interpreting this characteristic. In the first place, money was not always available from outside sources either because of heavy alternative demands on the capital market or because French bankers were reluctant to invest in industry.[41] Secondly, one should note the use to which these reserves were put, which was not to maintain the independence of firms, but often to promote takeovers and amalgamations. Finally, *auto-financement* may simply be a reflection of the fact that profits were high during this period and that owners preferred to plough money back into companies rather than to put it in banks which would then not re-lend it to the companies. The ultimate proof that *auto-financement* was not necessarily synonymous with economic inefficiency is that French ironmasters were able to achieve a considerable rate of growth during this period without resorting to outside borrowing. Whether they would have done even better by taking greater financial risks will never be known.

Thusfar, the French metal industry has been presented in terms of firms rather than men. What sort of men were the ironmasters? By 1914, there were two distinct types: those belonging to the traditional dynasties and those who had come up through company ranks as managers. Both were dynamic. The sixth generation of the

---

40. J.-P. Courthéoux, "Les pouvoirs économiques et sociaux dans un secteur industriel: la sidérurgie", *Revue d'Histoire Economique et Sociale*, no.3, 1960, 360–1.
41. Zeldin, *France*, i. 80–4.

de Wendel family proved as enterprising as the first. They invested heavily in steelmaking plants in Lorraine, owned coke in the north, in the Ruhr, and the Low Countries, and dominated the trade association of the industry. The Schneiders, now in the third generation, developed new armour plating, artillery, and warships; built railway equipment, bridges, electrical machinery and motors, which they sold all over the world; and constructed a steelworks in Russia.[42] Clearly, there were few signs of generational decay in these families. The second group of ironmasters, the managers, were to some degree the product of vertical integration and company concentration. This was the age of a new type of company executive. As companies grew larger through amalgamation and expansion , they came to be administered often not by the old style *patron* but by more anonymous technocrats who had started as engineers before ultimately becoming head of the firm. Among such engineers were Rogé, who was chief executive of Pont-à-Mousson, until he was replaced in 1900 by another engineer, Camille Cavallier; Adrien de Montgolfier at Marine et d'Homécourt; and Edouard Dreux, who became head of the Longwy Steelworks in 1910. The managers were as impressive in their achievements as the dynasts.

An important factor in the success of the industry during this period was the vital role played by the *Comité des Forges*. Attempts to form a trade association of ironmasters date back to 1833, though the *Comité des Forges* was not founded formally until 1864, under the new law on professional organisations.[43]

The *Comité des Forges* existed for two purposes. The first was to maintain order among the ironmasters themselves. To achieve this objective the *Comité* was constituted in such a way that it both reflected the relative strengths of ironmasters within the industry and attempted to preserve the balance of power. The vital decisions of the *Comité* were made by a Commission elected every three years. The Commission was dominated by the major companies, and seats were allotted on a regional basis in proportion to the importance of the area within the industry. Attempts to unbalance the status quo of the regions led to occasional major disputes within the *Comité* during the nineteenth century and would do so again during the war over the acquisition of sequestered German plants in Normandy.[44]

42. Palmade, *Capitalism*, 201–2.
43. Gille, *La Sidérugie*, 66, 67, 76, 193.
44. R. Priouret, *Origines du patronat français* (Paris, 1963), 183–4. See also Chapter 9.

The second purpose of the *Comité des Forges* was to defend the interests of the iron and steel industry against the outside world, whether the world took the form of consumers or the state. Initially, the *Comité des Forges* was merely an information service for subscribing members, with the chief purpose of ensuring that uniform prices were charged by members producing the same products. To this end, the *Bulletin du Comité des Forges* was published, and four meetings a year were held. Reorganised as a *syndicat* under the law of association of 1884, the *Comité* grouped three-quarters of France's iron and steel producers, despite the restraints placed on the activities of such organisations by Article 419 of the Penal Code, which banned monopolistic coalitions and *ententes*.[45]

In 1876 there had been another significant development in the French metallurgical industry: the *Comptoir de Longwy* was founded. Robert Pinot, who became secretary-general of the *Comité des Forges* in 1899, defined a *comptoir* as

> an essentially commercial organisation, responsible for the sale of a simple product which is truly identical from one factory to another, for whose factory of origin a buyer could not legitimately indicate a preference. The *comptoir* regulates sales on behalf of associated factories on the basis of amounts established by productive capacity, which are verified and periodically revised.[46]

Comptoirs were a legal fiction created to avoid the prohibition against professional associations like the *Comité des Forges* arranging for the sale of the products of their members. They were a useful device for grouping demands for metal products and redistributing them among members on a basis renegotiable every three years. *Comptoirs* minimised price fluctuations and stabilised production. In short, the *comptoir* was a mechanism which ensured that high prices for metal products would be maintained by limiting the expansion of productive capacity. Defenders of the *comptoir*, such as Robert Pinot, denied such allegations, claiming that nothing prevented the individual industrialist from increasing his productive capacity and demanding a higher share of the market when quotas came to be renegotiated.[47] He contrasted 'the supple and elegant form' of the *comptoir* with hardness and rigidity of the German

---

45. A. François-Poncet, *La Vie et l'oeuvre de Robert Pinot* (Paris, 1927).
46. Ibid., 142.
47. R. Pinot, *Le Comité des Forges de France au service de la nation* (Paris, 1919), 12, 13.

cartel or the American trust.

Examples of *comptoirs* were those established for the sale of springs in 1892 and girders in 1896, both created under the authority of the *Comité des Forges*, but the best known was probably the *Comptoir de Longwy*, which sold iron produced in the north-east of France.[48] In addition to this kind of *comptoir* which controlled the sale of individual metal products within France, there were also *comptoirs* organised for the sale of French metal products abroad, such as the *Comptoir d'Exportation des Produits Métallurgiques*, which also negotiated with foreign metallurgical cartels.[49] *Comptoirs* were to play a vital part during the First World War.

Under the direction of Robert Pinot, the commercial operations and the influence of the *Comité des Forges* were greatly expanded. Professional associations of manufacturers of railway material, ships, and munitions, as well as the general Union of Metallurgical and Mining Industries became affiliated with the *Comité des Forges*, sharing the same premises and the same secretary general. Under Pinot's leadership, the *Comité des Forges* worked actively to oppose Millerand's social decrees, which attempted to legislate for a minimum wage, the limitation of the hours of child and female labour, safer working conditions, and the establishment of workers' and employers' councils. On behalf of the metal producers, Pinot fought these measures tooth and nail. His biographer credits his love of liberty for the vigour with which he opposed state interference in industry:

> The state implies obligation, constraint; undoubtedly, constraint prevents less scrupulous employees from taking advantage of their absence of scruples to the detriment of their colleagues; but, at the same time, constraint kills zeal, emulation, and self-respect, which liberty, on the other hand, spurs on; under a system of obligation, one does what is required, nothing more, and often, it is not enough.[50]

Armed with this libertarian doctrine, Pinot organised the resistance of employers to strikes in the metallurgical industries. From 1905 onwards, he appealed to the public authorities for support against strikers to assure the protection of the right to work, to guarantee the liberty of citizens, and to maintain law and order.

By the eve of the war, Pinot had created a streamlined, efficient organisation to cater to the collective needs of the metallurgists. The

48. Ibid., 8.
49. Ibid., 17.
50. François-Poncet, *Pinot*, 167.

administration of the *Comité des Forges* comprised four sections, reflecting the diverse nature of the range of its activities: (1) The department of legislation, jurisprudence, and labour; (2) the section for tariffs, economic policy, and transport; (3) the technical section, which dealt with orders for material and construction contracts; (4) the secretariat. It is interesting to note that the first two sections of the administration of the *Comité* dealt almost exclusively with matters relating to government policy. As a result of work carried out by the third section, a standard classification system for metallurgical products was developed for subscribing members of the *Comité*, which facilitated the imposition of a common price structure. The *Comité des Forges* also acquired a strong financial ally in the form of the Banque Demachy, while individual member firms were closely involved with other banks; the Banque de l'Union Parisienne backed Le Creusot, the Crédit Lyonnais supported the Aciéries de la Marine, the Comptoir d'Escompte financed the Chantiers de la Méditerranée.[51] The *Comité des Forges* was administered by an eleven-member board, of whom the most prominent were François de Wendel of Les Petits-fils de François de Wendel; Eugène Schneider of Le Creusot; Camille Cavallier of Pont-à-Mousson; and Léon-Lévy of Châtillon-Commentry, Neuves-Maisons. It should be emphasised, however, that while the *Comité des Forges* counted among its members the biggest French metallurgists, grouping some 238 adherents by 1914, it did not contain all of them.[52] As will become apparent, the *Comité des Forges* attempted to use the war as a means of eliminating these small independent producers.

This, then, was the state of the French iron and steel industry on the eve of the First World War. Its strength was in large part attributable to the efficient exploitation of the great mineral resources of Lorraine; this advantage was to be forfeited in August 1914 when the Germans invaded the area. But whether they came from traditional dynasties or were newly-risen technocrats, the French ironmasters had a technical capacity and a genius for organisation which allowed them to recover from this loss and to use what resources remained to them to the fullest. They were able to adapt pre-war techniques, such as *auto-financement*, and pre-war structures, such as the *Comité des Forges* and the *Comptoir de Longwy*, to the wartime situation, though the dislocation of the traditional balance of power within the industry caused by the war would,

51. Edouard Barthe, *Chambre des députés*, 24 January 1919, 207.
52. Pinot, *Le Comité des Forges*, 20.

upon occasion, lead to a revival of geographic rivalries within the industry. Finally, the pre-war experiences of the ironmasters in dealing with the state, both bureaucrats and politicians, prepared them well for the confrontations that were to follow. The state hardly stood a chance.[53]

Chemicals

The French chemical industry before 1914 has had a bad press. J.H. Clapham wrote of it:

> France in spite of her tariffs was a great and growing buyer of foreign chemicals, in the five and twenty years before the war, while French chemicals were not prominent in the world's markets. Only an elaborate technical and statistical analysis could even suggest the extent to which this inferiority was, so to speak, culpable and to what extent it was inevitable.[54]

As has been indicated, however, recent studies have shown the industry to be far more dynamic than previously supposed. In the years from 1895 to 1913, it grew at an annual rate of 4.7 to 5.0 per cent.[55] But before one can speak with accuracy about the French chemical industry, one must distinguish between several main types of chemicals.

For the century preceding the 1914–18 war, soda was the foundation of the chemical industry. Soda was used in the manufacture of glass, ceramics, soap, photographic materials, carbonated drinks, dyes, pharmaceutical products, cellulose, and paper. As there was a shortage of natural soda in the world, the modern French chemical industry began in the nineteenth century with the creation of small soda plants employing the Leblanc method of producing artificial soda. This process required salt, coal or chalk, and, above all, sulphuric acid. The sulphuric acid acted on the salt to produce sulphate of sodium, which, when added to coal or chalk, produced soda. Salt, coal, and chalk were relatively easy to acquire, but chemical companies were required to invest heavily in plants to manufacture sulphuric acid. As with natural soda, natural sulphur was in short supply, but a process of baking iron bisulphate to yield sulphur was discovered during the nineteenth century and im-

53. See Chapters 2, 7, 8, 9 and 10.
54. Clapham, *Economic Development*, 257.
55. Markovitch, 'L'Industrie française', Table 2.

proved upon by Gay Lussac.[56]

The outstanding producer of soda and sulphuric acid in France before 1914 was Saint-Gobain, the oldest industrial firm in France. Founded by Louis XIV in 1665 as a royal glass factory, Saint-Gobain was a *manufacture royale* of the sort discussed earlier in this chapter. It was granted a *privilège*, giving it the exclusive right to manufacture glass in France, while its ownership and management remained in private hands. The company subsequently undertook the production of chemicals, and by the third quarter of the nineteenth century, Saint-Gobain had thoroughly integrated its soda and sulphuric acid production into an efficient vertical operation. It owned salt plants, iron pyrite mines, sulphuric acid factories, soda plants, and glassworks. However, the harmony of this operation was gravely upset by the discovery of the Solvay method of producing soda far more efficiently and cheaply than the Leblanc without using sulphuric acid. After the process was discovered, the production of soda in France increased from 300,000 tons in 1863 to 1.5 million in 1900, while the price dropped from 310 francs a ton to 100. With its heavy investment in mines and sulphuric acid plants, Saint-Gobain struggled gamely on with the Leblanc method until 1903, when it finally opted for Solvay.[57]

Happily, Saint-Gobain and the other owners of sulphuric acid plants in France found a new use for the product in the 1870s: the manufacture of superphosphate fertilisers. The discovery that the application of sulphuric acid to natural phosphate produced a highly soluble fertiliser led Saint-Gobain into an entirely new field of operation. From the 1870s the company began building superphosphate plants in the agricultural areas of the north and centre of France. Saint-Gobain also acquired interests in the vast natural phosphate deposits discovered in North Africa during the period. Once again, the company profited from vertical integration. By 1914, Saint-Gobain produced over half of the total production of sulphuric acid in France, nearly half of the superphosphates, and 100,000 tons of soda by the Solvay method. The Company employed 20,000 workers and 300 technicians and engineers and owned a soda plant, twenty-one factories, and an iron mine.[58]

Saint-Gobain had one major, though smaller, rival: Kuhlmann. Kuhlmann also produced soda, sulphuric acid, and superphosphates, but specialised as well in manufacturing chlorium, gelatine,

---

56. Boudet, *Affaires*, 174–7.
57. J. Choffel, *Saint-Gobain. Du miroir à l'atome* (Paris, 1960), 71–85.
58. Boudet, *Affaires*, 171.

copper sulphate, and ammonium.

As a result of the dynamism of the companies in this branch of the chemical industry, all of them French-owned, by 1914, France was entirely self-sufficient in soda and even exported a surplus. Eighty-seven sulphuric acid plants in France produced 1.2 million tons of acid annually, which compared favourably with the 1.65 million tons produced in Germany, and the 1.6 million tons produced in Britain. In 1913, France produced 2 million tons of superphosphates, more than Germany, Britain, or the United States.[59]

J. H. Clapham's strictures about the weaknesses of the French chemical industry apply more accurately to that branch which manufactured dyes. The process begins with coal-tar, which is distilled into benzol, which yields in turn a series of intermediate products, such as benzene, anthracene, naphthalene, and phenols; from these are manufactured not only a wide variety of dyes, but also nitrates, which are used to produce explosives and pharmaceuticals.[60] As with soda, this complex process encourages the vertical integration of operations and the squeezing out of small producers. Unfortunately, in this case, the small producers were French. In 1914, 87 per cent of the dyes used in France came directly or indirectly from Germany.[61] One single French factory, Saint-Denis, continued to manufacture both the intermediate products derived from coal-tar and dyes. Four other factories obtained their intermediate materials from Germany, six factories in France were entirely owned by Germans, and half of all dyes in France were imported directly from Germany.[62] How had this sad state of affairs come about? The decline of the French dye industry dates from the La Fuchsine affair in 1863, when the attempt of a company to monopolise production of France's first synthetic dye, Verguin's fuchsine, resulted in such enormous legal battles that both the company and its rivals went bankrupt, the manufacturers involved went into other lines of business, and the chemists left in disgust for Switzerland.[63] German firms quickly moved in to fill the breach. Saint-Denis valiantly carried on the fight, periodically inventing new colours, such as a brilliant orange in 1896, which the Germans promptly analysed and reproduced.[64] The Germans also kept down the

59. Ministère du Commerce, *Rapport Général*, ii. 31–2, 60, 101.
60. Boudet, *Affaires*, 173.
61. Palmade, *Capitalism*, 208.
62. Ministère du Commerce, *Rapport général*, ii. 206.
63. P. Hohenberg, *Chemicals in Western Europe: 1850–1914* (Chicago, 1967), 36.
64. Boudet, *Affaires*, 184.

French opposition by the dumping of dyes onto the French market. Attempts by French producers to raise tariffs on German dyes were ineffectual.[65] In 1914 there was virtually no French dye industry. Nor could there be said to be much of a French pharmaceutical industry. Pharmaceuticals constituted a third distinct, though less important, branch of the chemical industry in France. Pharmaceuticals are chemically related to dyes in that both are derived from coal-tar. Thus the Compagnie Parisienne des Couleurs d'Aniline, a German owned company, produced both dyes and drugs. German companies, like Merck of Darmstadt, and Bayer, drove most of their French rivals from the field.[66] Only one French company, the Société Chimique des Usines du Rhône, was able to challenge the Germans. As well as coal-tar based pharmaceuticals, it manufactured dyes, acetate for film, synthetic perfumes, and serums. It employed twenty-seven chemists, owned two factories in France, another in Russia, and maintained an office in New York. The company was one of the minor success stories of the French chemical industry before 1914 and eventually went on to become the chemical giant Rhône-Poulenc.[67]

The last major branch of the chemical industry was electrochemistry. France had taken an early lead in this industry, profiting from Sainte-Claire Deville's invention of a method of refining aluminium from bauxite at the Salindres factory of the Compagnie des Produits Chimiques d'Alais, Froges et Camargue, later known as Péchiney. From 1860 to 1889 this company was the only producer of aluminium in the world. The monopoly was broken by the discovery of the electrolytic method, and Péchiney failed to keep up with this new development. The company also produced more traditional products such as soda, acids, phosphate fertilisers, and copper sulphate for the wine growers of the Midi, as well as chlorate, from which chlorine could be extracted to produce shell fuses and explosives.

Thus the picture of the French chemical industry in 1914 is hardly one of unrelieved gloom; certain sectors were decidedly dynamic. Even more than in the iron and steel industry, the necessities of technology forced the concentration and vertical integration of companies. Dyes, explosives, pharmaceuticals, and perfumes, for example, were all linked by their common derivation from coal-tar.

65. R. Poidevin, *Les Relations économiques et financières entre la France et l'Allemagne de 1898 à 1914* (Paris, 1969), 224.
66. Ibid., 740.
67. Boudet, *Affaires*, 199.

By its very nature the chemical industry required considerable capital to finance research and development, to build, update, and eventually scrap complex machinery, and to purchase energy and materials. Large-scale operations also made it possible to use by-products in large enough amounts to be economically viable.[68] It is hardly surprising, therefore, to find the French chemical industry dominated by a few large companies in 1914. At one point, Saint-Gobain even contemplated a merger with Kuhlmann. As in the case of metals, *auto-financement* was the order of the day. Saint-Gobain financed all of its expansion and take-overs from its own reserves, and it was only in 1917, for the first time since its foundation in 1665, that the company borrowed money.[69]

So great were the demands for capital that most firms were of necessity originally floated by shares. The fact that no single family could afford the heavy costs of operating a major chemical company meant that the men who ran them were a special breed. Unlike the iron and steel industry, there were less clear distinctions between traditional industrialists owning a major interest in a company and managers who had started as company employees, since firms were usually founded by technicians who often converted them into share ownership or limited companies, and the managers who administered them thus had a better chance of becoming at least part-owners. As the industry was comparatively young, had experienced concentration from its beginnings, and required expert technical direction, the ownership and management of chemical companies tended to change more than in traditional companies. The firm of Kuhlmann had been founded in 1825 by a professor of chemistry from Lille, Frédéric Kuhlmann, as a simple joint-stock company. It was converted to a share ownership company in 1854 and a limited company in 1870. After Kuhlmann and his son died, the firm was administered by a technocrat and then reverted to Kuhlmann's son-in-law, Agache, who continued to administer it up to and during the war.[70]

The ownership and management of Saint-Gobain were a special case. Though the firm had become a limited company in 1831, with its 3,264 shares owned by 489 shareholders, only certain selected shareholders were informed about the operations of the company. Eventually a revolt of shareholders led to a minor reform: a perma-

---

68. Viallate, *L'Activité économique en France de la fin du XVIIIe siècle à nos jours* (Paris, 1937), 245–8.
69. Choffel, *Saint-Gobain*, 84.
70. Palmade, *Capitalism*, 162–3.

nent commission of delegates representing the ordinary share-holders was created to be given the information withheld from general meetings.[71] The management of the firm was dominated over the years by a few families, among them the de Vogüés, the de Broglies, and the Roederers. Since 1831, the firm had only one president who was an exception to the rules of dynastic succession, the renowned chemist Joseph Louis Gay-Lussac, who was president from 1844 to 1850.[72] The presence of traditional management, however, did not appear to be an inhibiting factor in the growth of the company.

The basic technology of chemicals created unique problems of production and marketing, and thus of organising the interests of the industry as a whole:

> From a technical point of view, the growth of production is almost limitless, while the consumption of this production is restricted by severe obstacles. The industry rarely creates a product consumed by a large clientele: often, only intermediary materials for some other product are manufactured. The industry is forced to study scientifically and develop technically an economic method of using its products; it must form and educate its customers, a task more easily accomplished by a collective organ. In addition, the fact that its technical possibilities are always superior to its economic possibilities creates the danger of overproduction; in the same way there is always the permanent danger of the discovery of new and more economic methods of production. Producers can only protect themselves against each other by *ententes*, which are, moreover, facilitated by the existence of the numerous patents characteristic of the industry, and by the small number of producers and clients.[73]

The technical complexity of the French chemical industry made it impossible to create one single co-ordinating trade association like the *Comité de Forges*. There was the Professional Association of Major Chemical Producers, but it does not appear to have been very effective. Instead, each branch of the industry made its own arrangements for marketing and production. Producers of soda and sulphuric acid remained unorganised, partly because of the competition of rival methods of production, but the French Syndicate of Superphosphates was highly organised, grouping almost all producers in four geographical regions, with a system of mutual technical and financial assistance, a fixing of prices, and an equitable sharing of profits.[74] On the other hand, industries which the Ger-

71. Choffel, *Saint-Gobain*, 79–80.
72. *1665–1965, Compagnie de Saint-Gobain* (Paris, 1965).
73. Viallate, *L'Activité économique*, 249–50.
74. Choffel, *Saint-Gobain*, 79.

mans monopolised were organised in international cartels. Under the direction of two German chemical giants, the Badische Anilin and the Bayer group, major European chemical companies made a series of agreements and arrangements covering the production and sale of dyes and pharmaceuticals. Aluminium producers were also grouped in a worldwide cartel.

There was less need for a trade association to represent the collective interests of the industry to the state than with iron and steel since there was relatively little contact between the two before 1914. The industry sold less than the ironmasters to the state and more to private industry, particularly since the state produced its own powder and explosives. The industry needed fewer favours from the government except protective tariffs, which were not particularly effective in stopping the Germans from consolidating their gains. The chemical industry was less affected by government social and labour policy.

What was the significance of all this for the war? The production of chemicals was obviously to be of critical importance to the war effort. Sulphuric acid was vital to the production of powder and explosives. Ammoniac became an important product, since it could be used to make nitric acid, which in turn produced powders, explosives, plastics, and varnishes. Chlorium was used to produce fuses, an explosive called cheddite, and gas. Dyes were needed to make uniforms. Pharmaceuticals were necessary for the war wounded.

The French chemical industry was considerably handicapped at the beginning of the war because the Germans had controlled certain branches of the industry before the war, and because they went on to capture a considerable number of chemical factories during the first weeks. The fact that the pre-war chemical industrialists were talented, efficient, and tough explains in some measure the success of their efforts subsequently, and their skill in dealing with the state. The pre-war organisation of the industry bears heavily on certain events that took place during the war: the struggle between Saint-Gobain and Kuhlmann, for example, or the attempt of Saint-Denis to take over sequestered German dye factories. Finally, the absence of a supreme organisation of chemical producers, the general disruption of existing *ententes* by the war, and the disappearance of international cartels meant that the state faced a less united industry than iron and steel and was ultimately better able to intervene for the purpose of regulating the activities of chemical companies and protecting the national interest.[75]

75. See Chapters 2 and 5.

Petroleum

Petroleum had first appeared in France in the 1860s. Alexander Deutsch de la Meurthe, a vegetable oil manufacturer, saw the possibilities in mineral oil and began importing it into France. Joined by his sons, Deutsch de la Meurthe expanded his interests to include a wide range of petroleum-based products, such as asphalt. Another major importer of petroleum was the Société Desmarais Frères, which brought crude oil in from the United States, Romania, and the Caucusus.[76]

By 1910, a group of ten firms, known as the *Cartel des Dix*, had established a veritable monopoly in supplying France with petroleum.[77] They owned virtually no sources of crude oil, they did nothing to prospect for oil in France or any of her colonies, they owned no refineries, they were merely the sole agents for importing refined petrol into France. The single source for this refined petrol was Standard Oil of New Jersey, which was, 'along with the Catholic Church, the greatest power in the world', as one deputy expressed it in 1913. France's tanker fleet consisted of three small vessels which together were capable of transporting only one-twentieth of the imported oil.[78] French port facilities were incapable of receiving large modern tankers of 10,000 or 15,000 tons, and all of the unloading, transportation, and distribution system for refined oil was completely outmoded.

Before the outbreak of war, there had been several proposals to bring petrol under state control. In 1903, the Chamber of Deputies had invited the government to institute a state petrol monopoly. In an annexe to a report on the wine crisis, drawn up in 1912, Etienne Clémentel had also proposed the creation of a monopoly:

> Since there is no other substitute for this product in France, a monopoly would not be a hindrance to any other French industry. Besides, petrol is a substance which lends itself so easily to a monopoly that a monopoly exists already; the state would give it legal consecration for the greatest benefit of the consumer. The execution of this decision would present no problems; the purchase of factories would be a simple operation.[79]

This proposal was greeted with howls of protest from chambers of

76. Palmade, *Capitalism*, 164.
77. R. Kuisel, *Ernest Mercier, French Technocrat* (Berkeley 1967), 22–4.
78. J. Manteilhet, *Vers une économie nationale. Le régime des consortiums* (Paris, 1918), 52–9.
79. *Rapport au nom de la Commission de la crise viticole sur les questions se rapportant au régime des alcools. Annexe.* 24 February 1912.

commerce and professional associations, and, generally speaking, governments of the day were also opposed to the idea of nationalisation because of the prohibitive costs involved. On 15 January 1914, de Monzie, a deputy, proposed a bill creating a *régie intéressée*, a mixed enterprise with private and public participation, for refining and importing oil into France. This formula would have avoided the expense of expropriation and the problem of the government suddenly being forced to produce qualified technical personnel to administer the industry. In March of the same year, de Monzie returned to the attack and proposed a 1 per cent tax on profits as well, to give the government at least 'a slight control over an industry whose operations and earnings are a mystery to us'. Clémentel objected to these propositions and said that companies would retaliate by moving their headquarters abroad. The Finance Minister said that companies would reject the *régie intéressée*, thereby forcing the government to take the unacceptable step of expropriating them. The bill died at the end of the session.[80] As shall be seen, wartime conditions ultimately forced the government to take complete control of the petroleum industry.[81]

From this survey of five French industries before the First World War, it should be apparent that generalisations about industrialists are dangerous. There were wide variations not only from one industry to the next but from one industrialist to the next. Nevertheless, in a general way it can be said that the French industrialists who would be dealing with bureaucrats and politicians during the war were capable and resourceful men; most of them had been successful in business in the years immediately before 1914; they were not the timorous, conservative, family-obsessed crowd depicted by Landes and Pitts; they were prepared to sacrifice some independence in the interests of economic efficiency through concentration, vertical integration, and the formation of trade associations and cartels; and they were not universally hostile to new techniques. Those industrialists who had had occasion to deal with the state before the war had been generally adept in minimising the effects of government intervention and maximising the benefits of government protection and patronage. It is a truism, but one worth stating, that industrialists were better equipped technically and commercially to deal with industrial problems than bureaucrats or politicians, and therefore better armed for negotiations than either group representing the state, since they were

80. F12 7716.
81. See Chapter 4.

operating on their own ground.

Politicians: the Politics of State Intervention

Before 1914, the whole rhythm of state intervention in industry was set by politics. Laws governing the organisation of companies, or the conditions of work in factories, or the acquisition of new state industries had all to be introduced in parliament, debated, and voted. Once enacted, it was the responsibility of bureaucrats to administer these laws. After 1914, the exigencies of war set the pace of state intervention, and the normal political process was often circumvented or distorted. Before these circumventions and distortions can be understood, however, the pre-war political situation must be discussed.

The politics of state intervention cannot be separated from the general context of French politics. A number of approaches to the subject suggest themselves. One could analyse politics in terms of parties and groups, their doctrines and their leaders. Alternatively, one could talk about political mentalities: Thibaudet's six categories of political ideas, Siegfried's three tendencies of Right, Left, and Centre, Goguel's two temperaments of the Established Order and Movement, or Zeldin's republican consensus.[82] Finally, there is the political system itself, ranging from local politics, public opinion, and the role of pressure groups, to parliamentary elections and the power of the president. In truth, all of these approaches must be taken into account and integrated. What politicians said must be distinguished from what they thought, and what politicians thought from what they did, faced with the constraints of the political system within which they were operating.

The best way to illustrate the interaction of these factors is to consider the example of a measure of state interference actually being legislated: the repurchase of the Western Railway by the state from 1906 to 1908. The selection of this issue might be contested. It could be argued that there was no real conflict of principle or party over this question and that the repurchase militated *against* the further extension of state power over industry, since the Western Railway was the only one of France's six private railway companies

---

82. F. Goguel, *La Politique des partis sous la IIIè République* (Paris, 1958). Zeldin, *France*, 633–4, 698. A. Siegfried, *Tableau des partis politiques en France* (Paris, 1930), 157–95. A. Thibaudet, *Les Idées politiques de la France* (Paris, 1932).

to lose money.[83] Moreover, this was not the first intrusion of the state in railway affairs: the whole system of railway concessions and financing had been intimately bound up with politics since the railways had first been introduced into France. Indeed, in 1850 and 1878, the state had already taken over certain money-losing branch lines and eventually created its own small company.[84] Finally, the whole operation has been portrayed as a mere financial and political boondoggle which overcompensated the shareholders of the Western while giving the Radicals new patronage in the west of France.[85]

Nevertheless, the repurchase of the Western caused the greatest single political controversy in France over state industrial intervention in the decade before the First World War. State control of the railways was an integral part of the programmes of both the Radical and Socialist parties. More important, many politicians of the day sincerely believed that the repurchase was an ideological, not a practical, question and that it represented a major advance of the state into hitherto uncharted industrial waters.[86] The fact that the issue was not a new one, or that financial and practical considerations were also involved, does not detract from but rather enhances the validity of the example. In politics there are few 'pure' cases. Finally, the measure is important because it was eventually enacted.

The background of the case can be quickly summarised. Private railway companies in France operated under a system of state concessions. Under laws passed in 1842, 1859, and 1873, the state guaranteed all loans undertaken by companies and all capital invested by them. In return, the concessions would automatically revert to the state in fifty, seventy-five, or ninety years, depending on the individual agreement. Thus by 1960 the state would have acquired all the concessions. The state also had the legal option of repurchasing concessions before they expired, and this is what was proposed in the case of the Western.[87]

The Compagnie des Chemins de fer de l'Ouest was one of the six networks organised during the reign of Napoleon III. By 1906 it owned 6,000 kilometres of track running through the underpopulated, unprofitable west of France, it was hemmed in by the Northern and Paris-Orléans companies, it was badly administered, lines

83. Goguel, *La Politique*, 132.
84. K. Doukas, *The French Railroads and the State* (New York, 1945), 58–62.
85. Zeldin, *France*, 704–5.
86. G. Bonnefous, *Histoire politique de la Troisième République* (Paris, 1965), i. 101–4.
87. H. Laufenburger, *L'Intervention de l'état en matière économique* (Paris, 1939), 37–8.

were crowded, shipments were delayed, and it continually lost money. In 1906, it owed the treasury 440 million francs in debts.

Proposals for the state to take over private railway companies go back as far as the building of the railways themselves. On 5 April 1849, for example, the *Programme de la presse démocratique et sociale* proclaimed the necessity of the state running the railways.[88] In 1872, the first of many proposals to repurchase all railway companies was made in the Chamber of Deputies, supported by such leading Republicans as Gambetta and Rouvier. From 1872 to 1905 the Chamber considered no fewer than fifteen separate projects to repurchase either all or some of the companies, and it had twice voted for such measures, only to have them overturned by the Senate. Specific bills to repurchase the Western had been introduced in 1895, 1899 (twice), 1900, 1901, and 1905, the last by the Railway Commission of the Chamber, but, an important point to note, until 1906 the measure had never formed part of the ministerial declaration and hence the official policy of any government.[89]

The Western Railway issue can be examined from two angles. First, in terms of what politicians said and did during the debate on repurchase, compared with the formal doctrines and programmes their parties and groups espoused: this is the interplay of ideology, mentality, and action. Secondly, from the perspective of the political process itself: the way in which the mechanics of the system influenced the passage not only of legislation involving state control of industry, but of all legislation.

The Ideology of State Intervention

One curious fact about the doctrinal aspect of the Western Railway issue should be underlined from the outset: though the measure was passed in the Chamber of Deputies by 364 votes to 187 on 7 December 1906, only 111 of the 592 deputies elected in May 1906 had included the proposal in their electoral programmes. Of the 111, many ultimately voted against the measure.[90] What makes this simple fact even more curious is that 247 Radicals and Radical-Socialists had been elected to the Chamber in 1906, and that from its foundation in 1901 to the war, the Radical and Radical-Socialist party consistently included the acquisition by the state not only of

88. J. Kaiser, *Les Grandes batailles du radicalisme 1820–1901* (Paris, 1962), Annexe 1, 313–14.
89. Doukas, *French Railroads*, 51–2. *Chambre des députés*, 7 December 1906, 2995.
90. *Sénat*, 18 June 1908, 788.

all railway companies, but also of all insurance companies and sources of energy, as well as the curtailment of all commercial, financial and industrial monopolies in its formal programme.[91] Radical theorists like Alfred Foullié and Léon Bourgeois had attempted to reconcile *laissez-faire* economics with state intervention, Social Darwinism with Rousseau's Social Contract, and Christian liberalism with socialism in a foggy philosophy called *Solidarité*, of which the control of the railways by the state was meant to be one concrete expression.[92] It is some indication of the seriousness with which party doctrine was taken that a majority of its elected members failed to include one of its principal tenets within their electoral programmes.

When Clemenceau formed his first government in 1906, it was dominated by six Radical ministers. Clemenceau himself had been advocating that the state take over railways, canals and mines, as well as implementing income and inheritance taxes, since the 1880s.[93] Clemenceau's ministerial declaration to the Chamber of Deputies on 5 November 1906 included the promise to repurchase the Western Railway, which was currently being run 'to the detriment of the general interest and of public finance'.[94] When, one and a half years later, he was finally able to wind up the debate in the Senate, he explained why the step had been taken.[95] He began by stating that the issue was not merely a practical one, it had a political dimension. He denied that the repurchase was statist or collectivist; rather, it was a means whereby the state could defend the public interest against the greed of the private companies, it was a way of exercising an element of control by using the future state railway as a test model against which their activities could be measured. It was private trusts and cartels which menaced individual liberty, not the state. Finally, he said, the repurchase should be construed as essentially a social reform.

Surprisingly few other Radicals spoke on the issue in either Chamber of the Senate. Even more surprisingly, one of the two that did, spoke against it. Viger, a Radical senator from the Loiret, denounced the measure as impractical, but more important, as a

91. F. Buisson, *La Politique radicale* (Paris, 1908), 208. C. Nicolet, *Le Radicalisme* (3rd edn., Paris, 1967), 31–42.
92. J. Scott, *Republican Ideas and the Liberal Tradition in France 1870–1914* (New York, 1966), 124, 173–7.
93. G. Bruun, *Clemenceau* (Hamden, Connecticut, 1968), 36. D. Halevy, *La République des comités* (Paris, 1934), 22–4. G. Wormser, *La République de Clemenceau* (Paris, 1961), 216–17.
94. *Chambre des députés*, 5 November 1906, 2387.
95. *Sénat*, 25 July 1908, 837–42.

fatal step down the slippery slope of collectivism: the Radicals, he said, 'are marching down the same road as the United Socialists and are doing their work for them at this very moment'.[96] It is mildly ironic to note that Senator Viger eventually became an agent of the collectivist state during the war, heading a government committee to control imports.[97]

In the end, a majority of Radical deputies and senators did finally vote with the government over the issue, as much to keep the government in power as for any ideological motivation. After the repurchase of the Western, the Radicals did little to promote other measures of state industrial intervention before the war; clearly, it is as well not to take their formal doctrine and party programmes on the subject unquestioningly at face value.

The main participants in the railway debate came from that large, amorphous collection of groups in the right of centre part of the political spectrum which shall, for convenience, be called the Republicans. It might have been expected that this group of deputies and senators would be hostile to state intervention in industry, or in any other sphere. In 1891, for example, that quintessentially Republican leader, Raymond Poincaré, had expressed his opposition to the growth of the state bureaucracy in the following words:

> I am willing to repeat that there still exists in France within the Administration certain outdated complications, a plethora of personnel who are sinister from all points of view, sinister because they incur considerable expenses for the state, sinister especially because they extract from the active life of the country, from the free life of industry, of commerce, and of agriculture the vital forces which could be better employed elsewhere in the best interests of the nation.[98]

Republicans like Poincaré rejected certain elements of the Napoleonic administration which had been grafted onto the Republic, preferring co-operatives, better private insurance, arbitrational tribunals for industrial disputes, and profit-sharing contracts for workers in private industry, to any state-imposed solutions. Poincaré duly voted against the repurchase, though he did not join in the debate.

Yet the curious fact is that of the Republicans who did speak on the issue, as many spoke for repurchase as against. Two of the most prominent supporters were Barthou and Caillaux, both moderate

96. *Sénat*, 29 May 1908, 667–75.
97. See Chapter 3.
98. P. Miguel, *Poincaré* (Paris, 1961), 123, 202–6, 227–9.

Republicans, both members of Clemenceau's ministry; their support was logical, particularly since they were, respectively, Minister of Public Works and Minister of Finance. The reasoning of each was completely different. Barthou's argument was essentially practical: the company was in a mess and it was less interested in self-improvement than in being overcompensated, the government was legally entitled to take the step, the railway workers of the Western would be better off, and Republicans from Gambetta in 1872 on had favoured repurchasing the railways.[99] Caillaux took the opposite tack: this measure was ideologically motivated, it was only the beginning, a pilot project preceding the repurchase of the other railways.[100]

Another Republican who voted for the repurchase was Alfred Mascuraud, which might at first glance seem odd, particularly in view of the vigorous campaign he was later to wage during the war against state interference in business.[101] Mascuraud was a small businessman who manufactured costume jewellery and was a political supporter of Waldeck-Rousseau, with whom he founded the *Comité républicain du Commerce, de l'Industrie, et de l'Agriculture* in 1899 to defend free enterprise and the interests of small business.[102] Yet it is because he was a small businessman that Mascuraud favoured repurchasing the Western. Republicans are often thought of as the party of big business, and the example is cited of Jules Méline's government from 1896 to 1898, during which measures were passed to protect sugar refineries, to reinforce the privileges of the Bank of France, and to give businessmen great advantages in French Equatorial Africa.[103] But Méline's policies favoured big business at the expense of small. The Mascuraud Committee was actually formed as a rival to the *Comité national républicain du commerce et de l'industrie*, a group of big industrialists who supported Méline financially. One interesting minor detail is that in 1899 the Mascuraud Committee shared offices and facilities in the rue Tiquetonne with the *Comité d'Action pour les réformes républicaines*, which eventually helped form the Radical party in 1901.[104] It was therefore logical that Mascuraud should

99. *Chambre des députés*, 5 December 1906, 2917, 2922–33; 7 December 1906, 2994–3001.
100. *Sénat*, 12 June 1908, 745–6.
101. See Chapter 3.
102. J. Jolly, *Dictionnaire des parlementaires français* (Paris, 1960–72), vii. 2396.
103. E. Beau de Loménie, *Les Responsabilités des dynasties bourgeoises* (1943–63), ii. 277.
104. Kaiser, *Les Grandes batailles*, 292–4.

support the repurchase of the Western, since the measure served to weaken the grip of big business on the country.

The Republicans who spoke against the repurchase were more predictable. A majority of deputies and senators from the West itself opposed repurchase, possibly fearing the effects of an increase of Radical patronage in the area. Some invoked practical arguments, arguing that the company was not as bad as it seemed. But the speakers who attracted the most attention were those who denounced the move as a Socialist plot. Rouvier's attack on the project in the Senate made a big impact, particularly (as Clemenceau was not hesitant in pointing out afterwards) in view of his previous support for the repurchase of the railways, beginning in 1872 and culminating in the state purchasing the Algerian railways under his presidency of the council in 1900.[105]

In short, one could not speak of a consistent Republican point of view with regard to issues of state intervention in industry before 1914, and one could not predict what the reaction of Republican groups and individual Republicans might be when faced with future issues of this kind; it depended upon the situation.

At either end of the political spectrum there was a greater uniformity of views. Few Monarchists and Conservatives spoke on the issue (there were few left anyway), as they were generally interested in other matters, such as state intervention in religious affairs. In the Senate, the vicomte de Montfort opposed repurchase on agricultural and military grounds, took the occasion to denounce the low quality of state arsenals, telephones, and matches, and said that civil servants were ruder than private employees.[106] In the final vote in the Chamber of Deputies, a lieutenant-colonel, a general, an admiral, two viscounts, two princes, three dukes, five barons, seven counts, and eleven marquises voted against repurchase.[107]

The Socialists took little part in the debate, except for the occasional ironic jeer from Jules Guesde and Jules Coutant. One Socialist deputy and one Socialist senator spoke in favour. An eccentric independent Socialist deputy from Finistère, Pierre Biétry, a former worker who had made something of a name for himself in Socialist circles by opposing the idea of a general strike and generally attacking both Radicals and Socialists, denounced the measure as an attack on individual property, to the amusement of the Chamber.[108]

105. *Sénat.* 23 June 1908, 823–9.
106. *Sénat*, 23 June 1908, 813–15.
107. *Chambre des députés*, 7 December 1906, 3016.
108. *Chambre des députés*, 5 December, 1906, 2930–3. Jolly, *Dictionnaire*, ii. 599–600. He eventually came to a bad end in Saigon.

The Socialists voted as a group for the project. It is hard to discover what the precise attitude of the United Socialists was to specific measures of state intervention in industry because they were unsure themselves. Jaurès, the leading force in the party from 1906 to 1914, was himself ambivalent towards state socialism, in favour of certain specific, practical proposals, such as the state taking over sugar refineries, but vague about the exact modalities of nationalising other industries.[109] The other dominant figure in the party, Jules Guesde, had little practical sense of what the state takeover of all industry would actually involve.[110] In any case, though their numbers in parliament were growing, the Socialists were essentially powerless, excluded from governments, sitting on the sidelines, offering advice, and voting as they felt appropriate on each issue that presented itself.

The debate over the repurchase of the Western Railway shows the danger of attaching too much importance to formal political doctrines about state intervention. Some parliamentarians saw the issue as one of principle, taking the 'thin end of the wedge' view of state interference if they were against it, or seeing the measure as one of social democracy if they were for it, but most deputies and senators spoke and voted as they did for mixed motives: to keep the government in power, to solve the practical problem of bad rail service in the West, to settle political debts, to divert attention from the difficulties caused by the separation of church and state,[111] to compensate shareholders, or to put a damper on the power of large, private companies running monopolies. Perhaps the true political significance of the repurchase for future cases of state intervention in industry is that, in the final analysis, the measure was a compromise solution to a practical problem. The idea of *partial* interference, of the government establishing a model company to monitor the activities of private industry, was to be a popular one during the war: the National Dyes Company and the Arsenal of Roanne are two examples.[112] The final passage of the repurchase of the Western Railway reflects the preponderance of political com-

---

109. G. Lefranc, *Le Mouvement socialiste sous la Troisième République* (Paris, 1963), 160–7. J. Jaurès, *Oeuvres* (Paris, 1933), vi. 363, 425. A. Zévaès, *Jean Jaurès*, (Paris, 1941), 65–79. *Jean Jaurès*, présenté par Vincent Auriol (Paris, 1962), 75–84.
110. C. Willard, *Les Guesdistes*, *Le Mouvement socialiste en France* (1893–1905) (Paris, 1965), 168–80.
111. One recalls Albert Thibaudet's celebrated *mot*: 'Le Parti Radical se trouva fort dépourvu quand la séparation fut venue.'
112. See Chapters 5 and 10.

promise, common sense, and consensus over formal doctrine and party programme in the French political system.

The Political System

So much for ideology and party policy: how did the mechanics of the political process affect the outcome of the affair? How, in short, did policy become law? The progress of the repurchase bill from Clemenceau's ministerial declaration on 5 November 1906 to its final passage by the Senate on 26 June 1908 will serve as a useful model of the political system to demonstrate certain features that were later to be of importance for the extension of state control over industry during the war. This exercise may at first seem an elaborate presentation of the obvious, but it provides a vital background to the wartime political situation.

Policies were made by cabinets. They became law in one of two ways: either they were proclaimed as ministerial decisions and decrees and took the force of law immediately, or they had to undergo the parliamentary process before being finally enacted as laws. Ministerial power fluctuated somewhat according to the seasons; it was said that France was governed by parliament during the eight months of the year it was usually in session, and by the ministers the other four months.[113] Normally, however, major government decisions had to be debated in parliament: such was the case of the repurchase of the Western.

In peacetime, the ability of a cabinet to enact legislation was dependent to a considerable degree upon the length of its tenure of office. Clemenceau's was one of the longer ministries of the Third Republic; it lasted two years, eight months, and twenty-five days. It took over a year and a half to push through the repurchase of the Western. The bill would not have been dropped automatically had Clemenceau's government been defeated earlier, but the fact that similar measures had been proposed in parliament since 1872 and twice voted by the Chamber of Deputies without ultimate success underlines the importance of ministries lasting long enough to see controversial bills safely through the machinery of parliament. A lack of ministerial continuity was one of the reasons that more far-reaching social and economic legislation was not passed by pre-war governments.[114] The first proposal to introduce income tax

---

113. J. Barthélemy, *Le Gouvernement de la France* (Paris, 1924), 45. E. Sait, *Government and Politics of France* (London, 1920), 89.
114. R. Soltau, *French Parties and Politics 1871–1921* (New York, 1965), 13.

had also been made in parliament in 1872; it was not fully legislated until 1917. It required the urgency of a wartime situation to speed up the legislative process or to allow governments to bypass it altogether.

The power of an individual minister to promote specific policies was related both to the continuity of the government in which he served and the period of time he held his ministry without interruption; the two were not necessarily the same. Barthou, the minister responsible for introducing the repurchase bill, held the Ministry of Public Works for four years, seven months, and nineteen days. He began under Sarrien in March 1906, continued under Clemenceau, and was kept on by Briand until he was finally forced out of office in a cabinet shuffle in November 1910.[115] The continuity of individual ministers increased the chances of a continuity of policies within the cabinet, particularly if the minister were a powerful figure in the government, though controversial measures would always require the united support of each new cabinet.

Continuity in office also gave the individual minister greater authority within his own ministry. The power of senior civil servants within a ministry stemmed from their permanence, their expertise and monopoly on information, and the fact that ministers had little control over their recruitment and organisation. The minister was able to impose his own will on the bureaucrats only by retaining the post long enough to master its complexities, to shape its organisation to his purpose, and to use his political authority to implement his own policies. The minister could not control the permanent civil servants single-handed, hence the need for his personal staff, or cabinet. The minister and his cabinet must be seen as a single unit, the link between the political and bureaucratic processes. The minister's personal collaborators were the extension of his power, they were directly responsible to him, it was they who assembled the information on which he based his decisions, it was they who kept watch on the permanent civil servants.[116] 'The Cabinet incarnates the authority of the minister. It lives his life, it share his fortunes: an unstable position but a privileged one'.[117] As has been mentioned previously, the quality of these men before 1914 was uneven; some were young and inexperienced, though the minister might also draw upon the staffs of the Council of State or the Court of Accounts. The cabinets were generally small: in 1913,

115. Barthélemy, *Le Gouvernement*, 114.
116. Sharp, *Government*, 141.
117. Sait, *Government*, 109.

the cabinet of the Minister of Public Works numbered six, while the Minister of Commerce had only three. The institution of the minister and his cabinet was to be of great significance in the decision-making process during the war.

The relationship between governments and parliaments calls for some elaboration. As in most democracies, in France parliament had an *ex post facto* control over ministries: 'The Government follows its own policy, inspired uniquely by its own conscience and the national interest. It is only when this policy is translated into acts that it comes under parliamentary control'.[118] This control was exercised in a number of ways. The government might be defeated in a vote of confidence in the Chamber of Deputies, or, more rarely, the Senate. This ultimate form of control was not employed by parliament during the repurchase debate and occurred only once during the war. More common was the control exercised through procedural manoeuvering, the moving of amendments, repeated debates on general government policy, opened by the interpellation of one or several deputies and closed by a vote on a motion of confidence (*ordre du jour*), and the daily questioning of ministers. In the repurchase debate, the government had a relatively smooth run. The discussion in the Chamber lasted only three days, while the Senate debated the issue over the period of nearly a month. In times of difficulty, however, the government could be so hounded and harassed on the floor of the Chamber and the Senate that no legislation could pass, and the government eventually had no alternative but to resign. This control by harassment was to be a distinguishing feature of the wartime political process.

The simple fact that the Chamber of Deputies and Senate elected their own presidents, who were not cabinet nominees, and set their own order of business independent of the leader of the government, reduced the effective direction of the government over the legislative process.[119] In the case of the repurchase bill, the Chamber considered the question a month after the government proposed the legislation, but the Senate allowed the matter to drift for a year and a half before taking it up.

The Senate rarely defeated a government outright, its tactics were delay, particularly when confronted with certain sorts of legislation it disliked:

The Chamber, in the heat of battle, adopts a measure; the project thus

118. Barthélemy, *Le Gouvernement*, 106.
119. Soltau, *French Politics*, 13.

voted goes to the Senate, which nominates in its own sweet time a commission, whose labours are interminable. During this period, the Chamber can no longer consider the problem, which has been removed from its deliberations. Gradually other problems come to occupy the public mind; the issue is buried. When, after several years, the reporter delivers his report, which is debated several months later, passions have decidedly cooled, intransigencies deflated. . . . [The Senate] is opposed to state control in all its forms; nevertheless, believing itself bound by political necessity, it voted for the repurchase of the Western Railway.[120]

The longer the Senate was able to delay consideration of a controversial issue, the greater the odds against the ministry sponsoring the bill surviving. In the end, however, should the government endure and persist, the Senate would give way; again, the political system reflected a deep-rooted sense of political realism and consensus, which was part of the basic mentality of French politicians.

The final, and perhaps the most daunting, form of control exercised over the government was by parliamentary commissions. The system of grand standing committees in the Chamber of Deputies and Senate had evolved gradually during the Third Republic.[121] In some ways, the committees performed the same function as a shadow cabinet in an English-based parliamentary system. For every ministry, there was a corresponding grand standing committee of the Chamber or Senate which monitored its activities and future legislation. Each committee of the Chamber was made up of thirty-three members, (increased to forty-four in 1910), who were nominated by officially recognised groups in proportion to their numbers in the Chamber. The same system applied to the Senate, except commissions had forty-four members. The power of the commissions came from the fact that they acted in the name of the whole Chamber or Senate, that they were permanent while governments were not, that they performed a central role in the passage of legislation, and that they could interfere with the internal workings of ministries.

The function of the commissions in the legislative process can be illustrated by examining the case of the repurchase bill. On 5 November 1906, the measure was announced to the Chamber in Clemenceau's ministerial declaration, then formally placed before the Chamber the same day by Louis Barthou, the Minister of Public Works, and sent to the Commission of Public Works, where it was

120. Barthélemy, *Le Gouvernement*, 76–9.
121. J. Barthélemy, *Essai sur le travail parlementaire et le système des commissions* (Paris, 1934). R. Gooch, *The French Parliamentary Commission System* (New York, 1935).

deliberated for three weeks. A report favourable to the project was drawn up and presented by the reporter of the commission, Emile Aimond, to the Chamber on 29 November. Meanwhile, the Budget Commission of the Chamber had also considered the measure and approved it. Before Barthou closed the debate, Aimond summed up the arguments in favour of the proposal on behalf of the Public Works Commission.

When the bill reached the Senate, it was forwarded to the Senate Railway Commission and the Senate Finance Commission, where it received a much cooler reception. The reporters of both Commissions delivered unfavourable reports to the Senate in May 1907 and March 1908 respectively. But despite the delaying tactics and hostile reports of the commissions, the proposal was finally debated by the Senate in May and June 1908. The reporter of the Railway Commission, Charles Prevet, took a leading part in the attack on the measure. He and the president of the commission, Emile Labiche, tried unsuccessfully to delay the matter further by claiming that important new material had just come to light which would require further consideration by the commissions. A last-ditch attempt by the commission to propose an alternative, milder measure was also defeated, and the bill passed.

The story is instructive in several regards. If delay was a prime tactic for frustrating the will of the government, it was the commissions which were largely responsible for using it. It was customary for the reporter of the commission to take a leading role in the debate, either for or against the measure. As the name would suggest, it was the reporter who drew up the commission's report, and, like the president of the commission and members of the government, he could speak as often as he wished in the debate. The prestige of the reporter was such, particularly in the case of the financial commissions, that he was often considered the equal of, and indeed a likely successor to, the incumbent minister. But as the repurchase debate also revealed, the power of the reporter and the commission was not limitless; in the case of conflict between the government and a commission, in the end it was the Chamber or Senate as a whole which acted as arbiter, in this case siding with the government.

Studies of ministerial instability reveal few instances of governments being brought down by parliamentary commissions, with the exception of the financial commissions of both chambers.[122] The

122. A. Soulier, *L'Instabilité ministérielle sous la Troisième République (1871–1938)* (Paris, 1939), 221.

Finance Commission of the Senate in particular became known as
the 'wrecker of ministries', or the 'committee of heirs apparent'.
The Budget Commission of the Chamber of Deputies and the
Finance Commission of the Senate were in a privileged position. To
begin with, the control of the budget has traditionally been the
strongest weapon of the legislative element of government against
the executive, and it was the financial commissions which wielded
that weapon. Moreover, this power was enhanced by the fact that
financial commissions also had the right to intervene on any issue
involving the expenditure of money. Most pieces of legislation,
therefore, as in the case of the repurchase bill, faced the quadruple
jeopardy of the two specific commissions concerned, in this instance, the Public Works Commission of the Chamber and the
Railway Commission of the Senate, and both financial commissions. The presidents and reporters of the two financial commissions had correspondingly greater prestige than those of the other
commissions. Unlike ordinary commissions, financial commissions
could meet when parliament was not in session. One special prerogative of the financial commissions, which was to be of considerable
significance for the war, was that under a finance law of April 1906,
amplified by a law of July 1914, members had the formal and legal
right to on-the-spot inspection of the state of war and naval material, which gave them a measure of unprecedented control of the
administration over the heads of the Ministers of War and the Navy.
Every year, each commission appointed two members for this
express purpose, and every year from 1906 to 1914 these members
warned of the insufficiency of military material.

   All commissions, ordinary as well as financial, had a measure of
indirect control over ministers and bureaucrats. They could request
ministers to appear at their meetings to justify themselves; though
the ministers were under no legal obligation to attend, they usually
did. Thus, a minister might have to appear at the meetings of four
different commissions as well as on the floor of the Chamber and
Senate to support one single piece of legislation. Commissions
could also summon civil servants to their hearings and, in certain
instances, inspect administrative services directly, though only in
the case of the financial commissions and war material was there any
legal stipulation for this.

   From this cursory review of the politics of state intervention in
industry in France before 1914, it can be seen that while politicians
were not unaware of ideological considerations, and were not
hesitant about invoking them in debate, in the end, the passage of
specific measures, such as the repurchase of the Western Railway,

was as much the result of practical politics as doctrine. Secondly, pre-war ministers and their bureaucrats were restricted in the exercise of their authority by the mechanics of the political system: ministerial instability, parliamentary debate, and the work of the commissions. War politics were characterised by an initial suspension of this process, followed by a resumption which was acrimonious to the point of self-destruction. It is time to consider these events in detail.

CHAPTER 2

The Influence of French Politics and British Pressure on Wartime Industrial Policy

For the first five critical months of the war in 1914, French ministers and bureaucrats were virtually free from political pressures in dealing with industrial problems; they failed to take advantage of their power, and the industrialists flourished. From 1915 to the end of the war, ministers and bureaucrats were subject to political pressure, sometimes intense, both from within France and from Britain; despite, and occasionally even because of, these pressures, the power of ministers and bureaucrats grew continuously. The chronicle of these later struggles between ministers and their bureaucrats, and industrialists, is outlined in the remaining chapters of this book; it is the purpose of this present chapter to describe the changing nature of the political arena within which these struggles took place.

1914

The Political Situation

On 2 August 1914, after the German invasion of Belgium, President Poincaré decreed all eighty-six departments of France and the three departments of Algeria to be in a state of siege. This decree was necessary to legalise the total mobilisation of the army and the navy which had taken place the day before, but its effects went far beyond military mobilisation. For France to be placed legally on a footing for war, parliament had to pass a law, or to ratify a decree of the President of the Republic, declaring the country to be in a state of siege. Two laws then came into operation, those of 9 August 1849[1] and 3 April 1878.[2] Individual liberties were suspended, the army could requisition arms and munitions as well as other forms of private property, publications could be banned, and citizens could be tried on security charges by the military authorities. Under these laws, however, there was no provision for requisitioning for civilian needs.

The state of siege laws left many questions unanswered. What were the rights and duties of the Chamber of Deputies and the Senate under a state of siege? How far could ministers and their subordinates go in making decisions without reference to parliament? How were wartime duties to be divided among ministers? What civilian administrative organisation would supply the material needs of the army? Who was to initiate the industrial programmes necessary to sustain the war effort? How was labour to be controlled, prices maintained, and materials in short supply dealt out?

The French General Staff had anticipated that the war would be short, that the production of 13,500 shells a day for the 75-millimetre field-gun, the basic artillery piece of the army, would prove sufficient, and that there would be no need to increase the number of men, 50,000 at the outbreak of the war, who were already employed in war industries.[3] Existing powder stores were expected to meet the requirements of the entire war.

Although it was not to be fully apparent until the myth of the 'short war' had been completely and tragically dispelled, the French government was aware from the outset that one logical corollary of total military mobilisation might be total economic mobilisation. It is significant that as early as 2 August 1914, a law of 1877 dealing with the requisitioning of industrial establishments by the military authorities was amended to define with greater exactitude how this was to be applied.[4] Although this power of direct requisitioning of private industry by the government was to prove more of a potential than an actual threat, the passage of such a bill in August 1914 indicates a certain governmental alertness to industrial problems in wartime.

On 4 August 1914, the Chamber of Deputies and the Senate met and ratified the government's state of siege decree, thereby

1. *Le Moniteur universel*, no.224, 12 August 1849, 2683.
2. *Journal officiel*, no.93, 4 April 1878, 3921.
3. B.W. Schaper, *Albert Thomas, trente ans de réformisme social* (Assen, 1959), 105.
4. *Journal officiel*, 3 August 1914, 2086.

relinquishing almost entirely any further share in the direction of the war, at least for the time being.[5] This task performed, parliament now adjourned to an indefinite date, leaving the government a free hand to prosecute the war without political constraint. Conscious of the need for national unity, and anxious to avoid partisanship, Viviani, who had led a government dominated by the Radicals since 14 June 1914, reshuffled his cabinet on 26 August 1914 to produce a non-partisan ministry of the talents which included, Briand, Delcassé, Malvy, Millerand, and Ribot, as well as two Socialists, Sembat and Guesde.[6]

The adjournment of parliament and the creation of a united government placed a moratorium on criticism during the early months of the war. The air of secrecy which necessarily enshrouded the formulation of wartime policy had the effect of screening the government's intentions from the view not only of the Germans, but of potential critics within France as well.

The way was now clear for strong, even dictatorial administration. The government ruled by executive decree, and the scope of its powers grew continuously. Transport, health, agriculture, commercial obligations, and industrial production all came to be regulated by decree. Financial control by parliament and its commissions disappeared when the government was empowered to open 'supplementary credits', as well as 'extraordinary resources', in the absence of the two chambers. British pressure had not yet begun. The powers of the French government to December 1914 were theoretically limitless.

Industrialists, Ministers and Bureaucrats

On 13 July 1914, Charles Humbert, a former army officer, senator from la Meuse, and reporter for the Army Commission, sounded a grim and prophetic note of warning to the Senate about the inadequacies of French military production. He demonstrated the inferiority of French field artillery compared to German, the mediocrity of French fixed artillery, the inadequacy of French mortars, and in general the lack of all munitions. French soldiers had outdated field equipment and lacked battle uniforms of neutral colours. He showed that there was a deficiency of two million pairs of military boots, and that the day war was declared, each French

5. *Chambre des députés*, 4 August 1914, 3116. *Sénat*, 4 August 1914, 1307.
6. *Journal officiel*, 27 August 1914, 7697–8.

soldier would have only one pair of boots, with another pair thirty years old in his pack. Reflecting the shock of the Senate, Clemenceau said, 'Since 1870, I have never attended as moving, as anguishing, as sorrowful a session of Parliament as I have today.' Messimy, the Minister of War, promised that most of the problems would be rectified by 1917.[7]

Within six weeks, the effects of years of inadequate industrial preparation for war were disastrously compounded. By the end of August 1914, the German army had swept through northern France taking 32,000 square kilometres of the richest industrial area of the country. Metals and chemicals were particularly badly hit. France lost 83 per cent of her iron ore, 81 per cent of her cast iron production, 74 per cent of her coal, and 63 per cent of her steel.[8] Sulphuric acid production was severely affected; Kuhlmann, for example, lost 95 per cent of its factories.[9] Territorial losses were made worse by the chaotic disruption of the labour force. In the first two weeks of the war, 2.887 million men joined the French army; with the indiscriminate conscription of skilled workers, industry was paralysed and, by the end of August, half of French factories were closed down, including the military workshops of Bourges and St Etienne. As a paradoxical consequence, in a time of mass mobilisation, there were 60,000 unemployed men in Paris alone.

The story of French industrial mobilisation during the rest of the war is largely the story of the continuing effort of the French government to compensate for these economic losses during the first weeks of the war. From the outset, the government clearly had the power to take industrial matters firmly in hand. That it failed to do so was in part because of the panic which gripped the country in September 1914; in part because the bureaucrats involved were inexperienced, few in numbers, geographically dispersed, and continuously restructured during this period; and in part because the ministers responsible were desperate to solve problems quickly, at any price, little anticipating the impact of these early decisions on later industrial policy. The attempts of ministers and bureaucrats to cope with the iron and steel and chemical industries in 1914 illustrates the problem well.

On 2 September 1914, the forty-fourth anniversary of the defeat at Sedan, the government was forced to flee Paris to the comparative

7. *Sénat*, 13 July 1914, 1199–1210; 14 July 1914, 1261–72.
8. A. Fontaine, *L'Industrie française pendant la guerre* (Paris, 1924), 40–2. Ministère du Commerce, *Rapport général*, i. 67.
9. Boudet, *Affaires*, 186.

safety of Bordeaux. Chaos prevailed. Hotels and schools were
jammed with deputies with nothing to do, soldiers who had been
mobilised but had managed to be transferred to a ministry rather
than to the front and, above all, businessmen, or would-be businessmen, of all complexions, who realised that rich contracts for military supplies were in the offing. A colourful coterie of camp-
followers pursued the men: the actress Nelly Beryl, mistress of
Malvy, the Minister of the Interior; the poetess Anna de Noailles
and the novelist Marthe Bibescu, both of whom established salons
where they received leading members of the government.[10]

The businessmen who flocked to Bordeaux did not come away
empty-handed. The immediate requirements of the army were filled
by ministerial orders, and to furnish them, a black market soon
sprang up in vital war materials: tents, flannel, sheets, shoes, socks,
barbed-wire, shirts, and belts.[11] Some manufacturers subcontracted
to English producers and kept half the money paid by the government. Such blatant abuses, however, proved relatively easy to
eradicate later in the war and form but a small part of the total
number of industrial contracts passed during the war.[12]

With the 'miracle of the Marne' in mid-September, which produced a more stable military situation on the front, the French
government was able to regain its breath and study the crisis in
army supplies in a more organised manner. On 20 September 1914,
Millerand, the new War Minister, summoned leading bankers,
industrialists, and representatives of the railway companies to Bordeaux for a conference to draw up plans for the immediate economic
mobilisation of the country. He announced that 100,000 shells a day
were required by the army, not 13,000. He divided the industrialists
into twelve regional groups and placed each regional group under
the leadership of one man, who was made responsible for sharing
out steel, distributing military contracts, and co-ordinating and
verifying their execution; investigating the industrial resources of
the region; utilising small industrialists, either singly or in groups,
to the maximum; and making certain that plants and personnel in
each region were being employed to achieve peak productivity.[13]
The first concern of all the industrialists was to be shell production.
Qualified metal workers such as turners and adjusters were summoned from the army by telegram, workers from small firms were

10. Beau de Loménie, *La Guerre et l'immédiate après guerre*, (Paris, 1954), 49.
11. Ibid., 71.
12. See, for example, *Archives nationales* 94 AP 71: *Services industriels et Inspections des Forges. Paiements et marchés*.
13. W. Oualid, C. Picquenard, *La Guerre et le Travail* (Paris, 1928), 48, 49.

sent to help larger ones, and the industrialists were soon to be given the right to hunt out the workers they required in the military depots.[14] On 24 September, the first census of metal workers in the depots was taken, and on 11 October, the generals received orders from the government to send back the workers of one hundred private firms immediately, for the production of shells.

At this early stage in the war, private industry was not slow to take advantage of the opportunities offered them by the government. The *Comité des Forges*, the powerful association of French metal producers, had volunteered its services to the government even before the flight to Bordeaux, through its secretary-general, Robert Pinot. Members of the association dominated the twelve regional groups established by Millerand. Such patriotism did not go unrewarded: the *Comité* was given a free hand in co-ordinating its members' productive capacities, centralising and distributing government contracts, allocating manpower, and hunting out exploitable industrial plants.[15] Pinot's immediate concern was that the first orders from the government for 75 mm. shells should be divided equally among the factories of members of the *Comité des Forges*, so that all of them might keep at least a portion of their personnel. On 23 August 1914, Messimy, the previous Minister of War, placed the responsibility for distributing government orders among industrialists directly in the hands of the *Comité des Forges*. He wrote to Pinot:

> I have asked the sections of my department which place orders with industrialists who adhere to your groups to put themselves in direct contact with you to assure *the distribution and execution of these orders.* I hope that in devoting your entire attention to the rapid execution of these orders you will strive to provide jobs for the workers of the greatest number of factories and plants possible.[16]

Thus, from the beginning of the war, the *Comité des Forges* received an almost blank cheque from the government to organise the supply of war materials. The *Comité* retained the initiative throughout the war by creating its own bureaucratic structure to supply whatever needs of the country for metal might arise. It was only towards the end of the war that the government began to counter-attack by proposing bureaucratic structures of its own, but by then, it was far too late; the *Comité des Forges* had become so firmly entrenched as

14. Schaper, *Thomas*, 106.
15. Ibid.
16. François-Poncet, *Pinot*, 194.

an integral part of the machinery for supplying metal and arms to the government that it could not be uprooted without causing serious disruption of the war effort.

One of the chief advantages for firms which co-operated at an early date with the government was that they were able to establish prices which were to be the basis of prices paid by the government throughout the war. These early prices were set at a time when the desperate need to supply the army immediately, the great expenses and risks involved in converting factories to armament production, and the inexperience of both industrialists and bureaucrats in ascertaining production costs led the government to offer maximum premiums for war material. The industrialists were soon able to rationalise and render economical their productive processes, and the capital risks of creating munitions plants diminished as the war went on, but the old price bases remained, principally because the ever-growing requirements of the army meant that industrial capacity was in continually short supply, and that producers could set the prices they liked.

The French chemical industry was one of the first to establish basic price lists. In November 1914, most of the chief manufacturers of sulphuric acid in France met in Bordeaux with government experts and determined the basic price of sulphuric acid for the duration of the war.[17] One of the chief companies to benefit from these negotiations was Saint-Gobain, which signed seven additional contracts from March to July 1915 with the state to produce various forms of acid, at the prices set at Bordeaux in November. It should be emphasised that the great profits which Saint-Gobain made during the rest of the war are directly attributable to the price bases negotiated in the fall of 1914. Saint-Gobain undertook a massive expansion and building programme, and the state guaranteed that in addition to fulfilling its regular contracts with the firm, it would purchase any surplus production. For Saint-Gobain, this was a veritable golden age.

In 1914, ministers solved the problem of creating a bureaucracy to deal with industrial problems in two ways. The solution of Millerand, the Minister of War, for armament production was to avoid the problem altogether by having private industry use its own bureaucracy, the *Comité des Forges*. This arrangement was understandable in view of the shortage of bureaucrats qualified in indus-

17. 94 AP 105: *Note sur les marchés d'acide sulfurique et d'oléum traités par la Cie. de Saint-Gobain avec l'Administration de la Guerre à la date du 23 octobre*, 29 October 1915.

trial questions in the pre-war Ministry of War, and it made for initially amicable relations between the iron and steel industry and the government, but it could hardly be said to have protected the national interest to the fullest.

The government took a different approach to the problem of the chemical industry. More accurately, it tried a number of approaches. Given the importance of chemicals in the manufacture of munitions, it might logically have been expected that the Ministry of War take charge of chemicals as well, but the hazards of war decreed otherwise. On 13 August 1914, the Minister of the Interior established a commission to investigate ways of providing the civilian population with medical supplies. Auguste Béhal, a member of the Academy of Médecine and professor at the Ecole Supérieure de Pharmacie, a man who was to become one of France's most influential wartime bureaucrats, prepared a report on pharmaceutical products, indicating needs and new programmes of production. He was then sent to London to an international conference on pharmaceutical products.

In the meantime, the Minister of Commerce, Thomson, had created his own commission to study the state of the chemical industry in France. On 17 October 1914, Thomson created by decree an embryonic Office for Chemical and Pharmaceutical products and appointed Béhal to be its head. Thus, within three months, the responsibility for a major industrial sector had been shifted from one ministry to another, and one man's report had grown into an entire office. The aims of the Office, as defined in October 1914, were vague, but left a great deal of scope for bureaucratic initiative: the Office was charged with the mission of assessing existing quantities of chemical and pharmaceutical products, evaluating production procedures, assuring the supply and distribution of raw materials, and finally 'developing a more intensive production of these same products in France and encouraging the manufacture of new products'.[18] It was with the hastily assembled, inexperienced, disorganised bureaucrats of this new Office that the leading chemical manufacturers negotiated sulphuric acid prices for munitions in Bordeaux one month later, in November 1914, even though the Office was attached to the Ministry of Commerce and not the Ministry of War.

It was not until 2 January 1915, long after the conference establishing basic prices for sulphuric acid, that an order (*arrêté*) created

18. F12 7698: *Notice sur l'Office des produits chimiques et pharmaceutiques*, October 1916.

an executive committee to direct the work of the Office. On 27 November 1915, fourteen representatives of various ministries with interests in the chemical industry were appointed to the committee. The personnel of the Office was in the meanwhile filled out with twelve wartime bureaucrats, who, like Béhal, were for the most part former chemists or professors.[19]

Thus, to the end of 1914, though ministers and bureaucrats were operating within a political vacuum, they were not able to take advantage of their great potential power to adapt pre-war bureaucratic structures quickly enough to deal effectively with industrial problems. Lacking numbers, experience, and organisation, bureaucrats lost the first, and critical, round of their negotiations with industrialists.

1915–1918

Politics

The impact of wartime politics in France on state intervention in industry can best be understood by considering the distinguishing political characteristics of three periods: (1) from the reopening of parliament on 22 December 1914 to the first secret session of the Chamber of Deputies on 16 June 1916; (2) 16 June 1916 to Clemenceau's assumption of power on 13 November 1917; (3) Clemenceau's government.[20]

22 December 1914–16 June 1916

Political considerations had relatively little influence on government industrial policy during this period, partly because that policy was as yet inchoate, and partly because the future chief architects of the policy, Albert Thomas and Etienne Clémentel, only took office in the middle and latter part of the period.

The first feature of the period was that on 22 December 1914, parliament reopened in Paris for the rest of the war. Once again ministers could be held politically accountable for their actions and were forced to spend time away from directing the war effort to appear before parliament and its commissions. Initially, it seemed that the moratorium on partisanship would continue. The deputies

19. See Chapter 5.
20. These divisions are a slight modification of those proposed by Soulier, *L'Instabilité*, 326–8.

voted that no elections should be held until after the war. All government expenditure since the last parliamentary session was approved, and credits for the first half of the 1915 budget were voted without debate.[21]

Soon, however, deputies and senators began to reassert their authority, at first tentatively, but then with ever-increasing stridency. The first warning was sounded on 14 January 1915 by Paul Deschanel, the President of the Chamber of Deputies. Taking a back-handed swipe at the government's conduct of the war to date he said:

> Certain unjust attacks have been made on the Parliament of the Republic. . . . I believe that one of the chief lessons of this war will be, in the future, the necessity of a stronger, more energetic control than ever. (*Universal and repeated applause.*) If Parliament had been more daring, if it had known more, France would be in a better situation today. (*The whole Chamber rises and applauds lengthily.*)[22]

The Socialists pressed successfully for a permanent sitting of the Chamber rather than the annual minimum five months stipulated by the Constitution of 1875. Thus, unlike the pre-war situation, from one year to the next ministers were virtually never free of parliamentary pressure.

Pre-war habits soon returned. In the first two months of 1915, ministers were bombarded with 1,200 written questions, most of them trivial.[23]

Another feature of the period, arising directly out of the reopening of parliament, was the revival of parliamentary commissions. Even before parliament resumed, there had been hints of trouble. Millerand, the Minister of War, met a cool reception in the Senate Finance and Army Commissions on 21 December 1914.[24] The first day the Senate convened in December, it enlarged and renewed the membership of the Army Commission, adding Clemenceau, Bourgeois, and Doumer, and placing it under Freycinet's presidency. The Senate Army Commission was concerned not only with military operations, but also with one important industrial problem, the manufacture of armaments and munitions. It is generally recognised that the Senate Army Commission and the Army Commission of

21. *Chambre des députés*, 22 December 1914, 3125; 23 December 1914, 3132–41.
22. *Chambre des députés*, 14 January 1915. 8.
23. Barthélemy, *Le Travail parlementaire*, 237.
24. A. Ribot, *Journal d'Alexandre Ribot et Correspondances Inédites 1914–1922* (Paris, 1936), 25.

the Chamber played a major part in shaking up the bureaucrats of the Ministry of War and forcing the creation of the Under-Secretariat of State for Artillery and Munitions at the Ministry under Albert Thomas in May 1915.[25]

The financial commissions of parliament were also active during this period, though they appear initially to have had less influence on industrial questions than the army commissions. In September 1915, the president of the Budget Commission of the Chamber of Deputies wrote to Albert Thomas complaining about the lack of information provided by the new Under-Secretariat of State for Artillery and Munitions. In particular, he resented commissions of parliament being presented with administrative *faits accomplis* which they were then asked to endorse.[26]

The last months of 1915 and the first months of 1916 marked the apogee of the power of the parliamentary commissions. On 30 October 1915, a new government was formed by Briand specifically to appease the hostility of the Senate Army Commission, now dominated by Clemenceau. The new government attempted once again to create greater political unity. It contained eight former presidents of the council; three Socialists, including Albert Thomas; a Conservative, Denys Cochin; as well as a general, Gallieni, who replaced Millerand at the Ministry of War; and an admiral, Lacaze, who took over the Ministry of the Navy. Etienne Clémentel replaced Gaston Thomson at the Ministry of Commerce.[27]

But the commissions would not be appeased. Georges Bonnefous gives a graphic description of parliamentary life during the stormy days of early 1916:

> The Chamber was in permanent session and the Government was literally tormented by parliamentarians. The Government was obliged to appear three times a week before the Commissions of the Chamber and Senate, and above all before the Senatorial Commission of the Army presided over by M. Clemenceau (who forced the President of the Council of Ministers and the Minister of War to appear before him eighteen consecutive times). The Commissions demanded that they be informed of all statistics (total strength of army, reserves, supplies . . .) and indiscretions resulted.[28]

Briand and Gallieni were most directly affected by the activity of

---

25. Gooch, *Committee System*, 237–8. P. Renouvin, *Les Formes du gouvernement de guerre* (Paris, 1925), 118–19.
26. 94 AP 103: President of the Budget Commission to Albert Thomas.
27. *Journal officiel*, 30 October 1915, 7812–14.
28. Bonnefous, *Histoire*, ii. 119.

the commissions, but all ministers suffered to some degree from this process of attrition. Etienne Clémentel, newly arrived at the Ministry of Commerce, was generally ignored by the commissions, but Albert Thomas at the Under-Secretariat of State for Artillery and Munitions was beginning to attract the unfavourable attention of the Senate Finance Commission, whose reporter was Raphäel Milliès-Lacroix, a combative sixty-six year old Radical-Socialist from the Landes with a great deal of financial and industrial experience.[29] The specific incident which triggered off Milliès-Lacroix's initial displeasure was Thomas's decision to advance money to Schneider to re-activate a formerly German-owned metallurgical complex at Caen in January 1916.[30]

In June 1916, the Chamber of Deputies voted to move beyond control by commissions to control by direct delegation:

> The Chamber decides to institute and to organise a direct delegation which will exercise on the spot, with the co-operation of the Government, an effective control of all services having the mission of providing for the needs of the army.[31]

The motion was passed by 444 votes to 80. Had the measure have become operative, war industries would have been directly controlled by parliament, but Briand resisted, and the direct delegation system was never implemented. The Senate passed a less drastic motion in July 1916 by 251 votes to 6: 'The Senate counts on the Government to take, with the collaboration of the Chambers and grand parliamentary commissions, whose permanent control is indispensable, all measures of organisation and action which serve to hasten the hour of victory'.[32] Though the commissions would continue their activity for the rest of the war, they would never dominate politics as completely as they did to June 1916.

16 June 1916–13 November 1917

This was the period when politics made their greatest impact on the government's industrial policy. Secret sessions of the Chamber of Deputies and the Senate exposed ministers to scathing scrutiny and criticism. Parliament and the press became generally more interested in industrial questions; both Clémentel's and Thomas's poli-

---

29. Jolly, *Dictionnaire*, vii. 2471–2.
30. See Chapter 9.
31. *Chambre des députés*, 22 June 1916, 1375–9.
32. *Sénat*, 9 July 1916, 667–9.

cies began attracting greater publicity and opposition. At the same time, parliamentary commissions did not let up their attack on the government; Thomas continued to draw heavy fire from the Senate Finance Commission. Finally, the full resumption of party politics and bitter partisanship first undermined Albert Thomas's position, then led to his resignation.

The crisis over the battle of Verdun led to a major new phase in French wartime politics: the implementation of secret sessions of the Chamber of Deputies meeting as a committee of the whole. Secret sessions could be held to discuss only specific issues, such as Verdun, and from 16 June 1916 to 10 October 1917, eight such sessions were held. Normally the subject of the session was a military matter, such as the quality of Joffre's command, or a diplomatic question, such as relations with Greece. Industrial issues were not discussed, except as they related to military problems; during the first session on Verdun in June 1916, for example, Albert Thomas gave a report on shell production figures to date, and he was attacked by Noulens, a Radical deputy, and Maurice Violette, a Republican, for the poor quality of French artillery.[33]

Secret sessions were an extreme form of the pre-war parliamentary method of controlling governments through harassment. Secret sessions led to the resignation of two Briand governments in November 1916 and March 1917,[34] but these resignations had little effect on French industrial policy, since both Clémentel and Thomas continued uninterrupted in their functions, the latter being made Minister of Armament in December 1916.

Of greater consequence to Clémentel and Thomas was the increasing attention paid by parliament and press to industrial questions. Clémentel came under attack in March 1917 when, under British pressure, he issued a general ban on imports into France, with exemptions being regulated by a government committee.[35] In June 1917, there was a major debate in the Senate over Clémentel's request to be given the power to requisition stocks of finished products held by private industry, as well as factories if necessary.[36] Both of these debates were characterised by a revival of the ideological arguments heard before the war during the repurchase of the Western Railway, but as in that earlier controversy, practicality prevailed and the measures passed.

33. Bonnefous, *Histoire*, ii. 207–10.
34. Soulier, *L'Instabilité*, 329–30. R. Poincaré, *Au Service de la France* (Paris, 1926–1933), vii. 275.
35. See the second part of this Chapter, and Chapter 3.
36. See Chapter 5.

The period of Ribot's and Painlevé's governments, from March to November 1917, have been characterised as a complete return 'to governments based, as before the war, on the tried and true combination of personal ambitions and political antagonism'.[37] Hounded in ordinary and secret sessions of parliament, weak when faced with crises such as the failure of the April 1917 offensive or the Russian Revolution, unable to cope with the deteriorating morale of the nation, these governments resorted to the pre-war technique of inventing distractions, such as the *Bonnet Rouge* spy scare. Clémentel emerged unscathed from these months of intense political instability, but Thomas did not.

In this period, as throughout the war, Clémentel's political position was practically invulnerable, and he was left untouched by changes of government. In December 1916, Briand had rashly offered Herriot the Ministry of Commerce without consulting Clémentel. Clémentel not only had enough political weight to scotch that plan, he was also able to add the Ministry of Agriculture temporarily to his ministerial portfolios.[38] Clémentel had the sense to avoid the temptation to switch to a more controversial and politically exposed ministry; in March 1917, for example, he refused Ribot's offer of the Ministry of Finance.[39] Clémentel survived politically for several reasons. He had the good fortune to be a Radical-Socialist in a parliament in which Radicals controlled the political centre. He had the advantage of heading the relatively uncontroversial Ministry of Commerce, which gave him great power administered through technically complex organisms that usually escaped public comprehension and notice. He was obliged to appear relatively rarely in parliament, since many of his reforms were executed by decree, and he was virtually free from the investigations of financial commissions, since these reforms rarely required the expenditure of money.

Albert Thomas's fortune was less great. To begin with, the whole question of armament production was an emotional political issue. Then, too, the work of Thomas and his bureaucrats was more susceptible to investigation by parliamentary commissions than that of Clémentel because it involved military matters and the expenditure of large sums of money. Both the army commissions and the financial commissions of parliament kept watch on Thomas; their reports received wide attention in parliament and the press. Thus,

37. Goguel, *La Politique*, 159–60.
38. M. Soulié, *La Vie politique d'Edouard Herriot* (Paris, 1962), 60. G. Suarez, *Briand* (Paris, 1938), iv. 77–8.
39. Ribot, *Journal*, 47.

when the Senate Finance Commission unearthed the scandal of the
uncompleted government arsenal at Roanne, the cry was taken up in
parliament and the newspapers in March 1917.[40] Nor was Thomas's
task made any easier by the passage of a finance bill on 30 June 1917
giving the financial commissions of both chambers the right to
supervise the use to which credits voted were being put as they were
actually being spent.[41]

Thomas's ministerial difficulties were worsened by his political
difficulties. Thomas was unfortunate in the choice of his political
and military allies. It was Thomas who had formally proposed that
Nivelle be made commander of the French army in December 1916,
and Nivelle's failure in April 1917 did nothing to enhance Thomas's
position.[42] Edouard Herriot and Thomas had been united in the
cabinet, but Herriot was no longer in the government by March
1917.[43] Thomas also had the misfortune to be linked with Malvy.
Poincaré had always had doubts about Thomas, Foch disliked him,
and Clemenceau attacked him.[44] Thomas's authority was further
undermined by the behind-the-scenes political manoeuvring of his
subordinate, Louis Loucheur.[45] From May 1917 on, Ribot began
giving Loucheur increasing responsibility for a variety of economic
problems, notably coal and shipping, without reference to Thomas.

In the days of the *Union Sacrée*, it had been a positive advantage
for Thomas to be a Socialist, even if there was a slight whiff of
tokenism about it, but the revival of partisanship in 1916 and 1917
turned that advantage into an increasingly heavy liability. The
ambiguity of Thomas's position as a Socialist became apparent in
1917 in conjunction with the Russian Revolution and the Stockholm Conference. On the one hand, his political prestige was at first
increased by his being sent on a mission to Russia to keep the
Provisional Government in the war. In May 1917, Thomas negotiated with the Russians on behalf of the Allies and reported directly
to Ribot and Lloyd George. In the same month, however, the
decision of the National Council of the Socialist party to send
delegates to a peace conference in Stockholm proved deeply embarrassing to Thomas.[46] Mutinies had just broken out in the French
army, and on 31 May 1917, Pétain told Ribot he could no longer

40. See Chapter 10.
41. *Journal officiel*, 1 July 1917, 5016–7.
42. Ribot, *Journal*, 35.
43. Soulié, *Herriot*, 61.
44. Poincaré, *Au Service*, vi. 207–11.
45. See Chapters 6 and 10. Ribot, *Journal*, 85–157.
46. Lefranc, *Le Mouvement socialiste*, 210.

control the army if French Socialists talked to Germans.[47] On 1 June 1917, Ribot informed the Chamber that no passports would be issued to any peace delegates. Socialists were also blamed for a rash of strikes which broke out during the same period. A further complication were the increasing attacks on Malvy, Ribot's Minister of the Interior, by Clemenceau in the Senate Army Commission. Malvy was accused of being a pacifist and a traitor, and certain associates of Thomas's were implicated. Many of these difficulties were aired during the two secret sessions of the Chamber held in June and July 1917, and Thomas came in for much of the criticism.

Nor was Thomas helped by the diminishing support within his own party for the governments of which he was a member. In April 1916, the National Council of the Socialist party supported the government by 1996 votes to 961; in August 1916, 1836 to 1081; in December 1916, delegates voted to allow Thomas to remain in the government by only 1637 votes to 1372.[48] The Socialist group in the Chamber also made life awkward for Thomas by voting against Briand in June and December 1916, and against Ribot in August 1917. There were 102 Socialist deputies in the Chamber after the 1914 elections, a group large enough to be politically embarrassing when they voted against the government, but not large enough to provide useful political support in times of crisis.

On 31 August 1917, Malvy resigned, followed by the rest of the government on 7 September. Thomas's role in the negotiations which followed as first Ribot, then Painlevé attempted to form a government is unclear.[49] The Socialists were divided on the question of Thomas's continuing participation in the government. Thomas claimed that he refused to serve in a government in which Ribot continued to hold the Ministry of Foreign Affairs. According to Ribot, Thomas was at first anxious to continue as Minister of Armament in a new Ribot government, and then, when he was negotiating with Painlevé, he insisted that he be given the Ministry of Foreign Affairs or the Ministry of War; Painlevé's refusal resulted in the withdrawal of Socialist participation in the new government, which was finally formed on 13 September. Ribot attributed Thomas's fall to an excess of personal ambition. Whatever the truth, Thomas's ministerial career, and thus, his industrial policies, were at an end; Louis Loucheur had become Minister of

47. Ribot, *Journal*, 139–41.
48. Soulier, *L'Instabilité*, 328–9.
49. Lefranc, *Le Mouvement socialiste*, 211. Ribot, *Journal*, 198–200. B. Schaper, *Albert Thomas, trente ans de réformisme social* (Assen, 1959), 155–9.

Armament. Clémentel, as usual, was not involved in this political crisis.

Painlevé formed two inner cabinets, one for the war, the other for economic matters. The economic committee included Clémentel, as well as the Ministers of Agriculture, Colonies, Transport, Armament, Food, and Finance, but it was ridiculed in the Chamber and made no impact on industrial policy before the government was ignominiously defeated in the Chamber on 13 November 1917, thereby giving Painlevé the unhappy distinction of heading the only wartime government to be beaten in a vote of confidence.[50]

Clemenceau's Government

In the last part of the war, the importance of political developments in the formulation of government industrial policy diminished. In part, this was because all parliamentary agitation and political partisanship subsided in the face of Clemenceau's iron will and utter dedication to winning the war. The disappearance of secret sessions of the Chamber and the abatement of the activities of parliamentary commissions once again allowed ministers and bureaucrats greater freedom of action. The last months of the war were to see a great extension of state authority over industry. Government industrial policies attracted considerable political controversy, but the policies went forward. Clémentel at the Ministry of Commerce and Louis Loucheur at the Ministry of Armament were able to carry out their plans with little reference to domestic politics.

Clemenceau's assumption of power on 16 November 1917 marked the end of effective parliamentary control over government policy. Clemenceau renounced all pretence of forming a truly representative government; the *Union Sacrée* was dead and buried, Socialists were excluded from power, and the cabinet was composed not of famous political names, but of 'hard-working, efficient, and responsible subordinates who would grasp and prosecute his policies'.[51] The key word is 'subordinate'. Clémentel continued at the Ministry of Commerce and Loucheur at Armament. They were joined by non-parliamentary technicians like Claveille at Public Works or political nonentities who would offer little resistance to Clemenceau's authoritarian rule.[52] Beneath the ministers there was a high proportion of businessmen and technocrats holding key posi-

50. *Journal officiel*, 13 September 1917, 7228–30. *Chambre des députés*, 18 Sept. 1917, 2322–4. *Chambre des députés*, 13 November 1917, 2954.
51. Bruun, *Clemenceau*, 133.
52. *Journal officiel* 17 November 1917, 9178.

tions in the bureaucracy, such as François-Marsal, connected with leading Protestant banks before 1914 and now in charge of economic and financial questions; Vilgrain, at the Ministry of Food, a grain specialist and owner of les Grands Moulins de Nancy; and Louis Louis-Dreyfus, a private grain merchant now involved in running the government's wheat importing operations. The participation of such businessmen in government did not mean, as some have claimed, that France was now in the hands of the suppliers as far as fixing prices and distributing raw materials were concerned;[53] the establishment of the consortia during this period effectively refutes this argument. It did mean that government was becoming more technical and less political.

Clemenceau's programme was simple:

No more pacifist campaigns no more talks with the Germans. No treason, no half-treason. The war. Nothing but the war. Our armies will no longer be caught between two fires, justice will be done. The country will know that it is being defended.[54]

Politically, this programme resulted in ending the secret sessions of parliament. Parliamentary commissions, too, played a less active part in politics; this was particularly true of the Senate Army Commission now that Clemenceau had gone on to greater things. There was a slight increase in the control of parliament over financial matters at the end of 1917 when normal budget procedures were reintroduced for the civilian expenses of the government. As one might expect, however, military expenses continued to be exempt from close parliamentary scrutiny.[55] This ambiguity surrounding parliamentary examination of military and related expenditure persisted as a factor in the unending drama of the arsenal of Roanne.

Clemenceau and his ministers ruled by executive power, reverting to the extensive use of decrees employed by the government in the early days of the war. As Clemenceau's economic and industrial policy was entirely subordinated to his preoccupation with military victory, Clémentel, Loucheur, and their bureaucrats enjoyed considerable freedom of action under the cover of Clemenceau's authority. In February 1918, a law was passed without opposition giving the government total decree authority over the production, distribution, and sale of products for human or animal consumption, which meant for Clémentel unprecedented potential power

53. Beau de Loménie, *La Guerre*, 126–30.
54. *Chambre des députés*, 20 November 1917, 2963.
55. Renouvin, *Formes*, 104–5.

over the domestic economy.[56] 1918 was the year of the greatest extension of state power over industry. Clémentel implemented the consortium system to cover the importation of all raw materials into France, giving the government tremendous leverage over private industry. The system was introduced by executive fiat in December 1917 with none but the most general reference to parliament. It was only in May and June 1918 that the consortium came under the fire of parliament and the press; this political opposition, however, had no effect in limiting the operation and extension of the system.[57] Similarly, the National Shoe, another of Clémentel's projects, was attacked in the Chamber of Deputies in February 1918 with no discernible results.[58]

Louis Loucheur, too, was untroubled by political pressure during this period. Immune from party squabbles because he was not a deputy or senator, respected as an industrial expert, able to lay the shortcomings of his Ministry at the door of his predecessor, Loucheur was free to devote his full attention and considerable talents to armament production and dealing with industrialists.[59]

The picture which emerges from this account of wartime politics is one of a period of initial political quiescence, followed by increasing parliamentary influence from mid-1916 to the end of 1917, ending with the ultimate restoration of the executive authority of the state under Clemenceau at the end of the war.

The first point to be made is that throughout most of the war, even when political agitation was at its height, ministers and bureaucrats had greater authority to implement new policies than had their predecessors before 1914. Ministers had wider decree authority, they could create bureaucratic structures *ex nihilo*, the significance of their policies was often masked by technical complexities, and by the time potential political critics had become aware of the full implications of the policies, it was usually too late to reverse them. Industrial policy, even with regard to munitions, simply did not capture political and public attention to the extent that military strategy, diplomacy, or internal security did. The biographies and autobiographies of the leading French political figures of the war reveal a very limited concern with industrial questions of any kind.

Ministerial instability, one of the most striking political features of the middle of the war, also had relatively little effect on industrial policy. In the case of Clémentel, one can detect no changes in his

56. Ibid., 101–2.
57. See Chapter 4.
58. See Chapter 5.
59. See Chapters 6, 7 and 10.

policy which could be attributed to changes of government. Albert Thomas was more affected by the revival of party politics: his ministerial career was ended by it. But as long as Thomas was in charge of armament production, his policies, too, were untouched by the cabinets which changed around him.

In assessing the political significance of parliamentary commissions, secret sessions of the Chamber, and general parliamentary tumult, a distinction must be made between political debate and the impact of that debate on government policy. Political debate on industrial questions began in earnest in 1916 and continued unchecked to the end of the war. The impact of the debate was limited to a few specific instances. The controversy over the Arsenal of Roanne in 1917 is a classic example of the way in which government policy could be brought to a halt by political discord. The imposition of the consortium system in 1918 illustrates the reverse and more typical phenomenon: a great deal of political debate with little discernable influence on government plans. Undoubtedly, continuous political sniping took up a great deal of time and wore down ministers' patience, nerves and strength, particularly in the case of Albert Thomas, but it rarely made them change their minds.

Nor were ministers much influenced by political pressures from special interest groups. Appeals, for example, by chemical industrialists to cabinet ministers against the creation by Clémentel of a National Dyes Company in 1916 fell on deaf ears.[60] A similar appeal to the cabinet from the de Wendel group against Thomas's Caen metallurgical project in February 1916 also failed.[61]

Ideology and party doctrine had little influence in shaping industrial policy. The fact that Etienne Clémentel was a Radical-Socialist and Albert Thomas a Socialist does not cast much light on the specific industrial policies each proposed. Government policy evolved on an *ad hoc* basis, in response to specific crises and pressures, and few general political principles were evoked to justify such policy. Necessity, not ideology, determined policy, and rare were the deputies and senators who were prepared to do battle with necessity in the name of principle. In the majority of decisions involving state intervention in industry, it was implicitly recognised by parliament that the government simply had no other choice than to take the action it had. As before the war, a basic common sense ultimately prevailed and a rough sort of political consensus eventually emerged. Thus, despite bitter debates over requisitions, pro-

60. See Chapter 5.
61. See Chapter 10.

hibitions of imports, and the extension of consortia, once deputies and senators had satisfied their consciences by denouncing such schemes, there was rarely any practical attempt made to block them. In short, the impact of politics on government industrial policy in France during the war was more apparent than real.

The British

> The economic history of the 1914–1918 war is nothing more than the account of the progressive depreciation of the three factors which make for the strength of nations: the capacity for credit, transport, and production; and of the measures taken by each state to alleviate this depreciation.[62]

In the early months of the war, the French government believed that despite the loss of the industrial north, there were sufficient stocks within the country to supply the needs of both the army and the civilian population without resorting to imports. But when the war did not end quickly, the government was increasingly forced to turn abroad to secure 'the three factors which make for the strength of nations': production, credit, and transport. Lacking productive capacity, France was forced to import vital materials, such as wheat, sugar, and coal; to pay for the imports, she was forced to borrow money; to bring the materials into the country, she was forced to borrow shipping.

Britain was able to supply all three needs, particularly shipping, and initially did so without imposing conditions for her help. But as the two nations became more bound together economically, France was obliged to alter her internal economic arrangements in two ways. First, the creation of each interallied economic organisation forced the creation of a parallel economic organisation within France; thus the joint purchase of wheat and sugar by the Allies abroad inevitably led to the establishment of grain and sugar distribution mechanisms in France, just as it had in England. Secondly, in the latter half of the war, Britain increasingly insisted that France demand of her industrialists the same degree of sacrifice that Britain demanded of hers. Specifically, in 1917, France was faced with the alternative of restricting the flow of imports into the country or losing the use of British shipping. France was also forced to accede to other British demands which followed logically from the restric-

---

62. E. Clémentel, *La France et la politique économique interalliée* (Paris, 1931), xv.

tion of imports, such as the creation of a single interallied agency to purchase raw materials abroad (the executive) and the subsequent establishment of an internal mechanism to supervise their distribution to French industrialists (the consortium). These measures in turn gave Clémentel and the bureaucrats of the Ministry of Commerce their principal instruments of control over French industry during the war.

Forging the Links 1914–1916

Britain was the logical country to which France would turn in her search for imports, credit, and shipping, not only because she was France's military ally, but because of Britain's economic strength and her pre-war trading connections with France. Britain's power stemmed from the combination of several great economic advantages: her vast industrial capacity, her sophisticated banking system, her worldwide commercial and financial network, her foreign investments and invisible exports, and above all, her commercial fleet of 10,000 ships whose 21 million tons represented 45 per cent of the world's total shipping.[63] Even before the war, Britain was the biggest market for French goods, followed by Germany, the United States, Belgium, and Russia. With the German and Belgian markets cut off, and the Russian market restricted, Britain's share of France's total exports increased from 13 per cent in 1913 to 24 per cent in 1919. Britain was also France's chief foreign source of raw materials before the war, providing coal, rubber, wool, iron, and steel.[64]

Imports. The first economic link established between the two countries during the war was the creation of an agency for the joint purchase of food. To reduce competition for foreign food bought for their respective armies and navies, the British and French created the *Commission Internationale du Ravitaillement* in London on 4 August 1914.[65] The arrangement, however, soon broke down, the two governments began competing, and food prices rose. As early as January 1915, fierce competition between the French *Intendance* and the British government for frozen meat forced them to accept a

63. P.R.O. Ministry of Transport Papers, Series 25, Vol. 67/29597/1922.'Historical Notes'.
64. L.M. Hinds, 'La Coopération économique entre la France et la Grande Bretagne pendant la Première Guerre Mondiale' (Paris *thèse de doctorat de troisième cycle*) 5, 8–11.
65. P. Larigaldie, *Les Organismes interalliés de contrôle économique* (Paris, 1926), 21–31.

common purchasing policy.

A more serious shortage in France was wheat. The 1915 harvest was 60 million, down from 70 million in 1914, which in turn was down from 87 million in 1913.[66] This shortage led to the creation of the Conference on Grain Purchasing at the *Commission Internationale du Ravitaillement* on 30 December 1915, with representatives of both governments charged with the responsibility for purchasing cereals, dividing the purchases between the two countries at a fixed price, and finding the necessary tonnage for its transport. In January 1916, Italy and Portugal jointed the arrangement, and the Conference became the Joint Committee on Grain Purchasing, which, in turn, was replaced by the Wheat Executive Committee at the end of 1916. The Wheat Executive represented the collective interests of France, England, and Italy, and the principle was established that each would pay the same price for wheat, no matter when or where it was bought. The creation of the Wheat Executive was of importance for future interallied economic relations, for it became a model for other interallied purchasing organisations.

The work of inter-allied grain purchasing organisations could only be effective, however, if supported by a parallel control of grain supplies within each of the participating countries. Clémentel, who became Minister of Commerce on 30 October 1915, set about to apply the provisions of the law of 16 October 1915 for requisitioning, buying abroad, and controlling imports of wheat, as well as fixing its consumer price.[67] Clémentel created the first of many new bureaucratic structures, the Wheat Consultative Committee. The power of the Ministry of Commerce over the domestic economy was particularly enhanced when the Wheat Executive became the sole purchaser of wheat abroad for the Allies at the end of 1916:

> the principle of equitable distribution made it possible, within the interior of each country, to implement a policy of rationing and economic use which was far stricter than any in force previously. . . . This fact shows once more the interdependence between interallied control and national control; without the latter, the former would be useless.[68]

A crisis in sugar supplies also brought the British and French closer together economically. From the 717,000 tons of 1913–14, produc-

---

66. Prompsat Archives T(2)3: *Rapport de M. Clémentel sur le Ravitaillement Civil* (8 Sept. 1914–31 December 1916), 6.
67. *Journal officiel*, 17 October 1915, 7442–5. See also Chapter 3.
68. Larigaldie, *Les Organismes*, 75–6.

tion in France had fallen off to 136,000 in the period 1915–16.[69] As with wheat, a consultative commission had been created in France, and purchases made abroad, but these measures proved insufficient. On 16 February 1916, England and France combined their purchasing operations for sugar. The British had also taken the lead in making the state the sole importer and distributor of sugar by creating the Royal Commission on Sugar Supply in 1914, with executive powers to purchase and distribute sugar on behalf of the civilian population.[70] The Royal Commission was another important model for future interallied economic organisms:

> Although the British Sugar Commission was strictly speaking only a British national organisation, it remained nevertheless the prototype of all organisms which were later created and the establishment of its purchasing system signified the creation of a stably-based embryo of interallied policy.[71]

As with wheat, the pressure was now on France to create a parallel supporting organisation within the country.[72] The French government had no qualms about becoming the sole importer of sugar into France, but it was extremely reluctant to take over the distribution of sugar within the country from the private sugar merchants. Accordingly, the government tightened its control over the sugar market in other ways. In May 1916, the Ministry of Commerce took the unprecedented step of buying the entire 1916 sugar crop from France's foreign suppliers, although distribution still remained in the hands of the private sugar merchants' syndicates. Once the 1916 crop had been acquired, however, the government took the sugar policy to its logical conclusion on 20 October 1916 by establishing distribution committees in every *département*, which, with certain exceptions, divided unrefined sugar among manufacturers, as the Royal Commission on Sugar Supply did in England.

Each time the British were called on to make up French losses of productive capacity, they demanded correspondingly greater internal controls within France. In May 1916, Runciman, of the British Board of Trade, and Sembat, the French Minister of Public Works, signed an agreement whereby Britain would limit the price and freight charges of coal imported into France. But the British im-

69. *Ravitaillement civil*, 8–9.
70. A. Marwick, *The Deluge. British Society and the First World War* (London, 1967), 173.
71. Larigaldie, *Les Organismes*, 40–1.
72. Clémentel, *France*, 44.

posed conditions which had serious implications for France's control of her domestic economy. 'In exchange, therefore, [Runciman] insisted that the French government impose a control on prices for the internal market and tax coal sold to the public in order to limit the profits of middlemen'.[73] The French were forced to create a *Bureau des Charbons* to centralise all applications for imports, to supervise the distribution of coal, and to fix the selling price to the French consumer.[74]

Thus French reliance on Britain for imports of wheat, sugar, and coal led to the increased intervention of the French state in the private sector of the economy. Though these early instances of intervention centred on food and coal, rather than directly on the industrial sphere, they were nevertheless important precedents for Clémentel and the bureaucrats of the Ministry of Commerce. Bureaucratic structures created within the Ministry to solve the problem of wheat and sugar provided the model for the creation of similar machinery for other materials.

Credit. Once the French government had decided to import certain materials, there still remained the problem of paying for them. Initially, France had hoped to finance the war, including imports, on her gold reserves. But as the importance of imports grew, and with it the problem of foreign credits, France put her gold supplies at the disposal of London. On 5 February 1915, the first formal arrangements were made between the finance ministers of Britain, France, and Russia; they agreed to pool their financial resources as they had their military resources. When this agreement turned out to be virtually meaningless, an accord was signed between Ribot and Lloyd George on 30 April 1915 whereby Britain would open credits for one and a half milliard francs to France to purchase war materials in Britain, Canada, and the United States in exchange for payment of one-third of the sum in gold. This arrangement was the basis for all future agreements between the two countries, and France was ultimately to obtain a total of fifteen milliard francs from Britain during the war.[75] Common financial policies were another important link between the two economies, and thus one more potential source of British leverage on France to force through joint policy decisions in other areas.

73. Hinds, 'Coopération', 57.
74. C. Fayle, *Seaborne Trade* (London, 1920), ii. 320–1.
75. Hinds, 'Coopération', 38–44.

Shipping. Increased imports depended upon one vital factor: shipping. The war ended almost all French land trade, since land frontiers were largely closed down by the German occupation. The takeover of the French railways for military purposes, the mobilisation of labour, and the loss of the industrial north added to the problem. Only the sea was open, but, even in peacetime, France was deficient in ships. 'Thus, in time of peace, between 60 and 70 per cent of French imports and exports were seaborne, but only about 40 per cent of the seaborne imports and less than 60 per cent of the corresponding exports were carried in French bottoms'.[76] When seaborne trade increased dramatically during the war, Britain was obliged to provide the shipping. The first French requests for British shipping came in September 1914. In October 1914, France was given requisitioned British ships for general purposes, and in January 1915, special arrangements were made to ship coal for the French railways. By the autumn of 1915, the shipping situation became critical as demands for British ships grew on all sides. On 10 November 1915, Britain created a Requisitioning (Carriage of Foodstuffs) Committee to provide shipping for food, and a Ship Licensing Committee to control the general use of requisitioned shipping. Both Committees came under the executive authority of the Shipping Control Committee, established on 27 January 1916 under Lord Curzon, which reported directly to the British Cabinet and had the power to seek information and enforce its opinions.[77]

The creation of centralised structures in Britain to deal with all demands for maritime transport, French as well as British, stemmed directly from economic links between the two countries in other spheres. Thus when the British and French created the Conference on Grain Purchasing in December 1915, it naturally followed that stricter arrangements for shipping wheat would also have to be made, and the British Ministry of Transport requested the *Commission Internationale du Ravitaillement* to centralise and establish priorities for all Allied demands for tonnage as far as possible.[78] Simultaneously, the 'oatmeal-steel' agreement was signed between the two countries in December 1915, whereby Britain allocated forty-five ships to France to import oatmeal and steel, both in very short supply in France, in the same ships.

The crisis in shipping deepened in 1916, with unrestricted attacks on merchant shipping by Germany from February 1916, insufficient

76. Fayle, *Seaborne Trade*, i. 11–12.
77. MT 25 67/29597/1922.
78. Fayle, *Seaborne Trade*, ii. 246.

construction of new cargo ships, the increasing need to import essential materials, particularly food-stuffs, as French harvests and the production of coal and other goods declined, and a three-fold increase in the number of ships required to import wheat from Australia, where the 1916 cereal crop was bounteous, instead of from North America, where it had fallen by 30 per cent to 40 per cent.[79] England lent France ships with increasing reluctance. The British Transport Advisory Committee complained about the French misuse of British shipping. The British also decided to economise on shipping by reducing their own imports, and in February and March 1916, they banned the import of many French goods. In April 1916, a Tonnage Executive was created in London to distribute shipping for interallied freight, but it had no practical effect. The same month, to placate the British, the French government took the first measures to control the use of tonnage placed at its disposal.[80] Concomitantly, the French government created the first rudimentary controls over imports into France.

In May 1916, the British Cabinet restricted British ships in Allied service to the tonnage held by each on 1 April 1916. In June 1916, there was an interallied economic conference at which it was agreed that the economic resources of the Allies would henceforth be pooled, but it brought no immediate resolution to the shipping problem. In the summer the British decided to restrict the import of luxuries in the near future.[81] Relations between France and Britain became strained in September 1916, when British consuls in French ports reported that nearly two hundred cargo ships could be found lying idle on any given day. Britain's Ship Licencing Committee began withdrawing dozens of British ships from French service, German submarines in the Channel tied up neutral shipping in English ports, and insurance costs for transporting goods soared. Coal and steel imports plunged correspondingly, which in turn slowed armament production. A noisy press row blew up between English and French newspapers.

To repair deteriorating relations between the two countries, an interallied economic conference was held from 27 November to 3 December 1916. Clémentel persuaded Runciman of the Board of Trade that a common Allied policy on shipping and wheat was necessary, and it was agreed that shortages would be shared proportionally among the Allies. It was this conference which pro-

79. Clémentel, *France*, 95–7.
80. Larigaldie, *Les Organismes*, 47–8.
81. MT 25 67/29597/1922.

duced the Wheat Executive Committee. In return for ships and wheat, France promised to process ships in her ports faster by freeing up more rail transport to clear goods through, although this could only be done by doubling passenger rail prices, cutting back on regular train services, eliminating *wagons-lit*, and even reducing leave for men at the Front.[82] For the moment Clémentel was able to forestall the demands of Curzon's Shipping Control Committee that Britain should further restrict imports coming from Allies and limit tonnage lent to them to the 1 April 1916 level, but the time was fast approaching when Britain would make far more explicit demands of the French in return for the imports, credit, and shipping placed at their disposal.

Applying the Pressure 1917–1918

The turning point in Franco-British relations came with the formation of the Lloyd George government in Britain on 7 December 1916, for it was Lloyd George who pushed for far greater economic and military co-operation with France than his predecessor Asquith, who had been opposed to any loss of British control to interallied organisations. But the price of greater co-operation was greater pressure on the French to align their internal economic arrangements with those of Britain. Increasingly, Britain refused to import from France or supply her with ships unless France first created a mechanism for restricting her own imports, then tightened control over the shipping placed at her disposal, then participated in interallied executives for buying foreign goods, and finally formulated a system of controlling domestic industry.

It was Etienne Clémentel, the Minister of Commerce, who would bear the brunt of British pressure in 1917 and 1918. In this respect, international developments set the pace for Clémentel's policy, and, in one sense, his room for manoeuvre continually decreased. But in another sense, his power grew, for as interallied economic policy prevailed at the national level, the policy of Clémentel prevailed with it, since he was a prime participant in interallied councils. If one compares the proposals which Clémentel made during these councils with the measures he introduced in France, his strategy becomes clear. Clémentel actively campaigned for increased interallied co-operation and co-ordination of policy, then turned to French producers and told them that he was forced by interallied pressure, with the greatest reluctance, to impose even stricter measures upon

82. Clémentel, *France*, 101–13.

them. For Clémentel, interallied policy was a useful weapon, the court of final authority for his domestic plans.

The Restriction of Imports. On 7 December 1916, Lloyd George formed his government. On 9 December, Sir Joseph Maclay was appointed Shipping Controller. On 19 December, the British government announced the complete takeover of shipping. On 21 December, the War Cabinet created an Import Restriction Committee under Lord Curzon, with the Chancellor of the Exchequer, the Minister of Munitions, the Secretary of the Board of Trade, and the Shipping Controller as members. On 22 December, a new Ministry of Shipping was established.[83]

The implications of these British measures to tighten control over shipping and imports were soon made clear to the French in an interallied naval conference held in January 1917. It was jointly agreed

> That it is of paramount importance that the Government of each Allied country, with a view to assisting the transport of articles which are essential to the successful prosecution of the war, should take immediate steps to restrict to the utmost extent the importation of all other articles.[84]

The need for Britain and France to take immediate concrete steps to reduce their respective imports became even more apparent after 1 February 1917, when Germany declared unrestricted submarine warfare against the Allies. From February to April 1917, 341 ships were sunk, as compared with 111 in the three previous months.[85] In Britain, on 9 February 1917, the Shipping Controller was given increased powers over merchant shipping. A Tonnage Priority Committee was established at the Ministry of Shipping, with representatives of each Ministry concerned with the nation's supplies. The Committee co-ordinated demands for tonnage with available shipping.[86] On 21 February, Curzon's Import Restriction Committee recommended further drastic reductions of imports, including many from France, to the War Cabinet. On 22 February, the War Cabinet decided to institute a system of import licences,

83. MT 25 67/29597/1922. P.R.O. Cabinet Papers, Series, 23, vol. 1, War Cabinets, December 1916.
84. CAB 23, vol. 1, War Cabinet 50, 31 January 1917, Appendix 11, Naval Conference Conclusions.
85. MT 25 67/29597/1922.
86. MT 25 45/45611/1920. War Cabinet Reports on Work of Ministry of Shipping 1917–1918.

controlled by the Department of Import Restrictions at the Board of Trade. The same day, Lloyd George informed French representatives in London of the new prohibition on the importation of many French luxury goods. He announced the measure in the House of Commons on 23 February, then went to a conference in France and explained the prohibition to Briand.[87]

France was already suffering a balance of payments deficit of 65 per cent in her trading relations with Britain before the British prohibition on imports. The French government had no alternative, however, but to accept the measure and to yield further to British pressure by restricting imports into France, thereby conserving British shipping. Lloyd George reported to the War Cabinet on his conversations with French officials:

> The French representatives state that it was the intention of the French Government to imitate the example of the British Government in further restriction of imports, and they insisted on the importance of close co-operation in this matter.[88]

In March 1917, the International Shipping Committee was founded and held its first meetings. In the second meeting, Royden, the British representative, explained how Britain had cut down on imports to save tonnage and

> suggested that the Allies should consider whether their Governments would examine the imports into their countries with a view to eventually effecting similar economies in the commodities carried.[89]

The French representative, Guernier, replied

> that the French Government would co-operate to the utmost to reduce the importation into France of unnecessary articles . . . within the last few weeks the French Government had also set up a Committee of Priorities, and that he would be supplied with the minutes of the Committee and would keep in touch with their proceedings.

On 22 March 1917, the French government duly decreed a prohibition on the import of all products not purchased for the government. To control exemptions from this general ban, Clémentel created a committee on the model of Curzon's Import

---

87. CAB 23, vol. 1, War Cabinets, February 1917.
88. CAB 23, vol. 2, War Cabinet 83, 1 March 1917, Appendix 111.
89. MT 25 6/7114. International Shipping Committee, 8 March 1917.

Restrictions Committee.[90]

The Control of Shipping. Despite this French concession, the British remained unsatisfied. They particularly objected to making over British shipping to the French without being able to monitor the use to which the shipping was being put. Lord Curzon's Shipping Control Committee had been responsible for balancing the demands of the Allies against the claims of Great Britain. In the words of a report on the work of the Ministry of Shipping sent to Lloyd George:

> This method was unsatisfactory as the entire responsibility for admitting or refusing a request from an Ally for tonnage fell upon the shoulders of the British Government, who had no adequate means of testing the soundness of the bases on which the requests were founded.[91]

In April 1917, Great Britain simply withdrew half of the tonnage she had previously made available to France. The tonnage agreements negotiated by Clémentel in December 1916 fell into abeyance. If the French refused to impose as strict a control over the use of shipping as the British, Great Britain threatened to withdraw all her ships from French service by June.

Faced with this ultimatum, a special meeting of French ministers and officials was called in Paris on 4 May 1917, presided over by Etienne Clémentel. Among those present were Violette, Under-Secretary of State for Maritime Transport; Loucheur, Under-Secretary of State for War Production; Nunzi, Director of Transport at the Ministry of War; and Guernier, High Commissioner in London. It was recognised 'that there was a great difference between English and French arrangements', and that the measures of control taken by the French over shipping were insufficient to prevent 'fraudulent and abusive operations'. It was unanimously agreed that British demands would have to be met by extending state control over French shipping. Loucheur commented on the importance of this decision: 'Agreements with Great Britain must be arrived at by all states taking control of their fleets. This is the revolutionary situation which is forced on us today'. It was also recognised that the state control would have to be imposed on other sectors of the economy.[92]

The records of meetings like this further demonstrate the point

90. See Chapter 3.
91. MT 25 45/45611/1920.
92. F12 7797.

that the British used their position of superior economic strength to force the French to extend state control over their own economy, and that the French both acknowledged this pressure and gave way before it. Defending a new decree for the chartering and purchasing of shipping by the state to the Chamber of Deputies later in May 1917, Violette said of Franco-British relations:

> From now on, you must understand that there are only two policies for us which are conceivable — I do not say reasonable — : on the one hand, isolation, and on the other, collaboration. I am not saying that both are reasonable because I need hardly add that the Government considers the policy of isolation to be an error for which it will never take the responsibility, and that from henceforth, if it is not to be the policy of isolation, we are inevitably led to the policy of collaboration on the basis established in 1916. From this emerges the imperious necessity, whatever individual opinions may exist, of realigning our legislation in accordance with English legislation, and thus the decree on the chartering and purchasing of shipping.[93]

The Executive System and the First Consortium. The British were still intent on discovering some method which would enable a more accurate estimate to be formed of the relative shipping needs of the different Allies. The methods adopted by the Wheat Executive after its creation in December 1916 indicated the way in which the problem could be solved.[94]

In August 1917, Clémentel held negotiations with the British in London. France obtained some relief from the British ban on imports of luxury goods, and the principle of special preference for French imports to allow her to improve her balance of payments was accepted.[95] The British also revoked their plans to withdraw shipping from the French, so that most of the advantages of the December 1916 agreements were regained.

Clémentel presented Ribot, the president of the Council of Ministers, with a lengthy account of the August meeting.[96] The British were becoming increasingly blunt in setting conditions for their support of France. Here is Clémentel's description of shipping negotiations:

> The British Government is prepared to put at our disposal all the English

---

93. *Chambre des députés*, 29 May 1917, 1257.
94. MT 25 45/45611/1920.
95. CAB 23, vol. 3, War Cabinets 208, 216; 9, 15 August 1917.
96. Prompsat Archives. *Rapport présenté à M. Ribot, Président du Conseil . . . par M. Clémentel . . . sur les négociations poursuivies à Londres.*

tonnage we are now using, at a uniform and reduced price, the day we impose on our nationals conditions equivalent to theirs, taking into account the particular nature of our shipping.

The pressure had the desired effect, for Clémentel wrote, 'How could we, in these conditions, wait one hour longer to take the measures which the gravity of the situation demands?' Specifically, Clémentel proposed the total requisition by the state of all French ships; the state would also carry out all future chartering and purchasing arrangements, as provided for in the May decree.

But British pressure was not confined to shipping questions. The British proposed the extension of the Wheat Executive system to all other raw materials. Executives would purchase and distribute materials on behalf of all the Allies, and the materials would be transported on British ships remaining under British control. The creation of further executives was a victory for the British in their campaign to recapture control of their own shipping and to create sole purchasing agencies for the Allies. The Oilseeds Executive and the Meats and Fats Executive were to be created immediately, with others to follow.

Sole purchasing agencies would only work, however, if the French government took a much tighter hold on private commerce and industry. Once again, the British proposed a model of internal control. On 9 August 1917, before the meeting with Clémentel, Sir Albert Stanley, President of the Board of Trade, had explained to the War Cabinet that because of inadequate supplies of raw materials and rising prices in the cotton industry, he had created the Cotton Control Board to regulate consumption of cotton and to reduce unemployment.[97] In his negotiations with the French later in the month, Stanley urged Clémentel to follow the British example in controlling French industry.

> He suggested that we organise a strict control of imports, as the British Government had done by assuring the distribution of raw materials through the organisation of a commission which included merchants, producers, the President of the Liverpool Exchange, and the delegates of the Board of Trade.

On 27 October 1917, Clémentel created the French Cotton Consortium, France's first consortium, which was to be the model for all future consortia in France.[98]

97. CAB 23, vol. 3, War Cabinet 208, 9 August 1917.
98. See Chapter 4.

Clémentel's confidential report to Ribot about his negotiations with the British in August 1917 supports earlier observations about the way in which Clémentel used British pressure as a weapon for extending state control in France. Clémentel reminded Ribot that what the British were now demanding was nothing less than that which he, Clémentel, had been proposing all along: a greater extension of state authority, particularly over shipping. 'It is undebateable that despite my reiterated requests, the French Government has not taken to the present moment the measures which the situation demands'. But it is also clear from British accounts of the August meeting that Clémentel did not merely react to British initiatives but used the occasion of the discussions to promote his own pet projects, notably a post-war Allied economic community. On 20 August, for example, it was reported to the British War Cabinet that Clémentel had proposed a twenty-year economic campaign against Germany after the war, with the Allies pooling all raw materials at their disposal and excluding the Germans from any access to them.[99] What Clémentel represented to the French government and public as British policies being forced on him by British pressure were often his own policies riding under the umbrella of British pressure. Clémentel played the game both ways: he used British pressure to force the French government to adopt his proposals, and he used his proposals, once adopted, as a bargaining token with which to placate the British. For instance, in a report delivered during the August meeting to Sir Joseph Maclay, British Shipping Controller, Clémentel pointed out that he had recently had the French parliament enact a law on the requisition of privately-owned goods and factories.[100]

The Milner Committee. In October 1917, Clémentel came to London and outlined the continuing seriousness of the French situation to Lloyd George.[101] He proposed the drawing up of a list of items absolutely indispensable to both countries, giving top priority to food, the complete pooling of Allied shipping, and its redistribution on a basis of need. The British agreed to provide as much tonnage as they could to feed the French, but from September to November 1917, the French still faced a deficit of 21 per cent in their requirements for cereals.[102]

99. CAB 23, vol. 3, War Cabinet 220, 20 August 1917.
100. *Rapport, Annexe 19*, 7. See also Chapter 5.
101. D. Lloyd George, *War Memoirs* (1st edn., London 1934), iii. 1343–5.
102. CAB 23, vol. 4, War Cabinet 261, 31 October 1917. MT 25 22/61759/1918. Tonnage Policy and Position 1917 and 1918.

On 3 November 1917, the Allies agreed to pool all grain supplies.[103] On 6 November, the British War Cabinet decided to centralise all Ministries and services dealing with the importation of food and other materials by creating a single interministerial committee under the chairmanship of Lord Milner. The Milner Committee was given the authority to rationalise the whole system of supplying Great Britain with foreign goods.[104] The Committee met on 27 November with Lord Curzon in the chair in the absence of Lord Milner. Faced with a deficit of 8 million tons of shipping in 1918, the Committee recommended further drastic cuts of imports. The significance of these restrictions for France was plainly spelled out in the last paragraph of a report on the meeting delivered by Lord Curzon to the War Cabinet:

> We are well aware that the recommendations which we are now submitting will, if carried into effect, not only cause grave dislocation to certain trades, but also involve great hardships and drastic changes in the life of the people. We believe that these burdens will be cheerfully borne, provided that some assurance can be given that our Allies are making equal sacrifices. At present we have only too much evidence that this is not always the case.
>
> We therefore recommend that His Majesty's Government should take such steps as may be necessary to ensure equality of treatment for this country and our Allies in these matters of economy and restriction of imports.[105]

Another recommendation was made to the War Cabinet on 27 November by Sir Edward Carson, chairman of the Economic Offensive Committee, for the introduction of uniform legislation in Britain, the Dominions, and the Allies to control the volume, direction, and priority of exports and imports of raw materials by licence.[106]

An opportunity of confronting the French with these views presented itself during the interallied economic conference held at the Quai d'Orsay in Paris from 29 November to 3 December 1917, and attended by the British, French, Italians, and Americans. The Allied Maritime Transport Council was created to assess the total capacity of Allied and neutral shipping and to allocate this shipping on a basis of need, as Clémentel had proposed.[107] Other interallied

103. MT 25 67/29597/1922.
104. CAB 23, vol. 4, War Cabinet 266, 6 November 1917.
105. CAB 23, vol. 4, War Cabinet 292, 5 December 1917, Appendix.
106. CAB 23, vol. 4, War Cabinet 283, 27 November 1917.
107. J. Salter, *Allied Shipping Control* (Oxford, 1921), 151–5.

committees were established to co-ordinate food production. In return for these favours, France was clearly expected to follow the British example in imposing further internal economic controls. Even before the interallied conference, almost as if to appease Curzon, Clemenceau had given some indication of the restrictions that were to come. In his ministerial declaration to the Chamber on 20 November 1917, he said:

> We are going to enter the path of food restrictions, following England, Italy, and even America, so admirable for her vitality. We will ask each citizen to participate fully in the common defence, to give more and agree to receive less. The army has made sacrifices. Let the whole country make sacrifices. (*Applause*).[108]

Immediately after the interallied conference, on 13 December 1917, the French government established the Executive Committee for Imports on the model of the Milner Committee.[109] Presided over by Clémentel, this interministerial committee included the Ministers of Armament, Food, and Public Works, as well as the Under-Secretaries of State for Food and Maritime Transport.

> Adopting a method of work and a nomenclature suggested by the British administration, the Executive Committee for Imports drew up a detailed programme of French needs on a basis of the 'zones of origin' of the products being imported.[110]

The power of this Committee over the French economy was subsequently increased in 1918 by the creation of a licencing system for imports, as Sir Edward Carson had proposed, which became ever more rigorous in its application, and by the further requisitioning of French shipping.

1918: Completing the System. Franco-British relations for the remainder of the war were characterised by a further linking of the two economies through interallied organisations, with a concomitant extension of internal economic controls in each country. The growing importance of America in the alliance became a prime factor. Faced with the mounting problem of payment by other Allied powers for American goods, the United States urged the Allies to make American purchases through a single official agency.

108. *Chambre des députés*, 20 November 1917, 2963.
109. See Chapter 3.
110. Hinds, 'Co-opération', 108–9.

It was American pressure which led to the creation in 1918 of the Interallied Council for War Purchases and Finance, presided over by Oscar Crosby, of the American Treasury.

But neither this Council nor the Allied Maritime Transport Council, created in December 1917, could function efficiently unless they were supported by subordinate interallied organisations responsible for supplying specific materials. Once again the Allies returned to the idea of the executive. This time the French took the initiative. During the interallied conference in Paris in November –December 1917, Jean Monnet, Clémentel's representative in London, proposed the immediate formation of interallied executives for all essential materials, along the lines of the existing Wheat Executive and Meats and Fats Executive. Monnet suggested that executives be created for three broad categories of materials: (1) food; (2) military products; (3) raw materials for domestic industry. The British fully supported the idea.[111]

In April 1918, during the second meeting of the Allied Maritime Transport Council, it was decided to establish executives, or 'programme committees', as they were alternately entitled, for all materials of interallied concern. Accordingly, executives were instituted in the spring and summer of 1918 for oil seeds, aircraft, chemicals, explosives, non-ferrous metals, steel, nitrate of soda, leather, wool, flax, horses, mechanical transport, petroleum, cotton, paper, and tobacco.[112] Each executive assessed the demands of all the Allies for the particular material and produced an agreed document listing total requirements. The Interallied Council for War Purchases and Finance and the Allied Maritime Transport Council then considered the documents of all the executives, the executives serving as the link between the two organisations.

> By this means the Allied Maritime Transport Council is spared the consideration of the relative claims of, say, France and Great Britain for cereals, and has only to consider the relative claims of, say, the Allied food programme as against the Allied munitions programme.[113]

The extension of the executive system virtually completed the economic union of the Allies. The last stage in the process came with the creation of the Interallied Munitions Council in June 1918 and the Interallied Food Council in July 1918.[114] An Interallied

111. MT 25 45/45611/1920.
112. MT 25 10/21068/1918. Allied Maritime Transport Council.
113. MT 25 45/45611/1920.
114. Larigaldie, *Les Organismes*, 144.

Council for Raw Materials was planned but did not come into being before the war ended.[115]

By the end of the war, the drive for interallied co-operation had extended beyond the bounds of maritime transport to almost every sphere of commercial and industrial activity. But each decision to create an interallied body implied the parallel creation of bureaucratic bodies at the national level to control that section of the domestic economy affected by the decision. Thus, the creation of interallied executives for raw materials led inexorably in 1918 to the creation by Clémentel of parallel interministerial committees and consortia within France for each of the executives.

Clémentel's power over France's economy in 1918 can be largely attributed to measures initially forced on the French government by the British in 1917 and 1918. The restriction of imports, the control of shipping, the creation of interallied executives, the establishment of the Executive Committee for Imports, and the extension of the consortium system in France all resulted in great part from British pressure. The way in which these instruments of power were utilised, however, and the long-term objectives to which they were applied can be understood only by examining more closely the career of Etienne Clémentel and the activities of the bureaucrats of the Ministry of Commerce.

115. MT 25 22/61067/1918. Interallied Control Bureau in London to be constituted by the Governments of Great Britain, France, Italy, Japan, and the United States. MT 25 10/21068/1918.

CHAPTER 3

Etienne Clémentel and the Ministry of Commerce and Industry

The Ministry of Commerce and Industry in August 1914 was singularly ill-prepared for the role it was eventually to play during the First World War. It was staffed by a small number of bureaucrats with limited pre-war experience in industrial and commercial matters. Gaston Thomson, Minister of Commerce in 1914 and 1915, had few ambitions for the Ministry or himself. Gradually, however, he was forced to respond to the twin crises of domestic and military shortages by extending the authority of the Ministry over the private sector of the economy, beginning with wheat. The mechanism for controlling wheat distribution later became the model for controlling the distribution of raw materials to industry. His successor, Etienne Clémentel, though under greater pressure from the British and more exposed to political criticism from within France, turned the pressure to advantage in expanding the control of the state over private industry. Clémentel's ideas of a state-directed economy developed gradually during his ministry, partly in response to British pressure, partly as he turned his mind in 1917 and 1918 to the problems of the post-war French economy. The implementation of these ideas began with the control of imports in March 1917, a measure which gave Clémentel and his bureaucrats the necessary first weapon to deal with industrialists. By 1918, the Ministry of Commerce had developed an elaborate bureaucratic structure, manned by a group of exceptional wartime bureaucrats who, in the last months of the war, became the equal of the industrialists in administrative expertise and industrial experience.

The Ministry of Commerce under Thomson 1914–1915: the Control of Wheat

Within a month of the outbreak of war, the first signs of a shortage of supplies for the civilian population began to appear in France, and the Ministry of Commerce was called upon to act. A decree of 8 September 1914[1] had created a 'Service for the Feeding of the Civilian Population' (*Service de Ravitaillement de la population civile*), which was placed under the authority of the Ministry of Commerce, where it remained until the end of 1916. It was this new attribution which gave the Ministry the initial foothold that eventually led to the establishment of its supreme authority over commerce and industry within France. Thomson was the Minister of the day, and he set himself three objectives: to maintain supplies of goods for the civilian population, to control prices, and to restore transportation. Thomson viewed the wartime role of his ministry in strictly limited terms: its chief function was to gather information about existing supplies and to make suggestions. The Ministry itself would not intervene in the market-place; such commercial operations as were necessary were to be undertaken by the chambers of commerce of the towns concerned. The problem of transportation was left to the Ministry of War. But as the war dragged on through the winter of 1915, it became increasingly apparent that Thomson's *dolce far niente* mentality was unsuited to the problems at hand.

Born in Algeria in 1848, the son of an Englishman settled in Oran, Gaston Thomas had made his career in publicity and journalism, collaborating first with Gambetta as editor of *La République Française*, then with Clemenceau as editor of *L'Homme Libre*.[2] Elected deputy of Constantine in 1877, a member of the *Gauche démocratique*, Thomson was to hold his seat continuously for fifty-five years. Thomson had been Minister of the Navy from 1905 to 1909, but he had been appointed to the Ministry of Commerce only on 13 June 1914, and the burdens placed on him by the war were manifestly beyond his capacities.

The first crisis was over wheat.[3] Smaller domestic harvests, higher prices, and difficulties with foreign wheat producers forced the Ministry of Commerce to act. Thomson was less concerned with related questions such as ensuring adequate transportation facilities

---

1. *Journal officiel*, 9 September 1914, 7874.
2. R. Samuel & G. Bonét-Maury, *Les Parlementaires français 1900–1914* (Paris 1914), 393. Further information about Thomson can be found in the Archives of the *Assemblée Nationale* in Paris.
3. See Chapter 2.

to deliver and distribute food or controlling dwindling supplies of coal, than with maintaining the basic prices of food staples in co-operation with the local authorities. Reluctantly, the Ministry of Commerce began to dabble in commerce; in particular, the Ministry purchased wheat and sugar to redistribute to the civilian population and also acted as sugar purchasing agent for the army. But the crisis of wheat shortages gathered momentum. By February 1915, the scarcity of wheat became acute, particularly in Paris, where existing siege supplies had been exhausted. To relieve Paris, the military authorities began to requisition supplies around the countryside, a measure which was suspended when local merchants and prefects protested against their areas being drained of wheat. At the same time, the price of foreign wheat rose dramatically. In May 1915, the Ministry of Commerce achieved a major break with the traditions of the pre-war era when it made its first purchases of wheat abroad and chartered its first ships to bring the cargo home. In June these operations were suspended until October when the necessary credits were voted and a satisfactory legal basis established by the law of 16 October 1915, but the psychologically necessary first step had been taken.[4]

The food crisis and the various attempts made by the Commerce Ministry to resolve it were of vital importance to the future relations of the government with private industry, for state interference in food provided the legal and administrative precedent for state interference in industry. As with food, the initial justification for increasing governmental control of industry was to be the shortage of raw materials; the pace for this increasing control was set by the evolution of the food crisis. It was only later that more sophisticated questions of war profits and government-owned industry arose. The shortage of raw materials was the vital key to the Pandora's box of private industry.

It will be recalled that the Ministry of Commerce had also found itself dealing with chemical problems and chemical companies when it created the Office for Chemical and Pharmaceutical Products in October 1914.[5] Thus by October 1915, when Etienne Clémentel replaced Gaston Thomson as Minister of Commerce, the Ministry of Commerce had acquired a certain number of attributions, bureaucratic structures, and bureaucrats on an *ad hoc* basis, but it lacked an overall plan a well-defined sense of purpose. It was

4. Prompsat Archives T(2)3: *Rapport de M. Clémentel sur le Ravitaillement civil* (8 Sept. 1914–31 Dec. 1916).
5. See Chapter 2.

only under Etienne Clémentel that the Ministry became ultimately responsible for controlling and directing all non-military industry in France.

Etienne Clémentel, Minister of the National Economy

Etienne Clémentel was born in 1864 near Clermont-Ferrand in the Auvergne. His father, a modest miller, died young, and Clémentel was raised in the small Auvergnat town of Riom by his mother, the daughter of a farmer. After studying law, Clémentel became the secretary of the deputy for the department. Following this introduction to politics, he became a *notaire* in Riom, then municipal councillor, and finally deputy mayor of Riom. In 1900, at the age of thirty-six, he was elected to the Chamber of Deputies as a Radical –Socialist. His early career as a deputy was marked by his successful efforts to pass a bill encouraging the creation of co-operative societies for the sale of agricultural produce. Minister of Colonies in 1905 and 1906 under Rouvier, Minister of Agriculture under Barthou, and briefly Minister of Finance under Ribot in 1914, Clémentel had also served as reporter for many of the budgets presented by the Budget Commission of the Chamber of Deputies. He became vice-president of the Chamber in 1909.[6]

Clémentel's pre-war political career was, in short, competent but unexceptional. There was little in the political record to suggest the dynamism, the tenacity and, above all, the imagination which were to be the hallmarks of his years as wartime Minister of Commerce. It is worth noting, however, that Clémentel's interests extended far beyond politics: he was a skilled artist and friend of Rodin and Monet, he was an amateur playwright, opera librettist, historian, and a student of science and mysticism.[7] This intellectual, artistic, and philosophical strain found its political expression in the visionary quality which Clémentel brought to the Ministry of Commerce during the war. In 1914, Clémentel had no economic plan, no discernible political doctrine, no programme, but he had the rare political gift — unexploited until the war began — of seeing far-reaching possibilities in currently unpromising situations.

6. *Le Temps*, 26 December 1936. R. Arnaud 'Etienne Clémentel, président-fondateur de la Chambre de Commerce Internationale 1864–1936', unpublished article (Paris, 1969).
7. *L'Oeuvre artistique d'Etienne Clémentel* (Paris, 1926). *Etienne Clémentel*, preface d'Edmond Haraucourt, (Paris, 1932). E. Clémentel, *L'Ame celtique* (Clermond-Ferrand 1898).

For the first year and a half of the war, Clémentel's chief contribution to the war effort was made in his capacity as president of the Commission of the Budget and the Army of the Chamber of Deputies. Although it was not strictly within his competence to do so, several times in 1915 he proposed a general economic mobilisation of the country. In the interests of social justice, he was particularly concerned that neither industrial workers nor industrialists should unduly benefit by the war, that both owed the fruit of their labour to the country as much as the soldier owed his blood. 'There must be no premium for being away from the front'.[8]

On 29 October 1915 Clémentel replaced Thomson as Minister of Commerce in Briand's first wartime government. Clémentel was fifty-two years old, experienced in politics, administration, and government finance, he had a great capacity for hard work and boundless energy, and he threw himself into the task with enthusiasm. He was to be Minister of Commerce for an uninterrupted period of five years until 27 November 1919, and during this time, his power and influence grew to the point that he became known by the general title of Minister of the National Economy. In addition to the Ministry of Commerce, he performed the Herculean task of holding as many as *five* other ministries and services simultaneously, including at various times, Food, the Post Office, Aviation, Technical Education, the Merchant Marine, Agriculture, and Labour. The normal authority which these posts conferred was greatly increased in wartime by the predominance of the executive element of government ruling by decree. Clémentel was never menaced politically; cabinets changed around him with no effect on his policy.[9] His long tenure of office gave him the time to reshape entirely the structure of the Ministry of Commerce, to build up a cadre of trusted collaborators, and with them to plan and execute radical economic changes.

Clémentel reigned supreme over many aspects of French economic life, but it was his power over industry which is of particular interest. This power was circumscribed by the realities of the wartime situation, notably pressure by the British to implement certain measures, and by the relative strength of industrialists *vis-à-vis* the state in bargaining sessions. When Clémentel first took office in October 1915, his immediate task was to resolve such practical difficulties as wheat shortages. But as the war proceeded,

8. Prompsat Archives T(2)3: *Rapport de M. Clémentel sur le Ravitaillement civil* (8 Sept. 1914–31 Dec. 1916).
9. See Chapter 2.

he gradually began to perceive his role in a broader context. He had a certain vision of a better world which he maintained throughout his life, and it is hardly surprising that he attempted to relate some of the major policy decisions he made during the war to that vision. Allowance must be made for the fact that some of these relationships may have occurred to him in hindsight, and that in the grand rhetorical tradition of the Third Republic the overall coherence of his policy decisions may have been more apparent than real, but nevertheless, Clémentel was no fool, and the force of his personality was such that he was unwilling to be merely a pawn of fate during the war, he was unwilling simply to react to the pressure of situations without any reference to longer-term goals. In short, he took advantage of the pressures, be they from politicians, industrialists, or the British, to advance his own views. Undoubtedly, the nature of the pressures and the decisions he was forced to take in response to them changed the nature of his ideas. The war made Clémentel think of specific problems and solutions which he had never considered before. As with any intelligent man, there was a dialectic between his preconceived notions and the exigencies of the situation.

Thus by 1917, Clémentel had developed plans for the general reform of French industry during and after the war, and within the bounds of the options open to him, he attempted to introduce them in the last years of the war. These plans are worth discussing since so many of Clémentel's major economic measures take on coherence and unity when viewed from the perspective of the post-war economic reforms he hoped to fashion.

Clémentel's vision of France could hardly be called revolutionary; he was far more a reformer, a gradualist, an adapter. But the implementation of his ideas would have had the effect of totally transforming France into a modern industrial state, for Clémentel believed that the advance of humanity was linked to material progress, and that this progress could only be achieved by modernising the basic economic structures of the nation. Clémentel thought that the most effective way to help the working class in France was not to increase salaries, but rather to control production. In February 1918, in a debate on the production of a National Shoe, he said:

> The first duty of the government is to turn towards the toiling masses who suffer the most, to attempt to improve their lot. This is my policy. It is not through the continual raising of salaries that we shall solve the problem. It is above all by forcing ourselves to create an equilibrium

between production and consumption. It is useless to increase salaries: when the consumer spends more than the producer earns, there is disequilibrium.[10]

As far as one can judge, what was meant by the phrase 'an equilibrium between production and consumption' was that working-class dissatisfaction in France stemmed from an insufficiency of basic consumer goods which led to price increases which in turn led to higher wage demands. If the government were to implement measures which would have the effect of increasing the production of consumer goods until working-class wants were satisfied, then true social justice would prevail. Clémentel was not exclusively preoccupied by the fate of the working class; in the same speech he said that the small businessman must also be protected. His view of society stressed the balance of classes rather than the predominance of any one of them.

Clémentel became above all the advocate of a state-directed economy. Drawing upon his experiences to date as the director of the national economy, in December 1917, he and his collaborators published a project to reorganise the Ministry of Commerce.[11] This is a remarkable document, for it attempted to create some order in the existing services while outlining wider post-war aims which were to be striven for simultaneously. In the opening sentences the motives for reorganising the Ministry were given: to prevent France from falling as far behind economically after the war as she had done before: 'It is necessary that from now on our industries adhere to a plan of action outlined by the public authorities in accordance with the best interests of the country and the requirements for its defence'.[12] In the post-war period, the Ministry had to maintain its expanded economic services; it had also to convert government factories to peacetime production and not allow them to fall into private hands. In the resurrected Ministry, provision had to be made to create an entire department exclusively devoted to economic planning (*organes de conception*). Naturally, it was the Ministry of Commerce which was to be responsible for orientating the economic activity of the country in the direction most favourable to the public interest.

In other words, the Ministry should indicate to industrialists and

10. *Chambre des députés*, 22 February 1918, 580.
11. *Projet de réorganization des services du Ministère du Commerce et de l'Industrie* (Paris, 1917).
12. Ibid., ii.

businessmen, and to the groups which represent them, the general plan by which their efforts should be directed, so that the actions of individuals would help rather than hinder the interests of the state. A nation, like a business or an industry, must have an economic programme, a plan of action. Until now, nothing like this has ever been done in France.[13]

The document dramatically contrasts the situation in France with that of Germany, where techniques of military strategy were applied to commerce and battle plans drawn up for the assault of foreign markets.

How was this planning to be done? Clémentel and his advisors proposed much closer contacts between the state and private industry in order that the views and desires of private industrialists might be known. The natural line of communication was the chamber of commerce, but these were too numerous and too weak to be effective. Clémentel advocated grouping and concentrating chambers of commerce in economic regions. In each region, the state was to be represented by a regional inspector from the Ministry of Commerce, who would maintain close ties with the consolidated chambers of commerce.

The Ministry's contacts with industry were to be further strengthened by the reconstitution of professional organisations of industrialists and businessmen (*syndicats*). As they presently stood, the *syndicats* were of no utility whatever to the public authorities, since they represented only a quarter of the total number of producers, and since their activity was frequently not restricted to one particular industry or type of business. It was imperative in the post-war era that a collective policy subscribed to by all members of *syndicats*, which would have to be greatly enlarged, replace the anarchy of individual effort. To aid exports, *syndicats* had to organise export boards (*comptoirs d'exportation*) to represent their collective interest abroad. The *syndicats* were not to be entirely autonomous; each was to maintain a dossier at the Ministry with information on its membership and organisation. The Ministry would force alliances and fusions of *syndicats* so that each amalgamated unit would represent the particular interests of one branch of commerce or industry.

Once the professional representation of individual industries had been thus rationalised, it would be relatively easy for the government to implement its general economic plans. In particular, Clémentel, ever the idealist, hoped that the collection of taxes on industrial and commercial profits would be greatly facilitated. In

13. Ibid., 2.

general, industries and businesses would be forced, for the first time in their history, to articulate in detail their economic objectives, and as with the regional groups of chambers of commerce, be expected to ally these objectives with the general interests of the nation. He pointed to the mixed industrial regime of Austro-Hungary, where the executives of economic interest groups contained bureaucrats, and to the Federation of British Industries as examples of the system he was advocating.

Nor did his proposals stop here. Clémentel was determined to increase the technical competence and knowledge of his civil servants, that they might be the better equipped to define economic priorities in a more informed manner, and to negotiate with industrialists from a position of strength. To this end, he planned a considerable expansion of the research and information gathering services of his Ministry. He intended to establish a force of permanent, trained investigators to undertake specified economic studies. He had already begun to expand his information services during the war by circularising all the producers of certain industries with questionnaires which pried more deeply into the private affairs of companies than any inquiry in the pre-war period would have dared. To force producers to answer, these questionnaires were frequently made an integral part of the process of applying to the government for raw materials. For example, before a producer of gums or other resinous products would receive an authorisation to import material, he had to answer questions concerning the nature of his production, sales, finished products, the date of his company's establishment, a detailed account of his imports in 1916 and 1917, and proof of his nationality.[14] Similar questionnaires were sent to metallurgists; here the emphasis was on pre-war imports and production: why had the company not produced these imported articles itself? Could the company manufacture products currently made in Germany?[15] The government also demanded detailed production statistics and information on stocks of reserves. The main purpose of these questionnaires was to increase production; dossiers were maintained in the Ministry of Commerce on most products produced in the country, with detailed information gathered by questionnaire on the primary materials, labour, transport, and credit facilities required by individual companies to intensify production.[16] Clémentel further proposed the annual publication of production statistics, the creation of a prices board to determine 'normal prices' through the expert assessment by bureaucrats of production costs, and the establishment of an industrial council, which was to be a state-supervised alliance of industry and science to ensure that French industry would remain in the vanguard of modern technological advance.

These claims made for the right of government to intervene in the private sector of the economy were wide indeed, astonishingly so for a man of such moderate political inclinations. The crux of the dispute between Clémentel and the industrialists was the issue of state-supervised industrial concentration versus a regime of rugged individualism. French industrialists valued their independence even above their profits and were anxious to regain it as soon as the war was over, but Clémentel believed that the control of the state over private industry should be continued indefinitely into the post-war period, and for two reasons: inside France, social and economic chaos would prevail when the break-up of wartime industrial ententes led to soaring prices; outside France, better organised economic enemies would take advantage of the divisions among French industrialists, and the nation would be reduced to that position of economic subservience and foreign bondage which she had suffered before the war. For Clémentel, the economic policy of France during the peace must be the pursuit of war by other means. Plans were drawn for the constitution of various committees to supervise the transition of the country from war to peace. Each committee was to devote its attentions to a major industry: metals, textiles, chemicals, and food, and these plans were advanced to the point that lists of possible members were made.[17] When the Import Control Committee (*Comité des dérogations*) was established in March 1917, Clémentel told its members that they were responsible not only for determining which foreign products should be allowed into France during the war, but for considering more long-range plans.

> After the war, there will be a whole series of problems to resolve; traditional instruments such as customs regulations and the like will not suffice. The solution to the problems of primary materials and production must be found now. Government and industry must form an alliance to search for primary materials at the lowest possible cost, to plan for the intensive exploitation of all our natural resources, and to determine the basic cost price of articles which must be manufactured by methods of mass production.
>
> Your committee will play an important role in this task. In a sense, I

17. F12 7661.

am entrusting to you our commercial and industrial destiny.[18]

This sophisticated brand of economic *revanchisme* might lead one to believe that Clémentel was a super-nationalist who put France's interests above all others, but this was not the case. Clémentel was a fervent internationalist and became increasingly so as the war continued. He believed that large economic unions would heal the differences between nations. Clémentel felt that France by herself could not withstand German economic domination after the war. What was called for was the continuation of the economic union of the Allied powers in peacetime. The success of interallied military and economic co-operation during the war had deeply impressed Clémentel. In a letter to Clemenceau on 19 September 1918, outlining the conditions necessary for negotiating peace with Germany, Clémentel warned that the Germans were already preparing their post-war economic offensive.

> It is therefore urgent that by negotiating a new agreement to replace the resolutions of June 1916 we achieve the formation by the Allied democracies, including America, of an economic union which will form the central link of the economic union of all free peoples. The executive of this future alliance exists already in the interallied economic councils which have been operating during the war, and it will be responsible for establishing joint import programmes for raw materials, for the collective purchase of certain of these materials, for the sharing of the credit facilities of some of the producing countries, and finally, for the pooling of all Allied shipping and its redistribution on a basis of equality and of the community of sacrifice, according to the most pressing cases of need, to ensure the victorious conclusion of the war and the preservation of the economic life of each ally while the war continues.[19]

These lofty ambitions were doomed to failure when the Allies stampeded back to the isolation of their prepared positions after the war. Nevertheless, this vision of an economic League of Nations must not be dismissed lightly, for it formed an essential part of the logic behind Clémentel's insistence on the concentration and supervision of French industry, since France could not otherwise participate in such a scheme.

18. Prompsat Archives T(2)5: *Comité des dérogations, Discours de M. le Ministre* 26 March 1917.
19. Prompsat Archives T(1)3: Clémentel to Clemenceau, 19 September 1918.

The Ministry of Commerce and the Control of Imports

Clémentel's economic plans owed much to British pressure, as outlined in the previous chapter. The British threatened Clémentel with a reduction of shipping until the restrictions which applied to British businessmen and industrialists applied to their French counterparts as well. Clémentel turned around and threatened French industrialists with a loss of imports unless they accepted his economic direction. It was the restriction of imports into France in March 1917 which gave Clémentel and his bureaucrats their first major weapon against the mass of French industrialists. The great expansion and restructuring of the Ministry of Commerce dates from this period.

The complete restriction of imports in 1917 was made necessary by the irresponsible and indiscriminate import practices of French businessmen. Clémentel denounced the greed of these importers:

> Since the beginning of unrestricted submarine warfare, there has been a rush on imports into France; importers pass orders unlimited by quantity or price, secure in the knowledge that they will make a profit on any product they bring into France. They never consider resisting in any way the excessive demands of freight agents.[20]

Paradoxically, while at the end of 1916 and beginning of 1917 the English were concentrating all their efforts on conserving their finances and freight supplies and were heading towards the absolute control of all elements of the economy, French public opinion ran strongly against the implementation of any such policy within France and clamoured for the preservation of free enterprise. As Clémentel remarked, 'The Frenchman is touchy, distrustful, and suspicious when faced with any government initiative'.[21]

The prohibition of imports into France was announced on 22 March 1917, at the height of the crisis in Anglo-French relations, when the French government, in an attempt to economise on shipping, decreed that from this day forward no product could be imported into France unless purchased for the account of the government. The Minister of Commerce established a committee to decide on exemptions to this general prohibition (*le comité des dérogations aux prohibitions d'éntree*).[22] This committee was presided over by Senator Viger, a Radical senator from the Loiret, a

20. Clémentel, *France*, 147.
21. Ibid., 137.
22. *Journal Officiel*, 24 March 1917, 305.

former Minister of Agriculture, an opponent of the repurchase of the Western Railway, and now president of the Senate Customs Committee.[23] Among the parliamentary members of the committee was Marc Réville, a Radical deputy from Montbéliard, a free trader, defender of small businesses and industries, former president of the Commission of Commerce and Industry of the Chamber and now president of the Chamber's Customs Committee.[24] On the face of it, Réville could hardly be described as an enthusiastic supporter of government intervention in commerce and industry. Another member of the commission, however, was Jean-Morel, a Radical-Socialist senator from the Loire, a former Minister of Colonies, an expert on customs questions, a man of liberal disposition and sympathetic to notions of commercial and industrial rationality.[25] The final parliamentary member was Louis Puech, a Republican deputy from the Seine of such an independent cast of mind that fellow Republicans referred to him as a 'dissident Radical'; he was also a former Minister of Agriculture and an opponent of wartime speculators.[26] The committee was thus basically Radical in its political disposition, but characteristically divided in its attitude towards state intervention.

Public reaction to the prohibition was swift and intemperate. On 26 March *Le Temps* classified the measure as a 'death sentence', while *Le Radical* more moderately entitled its article of 31 March 'an ill-considered measure'. The possible implications of the decree were outlined in an hysterical article in *L'Oeuvre économique* on 25 March under the heading 'Prohibitions! Exemptions!':

> M. Clémentel has leapt into incoherence with a sort of frantic drunkenness. . . . By a simple decree, the Minister has arrogated unto himself the right to decide the conditions of French production, he has decreed its ruin on the merest whim without the slightest regard for legality; he has given his so-called technical services dictatorial powers.
>
> All demands for imports are received, examined, granted or refused, by the delegates of the Minister; so much the worse for those without friends in high places, so much the worse for those who do not have the time to waste in the antichambers of the 'Masters of Exemptions'. The right to ruin or enrich people, on the slightest impulse, has become the preserve of the rue de Grenelle.

For all its frenzy, *L'Oeuvre économique* correctly foresaw the

23. Archives de l'Assemblée Nationale, *Dictionnaire des Parlementaires*.
24. Ibid.
25. Jolly, *Dictionnaire*, vii. 2515–16.
26. Ibid., 2763–4.

tremendous power which a general prohibition of imports gave the Commerce Ministry over the private sector of the economy. The state was to become the only middleman; all demands for raw materials would have to be justified to the state by private producers. The bureaucratic precedent in France for this strict control of imports came from the Interministerial Commission for Wood and Metals, which had been created by a decree of the War Minister on 11 May 1916. As Clémentel told the first meeting of the Exemptions Committee on 26 March 1917:

> This Interministerial Commission worked exactly in the same direction as you shall be obliged to work for the entirety of our imports. The Commission evolved towards the creation of a sole buyer. For a great many products, our policy must also tend towards the creation of a sole buyer.[27]

Only by absolute control of the importation of metal products had the state prevented disastrous price increases. The bureaucratic structure to which the Interministerial Commission had given rise would serve as a model for the expanded services of the Commerce Ministry which would result from the import prohibition. The technical services of the Ministry would have to be increased, specialised committees for individual products, co-ordinating bodies for bureaucrats and industrialists, and interministerial committees for products which were the concern of more than one ministry would all have to be created. The ultimate goal was that each major material should have its own single government purchasing agent, the 'sole buyer'.

To begin with, said Clémentel, the Exemptions Committee would be expected to divide all goods imported into France into three categories: (1) indispensable goods, to which a general exemption would apply, and no limits would be set on the amounts imported; (2) marginal goods, which would be imported in reduced amounts and divided equitably among French merchants and producers; (3) dispensable goods, such as luxury products, which were totally prohibited. But this classification of goods was only the beginning. The Exemptions Committee was expected to co-ordinate its efforts with the various *syndicats* of different industries to distribute among industrialists those materials which were in short supply, which in practice meant most materials. The Com-

27. Prompsat Archives T(2)5: *Comité des dérogations. Discours de M. le Ministre* 26 March 1917.

mittee was to undertake the technical studies necessary to assess the demands for materials. Industrialists would not be forced to join *syndicats*, and those who wished to remain outside would receive their fair share of material, but as the experience of dissident metal producers who had refused to join their *syndicat*, the *Comité des Forges*, had shown, independent producers might expect considerable delays. This gentle touch of blackmail was a warning the industrialists could not fail to perceive. It will be recalled that Clémentel was determined to force all producers into their respective *syndicats*, where he could control and centralise their endeavours to his own purpose.

Cries of alarm echoed through the land. On 4 April 1917, there was a full-scale debate in the Chamber of Deputies on the decree of 22 March.[28] The first speaker, George Ancel, said that this brusque suspension, from one day to the next, of almost all of France's overseas commerce, was the gravest economic development of the war. He blamed the current coal and wood shortages on bureaucratic red tape, and criticised the composition of the Exemptions Committee, which, despite the participation of such distinguished senators and deputies, would still be dominated by bureaucrats, capable bureaucrats, he conceded, but bureaucrats none the less. The voices of parliamentarians and the productive forces of the country would be stifled in such a forum. Ignoring the crisis in maritime transport and the resulting pressure from the British for France to discipline her industrialists and businessmen which had forced the government to issue the 22 March decree in the first place, Ancel proposed the old, completely impracticable, true-blue alternative: 'If you wish to save French industry of today and tomorrow, you would have done better to favour imports rather than restrain them: above all, live and let live' ('Hear, hear!'). Ancel's reaction was hardly surprising, given the fact that he was the head of an old ship-building and importing firm in Le Havre and was politically grouped with the Republicans.[29] Other speakers sang the same refrain with embellishments. How, asked Charles Lebouq, another Republican, could the Minister hope to increase exports if he decreases imports? How could he urge businessmen to maintain the economic life of the country and then without warning cut off imports? Even Louis Puech, one of the members of the Exemptions Committee, criticised the measure as being too violent a shock and maintained that the reverse pattern should have been followed, that

28. *Chambre des députes*, 4 April 1917, 1101–8.
29. Jolly, *Dictionnaire*, i. 370–1.

instead of a general interdiction on all imports, only luxury items should have been banned, allowing private businessmen free rein in searching for and supplying indispensable goods. Clémentel rose to speak. He began by emphasising the essential point, which was not the problem of increasing trade but the problem of allocating scarce shipping: 'Our means of transport are limited. They are and they will remain lower than the sum total of our requirements, both during the war and during the period which will follow the war'. In such a desperate situation, how could one allow all categories of cargo, indispensable, useful, and useless, to have equal priority? But the theory which lay behind the measure went beyond the issue of maritime transport. The government intended to direct the economy in the national interest, and import restrictions gave it the necessary leverage. The decree which dealt with the transport crisis was also designed to deal with the two other great crises of the wartime economy, credit and productivity:

> We wanted to avoid a new surcharge in our balance of payments deficit. We wanted to improve our domestic production by all the means at our disposal. When we control imports, we will direct the totality of our national production. We will strive with all our might to develop hitherto neglected productive capacities. . . . We have been equally concerned with encouraging the overall organisation of industry and commerce, which is being increasingly forced upon us.

Clémentel also gave notice that the period of speculation and unrestricted profits was at an end, and that Parliament would be asked to enact further legislation against those who took unfair advantage of a difficult situation. To the charge of acting brusquely and without warning, Clémentel pleaded guilty. How else could speculation have been avoided? He turned to alternative systems of control and rejected them; by banning all imports, then providing for exemptions, the measure remained flexible enough to accommodate an evolving situation. The system was all the more useful in negotiations with foreign governments for the export of larger quotas of French goods. He concluded by giving a clear warning to industrialists and businessmen of the future that was awaiting them:

> That ardent love of liberty and independence, which is one of the hallmarks of the French genius, must have as its corollary the spirit of sacrifice, the wish for total submission to the discipline of the nation. . . . Between disciplined producers, obeying the rules which govern all modern industry, and the most powerful individuals clinging obstinately to their outmoded methods, there cannot be an equal match.

Meanwhile, the Exemptions Committee had been working night and day classifying goods, and on 13 April 1917, the first lists were published. Faithful to its creator's wishes, the Committee and its subcommittees went on to determine the general requirements of national consumption and the capacities of national production, and to provide for the difference between the two by a limited importation programme. The Exemptions Committee became the all-powerful central body through which all imports were channelled. To it government departments made their requests for goods, to it the Finance Ministry made known the amount of foreign resources available for purchasing operations, and with this information, the Committee established priorities and granted permission to import. Although the system was initially limited to government expenditure, it soon spread to certain private purchasers who were fulfilling government contracts, and to such government-controlled organisations as the consortia. For the purely private purchaser, however, the process of assessing demands was an extremely difficult one for the Committee, requiring a large amount of documentation, considerable time, and delicate decision-making. Since the Committee had no wish to appear arbitrary, it erred on the side of generosity, with unsatisfactory consequences: 'The exemptions consequently multiplied, with the result that imports quickly reached an amount greatly in excess of that which would have been authorised by a definite programme drawn up in advance'.[30]

But before the government could curb imports by drawing up a long-range master plan, the machinery for processing applications had to be refined. This was done by the Orders of 8 and 15 July 1917, which strengthened the control of the state over transport and imports by reducing to a minimum exceptions to the system.[31] The Order of 8 September 1917 further simplified the system by reducing the number of categories for classifying goods from three to two: (1) unrestricted products, for the most part either food or raw materials for war industry; (2) prohibited products, which were divided into different groups to each of which was assigned a subcommittee to allow a more detailed study of the exceptions to be made.

The story of the progressive restriction of imports by the French government is a classic model of the interrelationships of industrialists, the British, ministers and bureaucrats, and politicians in

30. A. Aftalion, *The Effects of the War upon French Commercial Policy* (Oxford, 1923), 111–14.
31. Clémentel, *France*, 150.

France during the war. The story can be reduced to the following schema: (1) French industrialists, taking advantage of their commercial expertise and the confusion of the government's early attempts to restrict imports, make huge profits in the first years of the war by importing indiscriminately; (2) The British complain to Clémentel and insist that the abuses be stopped; (3) Clémentel yields to British pressure, uses his decree authority to restrict imports, but at the same time sees the long-range possibilities of creating bureaucratic machinery not only to control imports, but 'to direct the totality of our national production'; (4) There is a hostile political reaction from some deputies; it has no effect; (5) The first comprehensive bureaucratic machinery to control imports is created; (6) The industrialists immediately find flaws in the machinery and take advantage accordingly; (7) The machinery is strengthened, new structures such as the consortium evolve from Clémentel's initial concept of the *syndicat*, the industrialists are finally brought under control, and long-term reforms of French industry seem possible; (8) The war ends before these plans for reform come to full fruition.

The Bureaucracy of the Ministry of Commerce

Increasing controls imply increasing controllers. The growth in the authority of interallied agencies and the related growth of measures to control commerce and industry within France were reflected in the evolution of the administrative structure of the Ministry of Commerce in the last year and a half of the war. By 1918, in the realm of economic affairs, a discernable bureaucratic hierarchy had emerged in France, and it is the various organisms which made up this hierarchy which shall now be considered. The careers of a few key bureaucrats will be discussed to give some indication of the sort of men who could be found at the various levels of the hierarchy, and who, collectively, formed the elite of France's wartime civil service.

At the top of the pyramid came the interallied councils and commissions. The Interallied Council for War Purchases and Finance reigned supreme. French delegates to the War Purchases section of the Council were Clémentel, Louis Loucheur, the new Armament Minister, and Paul Bignon, a deputy. Paul Bignon was another deputy with family interests in maritime transports and exports, an opponent of income tax, and a Republican.[32] A number

---

32. Jolly, *Dictionnaire*, ii. 600–1.

of key civil servants supported the delegates to this and other interallied committees.

The Secretary-General of the Purchase Section of the Council was Max Lazard. Forty-three years of age in 1918, he had been trained as an economist before the war and was a co-founder of the International Association for the Campaign against Unemployment, and secretary-general and treasurer of its French branch, under the presidency of his distinguished fellow economist, André Fontaine. Officially classified for military purposes as a captain and interpreter-officer first class, he had begun the war in the French military mission attached to the British Army. In June 1915, at Albert Thomas's request, he took on a new assignment to organise the return of soldiers to war industry. From September 1915 to June 1917, he was in the United States with the French mission responsible for purchasing artillery. In July 1917, he returned to France to the Under-Secretariat of State for the Merchant Marine, where he was detailed to the section that determined transport priorities. In December 1917, he went to London to become Secretary-General of the War Purchase section of the Interallied Council. He remained at this post in 1918 while taking on additional duties as a member of France's Petrol Committee.[33] Lazard's career illustrates the exceptional mobility which leading wartime civil servants enjoyed with regard both to attribution and geography. The pre-war experience of such men in private enterprise or in economic organisations combined with the diversity of their activities during the war to create an exceptionally able class of administrators, and one completely out of the mould of the traditional bureaucracy. Hierarchy and seniority for once counted less than talent and expertise displayed under pressure, with the result that this was an elite of relatively young men.

Behind the Interallied Council came a host of other interallied organisations.[34] Some of these had very large French contingents, such as the International Food Commission, which had no fewer than

33. Information for this and other wartime bureaucrats comes from a variety of sources. The *Tout-Paris. Annuaire de la Société parisienne* was consulted for the years 1914, 1922, and 1927, as was the *Annuaire-Chaix. Les principales sociétés par actions* for the same years. Additional biographical information was found in F 12 8028, 'Affaires diverses', which contained a number of forms which bureaucrats filled out when applying for leave, which listed name, current employment, date of birth, rank, date of nomination to regiment, military career, decorations and honours, civil profession, state of health, reason for leave, and permanent address. Further information can be found in other cartons of the F 12 series.
34. F 12 7659.

twenty-two French delegates, each representing an interested ministry, or a service such as coal, or powders and explosives. Others had a French delegation of two or three men, such as the Interallied Chartering Executive, or the Wheat Executive, where Jean Monnet wielded great power. Jean Monnet, born in Cognac the son of a cognac merchant, was only twenty-six in 1914, and it was the war which launched him on the international career that was ultimately to lead to his contribution to European unity. Starting as an attaché second-class, assigned to the Commissariat, he had specialised in questions of food provisioning, becoming in 1916 French representative to the Interallied Food Commission and head of the French Food Bureau in London. In 1919 he was to become Under-Secretary-General of the League of Nations.[35] He undoubtedly owed his great wartime success in part to the fact that he spoke excellent English, and that Clémentel, who did not, was greatly dependent upon him each time he came to London.

Below the international commissions and agencies came the interministerial committees within France. Chief of these was the Executive Committee for Imports, established by decree on 13 December 1917, and charged with the task of 'centralising, in co-ordination with the corresponding Allied agencies, the import requirements entailing sea transport made by the various ministerial departments'.[36] The membership of the committee comprised several ministers, including Clémentel, who was president, and the Ministers of Armament, Agriculture and Food, and Colonies; as well as under-secretaries, representatives of the Army and Navy, and heads of government services and business associations such as Henry Bérenger, Commissioner of Petrols and Combustibles; Viger, President of the Exemptions Committee; Tardieu, Commissioner-General for Franco-American War Affairs; and David-Mennet, President of the Association of Presidents of Chambers of Commerce.

Henry Bérenger represents another aspect of the wartime bureaucracy, the politician-bureaucrat, or possibly the businessman-bureaucrat. He had already been a considerable personage before the war. Born in 1867, Henry Bérenger had been a brilliant student in philosophy at the Sorbonne, had published a study of Lavisse in 1891, written poems in the manner of d'Annunzio as well as a novel, and become involved in a movement designed to reconcile free-

35. *Who's Who in France* (9th edn., Paris, 1969), 1070.
36. F 12 7657: *Services de guerre du Ministère du Commerce, memorandum de M. Paisant*, 12 October 1918.

thinkers and young socialist-minded clergy. He founded the newspaper *L'Action* in 1903, became editor of *Siècle* in 1908 and *Paris-
Midi* in 1911. In 1912 he was elected senator for the island of
Guadaloupe as a Radical-Socialist and became an influential member of the Army Commission of the Senate. He also carried on a
press campaign against the introduction of the income tax. With the
coming of the war, he developed an interest in the production and
supply of petroleum, an interest which was to bring him into the
ranks of the wartime bureaucracy.[37] In addition to his functions as
member of the Executive Import Committee and Commissioner of
Petrols and Combustibles he was also President of the Petrol
Committee. In 1933, *Le Crapouillot* was unkind enough to suggest
even further wartime activities: 'The journalist Henry Bérenger,
vested with political influence, became the travelling salesman of
Schneider and Le Creusot, whose interests he represented in the
War and Navy Ministries'.[38] Whatever the truth of this charge may
be, his wartime career does not appear to have suffered for it.

After the Executive Committee for Imports came the interministerial committees for raw materials.

> These committees; in conjunction with the Technical Services of the
> Ministry of Commerce, have as their aim the supplying of the nation's
> industries with primary materials, and ensuring the best and most econ-
> omic use of these materials from the point of view of consumption. It is
> through the directives issued by these committees that the import con-
> sortia function.[39]

There were thirteen of these committees, the first to be created
being the National Press Office, on 3 June 1916, and the last,
the Interministerial Committee for Silk, on 26 September 1918.
In between lay an eclectic salad of wool, diamonds, cotton,
leather, paper, chemicals, jute, linen, medicinal plants, and
hemp. There were a considerable number of other interministerial bodies on which only a few key ministries were represented,
such as the Interministerial Commission for Metal and War Production, and separate committees for steel, copper, zinc, wood,
automobiles, and other materials and products. Many of these
commissions were centred on one ministry, which invited representatives of other ministries to participate in their deliberations.
The Ministry of Commerce was one of the main roosts for these

37. Jolly, *Dictionnaire*, ii. 547, 548.
38. *Le Crapouillot*, October 1933, 22.
39. Paisant memorandum.

interministerial committees.

Finally there were the committees and services of the Ministry of Commerce itself. The nerve centre of the Ministry was the Secretariat of War Services, which administered finances, edited documents for the Minister's signature, classified mail, and prepared subjects of discussion for the meetings of the various technical committees. This was a small but vital co-ordinating committee, headed by a former judge of the *Tribunal de la Seine* in Paris, Rieul Paisant. Paisant, who was forty-one in 1918, had begun the war as a lieutenant in the reserve, and served for twenty-one months as a brigade staff officer. It was only in May 1916 that he was assigned to the Commerce Ministry; he went on to become one of its most influential bureaucrats.[40] The full flowering of the bureaucracy came relatively late in the war, and ministers frequently drew on army staff officers who had distinguished themselves in administration.

The most important committee within the Ministry was the Technical Council of War Services. Presided over by the Minister, it included businessmen, industrialists, union leaders, and two bureaucrats, one of whom was recording secretary, who came together to discuss matters of common concern. The Minister's chief bureaucratic assistant was Henri Blazeix, who in addition to his membership of the Council, was also president of the Interministerial Committee for Fatty Materials, delegate of the Commerce Ministry to the Office for Industrial Reconstitution, and one of the Minister's chief negotiators with the *Comité des Forges*.[41] Blazeix was one of the Ministry's trouble-shooters and something of an all-rounder; he was responsible for drafting proposals for the Minister on several of the major problems of state-industrial relations.

Bureaucrats on the Technical Council were outnumbered by a powerful assemblage of captains of industry and commerce. Members included Charles Laurent, president of *L'Union minière et métallurgique*, president of the *Banque des Pays du Nord*, director of the *Chemin de fer de Paris à Orléans* and the Suez Canal Company; leading representatives of the cotton industry, the food industry, the chemical industry, and private maritime transport companies; and David-Mennet, head of the chambers of commerce of France. Finally, there were two union representatives, Briat, general secretary of the *Chambre Consultative des Associations ouvrieres de production*, and, less explicably, Keufeur, the head of the book workers' union.[42]

40. F12 7657, F12 7658, F12 7662, F12 8028.
41. F12 7657, F12 7672, F12 8044.
42. F12 7657.

The Technical Council met to discuss the establishment and operation of consortia, to tidy up scandals, to determine import priorities, and to attempt to resolve major crises arising from shortages or from clashes of will between government and industry. The Council was a useful forum for hammering out major policy decisions for the future, such as price controls, or the principle of the state as sole buyer. From the minutes of meetings, it is clear that after Clémentel, Henri Blazeix played the dominant role in the proceedings, seemingly expert on the whole range of questions which the council was called upon to answer.[43] The industrialists and businessmen tended to speak only on questions which directly concerned them, and the union leaders tended not to speak at all.

Beneath the Technical Council and the Secretariat for War Services came the technical services themselves. The functions and personnel of these services had a tendency to merge with those of the interministerial committees for primary products. As described by Rieul Paisant, these functions were: 'The organisation in collaboration with the Armament, Agriculture, and Food Ministries, and the Commissariat, of the distribution of all materials emanating from either supervised French production or imports made through the intermediary of consortia, *comptoirs*, offices, and other groups'.[44] There were ten of these services or sections, each specialising in a different material, each with its section chief, deputy chief, and deputies. The First Section, for example, specialising in metal, was divided into two subsections, one dealing with metal in general, the other with machines and motorised power. This section, the largest, required the services of eighteen bureaucrats.

Unbureaucratic Bureaucrats

This, then, was the bureaucratic structure of the Commerce Ministry and interrelated ministerial and Allied administrations by 1918. It was not until 29 June 1918 that a law was passed consecrating the legal form of this structure and it was only in the last year and a half of the war that the bureaucracy underwent the phenomenal growth in personnel, attributions, and power which the final edifice reflected. This evolution, compressed in such a short space of time, had begun on 22 March 1917 with the import prohibitions, and it was only from this date that the bureaucracy gained its real author-

43. F12: 7659: *Procès-verbaux des réunions du Conseil Technique.*
44. F12 7657.

ity and pre-eminence over private industry. A surprising number of those who were to become the most powerful bureaucrats in France by the end of the war, only came to the Commerce Ministry from the middle of 1916 or later. Some had fought on the Front and been wounded and invalided out of the army. Many were transferred from other ministries. They brought an unusual variety of pre-war experiences to bear on the problems they were confronted with in the Ministry: they were judges, teachers, professors, lawyers, engineers, economists, and industrialists. They were often non-specialists; they moved from one assignment to another with great frequency; they could and often did hold multiple livings. For the more capable, promotion was swift and the rewards in terms of power great.

Quite apart from their increase in numbers and in power, bureaucrats became more worldly. They were no longer restricted to the confines of one particular ministry, they met bureaucrats from other ministries on interministerial committees; they travelled to London to confer with bureaucrats of other nations on interallied organisations; and above all, they came into increasing contact with the people affected by their decisions: they met industrialists and businessmen on joint consultative committees, and met them as equals. With the increasing awareness caused by such communication came greater initiative and an increasing boldness of decision. Clearly a new breed of bureaucrat was emerging.

CHAPTER 4

The Consortium

The Creation of the Consortium System

To opponents of state intervention in private enterprise, the advent of the consortium seemed the fruition of a diabolical plot long prepared by the government. The historian, journalist and future leader of the *Redressement français*, Lucien Romier, wrote: 'The consortia seem to be the logical, if not necessary, conclusion of a rigorous evolution of the policy decreed by the public authorities in economic affairs since the beginning of 1916'.[1] First, the movement of imports into France had been restricted by the laws of 6 May 1916 and 22 March 1917; then various interallied agreements had further reduced the freedom of private businessmen; then all merchant ships were requisitioned by the Commerce Minister on 15 February 1918; then all credit facilities abroad were placed under strict government control by a series of measures culminating in the law of 3 April 1918. If perchance an importer should manage to bring his goods through despite all these restrictions, they could then be seized and requisitioned by the law of 5 April 1918. Only one problem remained: the state lacked any direct channel of communication with the individual producer who was receiving his share of the imported material. The consortium was designed to fill this gap. Its creation marked the logical conclusion of the emergence of the state as 'sole buyer'.

Definition and Origins

What exactly was a consortium? The description of Pierre Renouvin deserves to be quoted at length.

1. L. Romier, *Rapport sur les consortiums* (Paris, 1918), 3.

It is a group of businessmen or manufacturers, specialising in the same product, which centralises demands for raw material, buys the material abroad and resells it to members of the group, under the control of the state. In principle, the state assumes no financial role. . . . In practice, the consortium, which does not participate in general policy decisions, is attached to one of the state's executive committees, which are composed of bureaucrats and technicians. . . . It is this committee which controls the consortium, furnishes the means of transport, and fixes the prices.[2]

The consortium evolved from the *comptoir*, the product of interallied pressure, particularly from the United States, for France to create an organism to receive and redistribute material purchased by the Allied governments through representative missions sent to America: '*Comptoirs* . . . were groups of manufacturers engaged in buying foreign raw materials and transforming them into the manufactured products required by the government departments'.[3] Numerous *comptoirs* had been established, usually at the behest of the Armament Ministry, by manufacturers requiring various types of metals. But the Armament Ministry was interested only in acquiring scarce raw materials, not in maintaining or directing the economic life of the country, and as long as armament manufacture continued satisfactorily, there was little direct interference by the government in the running of the affairs of the *comptoirs*. Another antecedent of the consortium was the organisation created by the Agriculture Ministry to supply manufacturers with imported sulphur and superphosphates, but these were more transport co-operatives than anything else.

From both of these organisms, however, two of the vital features which distinguished a consortium were missing: state supervision of the redistribution of raw material among manufacturers, and the equalisation of the price of the material, no matter how much the price of acquisition may have varied from country to country and from one time to another. A third distinction may be added: the implicit limitation of profits which would result from closer state supervision of industry. As Romier, one of the more energetic advocates of the retention of the *comptoirs* noted: 'Whereas the consortium is very closely linked to the state by a contract, the *comptoir* is on more informal good terms with the state and, in particular, is free to share out its profits'.[4] It should be pointed out that later, during the heyday of the consortium, the term *comptoir*

2. Renouvin, *Formes*, 59.
3. A. Aftalion, *The Effect of the War upon Commercial Policy* (Oxford, 1923), 117.
4. Romier, *Consortiums*, 9.

came to mean something different. It was defined during a meeting of the Technical Council of War Services of the Ministry of Commerce as 'the organisations which distribute finished products, whereas consortiums distribute raw materials to industrialists, who, in general, transform it themselves into finished products'.[5] Thus, *comptoirs* were established in 1918 for such finished products as tubes and bicycles.

Another ancestor of the consortium may possibly be found in Germany, where raw materials had been an active preoccupation of the government from the outset of the war. In August 1914, a Raw Materials Section had been established, and by 1915, two full years before the French had come round to the idea, Walther Rathenau had created a series of War Materials Corporations, 'a system of private joint-stock companies established under government auspices to buy, store, and distributed raw materials'.[6] These corporations were considered to be serving the public interest, and as such, made no profits and distributed no dividends. Government officials and chamber of commerce members formed an intermediary governing body to mediate between the corporations and the government. Clémentel kept a close watch on Rathenau and his activities during the war, and it seems likely that he was influenced by the success of this German institution in his decision to create the consortium.

In Britain, two approaches were taken to the problem of allocating scarce imports among private producers. One method was to establish a purchasing union within a government department; this purchasing union would imitate all the methods and functions of a private commercial operation.[7] In Britain, this system was used for flax and jute; in France, for wheat. The other approach was to have a group of private traders take over the methods and functions of a government department. These groups were semi-official trade organisations and bore a strong resemblance to the consortium system.

> In the case of butter and cheese the buying organisation acting on behalf of the Ministry of Food was a committee of private traders called the Butter and Cheese Imports Committee. This Committee was established by the Food Controller in December 1917 to take over the responsibility for shipment, handling, inspection, storage, and distribution of butter

5. F12 7659: *Ile séance du Conseil technique*, 9 March 1918.
6. Feldman, *Germany*, 49.
7. E.M. Lloyd, *Experiments in State Control at the War Office and the Ministry of Food* (Oxford, 1924), 305–6.

and cheese under the direction of the Ministry of Food. Its financial operations were subject to control and audit by the Ministry and were guaranteed by the Treasury. A fixed commission of ½ per cent was credited to the Committee to cover the expense of administration.[8]

Since the creation of the consortium had arisen from the necessity of controlling the distribution within France of imported materials in response to British pressure, Clémentel may have found such British organisms as the Butter and Cheese Imports Committee, or the Cotton Commission, a similar organisation, useful models. As has been noted earlier, in August 1917, Sir Albert Stanley urged Clémentel to create an organism like the British one for importing cotton, and as shall be seen, Clémentel's first consortium was the cotton consortium, established two months later. Thus both the Germans and the British provided Clémentel with similar solutions to the problem of creating an importing and distribution organisation which would satisfactorily combine government and private interests.

Clémentel saw the consortium as a fair exchange of the resources of the state for the talents of private industry.[9] Only the state had the necessary transport and credit facilities to import scarce raw materials, and the other Allied governments would deal only with the state and its representatives. Industrialists, on the other hand, had a monopoly of industrial expertise and technical knowledge. What fairer bargain could be driven than to create an organism which would satisfy the interests of both?

The cotton consortium was the first example of the true consortium. In August 1917, the French High Commission in Washington sent Clémentel a report on the conditions under which the Americans would be willing to sell their cotton to France. The United States insisted on a single French purchasing agent. After consultation with the Ministry of War, the largest single purchaser of American cotton; the Ministry of Finance, which was responsible for financing American purchasing operations; and representatives of the cotton industry itself, Clémentel was able to draw up the convention which instituted the French Cotton Consortium on 27 October 1917. Like its German counterpart, the first French consortium was a private joint-stock company, with a capital of 10.692 million francs, to which all cotton manufacturers subscribed in proportion to their productive capacities. Its objectives were to undertake in the national interest all commercial operations

8. Ibid., 309.
9. F12 7662: *Commission du Budget, séance du Vendredi 16 mai 1918.*

'relative to the purchase, import, and sale of raw cotton destined to supply the cotton industry in France'.[10] Purchases of cotton in the United States were made not by the Consortium but by the French state, after consultation with the Consortium about the quantities and qualities required. The Consortium was legally obliged to repurchase all the cotton bought by the state upon delivery in a French port, and to pay all insurance, credit, transport, and administrative costs. An important feature of the agreement was that the Consortium resold the cotton to its members at a price set by the Ministry of Commerce. As a result, by June 1918, the price which the Consortium charged its members for cotton was 20 per cent lower than the price of the small amount of cotton still being sold on the free market.[11] In March 1918, an Interministerial Committee for Cotton was created and became the authority consulted by the Commerce Ministry on questions relating to the setting of prices of cotton and determining the amounts of cotton required to be imported. Previously the mechanism for the supervision of prices by the government had been unclearly defined, and in January 1918, the Technical Council had felt obliged to assert its right to review the price structure established by the cotton consortium.[12]

The Administrative and Legal Framework

From its first meeting on 10 December 1917, one of the chief concerns of the Technical Council of War Services was to be the extension of a system of consortia to cover all of French industry.[13] Clémentel asked this first meeting of industrialists and businessmen to consider other products to which the system could be readily applied. What means could be employed by consortia to reduce the price of consumer goods as quickly as possible? Was it advisable to eliminate all private middlemen from these transactions? Did members of the Technical Council think it a necessary corollary of the constitution of consortia for the government to create its own committee for every raw material, a committee which would control not only imports but all production decisions as well? These were far-ranging questions indeed. He concluded by offering the

10. J. Manteilhet, *Vers une économie nationale. Le régime des consortiums* (Paris, 1918; privately printed) 35, 36. Several copies of this work were discovered in the Prompsat Archives.
11. Ibid., 38.
12. F12 7659: *5ᵉ réunion du Conseil technique*, 14 January 1918.
13. F12 7659: *Iᵉʳᵉ réunion du Conseil technique*, 10 December 1917. See above, Chapter 3 for a description of the attributions and personnel of the Technical Council of War Services.

Technical Council a draft convention between the state and any further consortium which might be formed.

From Clémentel's questions, it was clear that the consortium was intended to strengthen the hand of the government considerably in controlling the economic life of France. Almost immediately the problem of finding a legal basis for justifying such intervention arose. One of the most curious features of the establishment of regime of the consortia, and indeed, of the formation of the entire economic policy of the war, was the extent to which major decisions were made by the bureaucracy and not by the legislature. The creation of the first consortium was a simple administrative decision of the Ministry of Commerce, and the subsequent proliferation and elaboration of the consortium system was the result of similar decisions. Critics of consortia such as Romier maintained that the conventions which established consortia were not really between the state and the consortium, but between the bureaucracy and the consortium:

> The basis and *raison d'être* of the consortium is to be found in the convention which the administration imposes on the group forming the consortium. We use the word 'administration' and not 'state' advisedly, since it is a well-known fact that this convention is the result of an administrative measure and not of a legislative one.[14]

Clémentel's defenders held that legislature had given its approval to the policy of consortia on two occasions, 7 February and 28 June 1918, but these were votes of confidence on his general administrative competence and not specific laws defining the legal position of this new organism.[15] It is interesting to observe that at a meeting of the Technical Council in January 1918, at which he proposed the creation of a number of new bureaucratic services, Clémentel suggested that rather than ask parliament for money to cover the running costs of these services, it would be preferable if consortia contributed 0.1 per cent of their income for this purpose. Clémentel appeared genuinely reluctant to involve the legislature in his policy decisions. A further impediment to the legalisation and codification of consortia was Article 419 of the Penal Code, which forbade any form of conspiracy among producers which might lead to the establishment of a trust or cartel. Clémentel was the first to admit that this article had been unofficially abrogated during the war, and he advocated its modification for the post-war period when French

14. Romier, *Consortiums*, 6.
15. Manteilhet, *Consortiums*, 29, 30.

producers would have to combine to compete with German cartels, but the article still remained on the statute books.

As more and more consortia came into being, the conventions which the administration signed with each of them became longer and increasingly sophisticated. The draft convention which Clémentel presented to the Technical Committee in December 1917, and which he thought would be suitable for all new consortia, consisted of thirteen articles, dealing with the form of the organism, which was to be a limited joint-stock company; the division of shares among members, which had to be approved by the ministers concerned, and which had as its basis the average portion of total imports of the raw material which each member had made in the period 1912–17; the distribution of imported material among members, which was in exact proportion to shares held; and the limitation of the profits of the consortium (as opposed to the profits of individual members) to 6 per cent, with any excess being used by the state for such general interests of the industry as research. The machinery for repurchasing material bought by agents of the government abroad was outlined in detail, as was the method of ensuring an equalisation of prices. The Minister of Commerce had the right to verify the accounts of the consortium at any time and to ratify personally the fees and emoluments paid to the chief executives of the consortium. He also had the power to resolve disputes between members of the executive. Provision was made for the reconstitution of the consortium six months after the termination of hostilities, to allow for the admission of new members.[16]

During the next few months, this draft document was found to contain a great number of imprecisions and loopholes, and every successive consortium which came into being during this period was obliged to adhere to increasingly stringent conditions. The bureaucratic structure which was to control the consortia became more elaborate. In January 1918, for example, Clémentel informed the Technical Council of the creation of a new inventory service to regulate the purchases of consortia on the basis of real military and civilian need; a new organisation for the direction and control of foreign purchases; a service to divide available shipping tonnage equitably among importers; and a central body to co-ordinate the work of the technical committees with regard to the administration of consortia.[17] On 18 June 1918, a Consultative Commission for Consortia was created, with the responsibility for:

16. F12 7662.
17. F12 7659: *6ᵉ réunion du Conseil technique*, 21 January 1918.

Studying from the legal, judicial, and financial point of view the establishment of consortia, their statutes, the conventions which govern their relations with the state, and in a general manner, the foundations upon which the functioning and control of these organisms rest.[18]

The membership of the Consultative Commission consisted of some of the leading bureaucrats of the Ministries of Commerce and Armament. It included Rieul Paisant, the head of the War Services Secretariat at the Ministry of Commerce; Gourdeau, one of the Ministry's directors of technical services; Texier, a lawyer who was second in command of the legal department at the Ministry; and André Matter, from the legal department of the Ministry of Armament.

The Commission set to work immediately to rectify some of the most glaring errors of the system. It was discovered that some consortia had been disregarding the advice of the Ministry of Commerce and its relevant technical committee in the distribution of raw material among members. The Commission declared that the consortia had to submit their rules for the distribution of material to the Minister of Commerce for his approval; the rules then had to be published and circulated to all those concerned. This division of imported material had also been criticised as being arbitrary and inflexible. To base the number of shares held in a consortium, and hence the proportion of an industrialist's share of raw material, on the average of his imports from 1912 to 1917 was to make no allowance for current needs and the requirements of specific production programmes. There was no reward for individual initiative and competence, and the most capable industrialists were frustrated and tied down by this rigid system. Accordingly, the primary consideration in dividing material was made to depend more directly on the capacity of the manufacturer to produce the finished product, and less on the number of shares he held in the consortium.

The debate within the Consultative Commission on this and other topics continued unresolved over the summer months of 1918. Should the division of material be based on 'work actually accomplished' or merely on 'the capacity for production'?[19] The Commission reaffirmed and strengthened the principle of the right of the state to equalise and set prices, but they fretted about the legality of such a principle. The problem of legality was continually being raised in one form or another. The minutes of the meeting of 4 July 1918 note:

18. F12 7662.
19. F12 7662: *Séance du 6 juillet 1918.*

The Commission discussed the question of whether the principles governing consortia should be formulated in a decree, in an order, or in a decision. A decree would give the necessary legal force, but seems useless. It is preferable not to give an immutable character to rules which should be variable.[20]

Another legal problem was whether the state could use the consortia as a means of collecting more war profits tax.[21] André Matter pointed to a law of 26 August 1789 which said that 'a tax may be increased, modified, or suppressed only by a law'. Again, on legal grounds, the right of the Minister of Commerce to arbitrate between disputing members of a consortium was declared to be out of order. Another problem which was never satisfactorily resolved was that of the admission of new members to a consortium during wartime.

As a result of all these discussions, a new general form of draft convention for consortia was drawn up, based largely on the statutes of the newly-created Drug Consortium. In the six months which had elapsed since the first general form, the length of the document had increased from eight to twenty-eight pages, and the number of articles in the convention had grown from thirteen to forty-five. The rules for admission were more precisely defined, particularly with regard to foreign-owned industries; the administration of the consortium was far more closely regulated, and the duties of the executive were outlined in greater detail; precise provision was made for the convocation and operation of general shareholders' meetings; and above all, the articles dealing with the bookkeeping arrangements and general financial administration of the consortium were tightened up considerably.

The Proliferation and Increasing Bureaucratic Control of Consortia

By February 1918 Clémentel's ambition to extend the system of consortia to all of French industry was becoming a reality. At the ninth meeting of the Technical Council, Guillet, one of his chief lieutenants, listed nearly fifty products or materials for which Clémentel had instituted or planned to institute consortia. These products included jewellery, wood, rubber, celluloid, varnish, leather, bicycles, electricity, soap, watches, ceramics, dresses, hard-

20. F12 7662.
21. F12 7662: A. Matter, *Les Consortiums et l'impôt sur les bénéfices de guerre*, 28 June 1918.

ware, silk, petrol, glass, and in fact, every major raw material required by French industry, and every major product for civilian consumption manufactured by it. The lines of distinction between raw materials and finished products, between *comptoirs* and consortia became somewhat blurred. It seems unclear, for example, why a bicycle consortium should be created when a *comptoir* had been established for the same product. In a further attempt to distinguish between importers of raw material and manufacturers of a specific finished article, the Commerce Ministry instituted a new organism called the omnium, which would group several consortia. Guillet drew the distinction in the following manner:

> The consortium groups members of the same industry, the omnium groups representatives of consortia which need primary materials of the same category: thus, the Soap Consortium includes soap manufacturers and will be represented in the Omnium of Fatty Materials and in the Omnium of Chemical Products, since its members need both fatty materials and chemical products.[22]

A new definition of the term consortium seemed to be emerging. A consortium could now also be based on a manufactured product, and the omnium became the organism which imported the raw material. The distinction became clearly necessary as the system was extended and grew in complexity, and conflicting claims for raw material from different industries appeared, but it implied a further tightening of state control over industry, particularly over production decisions and the prices of finished products. The loose control of the *comptoir* over manufactured goods was being replaced by the tighter control of the consortium, in a process identical to that which had occurred previously for raw materials.

By May 1918 so many consortia had appeared or were about to appear that a note was circulated to the heads of the technical sections of the Ministry of Commerce on the standard procedure to be undertaken in forming a consortium. If a section chief felt a material was ripe for a consortium, he was to send a note to the Director of Technical Services indicating the current tonnage and value of the imported material concerned, and outlining the advantages which would accrue from the formation of such a consortium. A meeting was then to be called at which the Director of Technical Services, the head of the interested technical section, the secretary-general of the relevant committee of industrialists and bureaucrats, and the presidents of the professional associations of the industry

22. F12 7659: *9ᵉ séance du Conseil technique*, 18 February 1918.

concerned were to appear. Prior to this meeting, the presidents of professional associations were to be sent a note explaining what a consortium was, and a copy of the draft convention. During the meeting these presidents would be asked to draw up a project for the consortium which took into account the information they had received. This proposal was to be examined by the head of the technical section, who would transmit it to the Director of Technical Services. The strict watch maintained by the Director ensured the close control of the consortium by the Ministry of Commerce.[23]

The effective control of consortia was wielded by the interministerial committee for the material for which the product had been created. Thus the Interministerial Cotton Committee was established on 19 February 1918 and given large responsibilities. The Committee was to centralise, co-ordinate, and control the requirements of the nation for raw cotton and all products manufactured from cotton. It was to determine which types of products made from cotton were to be manufactured in France rather than imported, taking into account the needs of the army, and the industrial capacity, raw materials, and manpower available; and it was within the power of the Committee to take any necessary measures to ensure this manufacture. The Committee was also to ascertain the cost of producing various products in cotton, and to set the maximum price which would be charged for the product at each stage of its production. The Committee was then to assess which products were to be imported, on a basis of transport available, and to draw up a list of priorities among imported products. Finally, it was made responsible for constituting reserve stocks of material, should this prove necessary.[24]

It will be recalled that these interministerial committees were composed of bureaucrats representing interested ministries and industrialists. In the case of the Cotton Committee, there were five members from the Ministry of Commerce, five from the Ministry of War, two from Armament, one from Finance, and one from the General Staff. Industrialists were represented by the President of the Cotton Consortium, two owners of cotton spinning mills, one industrialist who manufactured cotton thread, two industrialists engaged in cotton weaving, one cotton trader from the cotton exchange of Le Havre, one cotton textile manufacturer, and one wholesale cotton merchant. Bureaucrats clearly outnumbered industrialists and dominated the deliberations of the Committee. As

23. F12 7662: *Note pour MM les Chefs de Section*, 22 May 1918.
24. Manteilhet, *Consortiums*, 31.

Clémentel asked the Chamber of Deputies in June 1918,

> Would you allow me to have a majority of industrialists on these committees which are responsible for establishing the needs of the army at the same time as those of the civilian population? That would be inadmissible. Besides, the industrialists do not ask for this. On these committees the majority must rest with representatives of the government; that is indispensable.[25]

In short, the interministerial committees were supposed to be the effective executive committee of the consortiums and to make all their major policy decisions.

Once the consortium had come into being, and its administration had been provided for, there remained the difficulty of coaxing all the members of the industry to join. The problem was similar to that of a labour union operating in a factory in which certain workers refuse to join the union; why should these workers enjoy all the benefits of the union's struggles with management without participating in the costs? In a meeting of the Consultative Commission for Consortiums in July 1918, Rieul Paisant said that it would be difficult to force all industrialists to participate in a consortium as long as non-members continued to enjoy the same advantages of price and distribution of the raw material as members.[26] Paisant advocated a system of differential rules governing the price of the commodity, whereby non-members would at least pay their fair share of the operating costs of the consortium. This system of differential charges was incorporated into the conventions of a number of subsequent consortia, such as that for wire and nails, established on 30 August 1918, which contained the additional proviso that when non-members shared in the distribution of raw material, they tacitly accepted the rules of the consortium governing the resale of such material.[27] In a further attempt to coerce recalcitrant industrialists into an attitude of fraternity, Paisant also proposed that members and non-members alike be forced to participate in what amounted to a collective insurance agreement by which those industrial establishments which had survived the perils of war intact would be responsible for helping those owners of factories which had been burned out, occupied by the enemy, or damaged in any other way by the war.

25. *Chambre des députés*, 28 June 1918, 1839.
26. F12 7662: 6 July 1918.
27. F12 7662: *Consortium d'importation des fils, pointed, vis, et clous.*

The Control of Prices

The establishment of prices for imported materials was one of the most vexatious problems to beset the regime of consortia. Article Five of the first general draft convention of December 1917 said that prices would be fixed according to bases periodically established by the Minister of Commerce, after consultation with other interested ministers, on the recommendation of the executive of the consortium. Several kinds of prices were to be set. First, the price at which goods delivered by the state to the consortium would be resold to its members. This price would take into account all the costs necessary for the procurement, transportation, and insurance of the material, establishing an emergency reserve fund, and equalising the price for all members. Secondly, the state claimed the right, albeit indirectly, to supervise not only the price of raw materials but of finished products. The Minister of Commerce was to fix 'the bases for the sale price of manufactured industrial products, taking the prices charged by the Consortium to its members as a starting point'. The relevant technical committee would determine those products whose prices were to be fixed. Thirdly, the Minister would establish the quantities and prices of the material which were to be reserved for interested ministries.[28]

But what was the actual procedure by which these prices were to be fixed? At a meeting of the Technical Council in January 1918. Henri Blazeix announced that the general method for establishing prices would be that used by the French Vegetable Oil Consortium. As soon as the goods purchased abroad by the state had arrived in a French port, a provisional bill would be established by an agent on the Ministry of Supply, which would not take into account errors of weighing at the port of embarkation or losses en route, and the consortium would pay 90 per cent of this bill. The consortium would then verify the quantities and qualities of the product and draw up a definitive bill. In addition, the consortium would be required to make a deposit of 2.5 per cent of the provisional bill so that the state was protected against any loss resulting from a difference between the provisional and definitive price. This procedure covered the transfer of goods from the state to the consortium, but Blazeix was far less precise in describing the next and most critical stage of the operation, the transfer of the goods from the consortium to its members, and the equalisation of prices.[29]

From the meetings of the Consultative Commission from June

28. F12 7662.
29. F12 7659: *4ᵉ réunion du Conseil technique*, 7 January 1918.

1918 on, it is clear that this problem was never satisfactorily resolved. At the meeting of 26 June, members of the Commission agreed that it seemed unreasonable for the state to fix the price at which the consortium resold the material to its members, since it was the consortium, not the state, which was doing the selling, but concluded that it was only by the state fixing prices that prices could be equalised and eventually lowered as well.[30] Three days later, at their next meeting, members reassured themselves with the reminder that the decree of 28 January 1918 gave the Under-Secretary of Commerce control over consortia, and that this disposition could be used by the state to control prices.[31]

On 6 July, the Commission turned to consider the even thornier question of the prices to be set by individual members of the consortium when they sold their finished products to the general public. Rieul Paisant declared that any precise formula fixing these prices would be too absolute and incapable of amendment. Lemery, the Under-Secretary of Commerce, thought it useless to impose any detailed retail price structure on members of the consortia, and that only the bases for these prices should be specified. The Commission concluded its deliberations on an equivocal note: 'The state will draw up the rules which will be used to determine prices and control their application, but it is the consortium itself which will establish these prices'.[32] In later consortia, such as the Consortium for Wires, Spikes, Screws and Nails, the state attempted to find another formula to limit retail prices charges to the general public for manufactured goods. The Minister of Commerce would ascertain the cost price of these items by adding a certain percentage for labour and processing to the basic price which the industrialist paid the consortium for raw material.

> The retail price set by members of the consortium differs from the cost price of merchandise waiting to be sold in their warehouses. This difference, representing the general expenses and the net profit of the manufacturer, will be fixed periodically by the Minister of Commerce after consultation with the competent interministerial committee.[33]

This concern for controlling the prices set by members of consortia reflects the growing preoccupation of the Ministry of Commerce with the general question of limiting all retail prices.

30. F12 7662.
31. F12 7662: 29 June 1918.
32. F12 7662: *Commission Consultative des Consortiums*, 6 July 1918.
33. F12 7662: *Consortium d'importation des fils, pointes, vis, et clous. Convention.*

Increasingly Clémentel favoured the introduction of a system of 'standard products' (*produits types*), a few key products whose price would be pegged by the government in the hope that this would curb the price of other products. In April 1918, Clémentel outlined his scheme to the Technical Council.[34] He explained that there was no question of fixing the sale price of all goods, but rather of creating standard prices for five or six products for each category of material, leaving the rest free. He gave as an example the creation of a standard type of cloth and said that it might be necessary for the government itself to manufacture certain standard products, as it had done with the National Shoe. Blazeix added that these standard products were in the process of being defined for soap and vegetable oil as well. Initially, however, it was through the mechanism of the consortia that some check on consumer prices was to be maintained.

It will be recalled that Clémentel thought of the defence of the working and lower middle classes in terms of controlling consumer prices rather than raising incomes, and from the first draft convention in December 1917, his policy for consortia bore witness to this philosophy. There was something of the notion of the 'just price' behind Clémentel's view of the way in which the laws of supply and demand ought to be made to operate. As Manteilhet, one of the hardiest defenders of the consortium policy explained,

> The activity of consortia is evolving inexorably, at least for vital products of consumption, towards fixing prices at all stages of production, across the hundred processes of transformation from the raw material to the finished product. The brutal and blind taxes of an authoritarian state are replaced by a price structure which shows the cost price with a legitimate profit added, the joint achievement of the producer and the higher administration, which represents the totality of the consumers. . . . The consumer will pay the just price and the producer receive the just reward for their labour; the profits of this collective endeavour will be transformed into social wealth for all and not into an instrument of power for the few.[35]

Criticism of the Consortia

As can be imagined, the creation and development of consortia gave rise to a storm of controversy in France. The mechanics of establishing and operating consortia were extremely complex, and their constitution was, of necessity, hasty and imperfect. This was a period of intense experimentation, for the consortium had no real

34. F12 7659: *13ᵉ séance du Conseil technique*, 8 April 1918.
35. Manteilhet, *Consortiums*, 75.

precedent, no useful parallel. As André Matter, one of the leading bureaucrats of the Armament Ministry remarked, after advising against the use of consortia as a device for collecting was profits tax: 'Consortia are undergoing a trial period, and the greater the number of experiments we make in this trial period, the greater the light that will be shed on the form of their future organisation'.[36] The targets for criticism were consequently legion. The simple question of the admission of industrialists to membership in a consortium was complicated by the fact that only those industrialists who had been incorporated before 31 December 1917 and received their *patente* could be admitted immediately into the consortia. Otherwise, admittance had to be approved by the Ministry of Commerce. The purpose of this restriction was to discourage would-be speculators and war profiteers, but it also had the effect of forcing any French citizen planning a commercial or industrial venture in 1918 to apply for ministerial permission to do so.

One of the chief accusations was that the consortia simply did not work. The state was criticised for failing to discharge its obligations to supply the minimum amount of necessary maritime transport to importers, which, as one critic said, was the only tangible advantage it could have offered industrialists in compensation for the exorbitant control it had arrogated for itself.[37] This line of attack conveniently ignored the whole problem of the tremendous loss on tonnage as a result of submarine warfare, which more reasonable men might have considered an attenuating factor for the failure of the Commerce Ministry to live up to its promises. The state was also accused of not controlling price increases effectively; it was claimed that the government policy of seeking out and redistributing private stocks and reserve supplies of materials held by producers, far from preventing speculation and price increases as had been intended, had rather the reverse effect. Critics maintained that consortia suffered from over-bureaucratisation, that they lacked the decisiveness and flexibility of private organisations, that their operations were bogged down in a swamp of red tape and finicky procedural detail. Other critics said that the consortia created nothing and built no new factories, they merely divided existing materials, and did so inefficiently.

Clémentel devoted a great deal of his time in 1918 to answering these and other criticisms. At a meeting of the Budget Commission of the Chamber of Deputies in May, he denied that consortia had

36. F12 7662: A. Matter, *Les Consortiums et l'impôt sur les bénéfices de guerre*, 28 June 1918.
37. Romier, *Consortiums*, 9, 10.

been a failure. It was not true that consortia had created no new productive capacity; the problem was that the Armament Ministry had failed to provide some of the necessary building supplies, and that many of the new factories were closed down at present for lack of raw material to process. As for price increases, Clémentel pointed to the example of raw cotton, whose price had decreased by 20 per cent since the inception of consortia. The government was not systematically destroying stocks of materials; the Petrol Consortium had in fact increased its reserves. But the most telling argument against critics of the consortia was the fact that so many industrialists wanted to join: 'A phenomenon which is exactly the inverse of that predicted by economic theorists has occurred; we have been requested by industrialists to allow them to enter these organisations which have been depicted, in vain, as instruments of oppression'.[38] The demand had been so brisk that the government had been obliged to create a general convention formula which would be suitable for all future consortia.

On 29 June 1918, there was a sharp exchange in the Chamber of Deputies between Clémentel and one of the deputies, Emmanuel Brousse. Brousse was a Republican deputy from Perpignan, the publisher of *L'Indépendant des Pyrénées-Orientales*, and an advocate of greater economies in government.[39] Brousse said that consortia ruined small and middle-sized industry, they were dominated by the great industrialists, they were an alien German invention, and they were probably illegal. Clémentel replied by contrasting his policy with that of Rathenau, his German counterpart. Rathenau had ruthlessly suppressed small, inefficient industries: 'Our policy has been completely different. In order to preserve small producers, we have forced the strongest to help the weakest, and we have curbed the appetites of the most voracious'.[40] It is interesting to note that Clémentel saw consortia more as an instrument of protection for small firms than as an implement for introducing rationality into French industry. Clémentel reminded Brousse of the larger context of the war, of the demands of the United States for a rationalisation of Allied requests for American goods. He rectified an error which Brousse had not been the first to commit: the error of believing that consortia had a great deal of autonomous power. It was the state which controlled imports through its relevant technical committee.

Clémentel concluded by praising his subordinates, the men who

38. F12 7662: *Commission du Budget. Séance du vendredi 17 mai 1918.*
39. Jolly, *Dictionnaire*, ii. 782–4.
40. *Chambre des députés*, 28 June 1918. 1833–9.

staffed these committees. Any talk of the committees and consortia being dominated by traditional bureaucrats was nonsense.

> I would add that on these committees we have not only full-time bureaucrats, but a whole pléiade of military officers as well, in peacetime professors, engineers, and industrialists, men who could have, like so many of their colleagues, resumed their former occupations, but who preferred to remain enlisted men, placing their talent at the service of the state. Thus, on these committees, the formalist and sometimes pusillanimous spirit of the bureaucrat cannot predominate. ('Hear! Hear!')

Much of the opposition to consortia was clearly motivated by self-interest, both enlightened and unenlightened, for it is one of the great paradoxes of the war that an organism which ostensibly did so much to rationalise and reform an outdated industrial structure would have attracted so much hostility, even from those whom it was clearly intended to benefit. In an acerbic note drawn up for the Economic Information Service of the Ministry of Commerce in April 1918 by Alfred Puyfontaine, the head of Legal Department, the enemies of consortia were classified by three groups.

> First of all, we find ourselves faced with all those who gorged themselves with glory and money during the previous economic regime. The chambers of commerce are filled with these selfish people to whom all progress is odious. It would be easy to name names, starting with the Paris Chamber of Commerce.[41]

Next came a crowd of failed experts in commerce and politics, who assuaged their failure by forming important-sounding Leagues and Associations. They were insulted when they were not consulted by the government on matters of economic policy, and when their leading dignitaries were not offered automatically the presidency of various consortia. The habitat of this category of opponent was most frequently societies of economic expansion, which in turn were often manipulated by chambers of commerce. The third category of adversary was composed of those naive and mediocre individuals who were convinced that all of France was soon to be divided into consortia, and that it would no longer be possible to eat, drink, or clothe oneself without the permission of this new divinity. In their fertile imaginings, this timorous band saw consortia where there were none; they were even convinced that a Consortium of Candle Colours was soon to be inaugurated. Puyfontaine

---

41. F12 7662: *Note pour Monsieur le directeur du service de l'information économique.* 5 April 1918.

ended his note by repeating the view which he had outlined upon previous occasions, that consortia ought to be established only for essential industries, but that in this domain the state should not be afraid of shaking those who were hostile out of their torpor, nor of brushing aside those 'sterile bees who only know how to buzz around honey-laden hives.'

Le Temps, the most prestigious newspaper of the day, offered more sophisticated but equally implacable opposition. On 21 June 1918, an article outlined the growth and evolution of consortia up to date, and concluded that the state was intending to gather in its hands the totality of the productive forces of France by forcing all industrialists to enter consortia, which the Commerce Minister controlled absolutely, regulating purchases, transport, and sales prices. In that lofty *ex-cathedra* style which characterised the newspaper, the article went on,

> It is not to be believed that consortia in the final analysis are anything other than an accidental, if possibly defensible, means of assuring during the war the general supply of our country. From them one can expect none of the services which cartels render. The consortium is not and seemingly cannot be an instrument of internal equilibrium and external commercial conquest.[42]

The article then summarised the protests of the Chambers of Commerce of Bordeaux, Rouen, Nantes, Lyon, Marseilles, and La Rochelle, and ended with a dignified plea for the amendment of Article 419 of the Penal Code. The contrast was drawn between free associations of producers, which safeguarded commercial initiative, competence, and responsibility, and consortia which destroyed them. In other words, industrialists should be allowed to form cartels without any state supervision whatever, and the public be damned.

The fundamental opposition of *Le Temps* and the more serious critics of consortia was one of principle: the state had no moral right to interfere with the private sector of the economy. In an article in September 1918 on the formation of new consortia, *Le Temps* returned again to the question of responsibility. Under the old system, producers made production decisions at their own risk and peril, but now it was a government minister who decided such important matters as fixing prices. But what if he should miscalculate? If the price he set failed to correspond to economic realities,

42. *Le Temps*, 21 June 1918. 'La question des consortiums devant le comité parlementaire français du commerce'.

who would pay for the damage that might ensue? Government ministers were irresponsible since they did not have to support their financial decisions with their own money, and the implication was that this irresponsibility led to bad decisions. Clearly, Clémentel was out to impose the will of the state, its prices, its conditions of salaries and labour upon industry. Such a policy was doubly wrong: it was inefficient and it was immoral. It could only lead to 'the disorganisation of both free labour and modern France itself, daughter of the Revolution'.[43]

To combat such criticism, one of Clémentel's advisers proposed that the evolution of consortia might best be presented less as the product of a political philosophy than as a series of *ad hoc* administrative decisions.

> The creation of consortia does not proceed from an abstract political conception any more than it reflects a personal choice for a specific economic system. It is the consequence of a number of facts. At a certain moment, the French government realised the necessity of accommodating its economic action with that of the other Allied governments and creating organisations analogous with those which the particular circumstances of the war had already imposed on these governments. The fact which predominates and explains all others is the evolution which the war forced upon the old economic order, and which the entire world was bound to accept.[44]

In the light of what is known of British and American pressure on the French, this description of the development of the consortium system seems entirely accurate. Of particular significance is the acknowledgement that the French government was 'accommodating its economic action with that of the other Allied governments and creating organisations analogous with those which the particular circumstances of the war had already imposed on these governments.' At the same time, it should again be stressed that Clémentel and his men were not totally hopeless pawns in an economic game and that they attempted to reconcile the necessities of war with certain long-term economic goals. One indication of their intentions were the plans they drew up during the war to extend the economic revolution into peacetime, and it was the question of the fate of the consortia after the Armistice which occasioned the most impassioned polemics from critics.

But such was the force of this criticism that as early as May 1918,

43. *Le Temps*, 12 September 1918.
44. F12 7795: *Consortiums. Note pour Monsieur le Ministre.* 21 June 1918. *Dossier Simian.*

Clémentel was forced to concede that the consortia were doomed to extinction or at least to considerable modification. Commenting on the protests of the various chambers of commerce and their insistence that the current economic regime not survive the war, he said: 'As regards the post-war period, the cause which these gentlemen espouse has already been won; there can be no question of enclosing commerce and industry in a framework so rigid as to hamper their development'.[45] In reality, however, Clémentel did not give up so easily. A month later he asked the Chamber of Deputies: 'In preparing the new economic regime, cannot the consortia make a vital contribution?' Criticising the individualism of French industrialists he said: 'We shall oblige these men to group themselves together, to get to know each other. Certainly, this will not be done without difficulty, without effort, and sometimes even without slight coercion'.[46]

The debate on consortia continued unchecked until their eventual dissolution in 1919. Various attempts were made to convert consortia into voluntary associations which would be more amenable to producers. Lemery, the Under-Secretary of Commerce, proposed a number of reforms, starting with the scrapping of all existing conventions between the state and the consortia, and the modification of Article 419. In their place, he proposed converting existing consortia into straight private companies, to which industrialists would adhere voluntarily. Instead of the state acting as the defender of the public, consumers themselves would form a counter-balance by founding co-operatives.[47] But this and other schemes like it came to naught.

Even the most entrenched adversaries of consortia were forced to concede that at least during the war, some organisation had had to be created to resolve the anarchy of the untrammelled competition of producers for diminishing raw materials. It is tempting to interpret the intense criticism which consortia engendered as an index of their relative success. The fact that so many producers were demanding a restoration of commercial liberty might be taken as an indication of how effective consortia were in curbing excess profits and speculation in scarce materials. These cries of pain might lead one to believe that the government had won the confrontation with industrialists, that control was effective, that for the first time, and very much against their will, producers had been forced to renounce

45. *Commission du budget*, 17 May 1918.
46. *Chambre des députés*, 28 June 1918.
47. F12 7662: *Note sur les consortiums*, May 1918.

their sterile individualism in favour of fruitful collaboration under the watchful eye of the state.

Undoubtedly, much of the protestation was a tribute to the effectiveness of the Ministry of Commerce in controlling industry. But it should be borne in mind that many of the early consortia were less tightly controlled by the government. The earlier the foundation of the consortium, the greater its impunity from state interference. It was only in the last months of the war that the policy of retail price control by the state began to emerge, and that the campaign against excessive war profits was undertaken in earnest. The consortia themselves were limited to profits of 6 per cent, but individual members could make any profit they liked on manufactured goods sold to the army or general public. A closer examination of individual consortia reveals that some of them at least had been converted by canny industrialists into very profitable *de facto* cartels which earned handsome profits for their members. This makes the quasi-unanimity of criticism by industrialists and the representative bodies acting as their spokesmen all the more astonishing. If consortia were an effective means of government control, protest was understandable, but if the consortia were the source of great riches for their members, why should there have been such crocodile tears? The answer would seem to be that French industrialists valued their independence above even their profits.

The Consortium in Practice

To illustrate the way in which consortia could be manipulated either to the decided benefit of industrialists or to the clear advantage of the state, depending upon individual circumstances, let us consider two examples, the French Vegetable Oil Consortium and the French Petrol Consortium.

The French Vegetable Oil Consortium

In 1917, France's imports of oil-yielding seeds fell from one million to less than half a million tons.[48] There were two main sources for these seeds, Africa and the Far East, and with the intensification of submarine warfare, an enormous gap developed between the prices of comparable seeds from the two areas. It cost 600 francs a ton to ship peanuts from Sénégal, as opposed to 1,500 francs a ton for

48. Manteilhet, *Consortiums*, 42–51.

peanuts from India. Since the vegetable oil which this and other related substances such as copra, sesame, and cabbage-palm produced were of vital importance both to the army and to the civilian population, some manner of equalising the prices of products from the two areas had to be devised to keep total imports at the highest possible level. At the same time, it became apparent that some manufacturers were attempting to maintain their pre-war business contacts, even if those contacts might indirectly benefit the enemy. In June 1917, Clémentel informed the Senate that the Minister of War had discovered that supplies of vegetable and animal oils were being stocked by French businessmen in neutral countries to serve their traditional German clients.[49] On 4 September 1917, the government issued a decree making a declaration of all stocks of vegetable and animal oil held by manufacturers and merchants obligatory by 1 October.

In further response to the crisis, Violette, the Minister of Supply, announced that the state was purchasing the entire oil-seed harvest from Africa for 1917. The only logical way in which the government could ensure that an equitable distribution of the material might take place and that prices might be controlled was by creating a consortium of all interested industrialists. The alternative methods would have been either for the state to have auctioned off the crop to private buyers, provoking tremendous price increases, or to have instituted a system whereby bureaucrats would distribute the crop on a quota basis, a task which they were as yet manifestly unqualified to perform. The consortium was a compromise solution whereby the industrialists would form themselves into a company for the purpose of dividing the imported material, under the close supervision of the bureaucrats of the Ministry of Commerce.

The technical problems in forming a consortium were enormous. There were nearly two hundred different varieties of oil-yielding seeds, which came from one hundred and eighty ports located in twenty-two countries. Not all French plants could use the same seeds. Some industrialists also used animal fats in their manufacturing processes, and this posed additional problems of organisation.

The French Vegetable Oil Consortium (*le Consortium de l'huilerie française*) was officially constituted on 12 December 1917, with a capital of five million francs. The convention between the consortium and the state was a document of some forty-six articles, containing most of the general provisions which applied to all consortia. The feature peculiar to this consortium was that it con-

49. *Sénat*, 15 June 1917, 582.

stituted a tripartite alliance of the Syndicate of Vegetable Oil Manufacturers of Marseilles, represented by its president Rocca, and the Syndicates of Bordeaux, and the North and West, represented by their respective presidents.[50] Only one industrialist remained outside the consortium and he accepted the general rules governing the division of raw materials.

State control over the consortium was administered by the Interministerial Committee for Fatty Materials, which had been created on 13 July 1917 and endowed with the usual large powers for determining general policy. The Interministerial Committee was composed of twelve representatives of various interested ministries and six representatives of industry. Decisions of the Committee were executed by the Seventh Section of the Technical Services of the Ministry of Commerce. For all the theoretical powers held by the Committee, it was the Seventh Section which maintained what state control there was over the Consortium.

> The Seventh Section is in constant communication with the French Vegetable Oil Consortium and examines together with this Consortium all questions relating to the transportation and purchase price of raw materials, and in general, all questions emerging from the relations of the Ministry of Commerce with this Consortium, in conformity with the convention passed by it with the state.[51]

On 14 January 1918, the constituent assembly of the Consortium was held. Emilien Rocca of Marseilles was voted president, and shares were distributed to industrialists on the usual basis of the average of their imports over the years 1912 to 1917. On this basis, Rocca's company, Rocca, Tassy, et de Roux received 710 shares of a total of 10,000, which meant that if the total oil-seed import for the year was 600,000 tons, as anticipated, this firm would receive 42,600 of them.[52] In March a number of vegetable oil manufacturers from the north, notably the firm of Desmarais, which had lost factories through the German invasion, complained that they were not receiving their fair share of raw material, and manifested their opposition to Rocca's leadership of the Consortium.[53] At a meeting of the Technical Council in May, Clémentel announced that this particular question had been resolved to the satisfaction of all concerned, and that industrialists from invaded regions were to

50. F12 7662: *Consortium de l'huilerie française.*
51. F12 7717: *Attributions de la 7ème Section.* 14 December 1917.
52. F12 7719: *Assemblée constitutive du Consortium de l'huilerie francaise,* 14 January 1918.
53. F12 7719.

receive between one-tenth and one-twelfth of the material imported, a fair reflection of their productive capacity.[54] This development was touted as,

> a fine example of the fraternal collaboration which can be attributed to the honour of a group of men who were prepared to recognise the existence of interests common to all members of the same industry, bound together in national solidarity.[55]

But it is clear that this gesture of 'fraternal collaboration' was forced on Rocca and his reluctant colleagues by the firm pressure of Clémentel, and owed little to a spirit of spontaneous charity.

On 14 January 1918, the Technical Council entrusted Rocca and three other industrialists, Roerich, Meurillon, and Carrier with the following responsibility:

(1) To determine current prices for oil-yielding seeds, prices which are to be the basis of charges paid by members of the consortium.
(2) Using this scale of charges, to establish the prices which are to be set by merchants at various stages of completion.[56]

There can be no doubt that the hopes of the Ministry of Commerce were partially fulfilled and that the formation of the consortium brought considerable decreases in the price of raw materials delivered to manufacturers. Copra, which sold for 300 francs a ton in 1917, fell to 230; peanuts dropped from 140 to 120 francs.[57] What is less apparent, however, is the way in which these price decreases were transmitted by industrialists to the long-suffering consumer, since Rocca and his associates seemed considerably less prepared to carry out the second part of their charge, to establish a price scale for manufactured goods. Ferrière, a member of the Committee for Fatty Materials serving on the Prices Subcommission, in a letter written from Marseilles complained that the price of oil made from peanuts had risen from 400 francs in April 1918 to 500 in May. He pinpointed the weakness of this and all other consortia; the consortium itself was not to blame, but rather, the individual manufacturers, who could sell their finished products at any price. Regretting that the government was not moving faster in the direction of retail price control, he said that in the Marseilles area,

54. F12 7659: *15ᵉ séance du Conseil technique*, 6 May 1918.
55. Manteilhet, *Consortiums*, 51.
56. F12 7659: *5ᵉ séance du Conseil technique*, 14 January 1918.
57. Manteilhet, *Consortiums*, 49.

the producers, free to sell at any price they like, want to push prices as high as they can, and hope to delay by such dilatory tactics as attaching reservations to commitments, appeals, revisions, etc. . . . the moment when price fixing will put an end to these scandalous price increases.

Thus, while we are debating, producers are making enormous additional profits of 100 francs, and perhaps more, on every 100 kilogrammes of oil.[58]

Ferrière was careful to distinguish between the Consortium and the producers, and to attach blame only to the latter, but of whom was the Consortium composed? Of none other than these same producers. And who was the biggest producer of oil in the Marseilles area? None other than Emilien Rocca, president of the French Vegetable Oil Consortium, and the man charged with determining retail prices.

By May 1918, it had become common knowledge that membership of the Consortium had turned out to be a highly profitable venture. Even the Consortium itself, limited by convention to a profit of 6 per cent, registered excess profits of more than three million francs in the first six months of operations, and that without raising the sales prices of raw materials to its members. Under the conditions of the convention, money was turned over to the state to use for the general improvement of the industry, through research projects, technical training, and similar programmes.[59]

By October, a public campaign was developing against Rocca and his associates, and the government was forced to act. On 8 October 1918, an order was issued by the government creating an Interministerial Committee for the Supervision and Distribution of Fatty Materials to replace the Interministerial Committee for Fatty Materials. The change in nomenclature was significant. On 15 October, Edouard Barthe, one of the most persistent critics of industrialists during the war, addressed the Chamber of Deputies on the subject of consortia. The basic conception was good, he said, but certain individuals were compromising the whole scheme by their criminal behaviour. These individuals would have to be purged, and lest anyone have any doubt about the sort of person to whom he was referring, he would cite the example of the French Vegetable Oil Consortium. How was it, Barthe asked, that although France possessed the raw materials on her own soil and in her own colonies, that the price of the finished product was 200 francs per 100 kilogrammes more expensive than in neighbourhood countries?

58. F12 7662: C. Ferrière, 24 May 1918.
59. F12 7659: *15ᵉ séance du Conseil technique*, 6 May 1918.

Why was it that cabbage-palm used to cost 140 francs when delivered in Bordeaux and jumped to 330 francs when delivered in Marseilles? Now that this same material cost only 90 francs why should the oil made from it still cost 372 francs? Barthe had one final question to put to the government. Was it not true that a certain personage, who occupied a high position of authority within the consortium, indeed near its summit, had tried to bribe an adviser of one of the ministers, and that to his credit, this adviser, who was a lawyer, complained to the relevant professional superior, his *bâtonnier*? The *bâtonnier*, said Barthe, had promptly returned the money to its would-be donor.[60]

Two days after Barthe's speech, Clémentel asked the legal authorities to open a full inquiry into the affair. On 21 October, Firmin Laugier, a vegetable oil broker from Marseilles, wrote to Barthe to confirm that what he had said was true, and he offered under oath further information, which provided a fascinating insight into the activities of the Consortium in general and of Emilien Rocca in particular. Rocca had let it be known around Marseilles that he had high ministerial connections in Paris, and with reason, for he had executed two masterly coups. The first was in February 1915, when, in an effort to staunch the flow of vegetable oil from France, the government had placed an embargo on its export, but made an exception for cocoa butter, a product manufactured by the firm of Rocca, Tassy, et de Roux, with the result that vegetable oil continued to flow out of France in considerable quantities to Switzerland, Holland, and the Scandinavian countries. Flabbergasted by this loophole in export restrictions for a product so eminently useful to the Germans, the head of the export control bureau in Marseilles had gone to Paris and informed the relevant authorities of the dangers of this exemption. It was only after nine months of agitation, however, that cocoa butter was placed under the same embargo as other vegetable oils, in October 1915. This exemption had made the fortune of Rocca, Tassy, et de Roux, and Laugier calculated that the firm had earned sixty million francs profit thusfar from the war.

Rocca's second feat had been of a more personal nature.

Monsieur Rocca had a son, twenty-five years of age, tall and fat and ripe for the army: he obtained an exemption, and while the *poilus* died unpaid, for the honour of their country, young Rocca, installed in Paris, manoeuvred through thick and thin to defend Daddy's interests.

60. *Chambre des députés*, 15 October 1918, 2683.

And how were the members of the Consortium in the Marseilles area faring under the most recent scheme of the government to control prices at all levels of production? Not badly, said Laugier. One of the main by-products of cabbage-palm, once the oil was squeezed out, was oil-cake, a substance used to feed cattle. The government had set the wholesale price of oil-cake at 40 francs and the resale price at 47.5 francs. Rocca, as president of the local association of vegetable oil manufacturers, informed merchants that the wholesale price to them was to be 47.5 francs, explaining, 'We ourselves are retailers, our sale price is 47.5 francs, and I assume complete responsibility for this decision.' As these manufacturers sold 500 tons of oil-cake a day, this price difference represented 37,500 francs a day, or ten million francs a year, stolen from the pocket of the cattlemen and farmers. People had complained to the prefect, people had complained to government ministers, nothing had been done. So much for price controls.

Laugier concluded his letter on a bitter note:

> We are still paying 47.5 francs, but we at least have the satisfaction of reading every day in the newspapers exhortations from the Minister to increase our livestock and to plant more of our fields, or circulars from the prefect threatening the full penalties of the law for those who sell above the fixed price.[61]

The next day, 22 October, it was Emilien Rocca's turn to receive a letter, this time a touching tribute from a fellow vegetable oil producer in Marseilles. The only word for this campaign against Rocca was ignoble; it was based on an incident which was past history, an incident which was perfectly irreproachable. (It is unclear to which incident he was referring.) The whole thing had been done to put public opinion, which was forever being kept in ignorance of the real facts anyway, on the wrong track once again. Naturally, the fact that Rocca and his son were planning to resign would be misinterpreted as a confession of guilt. This producer, for one, felt it was Rocca's duty to stay at his post. 'If you think it necessary, find someone to lighten our burden, but do not abandon us.' Tactfully but firmly, he took a somewhat different view of the resignation of Rocca *fils*: 'As for your son, although it is our greatest wish that he should stay where he is, obviously we cannot speak in quite the same terms, since he is subject to a military authority

61. F12 7658: *Firmin Laugier, Courtier, 5, rue d'Arcole, Marseilles. 21 October 1918. à Monsieur Barthe, député.*

whose decisions we must accept'.[62] On the day of the Armistice, the French Vegetable Oil Consortium met and unanimously rejected Rocca's resignation from the presidency of the Consortium; a report of the meeting was duly sent to Clémentel on 13 November.[63] But by now the war was over, and it was evident that as the demise of all consortia was imminent, the question of who was to occupy their presidencies would soon be academic. On 2 December 1918, and again on 23 December, and 23 January 1919, decrees were passed and reconfirmed fixing the price of oil-yielding seeds and of the oil itself, but even if these decrees had been more effective than those which preceded them, it was shutting the barn door far too late.

When it came time to wind up the Consortium in 1919, it was calculated that the profits of the Consortium alone, quite apart from those of individual members, was 16.1 million francs.[64] This was at best an approximation, since the accountants sent by the government to verify the books of the Consortium found it impossible to make head or tail of what they found. On 22 June 1919, Boulangé, an inspector of finance, made a report on his findings. There was no unified accounting system, but rather, four completely autonomous systems, one each for the Consortium's head office, and the Committees of Marseilles, Bordeaux, and the north and west. No attempt had been made in 1918 to co-ordinate these accounts. Of the 250 boatloads of raw material cited in the books of Marseilles, only the figures for 70 of them tallied with the figures in the books of head-office. There was evidence in the different handwriting of head-office accounts of considerable alteration, and figures sent by the three Committees were often recopied without verification. Once again, the Marseilles Committee provided a useful illustration of the sort of error which could occur. Thirteen wagon-loads of material which the Marseilles Committee had acquired during the course of 1918 had still not been registered in the books of Marseilles, nor, for that matter, of Bordeaux, from whence, presumably, they had come. Unworried by these wandering wagons, head-office had merely duplicated the figures found in the books of the two Committees without questioning them. The accountant ended his report by concluding: 'It is therefore impossible to evaluate at the present moment the profits of the Consortium'.[65] A second accountant wrote of the Consortium's bookkeeping arrangements; 'It

62. F12 7658.
63. Ibid.
64. F12 7659: *Note pur Monsieur Chaudun. Bénéfices disponibles au moment de la liquidation de consortiums.*
65. Prompsat Archives M(1)10: *L'Inspecteur des finances, Boulangé.* 22 June 1919.

is worth noting that in the case of the direction committee of Marseilles, reports are generally so succinct and so imprecise that one would be unable to affirm that financial records were kept at all times'.[66] But none of these complaints appear to have been seriously investigated, and the Roccas, *père* and *fils*, seemed to retain their perennial popularity in ministerial circles. After all the accusations, it is surprising to find Emilien Rocca writing to Clémentel on 9 October 1919 enclosing a report on the present state of supplies of fatty materials in France, a report which Clémentel had requested in a meeting with the younger Rocca some weeks previously.[67]

The history of the French Vegetable Oil Consortium indicates the limitations of state control of industry during wartime. Theoretically, the regime of consortia gave government absolute power over private industry and business, to the extent of determining the price at which a finished product was to be retailed, yet in fact, the complexity of the mechanics of control, the lack of administrative precedent, the inevitable bureaucratic *longueurs* in creating appropriate control machinery, gave quick-witted industrialists ample time to turn the whole system to their own advantage. One technical loophole, such as the exception made for cocoa butter in the general export prohibition on vegetable oils, could mean millions of francs profit for a lucky firm. Industrialists could procrastinate in the face of official pressure, deliberately misinterpret rulings, as they did when Rocca and his associates sold at the retail instead of the wholesale price, they could play at ducks and drakes with their bookkeeping, with the net result that their large profits were never in any real danger. In short, industrialists could move much faster than the bureaucrats, who kept struggling along behind to produce new regulations and structures to keep up with them. Undoubtedly there was an inexorable advance of bureaucratic control as civil servants became more experienced in the animal cunning of business practice, and as we shall see presently, there is evidence that particularly in the latter half of 1918, bureaucrats were beginning to emerge victorious from their jousts with industrialists, but by then it was far too late. Many of the consortia worked more efficiently than this one from the government's point of view, if the complaints of the chambers of commerce are in any way to be believed, but there must also have been many unchronicled minor Roccas leading the state in the same merry chase over different terrain.

66. Prompsat Archives M(1)10: *L'Inspecteur des finances, Thomas.* 25 June 1919.
67. Prompsat Archives M(1)10: Emilien Rocca to Clémentel, 9 October 1919.

The French Petrol Consortium

Each industry which came to be incorporated into the consortium system had its own special characteristics which had to be accommodated. The French petrol industry was unique among all others in that its pre-war structure was virtually that of a cartel, and that relatively few changes needed to be made to convert this cartel into a consortium. If the French Vegetable Oil Consortium illustrates the way in which industrialists could exploit consortia, the Petrol Consortium is a good example of the inverse phenomenon, the attempt of reformers to utilise the wartime emergency to impose state control over private industry.

The full inadequacies of the French petroleum industry were mercilessly revealed by the war. From 350,000 tons of petrol a year, the requirements of the country shot up to a million tons. One day of battle could consume 1,600 tons. Without petrol, motorised troop transport, tractors pulling heavy artillery, aeroplanes, in short, the entire military effort, was paralysed. At the outset of the war, the government hurriedly signed contracts with the *Cartel des Dix* to arrange for the supply of the army and the civilian population on a priority basis. When Clémentel assumed office in November 1915, initially he saw no need to change this policy into a more active form of government intervention.

> The importation of petrol is undertaken by a small group of powerful commercial interests working in agreement with each other. It has proved sufficient for the Ministry and the Petrol Commission to ascertain that price increases requested upon several occasions were justified, that the quantities imported were adequate, and that they were distributed in a manner corresponding to the needs of the different regions.[68]

However, as the war continued, and petrol supplies became increasingly scarce, this complacent attitude faded, and once again there was a campaign to nationalise the industry. On 26 September 1916 Edouard Barthe denounced the excessive prices for petrol charged by members of the Cartel, and their bad faith in suppressing all refining of oil within France in favour of importing refined oil from Standard Oil. Petrol should be nationalised to prevent further speculation and excess profits, to protect the working class from further exploitation, and to reduce the drain on the state's finances. He pointed out that the Special Commission for Oil and

---

68. Prompsat Archives T(2)3: *Rapport de Monsieur Clémentel sur le ravitaillement civil (8 Septembre 1914–31 Décembre 1916).*

Petrol, instituted by the Ministry of Commerce, was already responsible for fixing retail prices in each *département*, and that the state was virtually running the monopoly, but the proposition came to nothing.

By 1917, however, the transportation crisis and the chronic shortage of petrol forced the government to act. Action was taken not by a law passed in parliament but by an administrative decree on 13 July 1917 creating the General Petrol Committee, under the presidency of Senator Henry Bérenger. The Committee was given the usual mission to 'examine, co-ordinate, and control the needs of the services of the state and the public', and to determine policy regarding priorities, exports, imports, transportation, and reserve supplies. Bureaucrats outnumbered industrialists on the Committee by eighteen to eight. The Technical Section of the Committee was headed by Professor Bordas, formerly of the *Collège de France*, and decisions were executed by the Board for Petrols and Combustibles at the Supply Ministry.[69]

The Committee accomplished a great deal of useful work in the next few months, modernising ports, constructing reservoirs and pipe-lines, obtaining tanker rail cars from the other Allied powers, improving the quality of refined petrol, importing castor oil for aeroplanes from the French colonies, and most important of all, stabilising prices. The progress towards complete state control was by now irreversible, and a bureaucratic structure capable of administering a state monopoly was steadily growing. In October 1917, a technical section for petrol was created at the Ministry of Commerce.[70] On 12 December, Bérenger informed the government that supplies of oil and petrol had declined to the point that should the French army become engaged in another battle like Verdun, existing petrol would last only three days, and that by 1 March 1918, France would be without a single litre of petrol.[71] On 15 December, Clemenceau appealed to Wilson for more tankers, and the crisis temporarily abated. By now, the state was responsible for so many of the operations involved in supplying France with petrol, that it seemed inconceivable that private firms should still continue to make vast profits. Etienne Clémentel described the situation in retrospect.

Could we, paying with money made available for the French government by the American government, having persuaded the American government

69. Manteilhet, *Consortiums*, 54, 55.
70. Renouvin, *Formes*, 63.
71. Kuisel, *Mercier*, 23.

to undertake most of the transport using American boats, continue to allow freedom of purchase to exist for imports? Could we allow refiners to keep the profits which had been created by importing a product paid for by the state with its own credits and transported on boats placed at its disposition by the American government? That would not have been possible.[72]

On 29 March 1918, the French Petrol Consortium was established, making the state the sole importer of petroleum. It is worth briefly examining the negotiations which led up to the establishment of the consortium, for they illuminate the sort of infighting which went on privately between representatives of the government and industrialists throughout the war. On this occasion, the government won a clear, if short-lived, victory.

By December 1917, the government had decided to institute a petrol consortium on the model of that created for cotton, and on 25 January 1918, a draft convention was drawn up which formed the basis for negotiations with the petrol industrialists.[73] The General Committee for Petrol was to submit a list of the country's petrol requirements, and this list would determine the purchases of petrol made by the state abroad. The Consortium was obliged to repurchase all material thus acquired by the state, at a price which would cover all procurement expenses. The most important feature of the Consortium was that the resale price of oil and petrol to distributors would be set by the Ministers of Commerce and Supply on the advice of the Consortium, after consultation with the General Committee. The retail price of petrol for civilian and military consumption would continue to be fixed by the Minister of Supply, again, after consultation with the General Committee. Either minister had the right to see the accounts of the Consortium at any time.

A period of negotiation with the petrol firms followed. On 4 February, Despeaux, president of the Petrol Producers' Association, and one of France's largest petrol importers, wrote to Bérenger, president of the General Committee, requesting assurances that the 'security of the commercial situation' of members of the Consortium would not be imperilled by the new sales conditions; in other words, that they be allowed a free hand in setting prices, so that they might continue to make their 'normal' profits. In reply to this, Clémentel wrote to Bérenger on 8 February to say that

72. *Chambre des députés*, 28 June 1918.
73. Prompsat Archives T(7)1: 25 January 1918. *Projet de création d'un consortium francais du pétrole et de l'essence.*

studies undertaken several years previously by the Finance Ministry indicated that the figures for the 'normal' profits were substantially below those given by Despeaux. Clémentel instructed Bérenger to inform the Producers' Association that it would form its consortium in the same manner as everyone else, that there could be no question of fixing prices before the constitution of the consortium, and that prices would be determined by the General Committee once the consortium was in operation. If members of the Producers' Association persisted in their procrastination, they should be warned that there were methods of dealing with them:

> If the preliminary condition of fixing prices is considered indispensable by the Petrol Producers' Association, the government will be obliged to take other measures as soon as possible, and obviously, these measures could go as far as the requisition of factories and personnel.

Faced with this threat, the Producers' Association surrendered and wrote to Bérenger on 16 February to confirm that they would form a consortium under the conditions outlined by Clémentel in his letter of 8 February.[74]

On 26 February, the legal department of the Ministry of Commerce sent its observations to Clémentel. A number of improvements for the draft convention were proposed in the interest of blocking loopholes and generally tightening the control of the state over the new organism. It was suggested, for example, that in view of the international interests involved, that it should be clearly set out that the administration of the consortium was to be entirely French. On 29 March, a final contract was signed by the government and representatives of the *Cartel des Dix*, but this by no means resolved the differences between the state and the industrialists.

On 19 April, Clémentel wrote to the Minister of Agriculture to comment on the general constituent meeting of the Consortium, which had taken place on 4 April, and he sent a copy of the letter to Fenaille, the newly-elected president of the Consortium, and a partner in the firm of Fenaille et Despeaux. Clémentel complained that instead of the ten companies involved each naming one of their senior executives to represent them on the Consortium, they had merely given the names of the companies. It was essential that the state deal with individual who would take full legal and moral responsibility for the sound administration of the great interests entrusted to them. The state had to be assured that the Consortium

74. Prompsat Archives T(7)1.

was composed of eminent, honourable, competent men, and he therefore refused to accept the nominations of merely the names of companies, which would have the effect of diminishing the responsibilities of their administrators and relieving them of the obligations and sanctions imposed by a law dating back to 1867. Clémentel proposed that these nominations be annulled and that a new meeting be called to name the heads of various firms as members of the Consortium.

On a minor note, Clémentel also refused to allow members of the Consortium the 60,000 francs a year they had voted themselves as directors' fees. None of the administrators of other consortia were paid, and Clémentel did not propose to break with this tradition.

In May, Clémentel once again called the Consortium to order.[75] He repeated his comments on the nomination of individuals to the executive of the Consortium and on directors' fees, and then went on to complain that he was not being kept completely informed of the operations of the Consortium. This was the only way of rendering legal associations of this type which totally controlled one particular product. He ordered Fenaille to send a complete copy of the minutes of every executive meeting to Bérenger, the Ministers of Agriculture and Supply, and to himself.

On 20 June 1918, Fenaille wrote a cold reply to Clémentel. After consulting legal experts, he still maintained that it was correct to nominate companies and not individuals to the executive of the Consortium, since joint stock companies were involved, not single-owner firms. Furthermore, there was the additional practical advantage of a company being represented by the specialist most competent to deal with the specific question being discussed at the time. As for supplying the Minister with minutes in order to maintain the appearance of legality, Fenaille could hardly restrain himself.

I must point out in the first place that if the holders of our type of merchandise have formed an association for their supply operations, it is the state which insisted upon it. In addition, it seems to me necessary to specify, without declaring for the legality or illegality of the fact, that, if this association is illegal, that is to say falls within the bounds of Article 419 of the penal code, it is not within the prerogative of the government to render it legal.[76]

75. Prompsat Archives T(7)1: Clémentel to le Président du Consortium d'importation du pétrole et de l'essence. 31 May 1918.
76. Prompsat Archives T(7)1: Le Président du Consortium français d'importation du pétrole et de l'essence to Clémentel, 20 June 1918.

Nevertheless, for convenience sake, the Consortium would accede to Clémentel's request. Finally, Fenaille turned to the question of directors' fees. He reminded Clémentel that in the contract signed on 29 March it was indicated that the emoluments of directors would be submitted to the Minister of Commerce for his approval. 'It is difficult to attach any meaning to this clause if it is the custom for administrators not to receive any remuneration.' As Clémentel insisted upon this condition, members of the Consortium would waive the right to collect fees, despite the onerous expenses which membership entailed.

In August 1918, the General Committee for Petrol, created the previous summer, was transformed into the General Commissariat for Oil and Petrol, still under the leadership of Senator Bérenger. This change further strengthened the hand of the government, as the Commissariat played a far more active role than the General Committee. It became the sole buyer and importer of petrol and oil of all kinds as well as the general controller and supervisor of all independent businesses and industries in France and her colonies.

As the war ground to a halt, advocates of state intervention in the economy hoped that the substitution of a state monopoly for that of a small group of private industrialists would be rendered permanent at last. There was no doubt that from the government point of view, the Consortium had been a great success. At the end of 1918, an interim report of the Inspector-General of Finance showed that the state had made a profit of twenty-five million francs in the first nine months of operations of the Consortium, merely by buying petrol abroad and importing it into France, which gave some idea of the order of the profits which the *Cartel des Dix* had made before the inception of the Consortium. These profits became public knowledge in June 1919, when yet another proposition was made in the Chamber of Deputies for the creation of a permanent government import monopoly, but by this time, opinion was running strongly against further state interference in the economy, and the motion was defeated.[77]

During the 1920s, there was a return to unrestricted private competition in France, with the big foreign oil companies, no longer content to work through French agents, buying up French companies of their own.[78] It was not until the end of the decade that the government once more acquired a stake in the petrol industry through a 25 per cent share in the *Compagnie française des pétroles*.

77. *Projet de loi instituant le monopole d'achat et d'importation des huiles raffinées et des essences de petrole.* 16 June 1919.
78. Kuisel, *Mercier*, 24–38.

Thus what might have been a revolution in the petroleum indus-try ultimately failed. Clémentel won most of the battles with the Cartel but lost the war. Unlike the French Vegetable Oil Consor-tium, the French Petrol Consortium was an example of how effec-tive government domination over an industry could be, given the proper conditions. In this case, the task was made easier by the existence of a small number of producers operating a virtual mono-poly, and consisted less of a fundamental reorganisation and re-grouping than a simple transfer of power from a group of private firms to the state. It should be emphasised that the private firms were still allowed to exist, and retained their right to retail petrol to the public, though under close government surveillance. They merely relinquished their importing role. The fact that the material involved was a simple one and did not take the multiplicity of form of oil-yielding seeds also made control simpler. Then again, the petrol consortium was established at a later date, when bureaucrats had more experience with this new organism and could benefit from past mistakes. Had the war continued into 1919, as was generally anticipated, it seems probable that tighter state control would have extended to the whole system of consortia.

Conclusion

By the end of the war, with nearly fifty consortia either established or about to be established, there was virtually no product in France for either military or civilian use which did not come under the jurisdiction of one or more of the consortia. Conceived initially as a method of conserving shipping and distributing scarce raw materials equitably, the consortia gradually became the instrument by which the state could impose its will on all aspects of industry, from forcing industrial concentration on its own terms to fixing prices and limiting profits. The rapid growth of government control over industry in the last months of the war made the fears for the post-war period of opponents of the consortia less improbable.

> Are these obligations and restrictions not destined to prepare the devel-opment of an economic policy which would have as its guiding principle the permanent control of the state over industry, or even, following a more recent formula, the participation of the state in industry?[79]

For Clémentel, the consortium was an implement with many uses. He conceived of it particularly as a weapon with which he

79. Romier, *Consortiums*, 11.

could attack war profiteers and speculators. His detractors accused him of wishing to eliminate all middlemen:

> The administration does not like businessmen, or in its parlance, "intermediaries", because trade, based almost exclusively on operations linked to the personality of the individual buyer or seller, is much harder to control than industry, whose entire activity is visible in its physical plant . . . At the present time, in several major branches, trade has been suspended and disorganised if not ruined, as a result of administrative intervention.[80]

Clémentel could reply that he merely wished to suppress those who were making unjustified profits. He expressed his policy in moral terms.

> We must render commerce moral by eliminating certain unqualified, fly-by-night intermediaries who have not only been speculators, but veritable despoilers, growing rich without risk at the expense of the labouring classes, to the detriment of France. By the organisation and discipline of the import business and of industry, these undesirables will be removed.[81]

But it is difficult to see how any broker, even the most honest, could have long survived had the regime of consortia continued into the post-war period. 'Only one industry has been killed or is dying,' said André Tardieu, 'that of the commission makers'.[82]

But consortia did not represent the ultimate extension of state authority over commerce and industry. As was demonstrated in the case of petrol, the government was prepared to requisition the factories of recalcitrant industrialists. Moreover, there were increasing indications that the state was prepared to dictate the actual conditions of production, from the design of the product to its final sale price, in the case of scarce consumer goods. The first of these was the National Shoe, which represented the full participation of the state in the productive process. It is to these wilder shores of government interference that we now must make our way.

80. Ibid., 10.
81. F12 7662: *Commission du budget*. 17 May 1918.
82. Manteilhet, *Consortiums*, 75.

CHAPTER 5

Requisitions, Shoes and Chemicals

The Power of Requisition

The power of the state over private industry in France during the
First World War might at first have appeared invincible, but it was
in reality a precarious, fragile thing. Relations between government
and industry could be likened to a poker game in which one player
owns all the chips but the other holds all the high cards. In any
contest of strength, industry could always win by threatening to
close down production. The highest card in the pack was the danger
of military defeat, and it could be played time and again against the
government, and never against private industry. Because industrial
capacity was always at a premium, despite all the threats and
imprecations government would always have to give in to industrialists' demands if the product concerned was vital enough to the
war effort. The state had no alternative, and the industrialists knew
it.

What the state lacked in cards, it had to make up in bluff if it
wished to retain any control whatever over industry. One such bluff
was the threat of requisition. The difficulties involved in actually
seizing a factory and making it work properly were so enormous
that there could be no practical advantage for the government in
taking such a step, and most probably the disadvantage of a decline
in production. But it was essential that in negotiations with industrialists over import restrictions, speculation, consortia, prices and
profits that the government at least have a threatening weapon in its
hand, even if the weapon was unloaded. The threat of sanctions was
an essential element in any bargaining session with industrialists. It
is in this light that the debate on requisitions must be seen.

When all is said and done, it is remarkable how few sanctions
were employed against industrialists during the war. In the rare

cases in which sanctions were invoked, they were often so minor as
to seem out of all proportion to the offence committed. In Albert
Thomas's papers, for example, there is a cryptic report in 1915 on
some obscure scandal, the *Affaire du Saut du Tarn* which sums up
perfectly the dilemma of sanctions: 'Necessity of sanctions, especially from the moral point of view. But no exclusion from future
contracts, in order not to hinder production. Dismiss the engineer
Leblond'.[1] Whatever the crime may have been, the punishment
could hardly have fitted it. The need to maintain production overrode all other considerations.

To overcome this powerlessness, the government began to investigate the possibilities of invoking its traditional rights of requisition
during wartime. Normally, this power was to be applied by army
officers for the purpose of billeting their troops at the expense of the
local citizenry, but one of the first decrees of the government after
the declaration of war in 1914 had been to strengthen the application of this power with regard to the expropriation of civilian-
owned factories and their personnel.[2] The motives behind this
legislation are not immediately apparent. If the war was expected to
be short, and existing supplies were thought to be sufficient, why
need the problem of requisitioning factories arise? In any event, this
power was left firmly in the hands of the military, not the civil,
authority. It was the Minister of War, not the Minister of Commerce, who authorised such requisitions and it was the army which
ran the factory once it had been seized. This decree was therefore of
no use whatever to Clémentel in his dealings with industrialists.

It is interesting to compare the situation in France with that in
England. The Defence of the Realm Act of 8 August 1914, with its
additions of 28 August and 27 November, gave the British government, acting through the Admiralty and the War Council, the
power to requisition factories employed in war production and
their output. In early 1915, for example, all supplies of old and new
sacking in the country were requisitioned when sandbags were
suddenly in short supply; manufacturers were paid generous prices
in compensation.[3]

France was slower in organising herself. In February 1917, a
group of deputies sought to amend the law regarding military
requisition so that all civilian-owned factories producing military
material would be obliged to reorganise themselves into a mixed

1. 94 AP 53: *Rapport du 19 août 1915.*
2. *Des réquisitions relatives aux établissements industriels, Journal officiel,* 3 August
   1914.
3. Marwick, *The Deluge,* 171, 172.

enterprise (*régie intéressée*)[4] under the control of the Minister of War. This control would be of a 'technical' nature, to ensure maximum operational efficiency and the most economical use of labour, particularly mobilised workers. The Minister could assign a representative to the management of the firm, with the power to direct technical, industrial, or commercial aspects of the factory's operations, and to supervise all production destined for the state. Should the productivity of these establishments fall below a certain level, they could be totally requisitioned by a simple order of the military authority. There was also a provision for war profits. There was to be a retroactive tax of 50 per cent to be levied on all profits earned since 1 August 1914 by factories producing war material, and in the future, all profits over 10 per cent were to be divided equally between the state and the producer. The bill was designed with two objectives in mind: to increase war production, and to satisfy growing public demand for an end to the scandalous profits being earned by military suppliers. The power of requisition would still have remained in the hands of the Minister of War, however, and Clémentel would still have been left without an effective weapon with which to menace recalcitrant industrialists.

On 12 June 1917, Clémentel asked the Senate to give him the power to requisition stocks of finished products held by private industry, as well as their factories, if need be. The first article of the proposed law read as follows:

> For the duration of the war, owners of factories producing materials necessary for supplying the indispensable needs of the civilian population may be obliged, by direct requisition by the civil authority, to place at the disposal of that authority all the resources of their factories, machines, raw materials, and finished products, and to furnish all relating processes of production, to undertake manufacture, and to provide repair facilities.[5]

He explained how he had already benefited from the War Minister's power of requisition in reorganising the distribution of scarce metal. Now he asked the Senate to give him the authority to requisition other scarce materials. Once again, said Clémentel, it was the pressure of the English which was forcing him to act. For example, France needed Australian wool, but the English had requisitioned all Australian wool and refused to make over any of it to the French

---

4. See Chapter I, and the proposal to create a *régie intéressée* for the petrol industry, made in January 1914.
5. *Senat*, 12 June 1917, 551–4.

unless it could be proved that no secret supplies of wool were being stockpiled by French businessmen. Clémentel could offer no such guarantees to the English until an inventory had been made of French stocks, and surplus materials had been requisitioned and redistributed among deserving industrialists. The honest business-man had nothing to fear from such an investigation. The fact that vegetable and animal oils were also being sold abroad in neutral countries was a further argument in favour of instituting the power of requisition.

> It is vital that the power of requisition be given to the public authorities as an effective weapon against speculators, whose taste for fraud is sustained by great skill.
> To stop unjustified increases in prices, the declaration of stocks con-stitutes the first vital step of furnishing us with information, and the power of requisition must be an indispensable corollary to this.

Clémentel gave a list of examples of industries in which individual companies had been forming large stockpiles of scarce materials; under the present law, there was absolutely no way of dealing with these companies. In conclusion, Clémentel described the measure as 'an imperious necessity of economic resistance, indeed, of national defence.'

This proposal gave rise to considerable debate in the Senate two days later.[6] The arguments are worth considering at some length, for the senators articulated many of the orthodox, conservative reactions to the threat of further government encroachment on private business which were current at the time. One of the oldest and most venerable of the senators, de Lamarzelle, led off the debate. De Lamarzelle was one of the Conservative deputies who had most interested himself in questions involving state interference with private enterprise before the war, and had been a stout oppo-nent of the introduction of income tax in 1914.[7] De Lamarzelle claimed that the power of unlimited requisition would be more of a hindrance than a help in achieving the intentions of the Minister of Commerce. Under this law, the state would have the exorbitant right to take the place of the owners and managers of an industrial establishment. What room did this leave for individual initiative? What would happen if a factory was actually requisitioned? All contracts were immediately suspended, all deliveries of finished goods would cease. Worse, how could any new contracts be signed

6. *Senat*, 14 June 1917, 561–9.
7. Jolly, *Dictionnaire*, VI, 2109–10.

under the menace of further requisition? This law stated that the civil authority could drive the head of an industrial establishment out of his own factory on the grounds of insufficient production. (He neglected to point out that this had also been a feature of the requisition law of 1877.) And who would replace the head of an enterprise? A bureaucrat. 'There are enough already,' yelled another deputy.

Clémentel began his reply by reminding the Senate of the grave economic difficulties which confronted the government, and in particular, the alarming shortage of raw materials. What lay behind this proposal? Nothing more than the desire to protect weak industrialists against the incursions of the strong. The metal industry had unanimously approved his policy of dividing scarce materials equitably and had recognised the necessity of such a measure in these grave times. Now he wished to extend that policy to other materials. Some businessmen were more capable than others, richer, stronger, more alert; there were strong industrialists and weak ones, and the system which de Lamarzelle advocated would result in the strong crushing the weak. 'Not true', shouted de Lamarzelle. But that is exactly what 'economic liberty' meant these days, answered Clémentel. The government was merely attempting to harmonise conflicting forces. It had no intention of directing private industry itself, rather, it needed a weapon against those stubborn, refractory businessmen who were clinging to their supplies of scarce raw materials, not to manufacture goods themselves, nor to provide other producers with materials, but for pure speculation. The case of the cotton industry illustrated the point well; the cotton manufacturers of eastern France claimed that the cotton importers of Le Havre had stocks sufficient for six months' consumption. The merchants of Le Havre replied that they had only three months' supplies, but that certain factories had supplies sufficient for a year. In a case like this, where did the truth lie? Even England, the home of commercial liberty, had in effect requisitioned the coal mines of Wales as well as all merchant shipping.

Finally, Clémentel endeavoured to lay to rest the spectre of universal requisition conjured up by de Lamarzelle. In practice, the power of requisition would probably be limited to certain specific materials, such as cotton, wool, leather, some foodstuffs, and a few vital war materials, such as tin. If the Senate would not vote this law, Clémentel refused to take the responsibility for the future economic disaster that would ensue. He vowed that he would use the power entrusted to him with the greatest discretion, keeping uppermost in his mind the principle 'that it is preferable that the industry of the nation administer its own affairs, under the control of the government.' His remarks were well received by the senators.

Clémentel returned to the fray the next day, when the proposal was voted article by article.[8] He insisted that the power of requisition against speculators be unlimited. There could be no enumerated list of specific materials to which the power would apply, for who could tell what new materials might be the object of speculation in the future? Nor was it enough that speculation be stopped, for it was essential that stockpiled goods be quickly redistributed to alleviate shortages. Only the power of requisition could ensure such rapid distribution. In extreme cases of bad faith, Clémentel insisted on the necessity of the power of expropriation without compensation. He hastened to assure the Senate that the actual requisition of a factory would be a very rare event. He did not aspire to become an economic tyrant. What was important was the psychological value of the threat. 'This weapon will be useful to me as a sword of Damocles, which I will be able to suspend over the heads of certain manufacturers and industrialists.' The law was voted virtually unamended.

On 25 June, *Le Temps* levelled a broadside against the new law. If the owner of a factory were dismissed for reasons of insufficient production, who would replace him? Clémentel had never answered this question. The law provided for indemnities, but only for 'direct' requisition. Who would pay compensation for the work which had been interrupted? Clémentel had claimed that the power would be limited to a few products of a few industrial establishments. But what if he were wrong, what if he abused his power? Furthermore, as Lamarzelle had said: 'Ministries change so often in France that what one minister promises not to do, his successor may well do'. There was no need for additional legislation to punish speculators and those who sold to the enemy; they were well provided for by the existing laws. As for the argument that the new measure was a Damocletian sword, if this were the case, crooks would have nothing to worry about, and only the honest would suffer. Interestingly, there followed a veiled reference to current fears of social revolution, presumably a reflection of rumours circulating about the army mutinies of the spring of 1917, and it was suggested that the latest piece of legislation was a sop to popular emotions. This law was an insult to French industrialists, concluded *Le Temps*.

8. *Sénat*, 15 June 1917, 588–9.

We should like to have seen the accusations brought against commerce reduced to their true proportions and real value, and to have seen this crowd of brave men defended as they ought to have been defended, these men to whom the country owes its material and ᶜmoral strength, the maintenance of its productive energies, the unending renewal of its credit. . . . The industrial and commercial world did not deserve this sign of mistrust.[9]

On 18 June 1917 the law on civil requisition came into force. The power of requisition should be seen in the wider context of the problem of scarce shipping and raw materials shortages which faced the Allies in 1917, and as an integral part of the control legislation which was being drafted accordingly within France at the time. Civil requisition was designed to be the threat, the potential sanction, which gave teeth to the rest of the government's programme of restrictions.

The National Shoe

But in addition to curbing speculation and strengthening the system of import restrictions, Clémentel had other uses for this new weapon as well. The power of requisition was essential to promote Clémentel's policy regarding consumer goods. As he told the Senate during the debate on requisitions, 'The principle is this: to obtain a reasonable price for indispensable articles of popular consumption, and to leave untouched more luxurious products'.[10] Why was the power of requisition a necessary part of this policy? Because without it, any industrialist could refuse to co-operate with the government and continue to manufacture luxury products which would earn him more money. Shoes were the particular product Clémentel had in mind.

In the annals of French footware, it is the scandals of military boot production which have been immortalised in literature, notably in Jules Romains's *Verdun*, where the sinister figure of Haverkamp produced boots made of badly tanned leather which soaked up water like blotting paper, sub-contracted most of his army contracts, and persuaded the government to advance him money for factories he would never build.[11] But there was no less a crisis in civilian shoes. It was only towards the middle of 1917 that boot

9. 'La Mise en réquisition générale', *Le Temps*, 25 June 1917.
10. *Sénat*, 14 June 1917, 568.
11. J. Romains, *Verdun* (Paris, 1938), 164–77.

production passed military needs. In the meantime, owing to the increasing demands of the army for leather since 1914, the price of men's shoes had increased from 20 francs in 1914 to 60 francs in 1917, women's button boots now cost 80 francs, and work boots had risen in price from 15 to 50 francs, a price well beyond the means of the average worker. At the end of 1916 the Ministry of Labour had appealed to the general public to buy as few shoes as possible, to choose low-cut models in preference to boots, to put studs in the soles and rubber on the heels, and to dry wet shoes as slowly as possible to conserve them. The Ministry recommended the wearing of wooden clogs; tram conductresses were already using them. In May 1917, 'trench clogs' went on sale in Paris for 60 centimes a pair; these consisted of a wooden sole and two leather straps.[12] Rather than see the civilian population of France go barefoot, Clémentel hit upon the idea of using leather left over from the production programme of military boots to create the National Shoe, cheap standarised footwear for the working class and *petite bourgeoisie*.

The idea behind the National Shoe was not for the government to produce shoes itself, but rather, to supply shoemakers with leather and order them to devote a certain percentage of their production to the manufacture of a simple shoe, with the threat of the requisition of their factories or workshops if they did not co-operate. The shoes were to be designed to government specifications and retailed at a low fixed price. The standard National Shoe was a high laced boot made of black box-calf with a sturdy leather sole. The design was intended to be simple, elegant, and solid. The men's model cost 28 francs a pair, the women's 23 francs, that for adolescents 18 francs, and children 16 francs.[13]

The obstacles to the implementation of such a policy were enormous. It was calculated that there were a hundred thousand shoemakers or repairers in France; how were scarce supplies of leather to be divided among them? Then again, if the requirements of the working class and lower middle class were to be satisfied, a very large number of shoes would have to be produced. Even if production reached one million pairs a month, this would still amount to only half the average monthly consumption of shoes in France before the war.

The National Shoe was officially created in September 1917, three

---

12. G. Perreux, *La Vie quotidienne des civils en France pendant la Grande Guerre* (Paris, 1966), 114.
13. Ibid., 114.

months after the passage of the bill on civil requisitions. There were
to be two categories of distributors: the first were all shoe merchants established and incorporated before 12 August 1917; the second
category was composed of co-operatives, corporative groups, unions,
charitable institutions, and municipal and departmental organisations.[14] In October 1917 30,000 pairs of shoes were produced, in
November, 259,000. In January 1918 484,000 pairs of town shoes
were made, and for the first time, 8,000 pairs of a work boot were
also manufactured. But demand far exceeded supply. National
Shoes were bought up within hours of their appearing in shops,
often by speculators, and they became increasingly difficult to
obtain.[15]

In February 1918, there was a debate in the Chamber of Deputies
on the results of the National Shoe project to date, during which a
certain amount of useful information on the way in which the
scheme was operating in practice was made public.[16] Most of the
deputies spoke favourably of the National Shoe, but qualified their
praise with practical criticism. Advocates of state intervention like
Giray wanted production increased immediately to one million
pairs a month, and complained that the basic model of the town
shoe was a luxury shoe, unsuitable for the working class. Giray
admitted, however, that since the appearance of the National Shoe,
price increases for other shoes had been checked, but he complained
that only big shoe chains received any of the new shoes. He urged
that the National Shoe be maintained in the post-war period, so that
renewed speculation would not once again put shoes out of the
reach of the working class. Giray knew whereof he spoke: a former
shoemaker from Lyon, like his father before him, and a Socialist, his
chief contribution to parliamentary life was to intervene on matters
relating to the shoe industry.[17]

Another Socialist deputy, Hippolyte Mauger, a leather tanner and
currier by trade, and the government's High Commissioner for
Leathers,[18] reminded the Chamber of the opposition of the shoe
manufacturers to the project. They had done everything within
their power to hinder the development of the National Shoe, since
they were anxious to prevent any limitation of their profits. The
government had allowed manufacturers and retailers to make a

14. Prompsat Archives M(1)9: *Note sur la Chaussure nationale*, Intendant Dadillon
    to Clémentel, 31 December 1919.
15. Perreux, *Vie quotidienne*, 114.
16. *Chambre des députés*, 22 February 1918, 567–82.
17. Jolly, *Dictionnaire*, v. 1842.
18. Ibid., vii. 2407.

modest profit under the new scheme, but this had left them gravely dissatisfied. However, Mauger believed that shoe manufacturers, like the rest of society, should be prepared to make sacrifices in the national interest.

Jules Nadi, a Socialist deputy from Valence (Drôme) and a strong advocate of higher taxation,[19] rose to make another accusation against shoe manufacturers. Whereas the average manufacturer could easily have produced 1,800 to 3,000 pairs of shoes a month, they had pledged themselves to only 150 pairs, or at the outside, 500 pairs a month: 'We have reason to say that the producers of the National Shoe have not, at any moment, made every possible effort to produce the National Shoe in sufficient quantity'. These remarks were greeted with enthusiastic applause from the socialist deputies.

At last one of the deputies, Louis Dubois, took up cudgels on behalf of the manufacturers. Dubois was a Republican deputy from the Seine, the son of a ship-builder, a newspaper publisher, the founder of a photogravure firm, a member of the committee formed to defend the economic interests of the Seine area, a critic of government railway policy, and Clémentel's future successor as Minister of Commerce in November 1919.[20] Why had producers not responded more enthusiastically to the government's initiative? Precisely because the small profit they were allowed did not take into account the rising costs of materials other than leather. Thread was up 30 per cent in price, cloth for the inside of the shoe 103 per cent, and the same was true of laces, nails, and other secondary materials. Little wonder that retailers were unenthusiastic about selling the National Shoe when commercial travellers made no commission whatever, and shoe merchants made a profit of only 12 per cent as compared with the profit of 25 per cent which was current in England for shoe retailers. All of the blame for the defects of the National Shoe were laid at the door of the state: 'If the government had interfered less, and if there had been fewer statutory prescriptions, we might perhaps have had a National Shoe at a cheaper price'. Dubois failed to explain how this might have been achieved, but he was warmly applauded by the deputies of the Centre and Right none the less.

Another deputy, Lefas, who was generally sympathetic to the project, proposed a ration card system to ensure that it was the workers who received the National Shoe, not the middle class. Lefas was a Republican deputy from Brittany who had made his reputa-

19. Ibid., vii. 2551.
20. Ibid., iv. 1506–8.

tion by defending the interests of families with many children.[21] Lefas said that the project as a whole had worked, and he pointed to the fact that the current price for the National Shoe was only 28.5 francs a pair, compared with 50 francs for other shoes. He was, however, opposed to any increase in production to the level of 80 per cent of total shoe production in France, as some had suggested, since this would involve great hardship for workers in the shoe industry, who survived on what they earned from manufacturing more expensive shoes.

Other deputies suggested that the leather from old shoes be used to produce new ones, or that the sale of National Shoes be limited to the poorest elements of the population, to prevent rich people from buying first.

Clémentel then spoke in defence of his policy. The first duty of the government, he said, was to consider the plight of the working class. The fact that a pair of National Shoes was still extremely difficult to acquire despite the production of nearly half a million pairs a month gave some measure of their success. He admitted that distribution had been a problem, but rather than create its own shoe stores, the government had been anxious to protect the small shoe merchant as much as possible. The solution devised by the government had been to say to shoe merchants: we shall oblige the manufacturers who supply you to deliver a number of pairs of National Shoes which will be a fixed proportion of the purchases you made from them before we created the National Shoe. A slightly greater proportion of shoes would be delivered to co-operative stores, since a high percentage of their clientele were workers.

But Clémentel refused to limit the purchase of National Shoes to the working class. He pointed to a social fact which tended to be overlooked: the sufferings of the lower middle class.

> In this war, we must not forget those who suffer the most, the class which formerly had small fixed incomes, whose incomes have lost part of their purchasing power; it is the owners of buildings, small buildings, notably in Paris, who no longer receive any income and who are obliged to work to survive; it is our minor civil servants, postmen, for example, who particularly suffer from the increased price of shoes.

In the face of this hardship, there was only one solution: to increase the production of the National Shoe.

Clémentel went on to announce a number of improvements in the

21. Ibid., vi. 2202.

programme. Agreement had now been reached with the Commissariat whereby all the secondary materials which were required to make a shoe would be subject to the same controls as leather. New credit arrangements with the Commissariat would further expedite production. More work shoes would be manufactured, and prices would be revised to make them compatible with the cost of living. Within two months, Clémentel estimated, 700,000 pairs of shoes would be made each month, and the ultimate goal was a million pairs a month. Finally, it was hoped that the shoe industry, and all others relating to it, such as tanneries, would show some initiative in grouping themselves together for the purpose of purchasing raw materials; in other words, they should form a consortium. Clémentel expressed the wish that groups of producers and retailers would develop contacts with groups of consumers and buyers, to create a completely rational production organisation.

This debate on the National Shoe was a revealing indication of the current mood of the deputies with regard to the social problems caused by the war. Like the power of civil requisition, the creation of the National Shoe was an attempt to placate an increasingly restive civilian population. The theme common to all the speeches was concern for the hardship of the working class and a willingness to make concessions to pacify it. It is worth noting that only one deputy spoke in defence of private enterprise, and that the threat of social revolution silenced the conservative voices which were normally only too willing to protest against measures of government interference with industry. The danger of revolution made far more impact than the danger of military defeat. Hence the milder tone of opposition to the National Shoe, which, both as a working reality and as a model for future state intervention in the production of common consumer goods, represented far more of a potential threat to the liberty of industrialists than the highly unlikely possibility of civil requisition.

It took longer than Clémentel predicted, but by August 1918, 765,000 pairs of town shoes and 54,000 pairs of work shoes were being produced under the National Shoe scheme.[22] August, however, was the high-water mark of the programme, and thereafter, production slipped steadily, with occasional resurgences (615,000 town shoes, 52,000 work shoes in April 1919). Parliament voted credits of 15 million francs on 23 November 1918, and it was intended that production should remain constant at 500,000 pairs a month for an indefinite period. In March 1919, however, there was

22. Prompsat Archives M(1)9: Dadillon to Clémentel, 31 December 1919.

a new general requisition of leather by the government, and it was decided to grant no more supplies of leather for the manufacture of National Shoes. The last shoes were produced in July 1919.

In a report summing up the results of the experiment, Ernest Dadillon, a permanent army officer who had been seconded to the Ministry of Commerce in 1916 as head of the technical service responsible for leather, described the way in which the programme had been generally received by the various elements of the population concerned.

> The National Shoe was welcomed with enthusiasm by the civilian population, which was tired of paying a price double the real value of shoes; with calm by merchants, who found the profit they were allowed a trifle small, but who were generally satisfied with it; and with a little resistance by the manufacturers in general. This resistance was characterised by a more or less concealed inertia which retarded production.[23]

The National Shoe project enjoyed considerable popularity near the end of the war, and there were plans afoot to manufacture other 'national' products. It is worth noting that the idea was not always received with hostility by industrialists.[24] Indeed, when in April 1917 Clémentel asked chambers of commerce to help control cloth prices, he was informed that the real source of the trouble was the intermediaries; it took only one middleman to provoke a general price increase. The Chamber of Commerce of Vienne, together with a group of cloth manufacturers, took the initiative themselves and proposed the creation of a National Cloth. It was agreed that industrialists would receive no profit whatever from the operation. Because the cloth would be in short supply, its distribution would be limited to refugees, old people, women who received grants from the state, those in charitable institutions, and poor children. Another suggestion was that the state should create a National Bicycle, but the war ended before this idea came to fruition.

It is intriguing to contemplate the possible extension of this system of national industries within France had the war continued into 1919. It is important to note that the industries were national, not nationalised, that the state directed production, it did not expropriate factories or workshops. In a sense, national industries were the next logical step after consortia. If the evolution of consortia tended towards the ultimate control of consumer prices, what

23. Ibid.
24. *Chambre des députés*, 22 February 1918, 579.

better way than for the state to supervise completely the production of a few key consumer goods? Creating a National Shoe had the triple advantage of providing the needy with shoes; of giving the state precise information on the cost of manufacturing a vital product, a powerful weapon in future negotiating sessions with industrialists who wished to win government contracts; and of introducing a rival product which would force producers to be more competitive in the prices they charged for their privately produced shoes. There was even a certain poetic justice in forcing the manufacturers to produce the rival product themselves.

The State and the French Chemical Industry

But plans for national industries were not restricted to this formula of the production of a few specific consumer goods. The war gave the French government a unique opportunity to develop a much more formidable form of national industry: a state-dominated chemical company.

Before the war, the French chemical industry had been severely challenged by the great German chemical companies, which not only exported chemicals to France, but owned factories in France as well. The war brought an abrupt end to this German domination, and French chemical companies suddenly found themselves operating within a completely protected domestic market. Of all these companies, the greatest by far was Saint-Gobain. From 1914 to 1918, Saint-Gobain completely dominated the French chemical industry. At a very early date the directors of the firm realised the tremendous potential for development which the war offered Saint-Gobain. It will be recalled that Saint-Gobain profited from early contracts signed with the government at Bordeaux in November 1914, which established the prices to be paid for chemical products for the remainder of the war. By 1915 Saint-Gobain appeared invincible.

Plans for a Comptoir and a Company

In October 1915, however, there was a tremulous note of discord. Lucien Dior, the deputy from La Manche, president of the French Superphosphates Producers' Association, and member of the Professional Association of Major Chemical Industries, a man whose relations with Saint-Gobain had not always been happy, wrote to Albert Thomas to propose a solution to the problem of the increasing shortage of sulphuric acid in France.[25] Under the present system, whereby the state signed contracts with individual companies, the supply of acid was not keeping pace with demand. The diversity of contracts which resulted from this system led to grave incoveniences, which were liable to provoke the sort of public criticism it would be better to avoid. Furthermore, the disorganised, rapid growth of the chemical industry during the war would lead to serious difficulties later, if some provision were not made immediately to utilise surplus productive capacity in peacetime. Dior proposed that the state sign a collective contract with all producers of sulphuric acid, which would force them to organise and rationalise themselves. Dior let it be known that the two professional associations with which he was connected would be sympathetic to such a project. He reminded Thomas of the great success of the German chemical industry since it had organised itself in this manner. What, in short, he was envisaging was an 'organisation taking a public form which will reconcile all interested parties'.

Thomas seized on the idea with enthusiasm; and gave it a more precise formula which differed substantially from the vague terms of Dior's letter. In a note to one of his subordinates, Thomas suggested that the project reflected the current state of Saint-Gobain's relations with Dior as much as anything else: 'But the idea itself is interesting. The idea of a sort of trust, neither public nor private, in which the state would intervene to impose a contract, is an idea which certainly merits consideration'.[26] Thomas decided to press on with the plan. A few days later, in conversation with another of his subordinates, he revealed that what he had in mind for the chemical industry in the post-war period was a 'great agency (*comptoir*) with the responsibility for regulating production, in which the state would intervene on behalf of its shares'.[27] Dior had certainly never contemplated this form of state participation. Thomas hoped that after the war chemical plants would be converted to the manufacture of dyes and pharmaceutical products, and that the industries which would consume these products would also participate in the *comptoir*.

A meeting of chemical industrialists was called for 4 November 1915. The industrialists were informed that the current production of sulphuric acid in France amounted to only 20,000 tons a month, whereas 30,000 tons were required. At the same time, France had to

25. 94 AP 105: Lucien Dior to Thomas, 16 October 1915.
26. 94 AP 105: Albert Thomas to Capitaine Cavalier, 18 October 1915.
27. 94 AP 105: Capitaine Breynart to Albert Thomas, 26 October 1915.

prepare for the post-war period. Plans for the creation of a *comptoir* were outlined in detail. Taking its inspiration from the *comptoirs* which already existed for metals, this organisation would assume the form of a private joint-stock company with a variable capital. Preference shares would be distributed to producers in proportion to their production of acid before 2 August 1914. Ordinary shares would be distributed on a basis of the productive capacity built since the beginning of the war. The *comptoir* would centralise sales of chemical products for the French domestic market, and these sales would then be distributed among preference shareholders in proportion to the amount of stock held, with any excess being distributed among ordinary shareholders. This system was very much weighted in favour of the established, traditional firms like Saint-Gobain, since the position of a company in 1914 would determine its position in the post-war period. Foreign markets were left open to all producers. This was a curious feature of the proposal, since it was commonly agreed that only by forming a large cartel on the German model could the French chemical industry hope to compare internationally. Thus the market which most needed industrial concentration was left unorganised. The most unusual feature of the agreement was that the state was also to own ordinary shares in the *comptoir* and would have the right to produce and sell acid on the same basis as other ordinary shareholders.[28]

Few concrete results emerged from this meeting with industrialists, but it was, none the less, an important event, for it was here that the idea of a national chemical company was truly born, an idea which was to undergo such change and transformation in the months ahead, but an idea which refused to die despite much determined smothering from the traditional chemical companies.

In December 1915, Fleurent, the head of the technical section responsible for dyes at the Ministry of Commerce, wrote to Béhal, the director of the Office of Chemical and Pharmaceutical Products to propose a project almost identical to that of the November meeting, grouping industrialists into a 'powerful company capable of creating large factories after the war to process raw materials and intermediate products to produce dyes'.[29] He tentatively suggested installing a factory at Lens. The suggestion that the new company should specifically produce dyes rather than some other form of chemical product such as sulphuric acid was an important alteration

28. 94 AP 105: *Note pour la réunion du 4 Novembre 1915.*
29. F12 7708: *Rôle du service technique dans les matières colorantes*, 7 February 1917.

to the original plan, since Saint-Gobain, with its primary interests in sulphuric acid and superhosphates, would be far less directly affected than firms like Saint-Denis, which specialised in dye production. Nevertheless, as sulphuric acid is one of the intermediate products required to produce certain kinds of dyes (such as alkali blue and alizarin red S), Saint-Gobain could not help but be affected to some extent by such a project. Béhal wrote to Clémentel newly arrived at the Ministry of Commerce, and Thomas, asking them to co-ordinate their efforts to draw up a plan to satisfy both civilian and military demand for chemical products. In February 1916, Clémentel and Thomas gave the deputy Denys Cochin the mission of touring major industrial cities to encourage chemical industrialists to create and develop new productive capacity. Cochin immediately went to Lyon, and by March, he was able to write Clémentel that several industrialists had agreed to form a company. These industrialists included Donat Agache, of the firm of Kuhlmann, Saint-Gobain's keenest rival within France, and several lesser industrialists, but they did not include representatives of larger traditional firms such as Saint-Gobain or Saint-Denis.

The Tactics of Saint-Gobain

In the meantime, Thomas had received a report on 20 February 1916 from one of his chief subordinates, Exbrayat, which provided a fascinating insight into the techniques employed by Saint-Gobain to sabotage the plans of its domestic rivals.[30] Exbrayat was particularly well qualified to investigate the business practices of a large company, since before the war he had been a director of the Banque Demachy, the bank of the *Comité de Forges*. During the war he became a civil servant at the Under-Secretariat of State for Artillery and Munitions and was made responsible for the procurement of tin. He also acted as a roving agent for Thomas and was detailed to draw up specific reports such as this one. Reading this report, it is difficult to believe that Saint-Gobain was aware that a war was in progress, and that France was desperate for chemicals, particularly sulphuric acid. Exbrayat's report was in response to Thomas's request for information on Saint-Gobain's activities generally during the war, and in particular on the firm's relations with other producers of sulphuric acid. In a revealing comment, Thomas admitted that he was reluctant to ask the Powder Service for

---

30. 94 AP 105: *Note pour Monsieur Albert Thomas, Acide sulfurique,* 20 February 1916.

information on this subject, since it was generally sympathetic to Saint-Gobain and had shown opposition when Thomas proposed contracts for sulphuric acid with other companies. Since the Powder Service was supposed to be a subordinate branch of the Under-Secretariat, this seems a considerable admission of weakness and loss of control over his own bureaucracy from the man who was ostensibly responsible for all war production.[31]

Since the beginning of the war, said Exbrayat, Saint-Gobain had been engaged in a policy of attempting to establish a chemical monopoly in France. This campaign had been directed specifically against Kuhlmann, which had lost most of its factories when the Germans had invaded northern France. Agache, the head of Kuhlmann, and several of his collaborators, had proposed to the government that they utilise their industrial experience by building a factory to supply sulphuric acid for the state. This arrangement contained considerable advantages for the state, since in return for financing construction costs, the factory would revert to the state after the war.

Under these conditions, Kuhlmann had built a factory capable of producing 100 tons of sulphuric acid a day, on 18 hectares of land at Port de Bouc, near the Canal du Rhône. Saint-Gobain promptly purchased 17 hectares of land one kilometre away from this site and began building a plant of its own, claiming that it had been instructed to do so by the Powder Service of the Under-Secretariat. Exbrayat said that it was natural for the Powder Service to request in a general way that Saint-Gobain build new acid factories, but it was certainly inexact to suggest that this be done at a location precisely adjacent to the Kuhlmann factory. Clearly Saint-Gobain was intent on crushing its neighbour by charging lower prices and blocking off any potential growth for this factory. The government must intervene:

> If we want to ensure that the considerable efforts which have been made to produce acid are not wasted after the war, if we want to try to help the development in France of a dye industry, of a glass and chemical industry, it is vital that the government not allow Saint-Gobain to ruin by a price war most of the new factories which have been built.

Exbrayat then embarked upon a survey of Saint-Gobain's general position during the war. The financial advantages for industrialists who received advances from the state were considerable, therefore, these advantages should be spread out equally among all manufac-

31. 94 AP 105: Albert Thomas to Capitaine Exbrayat, 1 February 1916.

turers, and not concentrated on a few, whether or not they were the biggest producers in terms of their former or present production statistics. This unfortunately was not the case. In the six-month period from January to July 1916, it was projected that the production of concentrated sulphuric acid would rise from 42,260 tons to 92,520 tons, and that Saint-Gobain's share would rise correspondingly from 23,000 to 37,000 tons, so that at the end of the period, Saint-Gobain would still be producing 40 per cent of the country's acid. During the same six months, Saint-Gobain's share of the oleum market (oleum is a by-product of sulphuric acid) would rise from 56 per cent to 66 per cent. All this was made possible because the state was financing Saint-Gobain's expansion through advances. A new factory cost 900,000 francs, of which the state would pay 500,000. At the end of the war, the buildings, factories, and rail connections reverted to Saint-Gobain, and the state could claim only certain machinery.

The state had done worse with each successive contract. Under the contract of 1 March 1915, Saint-Gobain had to pay the cost of building 22 new machines, and guaranteed delivery of acid at 8.5 francs per 100 kilogrammes to the state. The next contract on 6 May 1915 maintained the same price of 8.5 francs, but this time it was the state which financed the construction of another 22 machines. At first, when the state advanced money, it was to receive at least a portion of the machinery after the war, but soon even this slender advantage was lost, so that contracts such as that of 26 July 1915 provided for the construction of eight machines to produce oleum, with Saint-Gobain paying 2.4 million francs, the state 5.6 million francs, and all the machinery remaining the property of the company.

The state did much better in its dealings with other companies such as Kuhlmann. The cost of the plant at Port de Bouc had been financed entirely by the state, but in exchange, the state paid 6.5 francs per 100 kilogrammes of acid, not 8.5, and the factory reverted to the state after the war. An analysis of contracts passed with other companies revealed that the state often paid less money for the same product and was not obliged to participate in construction costs:

It would seem to emerge from this survey that the situation of Saint-Gobain with regard to the other producers of sulphuric acid, partly because of the enormous advantages it has been given, is in danger of compromising the great efforts which have been made in France during the war, if the state does not find some means of saving all producers of sulphuric acid, the middle-sized and small ones as well.

The peacetime requirements in France for concentrated acid were 900,000 tons annually. With its increased capacity, Saint-Gobain would be able to produce 530,000 tons. Left to its own devices, thanks to the vast profits it had amassed during the war, as well as the great reserves it had accumulated before, Saint-Gobain could lower the price of acid to the point of wiping out all competition. What was the state to do?

> The only solution seems to consist in the creation of a syndicate of all producers of sulphuric acid, who would pledge themselves to reduce their production in proportion to the capacity of each factory, in order to avoid any over-production. Saint-Gobain would undoubtedly refuse to enter this syndicate, but the government must profit from the present situation to force it to adhere officially to this pact.
>
> With the support of the Under-Secretary of State I am convinced that we shall succeed in uniting all the other producers.
>
> We shall also obtain, we believe, the acceptance of a price-fixing formula, such as the cost price with 10 per cent added, for example.

The Commission of Dyes

Armed with this information about Saint-Gobain's methods, Clémentel and Thomas pressed forth with their plans. Following up Denys Cochin's news of an impending agreement with the chemical industrialists of Lyon, Clémentel called a conference of these industrialists, only to discover considerable opposition to his plans. The industrialists claimed that the new organisation was useless, since they could finance any expansion in the Lyon area themselves, and that it seemed pointless to establish a factory near Rouen, as Cochin had suggested.[32] Undaunted, Clémentel summoned a new meeting of industrialists, this time including a much wider range of representatives from middle-sized and small chemical companies. He insisted on the necessity of creating a large company open to all interested parties, which would construct a series of factories at key points in France. The outcome of this meeting was the establishment of a Commission of Dyes for the purpose of creating a national dyes industry. Its members included Clémentel, Cochin, Béhal, Blazeix, four other representatives of the state, and three industrialists, of whom Agache, the head of Kuhlmann, was the most notable. Saint-Denis and Saint-Gobain were not represented.

The constitution of this Commission was another attempt by Clémentel to impose the will of the government over private

---

32. F12 7708: *Rôle du service technique.*

industry through the creation of a mixed body in which bureaucrats were in the clear majority. The office for Chemical and Pharmaceutical Products, which had been established with Auguste Béhal at its head in the opening months of the war, had performed a useful task as an advisory body,[33] and indeed, had also promoted the idea of a national chemical company, but it was unable to undertake the operations which the increasing intervention of the state in the chemical industry required. The Commission was designed to fill this administrative gap, but as shall be seen, it too was regarded only as a posting stage on the road to complete government control. The Commission was very much intended to be the organ which would implement Clémentel's policy rather than an independent consultative organisation.

The tone was set during the first meeting of the Commission on 30 April 1916, when Clémentel laid down the grand lines of his policy for the future development of the chemical industry. Clémentel began his exposition by pointing to the success of the German chemical industry during the war. German industrialists had formed a union of all their factories based on two conditions. The first was that in the case of the eventual loss of German-owned factories in enemy territory, the loss would be borne equally by all companies. The second was that all capital, patents, manufacturing processes, and research discoveries were pooled for the good of all the members. The only way in which the Germans were superior to the French was in their ability to organise, but experience in France thus far during the war had proved that the French were also capable of organisation and discipline. The war would force the French to place even more emphasis on these two qualities, and the good work would have to be extended into peacetime, 'which we must view as a period of commercial and industrial war'.[34]

Only the state could direct such organisation, particularly since the question had to be considered in the much larger context of interallied policy. Clémentel had already been in consultation with his British, Italian, Russian, and Belgian counterparts, and he now unveiled a grandiose scheme which provided for the creation not only of a national chemical company, but of an international chemical company with a capital of 350 million francs. The industrial management would be established in France and the commercial management in England. Commercial liberty would prevail among the participating countries for chemical goods, and a common tariff

33. See above, Chapter 2.
34. F12 7708: *Commission des matières colorantes, 1ère séance*, 30 April 1916.

barrier would be raised against the outside world. The principal objective of the company would be post-war competition with the German chemical industry. The project was to unfold in three stages. The first, the wartime stage, would ensure that a minimum production of essential dyes was maintained, using government factories. After the war, there would be an intermediate stage during which larger factories producing chemical products would be built. The third stage would be a world struggle against German chemical manufacturers. It was indicative of the moderate nature of French war aims that Clémentel could consider that the defeated Germans would still be able to maintain a chemical industry so strong as to require such formidable opposition.

Answering the criticism of Agache that this organisation would in effect be a trust and as such harmful to the interests of smaller firms such as Kuhlmann, Clémentel said that the company would be more accurately described as 'an international arrangement which has never been tried before,' than as a cartel or trust. The traditional arguments against trusts did not apply in this case, since operations were to be directed against the Germans rather than against domestic competitors. The executive of this new company would also take an experimental form, added Henri Blazeix. Agache had advocated the traditional board of directors, multiplied by a certain coefficient, operating in the usual way, but this new organism would have a unique form of administration adapted to this particular need, said Blazeix.

As was so often the case, the potential effectiveness of the Dyes Commission seemed greater at its inception than in its subsequent operations. In June 1916, the entire Commission went to England. It discussed tariffs with members of the British government and spoke to representatives of British Dyes, it toured factories, but little was heard from the Commission thereafter. Like the Office of Chemical and Pharmaceutical Products before it, its importance faded, it assumed a consultative role, and it lacked any real power to impose the will of the Minister of Commerce. The case of the Dyes Commission illustrates a general phenomenon of the war: the rapid devaluation of bureaucratic structures, and the subsequent need to create even more powerful organisms to deal with industry. Like insects, industrialists had the capacity to develop a resistant strain to any bureaucratic antidote which might be applied to their activities, and the government was therefore continually forced to develop new antidotes. The process was never-ending.

Despite its fundamentally innocuous nature, the establishment of the Dyes Commission still aroused strong opposition from the larger chemical companies, particularly those specialising in dyes, since one of its stated aims was the establishment of a national dyes industry. Senator Poirrier, the president of the Société Anonyme des Matières Colorantes et Produits Chimiques de Saint-Denis, wrote to Clémentel on 2 June 1916 to complain that the government seemed to be unaware of the fact that several dye companies already existed in France, including the one of which he had the honour to be president, and that if the company were provided with the necessary raw materials and manpower, it would be in a position to satisfy the most pressing demands of French consumers.[35] When such industrial capacity existed, was the state contemplating the creation of a national dyes industry which would compete directly with private firms? Would such a national industry, armed with the moral support of the public authorities and the financial support of the Treasury, not be in a privileged economic position which would render all competition by existing companies impossible? Poirrier concluded indignantly: 'Have you envisaged the moral responsibility which would result for the state from its intervention, with regard to the shareholders who have provided the capital for the private firms?'

The National Dyes Syndicate

The next stage in the development of a national chemical industry took place within a few days of the constitution of the Dyes Commission. A National Dyes Syndicate was established. The Syndicate was in some ways a separate initiative from the Commission, since it was concerned not with the establishment of an interallied company, but was conceived rather as the prototype of a specifically national chemical company. From its inception, the Syndicate was intended to be only an intermediate step to the creation of a company proper. The founders of the Syndicate included the same middle-sized and small chemical industrialists, unified in their opposition to the chemical Goliaths, Saint-Gobain and Saint-Denis, who had continually agitated in favour of some form of union of chemical producers.

The organisers launched their plans with a great deal of astuteness. They were determined, above all, to appear fair minded and to avoid any impression of ganging up on big brother.[36] Accordingly,

35. F12 7708: Senator Poirrier to Clémentel, 2 June 1916.
36. F12 7708: *Note No. 3 sur la constitution du syndicat national des matières colorantes*.

they invited every chemical industrialist and every consumer of chemical products known to them to take part in the Syndicate, and they advertised the project in the relevant trade journals. It was therefore safe to say that 'No one was excluded from participating and it would be impossible to cite the name of a single person or of a single company which wanted to subscribe but was prevented from doing so.' The fixed capital was immediately subscribed by the founders, who were then prepared to resell shares to all who subsequently applied to join.

As a further conciliatory gesture, the organisers cleverly offered the position of honorary president of the Syndicate to one of their leading critics, Senator Poirrier himself; and his company, Saint-Denis, was offered a share of 3 million francs in the Syndicate as well. They offered another of the largest French chemical companies, les Usines du Rhône, a share of 5 million francs. As was anticipated, both companies declined these proposals 'in almost identical terms', in letters of 2 and 3 August 1916 respectively. There was a strong suggestion that the two firms had been in close consultation with each other before drafting their replies. Saint-Gobain had also been approached with the same offer for a share in the Syndicate and had also declined. The gist of the reply made by representatives of Saint-Gobain in negotiation was that

> this company was only interested in projects in which it could be assured of having more than 50% of the capital, and moreover, the company was currently utilising all of its resources either to build factories to replace those captured by the enemy or for the harnessing of hydroelectric resources which it owned.

Thus, said the founders of the Syndicate, they had been more than reasonable in soliciting the participation of all interested parties in the scheme, and they had in no way attempted to reserve the profits of the enterprise for themselves. The big chemical companies had nothing to complain of since they had been offered their chance and refused.

On 11 September 1916, a contract was signed between the Minister of War and the National Dyes Syndicate. The primary justification for this contract was that the Minister of War was planning for the post-war period and wanted to make some provision for the munitions factories which had been built during the war. What was the point of preserving powder and explosives plants in peacetime, if there was no source of primary materials to supply them? If left to their own devices, industrialists would close down the excess productive capacity of their factories, and it would require a considerable new effort to start them up again. If the factories producing secondary products such as powders and explosives closed, the plants which produced the necessary primary products would also close. To avoid this problem, and to encourage industrialists to maintain their plants in a state of readiness, explosives plants had to be converted to the production of closely-related goods such as dyes, which would continue to provide a market for primary materials. Thus, for military reasons, a powerful company would have to be formed to take over unwanted chemical plants after the war to keep them prepared for a rapid reversion to their original function as producers of war material. The state would thereby have at its disposal the necessary trained technical personnel.[37]

The National Dyes Company

To the original case presented by Clémentel for the creation of a national chemical company for the purpose of doing commercial battle with the Germans after the war, this second military motive was added, the need to maintain French industry in a state of alert after the war in preparation for any possible new conflict. The ground was now prepared for the implementation of the ultimate stage of the operation, the creation of the company itself. This final step was carefully planned. By August 1916, the project had advanced to the point that Clémentel could write to the Under-Secretary of State for the Commissariat and Supply to give precise details about the nature and form of the new company.[38] The National Dyes Company would be formed to develop an independent dyes industry in France, as well as to participate with British Dyes in the creation of the new interallied dyes company, which would free the Allied nations from their dependence on German companies. The new company would receive raw materials and partially processed materials from British Dyes, which it would convert into finished dyes.

The evolution of the French government's relations with the chemical industry which led to the establishment of a National Dyes Company was to a certain extent the parallel of the British experience. In Britain, the Committee on Chemicals had decided to create a national joint-stock company to produce aniline dyes.

37. F12 7708: *Projet de loi tendant à la ratification du contrat conclu le 11 septembre 1916, entre le Ministre de la Guerre et le Syndicat National des Matières colorantes.*
38. F12 7838: 17 August 1916.

British Dyes Limited was a compromise between government spon-
sorship and private shareholding and, as in France, the scheme
nearly failed in the face of determined opposition on the part of
private manufacturers. It required a government subscription of
£1.7 million to keep the company afloat until the end of the war,
when it was amalgamated with a private firm.[39]

In October 1916, the board of directors of the new company was
named.[40] The president of the new Société Nationale des Matières
Colorantes was to be René Massé, the president of the professional
association of the French Gas Industry. Other directors included
Donat Agache, of Kuhlmann, and seven other representatives of
smaller chemical companies, or companies which consumed their
products, such as dye works. In addition, Clémentel had adroitly
enlisted the help of powerful allies outside the government and the
chemical industry. Major banks were represented by Alfred Bon-
zon, of the Banque de l'Union Parisienne, and Gaston Griolet, the
president of the board of directors of the Banque de Paris et des
Pays Bas. Equally important was the presence of three metallurgists,
the patriarchial Théodore Laurent, of the Forges et Aciéries de la
Marine et d'Homécourt, Ernest Métivier, of Schneider, and Jean
Neyret, president of the Société des Aciéries et Forges de Firminy.
The only board members not drawn from private business were
Gaston Guiot, a minister plenipotentiary, and Raphaël-Georges
Lévy, a member of the *Institut*.

Thus, from the outset, the government seemed determined to
show that it would not exercise undue influence over the new
company. Indeed, from the constitution of the board of directors, it
was not immediately apparent how the state would exert any
influence whatever. The formation of the board, however, was a
stroke of genius, for by enlisting the services of prominent businessmen and industrialists to run a company to rival Saint-Gobain,
Saint-Denis, and les Usines du Rhône, Clémentel was effectively
playing off one group of businessmen against another. Now it was
no longer the government which would clash directly with private
industry, it was one group of industrialists sponsored by the
government which would compete with other industrialists. All the
disadvantages and inexperience of bureaucrats operating in industrial affairs were overcome by the simple expedient of employing
industrialists to do the task instead.

In November 1916, the Banque de Paris et des Pays Bas arranged

39. Marwick, *The Deluge*, 173.
40. F12 7708: *Conseil d'Administration*.

the financing of the new company, and organised a financial group to raise the 40 million francs capital required.[41] On 16 December 1916, the National Dyes Syndicate officially founded the National Dyes Company. According to Article Two of the statutes of the Company, its aims were:

> the production and sale of all organic chemical products and of dyes, as well as all other products related to such production, in order that those products furnished by Germany before the war may be replaced by those manufactured in France; the execution of the contract signed with the state, with the purpose of using explosive factories built for war production, which will be provided by the National Dyes Syndicate.[42]

With such extensive ambitions, the concern of the larger chemical companies was understandable.

But which were the factories which the National Dyes Syndicate was to contribute to the new company? In lieu of direct financial participation, the state would turn over its own explosive plants, which were administered by the Under-Secretariat of State for War Production, when the war ended.

The Battle for German Factories in France

But there was one remaining source of unexploited industrial capacity in France which could be used for the production of dyes: German-owned chemical factories, which had been operating at reduced capacity or lying idle since the beginning of the war.

These plants had been the subject of a long and complicated debate ever since their initial sequestration by the government.[43] Three specific plants were involved; the Creil factory of the Compagnie Parisienne, which was owned by Fabwerke Höchst; the Manufacture Lyonnaise, owned by Frankfurter Anilin Farben Fabrik; and the St Fons factory of Aktion Gesellschaft für Anilin Fabrikation. The French textile industry in general and the Lyon silk industry in particular were dependent upon the dyes of these plants and, from November 1914 on, there was a series of letters from representatives of the textile industry to the government requesting that these plants be kept operating.

French dyes manufacturers, however, viewed things differently.

41. F12 7708: 6 November 1916.
42. F12 7708.
43. Unless otherwise stated, the letters which follow were all found in F12 7838: *Fonctionnement des usines séquestrées 1915–1917.*

For them, the war seemed a heaven-sent opportunity to dispose of their German rivals and establish their own domestic monopoly in France. Accordingly, they opposed any plan to preserve the three German factories. On 17 December 1915, Senator Poirrier, the president of Saint-Denis, wrote to the Office for Chemical and Pharmaceutical Products to complain that the Manufacture Lyonnaise, although sequestered, was continuing to operate in competition with French firms, and requested that it be closed. The Office dismissed the complaint by saying that as the stocks of material which the Manufacture Lyonnaise held were rapidly disappearing, the company would soon cease to enjoy any special advantages over its French rivals.

It is worth noting that initially there was never any question of outright confiscation without compensation of the plants by the government, and that all of the ultimate participants in the debate were prepared to reimburse the Germans in the event of the factories being utilised in any way. It should also be observed that the first impulse for exploiting these factories came from private industry, not from the government. But on 20 July 1916, there was a significant new development. The president of the National Dyes Syndicate, Jeamard, wrote to Clémentel proposing that the sequestered factories be run not by private enterprise but by the Syndicate itself. Jeamard referred to the recent agreement with British Dyes to furnish France with primary chemical products; to use these products, it was necessary to increase the capacity of the dyes plants which consumed them. The Syndicate considered itself in a position to operate these plants and proposed an arrangement whereby sequestered factories would be rented in exchange for 25 per cent of the profits. This solution avoided the problem of payment to the Germans in neutral countries, since the rental money would be kept in trust for the German owners by the government.

Throughout the affair, a number of legal difficulties arose to obstruct the path of the government. The *Garde des sceaux* informed Clémentel that from a legal point of view he had no right to rent out the sequestered factories. The administrators of the plants concerned made the same objection. It was also questionable whether patents, industrial and commercial dossiers, and technical secrets could be used by any new occupant of the factories. Finally, there was the delicate problem of consulting the German owners about their wishes. In the end, all the obstacles were overcome, and arrangements were made in early 1917 for the National Dyes Company to rent the factories.

At this point, the storm broke. Cotelle, the president of Saint-

Denis and son-in-law of the former president, Senator Poirrier, who had just died, wrote directly to Peytavin, the chief administrator of the Manufacture Lyonnaise while it was under sequestration, to protest against any sale of the factory to the National Dyes Company. Cotelle countered the offer of 1.6 million francs, which the Company had made, with an immediate offer of 1.7 million, but he insisted that ideally the sale of the Manufacture Lyonnaise should be arranged by regular public auction. This was the signal for a flood of letters and telegrams protesting against the sale of the Manufacture Lyonnaise to a state-controlled company, which the *Garde des Sceaux* diligently diverted to Clémentel.

A few days later, Cotelle launched a parallel attack on the Cie Parisienne. On 27 March, he wrote to Navarre, the chief administrator of the firm, to protest against any contract with, rental by, or sale to the National Dyes Company, without public notice and a competition open to all chemical companies. Cotelle demanded that an engineer from Saint-Denis be allowed to tour the Creil factory with a view to making a fair bid for it. Then Cotelle brought his heavy guns to bear. He informed Navarre that if his wish was not granted immediately, he would write the following day to Ribot, the President of the Council of Ministers, Viviani, the Minister of Justice, Clémentel, the Minister of Commerce, the President of the Civil Tribunal of Paris and the Attorney General of the Republic. Undaunted by this massive threat, Navarre replied that he could not comply with the demand, since a tour of inspection would reveal secret manufacturing processes and techniques to unauthorised personnel. In any case, said Navarre, it was too late, because he was already involved in arranging for the merger of the Cie Parisienne with the National Dyes Company. Preparations were well advanced and had not resulted from any personal initiative of Navarre, but from the decisions of his superiors.

Two days later, on 29 March 1917, Cotelle wrote a blistering note to Clémentel:

> I feel it my duty to send you a copy of the dossier which I have just delivered to the President of the Council of Ministers to draw his attention to this mysterious affair in which the most experienced and honorable firms have been dismissed in favour of a company which only exists on paper, and whose creation gave rise to exceptional criticism by the Minister of Finance.

But it was too late. In April 1917, the National Dyes Company was officially given the right to rent sequestered German factories.

Cotelle, on behalf of Saint-Denis, raged furiously, and sent another letter to Clémentel on 22 April insisting on 'an equitable distribution of sequestered factories', but to no avail. For the remainder of the war, Saint-Denis peppered the government with further demands to rent German factories, and each time was rebuffed.

Why was it that Saint-Denis and not Saint-Gobain led the fight against the state? One can only speculate, but it seems probable that they were concerting their efforts against the government, and that Saint-Denis was chosen as the spokesman for the larger companies rather than Saint-Gobain, since its intentions were less obviously monopolistic, and since it had a more direct interest in dyes production. The fight over German factories was not only between the large companies and the government, but between the large companies and the small companies, who sought the state as their ally. Paradoxically, the establishment of a national chemical company helped the small companies since it acted as a counterweight to the leviathans. The National Dyes Company also gave the government a more practical working knowledge of the chemical industry and the technical expertise required to legislate and control private chemical companies.

The Committee for Chemical Products and the Chemical Products Consortium

In the meantime, the government was continuing to construct elaborate bureaucratic structures to encompass the chemical industry still further. On 27 August 1917, the Committee for Chemical Products was created. As an interministerial committee, it was endowed with the usual impressive authority to 'determine, centralise, co-ordinate, or control the needs of the services of the state and of the civilian population',[44] and it was given the power to distribute monthly supplies of raw materials among the private chemical companies, and to determine the prices which these companies could charge for manufactured goods. In addition to the representatives of various interested ministries, there were four industrialists, and this time, two of them represented major companies, Boyer, the chairman of the board of les Usines du Rhône, and Choffel, of Saint-Denis. Once again, however, Saint-Gobain was not represented. The Committee was designed with several objectives in mind. Auguste Béhal, a member of the Committee, as of every other bureaucratic body created during the war to deal with

44. F12 7700.

chemicals, outlined the plans of the government for the chemical industry at a meeting of the Committee in October 1917.[45] The Committee had an immediate goal: to co-ordinate the production of chemical products for wartime. But it also had a long-term aim: to capture a large section of the world's chemical market in the post-war period. Conditions would never be better than they were at present, with the potential disappearance of German producers, but it required great changes on the part of French industrialists.

As in politics, you must create a union of all producers, the notion of competing firms must disappear, you must unify your productive capacities, you must form cartels to satisfy the requirements of England, of the other Allied states, and of neutral countries.

Industrialists must be prepared to make sacrifices; in the interest of being more competitive, prices would have to be lowered.

Béhal did not explain how all this was to be accomplished, but his ideas of a union, a cartel of all producers, had tremendous implications. Notably, it implied that the task of co-ordination, of determining who should sacrifice what, of ordering fusions and price reductions, of preventing excessive domestic competition, should be undertaken by the government. Thus, in the post-war world, the government would not only have its own dyes company it would impose its control over all other chemical companies. It should be noted that this cartel would have covered all chemical products, not merely dyes.

The Committee itself could not force such a revolution; indeed, the minutes of its meetings reveal that its primary concerns were ones of routine administration, determining imports and exports to facilitate the war effort, and resolving minor technical problems. How, then, were these great changes to be accomplished? Once again, it was the ubiquitous consortium which was intended to pave the way to the future. In early 1918, the Technical Council began to consider the possibility of creating a Chemical Products Consortium. Initially, it seemed that there was one insuperable obstacle: Saint-Gobain. As Henri Blazeix remarked at a meeting of the Technical Council on 25 February 1918, Saint-Gobain dominated the chemical industry to such an extent that it practically constituted a consortium by itself. Some special formula would have to be found to overcome this difficulty.[46] In the end, it was decided that

45. F12 7700: *Comité interministériel des produits chimiques, Procès-verbal de la 2ème séance du 8 Octobre.*
46. F12 7659: *10ᵉ séance du Conseil Technique*, 25 February 1918.

the simplest solution was to treat Saint-Gobain on the same basis as all other chemical producers, and the idea of a special formula was abandoned. The Technical Council pressed on with its task, and the Consortium was duly founded.

In June 1918, the definitive convention between the state and the Chemical Products Consortium was drawn up. It contained the standard features of other consortia, but as one of the later consortia to be constituted, the control of state was more elaborately defined and enforced. One interesting feature was that membership in the Consortium was no longer voluntary; all importers of chemical products who had been in business before 31 December 1917 were obliged to join the Consortium. Thus the option of non-co-operation was firmly closed to companies like Saint-Gobain and Saint-Denis. The authority of the state, administered through the institution of the Consortium, would apply to all chemical companies, large and small.

The Bureaucracy and the Chemical Industry

By the last year of the war, there was such a profusion of bureaucratic organisations responsible for supervising the chemical industry in France that on 23 March 1918, Fleurent, the head of the Third Section of the Technical Services of the Ministry of Commerce, which was concerned with chemicals, sent a note to Clémentel which defined the relationship of these various bodies to each other.[47] At the top of the bureaucratic hierarchy came the Committee for Chemical Products, which determined general policy, benefiting from the larger perspective which the participation of representatives of various ministries assured. Next came the Third Section of the Technical Services, which represented exclusively the authority of the Ministry of Commerce and was responsible for 'exercising control over the totality of internal and external commerce, and charged with the practical application of decisions taken by the Committee.'

Then came the oldest of the organisations, the Office for Chemical Products, which had come into existence in October 1914 and had played a supervisory role

> to determine existing quantities of chemical and pharmaceutical products; to evaluate their annual production; to assure their supply and distribution; to develop a more intensive production in France of these same products and to encourage the manufacture of new products.

47. F12 7700: Fleurent to Clémentel, 23 March 1918.

The old function of dividing up imported raw material among different producers and consumers was taken over by the Consortium, but the Office was still responsible for providing the statistical information which the Third Section used to plan the future activities of the Consortium. Thus the Office had become an information-gathering body, the research department, and the intelligence service of the Ministry of Commerce, but it lacked the power to implement its own recommendations.

Finally, there was the Consortium itself, 'a veritable commercial company, which centralises the demands of its adherents, groups them under the authority of a sole purchasing agent, and divides material in the best interests of national production'. From this account, it was clear that the vital link in the mechanism was Fleurent's own Third Section, because this was the body that wielded real power, translating the vague proposals of the Committee into concrete action, harnessing the Office as a subordinate agency, and giving the Consortium its orders on behalf of the government. This nexus of power was summed up by Fleurent in the following way:

> The Third Section of the Technical Service, in order to fulfil the directions given it by the Committee for Chemical Products, and, in consequence, to wield its authority effectively over the Consortium, can only do so on the condition that it has continuous information about the activities of the Office for Chemical Products, so that the action of this agency will be co-ordinated, not divergent.

Fleurent's note is one of the most revealing commentaries available on the way in which the welter of wartime bureaucratic bodies actually worked in relation to each other. Taken at their face value, it might be thought that the interministerial committees for various products were the supreme authority, as indeed, in the official bureaucratic hierarchy they were. But in fact it was the technical sections of the Ministry of Commerce which had the greatest contact with and influence over non-military private industry in France during the war. The heads of these sections, men like Fleurent, were Clémentel's agents, the extension of his will and power, because they shared his convictions about the necessity of increasing the power of the state over private industry. It was the technical sections which gave the wartime bureaucratic structures their coherence and their direction. They were the Minister's vital command posts.

Post-War Plans

As the war drew to a close, Clémentel began to plan more con-
cretely for the future of the French chemical industry after the war.
He asked his subordinates to prepare recommendations, particularly with regard to the future of the National Dyes Company. On
28 October 1918, he received the report.[48] The report was more
interesting for what it revealed about the difficulties of the current
state of the chemical industry than in its proposals for the future.
The authors pointed to the great problem which had resulted from
the creation by the state of the National Dyes Company: because of
the special relationship between the state and this company,
whereby the company seemed unfairly favoured and protected
above all others, it was impossible for the state to create an *entente*
with the other chemical companies: 'It is difficult to have, therefore,
a sincere and fruitful agreement between private firms and the
National Dyes Company as long as this latter remains a direct
competitor backed by the state.' In other words, the state could not
have both a union of all chemical companies with a view to competing with the Germans, and at the same time, its own national
chemical company. Therefore, the state should intervene only over
problems which private companies could not resolve. Undoubtedly,
there should be a central organism in France to integrate the
industrial, commercial, and financial forces of the dyes industry,
and to co-ordinate the importation of raw material and the production of finished products. But was the National Dyes Company the
organism required? There were certain conveniences to be derived
from maintaining the company. Only the National Dyes Company
had signed a general contract with the state. This arrangement had
the advantage of allowing parliamentary commissions to exercise
some control over the Company by means of the contract. Accordingly, the authors of the report proposed that the National Dyes
Company be preserved, but that its form be modified so that all
private chemical companies might participate and thereby be bound
by the general contract signed with the state.

Specifically, they proposed that the company give up its productive operations and transfer them to private industry to avoid a
conflict of interest. The National Dyes Company should represent a
community of interests between the state and the private companies. To this end, the Company would buy shares in all the private
chemical companies in France, and it would have its own member

48. F12 7708: *Note sur le projet d'organisation de l'industrie des matières colorantes,*
    28 October 1918.

on every board of directors to represent its interests. In turn, all of the private firms would subscribe to shares in the Company; the general public would be invited to participate as well. The Company would no longer own factories, but it would have a very real commercial function:

> The National Dyes Company would be the only purchaser and distributor, on behalf of the subscribing companies, of imported materials and products, and of raw materials and products produced in France. In addition, it would be the only sales agent of products manufactured by the affiliated companies.

This ingenious proposal would have converted the Company into the sole purchasing and sales agent of the French dyes industry. The Company would have combined the importing role of the consortium with the sales mechanism of a cartel. All of Clémentel's conditions for the post-war battle with the Germans would thereby have been fulfilled, while at the same time, a maximum of productive freedom would have been maintained by the private companies. Why, then, did the scheme fail? The principal reason would seem to be that in the general rush to disband all bureaucratic structures and controls over private industry during the six months which followed the war, any plan which consolidated and strengthened the administrative hold of the government was doomed to failure. Since all consortia were being liquidated, how could a super consortium be created? Then again, one can only suppose that the big chemical companies still thought they might be able to profit from the chaos of the post-war period to consolidate their domination over the industry by driving smaller rivals out of business, using the enormous financial resource at their disposal to engage in a price war until the smaller firms collapsed. This, Exbrayat had predicted in his report in February 1916, was the long-term policy of a company like Saint-Gobain, and there is little reason to suppose that the policy had changed significantly during the war. The bigger firms thought they could do better on their own, and refused to take part in any general organisation of any part of the chemical industry.

But the French chemical industry did not quite relapse to its unreformed pre-1914 state in 1919. For one thing, its greatest enemy, the Germans, had been temporarily confounded. Under the economic clauses of the Versailles Treaty, the Germans were required to place 50 per cent of the country's stocks of dyes at the disposal of the Allies. For this, they were to be compensated by pre-war prices to be decided by an interallied commission. Furthermore, for a five year period, German dyes factories had to deliver an amount of their dyes production equal to 25 per cent of their pre-war production to the Allies, at cost price 'with a reasonable profit added'.[49] Moreover, if French chemical companies refused to unite themselves under government supervision, they could see the advantage of establishing an organism to determine a common sales policy, as the metal producers had done in creating the *Comité des Forges*; thus, in November 1919, the Union of Producers and Consumers for the Development of the Dyes Industry in France was created.[50] To this extent, at least, part of the chemical industry had learned the lesson of organisation taught by the war.

Conclusion

Requisitions, the National Shoe, and the National Dyes Company; taken together, these three developments represent the greatest extension of the authority of the Ministry of Commerce over private industry during the 1914–18 war. The first, the right to requisition privately-owned factories, was paradoxically the most hotly-contested and the least operative of the government's new powers. And yet, the importance of this measure should not be minimised. It gave the government an arm with which to threaten recalcitrant industrialists, as, for example, during the formation of the Petrol Consortium when Clémentel invoked the menace of requisition against the petrol industrialists when they seemed re-luctant to co-operate. In this case the industrialists immediately gave way under the menace, thereby demonstrating that the power of requisition was not totally ineffective as a bargaining weapon. The threat of requisition should be seen in the larger context of implementing Clémentel's general policy of raw material controls, consortia, price fixing, and curbing speculation and profiteering; without the threat of sanctions, the government was powerless in the face of industrial resistance to any of these measures. The debate to which the proposal gave rise illustrated the almost pathological fear of government interference with the private property of indus-trialists which men like Senator de Lamarzelle sincerely felt. Private property was sacred no matter how great the danger of military defeat. Men's lives could be requisitioned, but not property. As *Le Temps* never ceased to remind its readers, private property was one

49. *Traité de Paix (Annexe 11 de la part VIII).*
50. F12 7709.

of the essential features of *La France éternelle* which her soldiers were fighting to defend.

The National Shoe attracted less adverse publicity, but had far greater practical effect. In this case, the government would not take away the factories of shoemakers, it merely ordered them to make shoes according to certain specifications. The inviolability of private ownership was thus preserved, and the public debate was correspondingly cooler and more rational. At the same time, there was the added impetus of defusing a potentially dangerous social situation. And yet, the implications of this measure were far-reaching, and indeed in a sense revolutionary, for it challenged the very notion of the diversity of consumer products which has been one of the most prominent characteristics of French business. Had the system of National Shoes, National Bicycles, and National Cloth been extended to include other basic consumer products, a development contemplated by Clémentel and his advisers, the resulting standardisation of goods would have been one of the most significant developments in the social history of modern France. It is astonishing that this potential revolution in consumer products should have begun at all, particularly with an industry dominated by small, independent producers with a strong tradition of dissent.

The creation of the National Dyes Company represented a different form of national industry. As with the National Shoe, the principle of private ownership was preserved, since shares in the Company were held by private firms. But the contribution of its own explosives plants and the sequestered German factories under its control gave the state the right to supervise closely the operations of the new company and to determine its general policy. The National Dyes Company, like British Dyes Ltd., was a curious hybrid animal, not fully nationalised, not directed by bureaucrats, but yet an instrument of state policy, defending the interests of one group of chemical industrialists against another, and the potential base for the establishment of a state controlled chemical cartel in the post-war period.

In the end, French chemical companies emerged from the war greatly enriched, with their independence virtually intact. Saint-Gobain continued to dominate the industry to the present day; in 1962 (before its merger with Péchiney, and later Pont-à-Mousson, in 1970) the company was still the biggest producer of sulphuric acid, superphosphates, and fertilisers in France.[51] Undoubtedly, the remarkable success of the firm can be ascribed in part to the great development which it underwent from 1914 to 1918.

51. *Saint-Gobain 1665–1965*, 110.

CHAPTER 6

Albert Thomas and Louis Loucheur

For Jaurès, to use a biblical expression, in the beginning was
the Word. For Thomas, it was the Act.

(Emile Vandervelde)[1]

Albert Thomas was very much a socialist in the style of Millerand
and Bernstein, less concerned with doctrine than with concrete
action. Lacking the passion and the vision of a Jaurès, Thomas saw
his role as that of the reasonable man, the moderator, reconciling
the ideological differences of his fellow socialists through compromise based on common sense. Thomas was anti-revolutionary; he
favoured Jaurès's formula of 'revolutionary spirit, reformist action';
he opposed any form of violence by the working class in the
assertion of their rights; and he advocated legal change through the
development of strong organisations such as labour unions. Even
during the most troubled period of labour relations in France from
1906 to 1907, when the Courrières disaster in which 1100 miners
lost their lives dramatically exposed the appalling conditions in the
mines, and Clemenceau sent in troops to suppress the ensuing
strikes, Thomas remained steadfast in his opposition to acts of
sabotage, and even to strikes, which he felt weakened the union
movement.

Thomas's moderation is partially explained by his background.
Born in the Paris suburb of Champigny-sur-Marne in 1878, the son
of a baker, his first-hand experience with the grim realities of the life
of the French industrial working class was extremely limited. His
exceptional intelligence was recognised at an early age, he devoted
himself entirely to his studies, and he succeeded brilliantly. Upon

1. Quoted in Schaper, *Thomas*. The principal sources for the first part of this
chapter are Schaper, *Thomas*; *Albert Thomas 1878–1932* (Annemasse, 1932); and
Albert Thomas vivant (Geneva, 1957).

181

graduation from the *Lycée Michelet*, he won a place in the *Ecole Normal Supérieure* and a trip to Russia, offered by the Grands Express Européens. He stood first in his history class at the University of Paris in 1900, obtained his diploma in history and geography in 1901, and in 1902, came first in the *agrégation*. In the following years, Thomas travelled, spending six months in Germany, tutored Jean Hugo, a descendant of Victor, taught in a girls' school, edited socialist magazines, attended socialist congresses, wrote socialist histories, and frequented socialist salons, but his actual contact with workers and their problems remained tenuous. His initial interest in socialism seems to have been academic, arising from his studies of working-class movements in France since 1830, and from conversations with men like Charles Andler and Arthur Fontaine, whom he met at the *Ecole Normale* and elsewhere. Thomas's socialism was logical, cool and eclectic; he shunned Marx in favour of indigenous French social theorists such as Saint-Simon, Louis Blanc, and Proudhon. He was attracted by 'the socialism of 1848', by the 'integral socialism' of Benoît Malon, and he maintained a great veneration for Michelet. Questions which inspired his contemporaries, such as the relation of the trade union movement to the Socialist party, left him indifferent.

What, then, motivated Thomas? Undoubtedly, he was ambitious and compulsively hard-working. From an early age, he seemed determined to carve out for himself a *belle carrière* in politics, and to this end he chose a path as well worn as that taken by Clémentel. The *Ecole Normale Supérieure* was an acknowledged training ground for politicians: Jaurès, Blum, Painlevé, and Herriot were all graduates. Those who had been to the *Ecole Normale* formed the French equivalent of an old-boy network, and at least four of Thomas's friends from the school followed him into armament production during the war as top advisers, and later into the International Labour Organisation. In this respect, at least, the *République des Camarades* applied to socialists as much as to radicals. Like Clémentel, Thomas took part in local politics, becoming a member of the municipal council of Champigny in 1904, and mayor in 1912. After two unsuccessful attempts in 1908 and 1909, he became deputy of the Seine for the Sceaux district in 1910 at the age of thirty-two. This was the *annus mirabilis* of the Socialists when the number of their deputies elected increased from 55 to 74. Between 1910 and 1914, Thomas was a member of the Public Works, Finance, and Railway Commissions of the Chamber, and he helped shape legislation for stricter mining regulations and for workers' and peasants' pensions. From 1911, he laboured hard and long for the purchase, as opposed to the expropriation, by the state of privately-owned railways.

One of the more equivocal aspects of Thomas's socialism was his personal friendship with a number of leading industrialist families in France. Consider, for example, his relations with the Ménard-Dorian family. During his years at the *Ecole Normale*, he frequented the salon of Mme Ménard-Dorian, whose father had been a gun manufacturer for the 1870 war, and whose husband owned steel mills. From an early age, Thomas had made useful social contacts with members of the *Comité des Forges*, and this at a time when the *Comité* was campaigning vigorously against the social legislation of Millerand, who was, paradoxically, one of Thomas's great heroes. It is unsurprising that with such ubiquitous social tastes, Thomas should have been undogmatic on the vexed question of *ministérialisme*: whether Socialists should participate in governments in which they did not form the majority. Unlike Millerand, Briand, Viviani, and Laval, Thomas never officially abandoned his socialism. Armed with the example of Guesde and Sembat before him, he entered the *Union Sacrée* government in 1915. His participation in a non-socialist government posed no philosophical problems for him. He viewed the question pragmatically, not ideologically, and decided that he could make his most effective contribution to the war effort as a member of the government.

The Organisation of War Production

When the war broke out, after a few weeks' service in a territorial regiment, first as a sergeant, then as a lieutenant and flag-bearer, Thomas was recalled to organise the running of the railways. Acting as a liaison officer between the General Staff and the Ministry of Public Works, he arranged the evacuation of Paris. In October 1914, his old hero Millerand, by now the Minister of War, asked him to take over war production. He immediately set about to rectify the alarming shortage of trained armament workers by having qualified men recalled from military depots by telegram. From October 1914 to May 1915, Thomas toured the country, investigating potential armament plants, and converting and expanding existing automobile and bicycle factories. As for the maintenance of decent working conditions in munitions plants, Thomas took the words of Millerand to heart: 'There are no more workers' rights, no more social laws, there is only the war.' Thomas allowed existing social legislation to be suspended, the limitation on the hours of work to be lifted, and instructed factory inspectors to ignore all abuses. By May 1915, there were 40,000 75 mm. shells being produced in France every day, but this proved far from sufficient, for by now the Army required 100,000.

Until May 1915, armament production in France had been improvised and had been the responsibility of no special bureaucratic body. Once it had become apparent that the war was going to last for some time, however, it was imperative that a separate organisation be created to deal with armaments. The Commissariat section of the Ministry of War, whose tasks had been multiplied to the point that supplies were in danger of breaking down altogether, was subdivided into various under-secretariats, of which one, the Under-Secretariat of State for Artillery and Munitions, was placed under the direction of Albert Thomas. The Under-Secretariat was composed of three bureaux and seventeen sections.[2] For his immediate subordinates, Thomas chose a number of men who had been with him at the *Ecole Normale*, men like Roques, and the economists Simiand and Oualid, who were to exercise a great deal of authority during the course of the war.[3]

'The factory of war and the union of classes.' This caption was placed under a photograph of Thomas visiting the Schneider armament works at Creusot, which appeared in *L'Illustration* shortly after the creation of the Under-Secretariat.[4] The slogan summed up perfectly the logical difficulties inherent in a situation in which a Socialist was asked to play the role of entrepreneur and industrialist. The 'Union of classes' was a verbal conceit which could not disguise the fundamental contradictions in Thomas's position. On the one hand, he was obliged to supply industrialists with the workers they required and ensure that each worker yielded maximum productivity, even if this entailed by-passing existing social legislation. On the other hand, as a Socialist he was expected to defend the interest of the workers. Thomas created a Worker Service to regulate the control of manpower in armament factories. In a circular announcing the imposition of this control by the Under-Secretariat on 15 July 1915, Thomas defined the fundamental aim of the new Service: 'I affirm my wish . . . to keep at the top of the list of my concerns the productivity of our factories, with regard both to quality and quantity'.[5] But at the same time, Thomas had to consider the welfare of the workers. Industrialists were no longer

2. Renouvin, *Formes*, 56.
3. Schaper, *Thomas*, 208.
4. *L'Illustration*, 4 September 1915.
5. Oualid, *La Guerre*, 71.

allowed to go to military depots to select workers, but were required to make their requests through the machinery of the Worker Service. The state would protect the worker, it would make certain that he was equitably paid, and that the conditions of labour were tolerable, insofar as this was compatible with maximum productivity. The inescapable dilemma was reflected in the reports of factory inspectors to the Under-Secretariat. One such typical note reads: 'At the Forges of Foulain, the period of work is 16 hours a day, which is excessive but necessary to ensure the delivery of orders in the required time'.[6] On 31 December 1916, the Under-Secretariat of State for Artillery and Munitions officially became the Ministry of Armament and War Production. This change gave formal recognition to the growing power of the Under-Secretariat in its position as the industrial organisation of the army. Under the decree which provided for its creation,[7] the Minister was responsible for the preparation, production and use of all war materials, and he was given complete power to search out supplies and organise production to this effect. The Minister was charged with the purchasing, manufacturing, supplying, and maintaining of armaments, and with planning for future production on the recommendations of the High Command. All the technical and research facilities required for this task were placed at his disposal. Under Article Three, the Minister was exclusively responsible for making contracts with industrialists on behalf of the various military services. The Minister purchased all the necessary raw materials for war production at home and abroad. He arbitrated between the competing demands for armaments from various bodies and services. He was responsible for promoting military inventions, he had the power to requisition material if necessary, he had the use of all hydraulic power on non-navigable waters, and he controlled all military manpower in war factories. But above all, the Minister of Armament was the link between the government and that sector of private industry which produced war material: 'The Ministry co-ordinates the public services: buyers, consumers, and producers; and the private sector: scientific research, industries, hydraulic power, and manpower.'

On 2 January 1917, a further decree was issued which outlined the organisation of the new Ministry.[8] There were to be two under-secretariats, one for inventions, and one for war production. In addition, six services were to be created to deal with artillery,

6. 94 AP 53: *Rapport mensuel No. 121. . . pour la période du 13 novembre au 13 décembre 1916.*
7. 31 December 1916. *Journal Officiel*, 1 January 1917, 10, 11.
8. *Journal Officiel*, 6 January 1917, 234.

powders, bookkeeping, production, manpower, and technical studies.

The elevation of the Under-Secretariat to the status of a ministry involved a considerable expansion of the powers and functions of the civil servants working under Thomas. For example, there were twenty-two inter-ministerial committees for various raw materials which required the participation of separate representatives from the Ministry of Armament.[9] Some of these committees necessitated the presence of as many as six delegates from the Ministry.

Albert Thomas, Etienne Clémentel and their Ministries

Many similarities can be found between the bureaucratic structures of the Ministry of Commerce and those of the Ministry of Armament, and what has been said of the one often applies equally to the other. But there were fundamental differences between the two in their relations with private industry. In the case of the Ministry of Commerce, the principal point of contact with industry was the power of the Ministry to distribute scarce raw materials. From this single authority, all other relationships flowed: consortia, price fixing, requisitions, and national industries. In the case of the Ministry of Armament, the principal relationship was that of the buyer to the seller. Unlike the Ministry of Commerce, the Ministry of Armaments commissioned industrialists to produce war materials, it signed contracts, it haggled over prices. The basic weapons of the Ministry of Commerce were the withholding of raw materials from an industrialist or the threat of requisitioning his factory. The Ministry of Armament, on the other hand, could refuse to buy from an industrialist, and as the Ministry was the only purchaser of military supplies in the country, this refusal could ruin the industrialist who was heavily committed to war production. The essential difference between the Ministries was one of financial resources; the enormous credits of the Ministry of Armament gave it correspondingly greater power.

Thomas's career as director of French armament production, which ended in September 1917 with the formation of the Painlevé government, was on the whole a successful one. Under his administration, the number of people employed in war industries in France rose from 50,000 in August 1914 to 1.7 million in September 1917. The production of shells for the 75 mm. gun alone increased

9. See Chapter 3.

from 13,500 a day to 212,000, a considerable feat for a country which was as unprepared industrially for war as France in 1914. Similarly, for the 155 mm. shell, production rose from 405 a day to 45,000.[10] To put the French achievement into perspective, in July 1916 the British were producing just over one million shells of all calibres *weekly*.[11] Undoubtedly, there were serious failures in war production. Heavy artillery and aeroplanes were in extremely short supply throughout the war. On the whole, the French placed too much faith in huge stockpiles of light ammunition. Moreover, as will be seen, Thomas made considerable errors of judgement on a number of occasions, and at times, appeared to lose control of situations. By way of contrast, Clémentel's career at the Ministry of Commerce was untarnished by such mistakes, although Thomas was clearly in a more exposed and vulnerable position in supervising armament production. Thomas's enthusiasm and good-will led him to make promises to the Army which he was often unable to keep. In September 1916, the Supreme Council for National Defence, after stressing the need for the production of shells to be increased, felt compelled to remind Thomas to be realistic.

> It is necessary for the Under-Secretary of State not to promise more than realisable possibilities, to prevent the High Command from engaging in operations for which we would not be able to furnish the promised quantities of large shells.
>
> One need only consult the monthly statements of production statistics to observe that each time Monsieur Albert Thomas has made an urgent appeal to industrialists to ask them to make an effort to produce some shell which is required for anticipated operations, the industrialists, understandably, have promised a great deal but have never, for all their good-will and devotion, fulfilled their obligation.[12]

This was a serious charge, for this tendency to make overly-optimistic predictions about armament production could have disastrous military consequences through fundamental miscalculations about available supplies of material.

It is instructive to compare the wartime careers of Clémentel and Thomas. For all his avowed socialism, Thomas never envisaged the war as a potential vehicle of change, either social, economic, or institutional in the way in which Clémentel did. His essentially pragmatic approach to wartime problems prevented him from envisaging any great post-war goals towards which his efforts

10. Schaper, *Thomas*, 111.
11. *History of the Ministry of Munitions* (London, 1922), ii. Part 1, 30.
12. 94 AP 72.

would be continually directed. In terms of social policy and theory, he had little to offer. He talked of 'the socialism of war', or 'the socialism of Le Creusot', this latter a curious juxtaposition of words when one considers the reactionary, paternalistic nature of that great metallurgical complex. It is never clear what he meant by these phrases. Certainly Thomas instituted a number of practical social measures during the war. He created mixed commissions of workers and employers to study such problems as conditions of work, female labour, and hygiene. He encouraged the co-operative movement, so that workers might purchase food and basic consumer goods more cheaply.

But how were these measures to be transferred to the post-war world? One specific issue on which Clémentel and Thomas collaborated was the National Dyes Company. In this case, it was Clémentel who ultimately brought the project to completion, and it is difficult to discern Thomas's exact role in promoting the Company. There are curiously few references in Thomas's papers to his views of the post-war period, except in one dossier.[13] There is evidence that once he had left office, he consulted with a number of people about the form of 'economic socialism' which should exist in France after the war, and that he contemplated the possibility of creating a system whereby all industries would be owned and controlled by three elements: those who provided the capital, those who provided labour, and the state, but this idea remained vague and unelaborated.[14] Thomas devoted more thought to the problem of nationalisation. He distinguished between an enterprise being nationalised 'in the general interest of the national collectivity', of which he approved, and nationalisation being carried out in the name of 'the interests of the state government', of which he disapproved. Industries would be governed by three groups: the producers, which consisted of trade unions of workers and engineers unions; the consumers, as represented by co-operative societies, chambers of commerce, and professional associations of producers; and the state. Nationalised firms would be semi-autonomous bodies over which the state would have but little control. This was to encourage financial responsibility. 'Experience has proved it: the possibility that a firm might go bankrupt is the beginning of wisdom.' The state would merely receive its share of the profits and ensure that the prices charged by the company were just. This

---

13. 94 AP 366: *Socialisme économique; le Monopole des pétroles. Bénéfices de guerre; assurances (1917–1919).*
14. 94 AP 366: *Note sur l'Après-Guerre. Conversation avec M. de Verneuil,* 8 November 1917.

concept of the total administrative and financial independence of nationalised firms was extremely important, for it was the principle which guided the creation of the Arsenal of Roanne.

Thus, unlike that of Clémentel, Thomas's vision of post-war France was limited to one or two vague ideas which were never fully elaborated and for whose implementation no plans were laid. But there were also fundamental differences of approach in solving the immediate problems of the war which separated the two men. These differences in part resulted from the particular nature and interests of the respective ministries to which the two men were assigned. One issue over which they were in total disagreement was the problem of the importation of scarce raw materials. Thomas, quite naturally, was concerned that as much of this material as possible should be employed in armament manufacture. Clémentel, on the other hand, had to defend the interests of industrialists producing non-military goods, and was therefore determined to prevent the Ministry of Armament controlling completely all supplies of raw materials. As a consequence of this difference of interests, a difference in policy developed between the two ministries. The president of the Interministerial Commission for Wood and Metals, Gaillard, a bureaucrat from the Ministry of Armament, contrasted the two policies in the following way:

> The thesis of the Ministry of Commerce is entirely different from that of the Ministry of Armament. The Ministry of Commerce is of the opinion that the moment a product becomes scarce, the gates must be opened wide to all imports, while, on the other hand, we believe that it is preferable in such a situation to prohibit imports, not so that they will be diminished, but in order that they may be supervised in such a manner as to obtain the best possible distribution of imported materials and to avoid at the same time increased prices abroad, which would be disastrous for the Treasury.[15]

What the officials of the Ministry of Armament implied by the word 'supervision' was that they alone should control the distribution of raw materials. The alternative 'open door' policy of the Ministry of Commerce did not mean unrestricted freedom of commerce, but rather that the two ministries should share in the control of raw materials. In truth, the Ministry of Commerce also subscribed to the method of a general ban on imports, with a bureaucratic body to provide for exemptions, but it believed that this body should come

15. 94 AP 110: *Commission interministérielle des bois et des métaux, Procès-verbal de la séance du 28 mars 1917.*

under its jurisdiction rather than that of the Ministry of Armament.

This rivalry between the two ministries was well illustrated by a dispute over the constitution and functions of the Interministerial Commission for Wood and Metals. Trouble arose over the question of whether or not the Ministry of Commerce had a guaranteed right to a certain portion of imported metal which it would redistribute to hard-pressed domestic industries. On 3 October 1916, Clémentel sent a strong protest to Thomas about the proposal of the Commission to suppress 'all imports which are not strictly necessary for National Defence'. Clémentel said that the decree creating the Interministerial Commission had been designed to furnish both ministries with vital imported materials, and that the decision to restrict imports to those necessary for war production was a flagrant abuse of the agreements signed by the two ministries. He warned Thomas that unless the two of them came to some arrangement, he would be forced to raise the issue at the Council of Ministers, and in the event of his failing to obtain a firm assurance that domestic industries would continue to be supplied with raw materials, he would immediately resign his ministry. Clémentel cited the example of the firm of Pleyel which needed only 800 kilos of metal to complete 1,200 pianos. Only since the beginning of the war had French industry succeeded in its efforts to manufacture many of the products formerly supplied in great quantities by Germany, but this industrial renaissance had been placed in great jeopardy by the shortage of vital raw materials. Clémentel therefore asked Thomas to recant and to assure the Minister of Commerce of a minimum contingent of at least 15,000 tons of imported metal a month, an amount which would not have to be verified by the Interministerial Commission.[16] Defenders of the Commission replied that an overall control of metal had to be maintained, otherwise the problem of supply would become insoluble. Only the Commission had the power to impose such control. The question of which ministry controlled the Commission was glossed over.[17]

On 8 March 1917, Clémentel wrote Thomas to remind him once again that the Council of Ministers had agreed that the Ministry of Commerce should have a share of imported materials in order to prevent the ruin of all non-military industrial production, particularly that of agricultural machinery. Clémentel went on to protest against the creation of commercial committees attached exclusively

16. 94 AP 110: Clémentel to Thomas, 3 October 1916.
17. 94 AP 110: *Observations sommaires du Colonel Costes sur la lettre du Ministre du Commerce.*

to the Ministry of Armament, such as the Interministerial Commission. The Council of Ministers had agreed that both ministries should share in the creation of such committees, and that as it was presently constituted, the Interministerial Commission belied its name.[18]

This dispute between Clémentel and Thomas was in part an argument between two advocates on behalf of their respective clients, the one defending the interests of private non-military industry, the other the interests of the army. Yet there was also the element of a power struggle between the two men on behalf of their respective bureaucrats. For Clémentel, the question of which ministry controlled the Interministerial Commission for Wood and Metals was every bit as important as defending the rights of non-military industrialists. The two issues were inextricably linked, since by obtaining more authority within the Commission, the Minister of Commerce would be in a better position to defend the rights of his industrialists, but there was the additional aspect of personal rivalry and prestige which was also involved. The struggle between bureaucrats and industrialists during the war should not obscure the parallel struggles which were being waged between rival groups of bureaucrats, and ultimately between rival politicians, for greater power. The differences between Thomas and Clémentel were in part founded on rival claims for authority.

Thomas's Vulnerability

There were also profound psychological differences between the two men which ultimately found expression in their respective careers. Throughout the war, Thomas was subject to pressures which Clémentel never knew. The strain of being a Socialist while performing the functions of a capitalist as director of the nation's wartime industrial programme undoubtedly left its mark on Thomas. He was attacked throughout the war by both the Left and the Right on a whole range of issues. He was accused by the Left of failing to defend the interests of the armament workers under his jurisdiction sufficiently. He was accused of selling out to the industrialists. He was attacked for being too sympathetic to Kerenski and the provisional government in Russia, and not sympathetic enough to the Bolsheviks. He was criticised for defending the old-fashioned concept of nationalities forming their own states in

18. 94 AP 110: Clémentel to Thomas, 8 March 1917.

central and eastern Europe instead of being more concerned with
the social problems in these areas.[19]

But it was the Right which really heaped fire and brimstone upon
him, particularly after he left office. He was accused of dealing with
the enemy in Switzerland,[20] of buying a château on the profits of his
period of office,[21] of prolonging the war eighteen months in order
to make even more money, of collaborating with 'the Jew Citroën'
to make enormous profits,[22] and of being entirely responsible for
the high cost of living, since he had raised the salaries of armament
workers.[23]

The attacks came from all quarters. In the police archives, there is
a series of reports from informers on the source of subsidies for
various newspapers. One such police 'correspondent' claimed in
1919 that Albert Thomas distributed money given him by the
Banque Demachy to the smaller newspapers of the boulevards to
buy for himself more sympathetic publicity.[24] As the Banque Demachy was the bank of the *Comité des Forges*, the charge, if true,
was sensational. Thomas, the Socialist, former Minister of Armament, was using money provided by metallurgical interests to
further his own career. But Thomas came under such heavy fire
from all sides that charges like these merely form a small part of the
general, unsubstantiated stream of abuse to which he was constantly
subjected. There were reports emanating from as far away as New
York that Thomas had been greatly enriched by the war, that he was
compromised in the Goldsoll scandal,[25] and had been involved with
Caillaux and Malvy into the bargain.[26]

Thomas's position in the *Union Sacrée* government was also
extremely insecure. The details of his failure to be reappointed as
Minister of Armament in September 1917 are still obscure, but the
ostensible reason for his departure was his objection to the placing
of the anti-socialist Ribot at the Ministry of Foreign Affairs, when

19. These, and the accusations which follow, can all be found in the dossier 94 AP
	362: *Attaques de gauche, attaques de droite.*
20. *Démocratie Nouvelle*, 4 October 1918.
21. *Démocratie Nouvelle*, 5 October 1918.
22. *Le Reveil de l'Auxois*, 18 November 1919.
23. *L'Avenir*, 11 July 1919.
24. F7 12, 842: Report F. 5, 444. 8 February 1919.
25. 94 AP 157: Frank Goldsoll, born in Cleveland, Ohio in 1874, started a chain of
	theatres and shops in Germany, went into the film industry in France, and
	eventually emigrated to the United States, where he acted as a purchasing agent
	for lorries on behalf of the French government, and embezzled 3.5 million
	dollars in the process.
26. 94 AP 417: Martellet to Thomas, New York, 25 August 1918.

Painlevé formed his new government on 10 September.[27] Attacked by Clemenceau, reputedly despised by Foch, linked unjustly with Malvy, undermined by his subordinate Loucheur, Thomas's life at the Ministry of Armament was never easy.

Thomas also had a capacity for arousing passionate popular resentment and even hatred for his continuing support of the government as the working class became increasingly disenchanted with the war. There is a whole dossier in the archives of insulting letters and threats on his life. Again, the abuse came from all sides. Telegrams, postcards, letters, stickers, posters, pamphlets, and cartoons poured into the Ministry, universally hostile, often to the point of violence.[28] Letters arrived addressed to 'Monsieur Albert Thomas, Minister of Armament, Friend of War Profiteers, Accomplice of French Bolsheviks', or to 'Thomas, Political Joker, Thug of Big Business, Great Dupe of all the Russias'. Thomas was accused of favouring the workers at the expense of the soldiers. One soldier described the workers as: 'Lazy, drunk, saboteurs, and lustful; since they have returned from the front, using the pretext of the high cost of living, they have not ceased to demand increased salaries'.[29] Alternatively, Thomas was called an enemy of the workers because he was prepared to send some of them back to the front. He was blamed for every aspect of government policy, including calling up the classes of 1914, 1915, and 1916. There were pathetic letters, often badly-spelled and written in a semi-illegible scrawl, from mothers who had lost one or more sons.

> Monsieur I ask you what hatred you can have in your heart against our poor children, you keep saying the young men must be slaughtered first, don't you find enough of the classes of '14, '15, and '16 have fallen already, why the young rather than the old, it seems to me that men of 40 or 50 have lived and had a good life which the young ones will never have because you are having them all hacked to pieces . . .[30]

And throughout all the letters, the constant refrain that he was profiting from the war, a charge for which no evidence exists whatever.

Under such tremendous, unceasing pressure, it would have been astonishing if Thomas had not felt the strain. A man beset upon by enemies, betrayed by subordinates, a man with few natural political

27. Schaper, *Thomas*, 155–9. See Chapter 2.
28. 94 AP 155.
29. 2 August 1917.
30. 27 November 1916.

allies, lacking the trust in a doctrine or ideology which might have given him a clearer indication of what he was to do, Thomas began to lose his nerve at the end of his period of office at the Ministry of Armament. As several of his projects went disastrously astray, as the attacks of his enemies mounted, Thomas began to lose not only his self-confidence but his sense of judgement. Nowhere is this sense of failure and uncertainty better conveyed than in a letter he wrote to General Gamelin on 18 March 1918.

I am envious of you. At the front one's duty is simpler, and one is aware of a sense of total accomplishment. The life of those at the rear, and especially in political life, is more complicated, and one always has the bitter feeling of not being able to accomplish all that one should.[31]

When Thomas began his organisation of war material production in 1915, his admirers called him 'the Joffre of our factories'. As the war dragged on, the appellation came to have a sad, ironic fitness which its originators could never have foreseen.

Louis Loucheur

A greater contrast with Albert Thomas could hardly be found than in the person of Louis Loucheur. Born in Roubaix in 1872, Loucheur's family background was more prosperous than that of Thomas; his father was an architect, albeit undistinguished. Like Thomas, he did well at school, winning a scholarship to the *Lycée* at Lille. After graduating as an engineer from the *Ecole Polytechnique*, he joined the Chemins du fer du Nord, controlled by the Rothschilds, in 1893. In 1899 he and Alexandre Giros, a friend from the *Ecole Polytechnique*, founded a construction firm, Girolou. Loucheur specialised in electricity and won several important contracts to build electrical plants. In 1908 Loucheur and Giros formed the Société Générale des Entreprises to raise the capital necessary to undertake more ambitious construction projects. The company founded several sizeable local electricity companies, such as Energie Eléctrique du Nord de la France, and also built dams and tramway networks. In 1909 the firm began building local railways, such as that for Haute-Vienne. In 1910 Loucheur extended his activities abroad and was commissioned to build 9,000 kilometres of railway in Turkey. The following year, he won a contract to bring elec-

31. 94 AP 415.

tricity to Turkey, and he formed a financial consortium for the purposes of building public utilities in Morocco. In 1913, he formed a Russian subsidiary. In 1914, he had railway projects in Italy, Spain, Macedonia, and Thrace, and he was contracted to build a power station in St Petersburg. In short, Louis Loucheur was the very incarnation of rugged, expansionist, free enterprise.[32]

When war broke out, he was attached to the artillery as a lieutenant, but as his biographer comments on the entries in his diary during this period: 'We feel the presence of the man who vibrates with each pulsation of France at war. No, Loucheur could not remain a simple artillery officer'.[33] And indeed, he did not. He returned to his office at the Société Générale des Entreprises and began to build armament factories. He built two factories which produced 155 mm. and 220 mm. guns, in association with Schneider et Cie. Loucheur was one of the first industrialists to use female labour in arms factories, and he also introduced modern methods of assembly-line production. In July 1915, Loucheur and Louis Renault formed a partnership to manufacture shells.[34] Loucheur also carried out research into the possibility of making poison gas.[35]

It was one of the principal subsidiaries of the Société Générale des Entreprises, Eclairage Eléctrique, which specialised in armament production during the war. From all accounts, Eclairage Eléctrique reaped vast profits during the years Albert Thomas was in charge of armament production. An analysis of two contracts for shell fuses signed by the government, one with Eclairage Eléctrique, the other with Hervais, a firm in Clermont-Ferrand, in 1916, reveals that the prices charged by the former were at least 78 per cent higher than those charged by the latter.[36]

Like so many other industrialists, Loucheur had gone into armament production with a total lack of experience in the field, with no suitable factories, and little money. His munitions empire was to be built up entirely with the use of government advances. He built factories at Suresne, Lyon, Blanc-Pignon, Pont de Claix, Baux-Roux, Paris, and Saint-Ouen. His relations with Albert Thomas during this period were strictly those of buyer to seller. Like other industrialists, he had a tendency to promise more than he could

32. Louis Loucheur, *Carnets secrets 1908–1932*, ed. Jacques de Launay (Bruxelles, 1962).
33. Ibid., 17.
34. 94 AP 53: *Rapport du Sous-secrétariat d'Etat*, 2 July 1915.
35. Beau de Lomenie, *La Guerre*, 81.
36. 94 AP 74: *Rapport No. 53 du Contrôleur de l'ère classe Gache ... sur les marchés de fusées d'obus*, 30 December 1916.

deliver. In August 1915, Milliès-Lacroix, reporter of the Finance Commission of the Senate, wrote to Loucheur to complain that he had undertaken to produce 1.8 million shells and had delivered only 228,000.[37] Loucheur replied that there had been technical changes in the type of shell produced, steel was in short supply and of poor quality, there was not enough available labour, and there were no supplies coming in from Le Havre.[38] During the same period, Thomas wrote to Loucheur to propose some limitation on the profits of Eclairage Eléctrique. There were sharp exchanges in 1915 about the price Loucheur was charging for shell casings.

> The Société d'Eclairage Eléctrique complains of delays caused by shortages of materials and insists on a corresponding postponement of delivery dates . . . We reply that the high prices granted to the supplier are designed to cover the various risks resulting from the events of war and from the difficulties and assorted risks of production during a period of this nature, which are no grounds for giving this industrialist more favourable conditions in this respect than to the rest.[39]

There is other evidence to suggest that Loucheur tried to obtain special favours for Eclairage Eléctrique which Thomas refused to grant. In one letter, Thomas told him: 'It would be impossible to treat you, as you suggest, as an equal of the arsenals of the state, and your firm can only be dealt with under the same conditions as other factories'.[40] Thus even at this stage of the war, relations between the two men were not altogether harmonious. They were to become even less so in the future.

On 12 December 1916, Loucheur resigned his position as head of the Société Générale des Entreprises and its affiliated companies. In the words of his hagiographer: 'At the age of 44, he sacrificed all his past achievements, a career which he loved and to which he had devoted 25 years. Thus he abandoned all hope of an extraordinarily brilliant future in order that he might serve the more.'[41] Up to this point in the war Loucheur had been careful to cultivate useful contacts in governmental circles. His opportunity to exploit these contacts came when he lunched with Briand, the President of the Council of Ministers, on 7 December 1916. Briand asked him what he thought of Albert Thomas. Loucheur replied in the best 'Brutus is an honourable man' tradition.

37. 94 AP 76: Milliès-Lacroix to Loucheur, 19 August 1915.
38. 94 AP 76: Loucheur to Milliès-Lacroix, 3 September 1915.
39. 94 AP 53: *Rapport du Sous-secrétariat d'Etat*, 13 August 1915.
40. 94 AP 76: Thomas to Loucheur, August 1915.
41. Loucheur, *Carnets*, 18.

I praised him fulsomely, I recalled his hard work, his patriotism, his luminous mind, but I referred at the same time to his weaknesses, which he owes to his connections from the past. I indicated that Claveille had utterly failed with him because he never wants to delegate authority; he was almost jealous of Claveille. He is a weak authoritarian.[42]

Briand was anxious to keep Thomas at his post, but he used the occasion of the creation of the Ministry of Armament at the end of the same month to make Loucheur an Under-Secretary of State within the Ministry, responsible for war production. Loucheur insisted on almost total autonomy from the Ministry, and he also demanded a seat for himself on the War Council.

From this moment on, it seems clear that Loucheur was actively plotting for Thomas's overthrow. Loucheur became friendly with Clemenceau, and at the same time, he made suggestions to Painlevé: 'I told him that in my opinion Thomas should be made a minister without portfolio, responsible for foreign relations, going off to negotiate with the English, the Russians, the Americans'.[43] In other words, the further away from France the better. Loucheur was too modest to suggest any possible successor to Thomas at the Ministry of Armament. Meanwhile, he persistently undermined the authority of his minister by discreetly campaigning for a harder line on munitions workers in particular, and labour troubles in general. As we shall see, there is evidence to suggest that his role in the *débâcle* of the Arsenal of Roanne was not altogether creditable.

When in September 1917, Painlevè was preparing his ministry, he asked Loucheur to take the Ministry of Food. Loucheur refused and was duly offered the Ministry of Armament, which he accepted. The poacher had turned gamekeeper, and in some ways, Loucheur's period of office was more successful than that of his predecessor. By his background and disposition, Loucheur fitted more nearly the mould of an ideal Minister of Armament. Unhampered by political connections or obligations to any political party, experienced in the world of business and industry, Loucheur ran the Ministry like a large company. By nature an authoritarian, Loucheur did not hesitate to use the full power of the state against his former fellow industrialists. Paradoxically, the great free enterpriser proved in some ways to be a more enthusiastic advocate of state intervention than his socialist predecessor. As Henri Hauser, one of Clémentel's chief collaborators, commented in 1918:

42. Ibid., 22. Claveille was director of French railways during the war and a member of the Contract Commission.
43. Ibid., 38.

We appointed a very big industrialist to be the head of several of these great services of the state, and people said that state intervention was at an end. But what did this big industrialist do as soon as he became minister? Immediately, in the interests of the nation, he imposed a discipline on French industry which was infinitely more severe than the timid parliamentarians of the previous regime would have dared imagine.[44]

Both Clémentel and Loucheur shared the view that the government should tell each industrialist exactly what he was to do, and that the industrialist should be allowed to do nothing other than this one specific task. This was *dirigisme* with a vengeance.

Loucheur applied industrial techniques to the running of the Ministry of Armament. He introduced a method of cost analysis based on his own experience as an armament manufacturer. He was able to lower the prices which industrialists charged for armaments by comparing the manufacturing costs of various products produced by the Société de l'Eclairage de Lyon, and Thomas-Houston,[45] two firms with which he had previously been associated. This did little to increase his popularity in industrial circles, but it helped lower prices. Loucheur also took a firmer line on labour unrest. At a conference on 6 October 1917 with armament manufacturers, he announced that he intended to maintain good relations with workers and to guarantee them reasonable salaries, but that it was only fair to the troops at the front that mobilised workers in munitions plants should be expected to do their duty and forbidden to strike.[46]

While Loucheur was Minister of Armament, his old company, the Société Générale des Entreprises, was by no means idle. Indeed, it was claimed after the war by the deputy Edouard Barthe that the Société Générale made a profit of 2 million francs in the month of March 1918 alone.[47] Loucheur merely scoffed at the charge.

After the war, Loucheur became Minister of Industrial Reconstruction. Again, there are suggestions that the line which separated his public and business careers at times became blurred. While Loucheur ran the Ministry, Giros, his business associate, ran the Société Générale, which profited handsomely from the reconstruction of the post-war period. Giros created two companies for this purpose, the Société d'Etudes et de Travaux, and the Société de Reconstruction des Usines Sinistrées.[48] This parallel interest in

44. *Le Musée sociale*, no. 3, 1 May 1918, 75.
45. Loucheur, *Carnets*, 29.
46. Ibid., 45.
47. *Chambre des députés*, 24 January 1919, 205.
48. Beau de Loménie, *La Guerre*, 213.

reconstruction may have been purely coincidental, but the least one can say is that Loucheur does not appear to have been over-sensitive to the possible accusation of conflict of interest.

Thus armament production in France was successively directed by two men whose pre-war careers, political affiliations, and administrative approaches were poles apart. For reasons of available archival material, we shall concentrate for the most part on relations between industrialist and the bureaucrats of the Under-Secretariat and Ministry during Albert Thomas's tenure of office, but Louis Loucheur will always be found lurking in the background.

CHAPTER 7

Bureaucrats versus Industrialists: Struggles, Profits and Scandals

Bureaucrats versus Shell Producers

The power of the bureaucrats of the Under-Secretariat of State for Artillery and Munitions stemmed from the vast financial resources placed at their disposal with which they were to procure all the arms and equipment necessary to maintain the French Army in the field. It was to these bureaucrats that industrialists who wished to produce war material were forced to apply. Given the nature of this buyer-seller relationship between bureaucrats and industrialists, the question of contracts came to assume paramount importance.

The Contract Commission

A standard procedure for examining contracts gradually evolved at the Under-Secretariat. In September 1915, Albert Thomas sent out a circular to announce the creation of a five-man Contract Commission. Any contract signed by the Under-Secretary worth more than 50,000 francs was to be submitted first to the Contract Commission and then to the legal department of the Under-Secretariat. Both the Commission and the legal department were to give their approval within eight days if the contract appeared acceptable. If either body raised objections, the Under-Secretary himself was to make the final decision. To facilitate the work of the Commission, the various services within the Under-Secretariat were ordered to reduce the different kinds of contracts passed to a few standard models.[1]

1. 94 AP 69: *Circular*, 7 September 1915.

The creation of a Contract Commission by no means resolved all the problems relating to contracts. In 1917, Perchot, a left-leaning Radical-Socialist senator from the Lower Alps, a scientist with a background in industry, and a parliamentary specialist in economic questions, delivered a blistering criticism of the operating methods of the Contract Commission for determining prices.[2] The establishment of the Commission had made scarcely any impact on the enormous profits of arms producers. For example, instead of taking the cost-price of producing 75 mm. shells as the basis for determining the price to be paid to manufacturers, the Commission had chosen a large contract with a major metallurgical firm as typical, reasoning in the following way. First, the officers of this company, who were honourable men, had affirmed that under this particular contract, worth 92 million francs, the firm had made only a normal profit. Secondly, the Commission compared the price paid under this contract with the cost-price of producing the same shell in a state arsenal and discovered a difference of 75 per cent. Conclusion: the normal profit which the state should pay shell manufacturers was 75 per cent. 'The syllogism, gentlemen, is elegant, but the interests of the Treasury are but weakly defended.'

Meetings of Shell Producers and Bureaucrats

Another forum in which bureaucrats and industrialists met were the various meetings held to discuss problems of mutual interest with regard to the production of certain materials. One of the most important of these series of meetings was that held to discuss the production of large shells. Nothing conveys more vividly the stresses and strains in the relationship between industrialists and bureaucrats than the minutes of these meetings.[3] Many of the main points of dispute between them were aired at these meetings, and it is therefore worth examining some of the questions which were discussed. The first meeting was held on 28 May 1915, shortly after the creation of the Under-Secretariat. Albert Thomas presided over the meeting, supported by three generals who had been seconded to the new Under-Secretariat, as well as by other bureaucrats. The industrialists were also fully represented. After the spokesmen for the various armament manufacturers gave a report on the production, both actual and anticipated, of shells to date, the real debate began. In this first meeting, for example, the question of sub-

2. *Sénat*, 28 March 1917, 330.
3. These can be found in 94 AP 72 and cover a period of time from May 1915 to March 1916.

contractors was raised. One industrialist said he could increase his production of shells if he were given the authorisation to sub-contract part of the work to several firms in Nantes, to which one of the bureaucrats replied that most of these firms were totally incapable of doing the work required. In the end, the matter was resolved by a compromise whereby only reliable firms would be used for sub-contracting and smaller firms would be excluded.

Shell Prices

Unsurprisingly, the major topic of discussion at these meetings was prices. In one meeting,[4] Ferry, an industrialist representing the firm of Ferry-Capitain, complained of the inequality of the prices which the government paid for 90 mm. shells. There was a difference of 40 per cent, to his disadvantage, between the price which he had been paid and the price which certain other firms had been paid. Like the labourers in the vineyard who arrived early in the morning, he did not dispute that he had been paid fairly at the agreed price, but he resented the fact that other firms had done even better, and for this reason alone, he demanded an upward revision of the price for shells stipulated in his original contract. On behalf of the government, Colonel Chevillot observed that the prices were different because the contracts had been signed at different times and under different conditions, and he reminded Ferry that no industrialist had been forced to sign any contract. Albert Thomas added that any uniform price for the same product would be even more unfair, and that the difference in price probably reflected a difference in cost-price. Ferry insisted that in view of the satisfactory production of his factory, he ought to be paid a higher price for his shells in any case, but his request does not appear to have been granted.

In August 1915, outside the regular meetings, Léon-Lévy, representing the firm of Chatillon, Commentry, et Neuves-Maisons, raised the important issue of revising the price of shells, particularly of 155 mm. shells, in the light of the increased cost of raw materials.[5] The bureaucrats of the Under-Secretariat counter-attacked by proposing that any revision of prices should also take into account other considerations, such as the fact that earlier prices paid for shells had been designed to compensate the industrialist for the costs of building new installations, costs which were now completely amortised. Under Colonel Chevillot, the bureaucrats set

4. 25 June 1915.
5. 94 AP 53: *Rapport du Sous-secrétariat d'Etat du 5 Août 1915.*

to work establishing the cost-price of producing various shells. If necessary, the results of their findings should be made public, they believed, to enlist popular support against the industrialists. Later in the month, General Bourgeois drew up plans to create a consultative commission comprised of industrialists and bureaucrats to discuss the revision of prices.[6]

Insufficient Shell Production

Soon after the meetings between shell-producers and bureaucrats were instituted, the problem of insufficient production — inextricably linked with the problem of the revision of prices — increasingly began to dominate discussions. At a meeting at the end of August 1915,[7] after the reports on shell production had been read out, Thomas expressed his regrets at the insignificant progress that had been made during the month in achieving a higher rate of production of large calibre shells. Not nearly enough 220 mm. shells had been produced, and as for 155 mm. shells, industrialists had pledged themselves to deliver 2,240 a day during the month, but in fact had produced only 1,800. Now they promised to produce 2,500 a day during September, when 12,000 a day were required. Robert Pinot, the Secretary-General of the *Comité des Forges*, replied soothingly that he was sure that industrialists would respond to the Under-Secretary's appeal to increase production, in the interests of the National Defence, and he terminated his remarks by saying that industrialists would 'leave the question of prices which have been submitted to the Under-Secretary entirely to his sense of fair play.'[8]

It was clear that the matter of the revision of prices was far from settled. At a subsequent meeting of industrialists in August 1915, Thomas partially capitulated over price revision and announced that in view of the increasing cost of raw materials, the price paid for 75 mm. shells would be increased when current short-term contracts with manufacturers were renewed. Thomas drew attention to the obvious correlation between the poor response of industrialists in producing certain shells, notably the 155 mm. shell, and the apparent low price currently paid by the state for this shell, and he said that these prices would also be increased. He concluded on a note of wistful thinking, which echoed the remarks of Robert Pinot the previous day:

6. 94 AP 53: *Rapport du S.S.E. du 21 Août 1915.*
7. 27 August 1915.
8. 27 August 1915.

The Under-Secretary of State asked industrialists to have confidence in his spirit of fair play for all these questions, and he appealed to their sense of patriotism to prevent any slow-down in their production, to the detriment of the needs of National Defence.[9]

In the meantime Thomas's bureaucrats were casting about for a means of increasing productivity while at the same time satisfying the seemingly insatiable demands of the industrialists for greater profits. One such solution was proposed by a young engineer named Hugoniot, one of Thomas's chief advisers, and a man whom we shall be meeting later in a different context. He suggested that a system of premiums be created whereby industrialists would be given extra money if they achieved a greater production than had been specified in their contract, while reducing to a minimum the number of mobilised workers they employed. Hugoniot admitted that there were drawbacks to the scheme: 'It must be said that this system of premiums will favour large industry at the expense of small, but I believe, in all good conscience, that this is the only practical way of achieving greater productivity'.[10] The system would also be cheaper than importing shells from England.

By October 1915, Thomas had come to the conclusion that industrialists were trying to blackmail him over prices. It had been suggested at one of the meetings that in view of the enormous profits which shell manufacturers were making that prices by adjusted downwards:

> During the course of a survey which has been started on this subject, certain remarks have been made and certain industrialists . . . seem to have declared themselves unwilling to continue production if the prices paid up to the present were diminished. The Under-Secretary of State does not want to believe that such words have been uttered.[11]

Nevertheless, he hastened to assure industrialists that for the moment no such reduction was contemplated, and therefore, industrialists should under no circumstances reduce production. Once again it was Robert Pinot, speaking on behalf of the *Comité des Forges*, who poured oil over the troubled waters. He was sure that these reports of what industrialists had been saying were exaggerated, and he proposed that certain administrative changes be made to centralise demands for raw materials and to work out a more

9. 28 August 1915.
10. E. Hugoniot, *Rapport du Service industriel*, 28 August 1915.
11. 1 October 1915.

equitable method of determining prices. But the honeyed words of Robert Pinot in no way solved the problem. A month later, one of the officers working under Thomas, General Dumézil, complained that industrialists were still not producing shells of calibres from 274 mm. to 400 mm. in any quantity. One of the industrialists replied that this was because of uncertainty over prices. Robert Pinot pointed out that industrialists were merely being logical in the choice of shells they produced

> since each industrialist has the choice of several calibres which the services wish to be built and naturally takes those which seem to present the least difficulty in producing and for which there is the least difference in price between his estimate and that of the Ironworks Administration [Direction des Forges].[12]

Meanwhile, outside the framework of these meetings, the bureaucrats of the Under-Secretariat were still wrestling with the problem of curbing excessive prices. In December 1915 they were busy at work preparing a law which was ostensibly designed to oblige industrialists to declare their stocks of material but which also contained provisions to limit prices. The authors of the law said that the period of improvisation, during which industrialists had obtained high prices to cover the risks involved in building and expanding their plants, was at an end. Now that war production had been organised on a regular basis, the great risks no longer existed, and producers had a guaranteed market, so that the state should proceed to a methodical revision of all contracts and all prices. The Contract Commission had attempted to carry out this policy and had succeeded in the case of certain products, such as aluminium. The law provided not only for the revision of prices paid by the government, but also for the prices paid by private firms for metal repurchased from the great metallurgical companies, since the smaller firms were often working indirectly for the state.[13]

But try as they might, the bureaucrats could not force down prices. The laws of supply and demand proved stronger than any legislation they could devise, and they were forced to continue to grant favourable conditions to the industrialists in the interest of maintaining production. By the beginning of 1916, the appeals of Thomas to industrialists to make a new effort to increase production had become virtually ritualistic, as had the responses of the industrialists: 'Monsieur Cavallier asked, for his own part, that the

12. 26 November 1915.
13. 94 AP 347: 2 December 1915.

Under-Secretary of State himself attempt to obtain from the Ministry of War a new effort to furnish the manpower which was still required'.[14]

Government Loans and Advances

Another major topic of discussion at these meetings was the problem of government loans to industrialists to finance the expansion of old factories or the construction of new ones. This issue has already been encountered with regard to the chemical industry, and in particular, Saint-Gobain, but in the case of shell producers, the government appears to have taken a more aggressive attitude. As early as August 1915, for example, when the Consortium du Nord, a group of munitions manufacturers, asked for a loan, Colonel Chevillot, one of the leading bureaucrats of the Under-Secretariat, insisted on more information about the intentions of the group and the regularisation of its constitution before granting any loan.[15] Previously, however, loans had flowed from the Under-Secretariat like water. From October to December 1914, Loucheur's company, the Eclairage Eléctrique, had received a total of 6,714,132 francs in advances. On 8 February 1915, André Citroën received a single loan of 6 million francs. Louis Renault received 3.48 million francs in March, while Delaunay-Belleville received 7.3 million francs. Relatively unknown firms did equally well; the Société des Forces Motrices et Usines de l'Avre netted a colossal 18.07 million francs between January and September 1915. Long lists of other industrialists who were granted similar sums could also be cited. Rates of interest were extremely favourable to industrialists and they could take up to ten years to repay.[16]

In December 1915, the Ministry of War announced its intention to insert in all future contracts with industrialists in which loans were involved a clause to the effect that the state would have the option of repurchasing factories whose construction it had, in effect, subsidised through generous contracts.[17] This provoked a vigorous reaction on the part of the industrialists, led by Léon-Lévy. Léon-Lévy grouped factories producing war materials under three headings. The first were factories which had existed before the war and which had been modified and extended to enable them to execute war contracts. For these factories, Léon-Lévy said, any

14. 26 January 1916.
15. 94 AP 53: *Rapport du S.S.E. du 3 Juillet 1915.*
16. 94 AP 71: *Avances aux industriels 1915–1917.*
17. 30 December 1915.

repurchase clause would be a nonsense, because the state could not take over a fraction of the plant. In any case, the tooling machinery of armament plants was rapidly worn out, and the state would be obliged to replace all the machinery at the end of the war before plants could resume their normal activity.

The second category were factories in territory currently occupied by the Germans. In this case, the state had helped the industrialists to buy equipment to replace that which had been stolen by the enemy in order that production might be resumed as quickly as possible once the territory had been liberated. It made even less sense for the state to have the right to purchase these factories, since this would hinder the rapid economic recovery of the occupied zone.

In the third category consisted of factories which were entirely new and had been created specifically to fulfil war contracts. Here, Léon-Lévy admitted, the state had a better case, but he objected to the mechanism by which the operation would be carried out. Specifically, he cited the problem of the date at which the state would take over the plants and the resulting uncertainty and financial risk involved. If the state still insisted on repurchasing this third group of factories, then it should be prepared to subsidise construction costs entirely. Finally, said Léon-Lévy, for all three categories of factory, industrialists had a right to complain that this power of repurchase was a completely new element in negotiations between industrialists and the state, that industrialists had received no warning of this possibility when they had originally bid for contracts or built new factories, and that it was impossible to apply such a measure.

Claveille, the director of the state railways and a member of the Contract Commission, replied on behalf of the government. In the first place, this repurchase clause would not be applied retroactively to contracts already signed. The chief motive behind the framing of this clause was to find some formula which would compensate for the present situation in which industrialists were able to amortize the cost of expanding their plans completely with their first contract, so that when contracts were renewed on the same conditions, they were receiving an unwarranted bonus for material which had already been amortized. Claveille also insisted that the value of plants should be assessed at the moment contracts were signed, with a view to calculating their eventual worth in the event of purchase by the state. Only in this way would the interests of the state be protected. Léon-Lévy strongly opposed such a step, declaring that industrialists could never calculate accurately the expenses which would be involved in building or expanding their plants at the moment when they signed a contract with the state, and that any attempted calculation might lead to grave injustices. The repurchase clause became a dead letter.

Penalties

The last major question to be discussed at these meetings of bureau-crats and shell-makers were the penalties which industrialists were to pay in the event of their failure to fulfil contractual obligations with the state. The question was raised in June 1915 at one of the earliest meetings of the group by General Bourgeois, who outlined a scheme prepared by Louis Loucheur which provided for a system-atic check of lots of 200 shells.[18] If more than a certain percentage were found to be defective, each shell in the entire shipment would be checked individually, and all the defective ones replaced. If more than 100 shells were found to be defective, a system of penalties would come into play whereby each defective shell over 100 would cost the industrialist 11.5 francs. Industrialists like Louis Renault wanted a maximum penalty of 500 francs per 200 shells, while the Under-Secretariat demanded the full maximum of 1150 francs.

It is revealing of the low quality of shell production during the war that such a significant number had to be defective before penalties were introduced. But industrialists were resentful even of these sanctions. The next day, 27 June, the bureaucrats were forced to redraft the penalty clause to make it milder and more amenable to industrialists, since it seemed impossible to apply in its present state.[19] At a subsequent meeting in November 1915,[20] Léon-Lévy said that he could understand the argument in favour of penalties in cases of grave mistakes, bad faith, inertia, or incompetence, but that in wartime, delays in delivery and faulty production could more often be attributed to cases of *force majeure*, such as delays in the shipment of raw materials and tooling machinery, and that legisla-tion for penalties could not be framed in such a way as to take these situations into account. Louis Loucheur, speaking in his capacity as an industrialist, gave the example of one such delay in the produc-tion of shell fuses, for which he had a contract with the government: it was caused by a complete shortage of brass with which the Ironworks Administration was supposed to supply him. Calveille

18. 26 June 1915.
19. 94 AP 53: *Rapport du S.S.E. du 27 Juin 1915.*
20. 27 November 1915.

replied that the government was not willing to abandon the principle of penalties.

Undoubtedly, the problem of delays in the fulfilling of contracts was a serious one. Even the most reputable firms, such as Le Creusot, Commentry, and Pont-à-Mousson, frequently fell behind in their deliveries.[21] In March 1916 there was a further dispute over penalties, this time because the government refused to allow the plea of a shortage of military labour as sufficient excuse for the failure of an industrialist to adhere to the conditions of a contract.[22] With a single voice the industrialists protested against this decision, which seemed to contradict an assurance given earlier by Thomas that a labour shortage constituted a justifiable case of *force majeure*. Certain industrialists claimed that they had been practically forced to accept contracts in the first place, and they made a thinly-veiled threat that if the penalty clauses were maintained, they would be forced to reduce their commitments to produce shells. Thomas replied that a study of cases in which the government had contemplated imposing penalties had revealed that the excuse of labour shortages had been used systematically by industrialists as an automatic escape clause, and that for this reason, the excuse could no longer be accepted in the future. Refusing to be blackmailed by threats of diminishing production, Thomas recognised that the result of the enforcement of penalties might be a reduction of commitments to produce, but that it was preferable to have smaller commitments which would be fulfilled than great promises which led to cruel disappointments when they were unrealised. Hence penalties would be maintained.

Privately, however, Thomas admitted to his closest associates that he was still deeply worried by the question. In April 1916, he sent a memorandum to one of his advisers in which he admitted that for all his display of unflinching firmness in negotiations with industrialists, he might in the end be forced to yield ground to them:

> I would like to take up the question of penalties with you again. It aroused the emotions of our industrialists rather more than I anticipated. Naturally, I maintained the principle with great firmness at the conference. Several people have even criticised me for this; but it will be necessary that we reconsider the question among ourselves . . .[23]

---

21. Various reports on late deliveries can be found in 94 AP 24.
22. 31 March 1916.
23. 94 AP 24: AT/AA (Albert Aftalion) 3 April 1916, no.2836.

The Reports of Government Inspectors

The effectiveness of imposing penalty clauses depended largely on the willingness of the government to accept reports made by inspectors on the conditions of production prevailing within armament factories. There is evidence to suggest that Thomas failed to support his inspectors when they criticised the methods of the industrialists whose factories they were inspecting. Government-appointed inspectors frequently clashed with industrialists over the quality of shells being produced. In October 1915, Thomas received a lively report of one such clash with André Citroën from an outraged inspector called Virlogeux.[24] The report is interesting for what it reveals about Citroën's manufacturing techniques.

There had been a number of quarrels between Virlogeux and Citroën about the quality of shells being produced in Citroën's Paris plant, and on 10 October 1915 it was decided to send a military mission consisting of General Dumézil and Colonel Payeur of the Under-Secretariat to settle differences between the two men. Virlogeux's report was an account of this visit. On 11 October, Dumézil and Payeur arrived at the plant and were promptly ushered into Citroën's office. Virlogeux was told to wait outside until they had finished. When Dumézil and Payeur emerged from the meeting, Virlogeux attempted to explain why, under the manufacturing conditions which prevailed currently at the plant, defective shells were being produced. With military directness Dumézil replied, 'Je m'en fous.' Somewhat surprised and taken aback but still determined, Virlogeux then pointed out that only 2,000 shells were being produced every ten days, whereas Citroën claimed that 4,000 were being manufactured, and that within a month, 10,000 would be produced. General Dumézil ignored this observation completely. Virlogeux and Citroën then clashed over the number of shells which had been finished and stockpiled, Citroën claiming 37,000 to Virlogeux's 15,000. Again, Dumézil paid him no heed.

Sorely tried, Virlogeux accused Citroën of bad faith, and of deliberately misrepresenting the work of government inspectors. 'Cela m'emmerde,' was the terse reply of the General. 'You are free to use those expressions if you wish,' retorted Virlogeux. At this point, General Dumézil gave a long lecture on the role of inspectors, accusing Virlogeux of 'excessive rigour', and without waiting for Albert Thomas's final decision, he announced that on the recommendation of Citroën, less rigid standards and tolerances would henceforth be applied in the inspection of shells. Undeterred,

24. 94 AP 73: Le Chef d'Escadron Virlogeux to Thomas. 11 October 1915.

Virlogeux told Dumézil that his inspectors were utterly devoted to their work and had never rejected any shell which satisfied basic standards of quality. He calculated that the number of shells rejected under these standards amounted to no less than 50 per cent of those produced, and furthermore that Citroën had engaged in genuinely fraudulent practices, of which he, Virlogeux, had proof, and that he would send two depositions of former inspectors of the factory to this effect.

Virlogeux concluded his report by appealing directly to Thomas to mount an official inquiry, in the interests of National Defence, to discover what was really happening in the factory, and that if necessary charges should be laid against Citroën for misdemeanours committed in supplying the government. Virlogeux felt obliged to add that only Payeur had come to the defence of the government inspectors when Citroën had claimed that the instruments they used to test shells were inaccurate. The truth of the matter was that the factory used a machine in its production process which was incorrectly adjusted, and that this had been clearly demonstrated before the General's very eyes. Virlogeux ended by pleading for more government inspectors in armament factories. A supplementary report by another inspector, Mignot, was appended which supported Virlogeux's contentions about the Citroën plant.

Virlogeux's report corroborates in detail observations made earlier in the chapter about the alarmingly low quality of shell production in France at this stage in the war and the consequent concern of industrialists that the lightest possible penalty clauses be applied. Albert Thomas's reaction to this report has not survived, but it seems unlikely that much was done to vindicate the claims of his inspector. For all the alleged dishonesty in his methods, Citroën was still too large a producer of shells and other war materials to offend. Armed with the most solid proof, there was little Thomas could do if he did not wish to imperil existing shell production. When government inspectors complained too vigorously about the production methods of an industrialist, their zeal was generally rewarded with a recall. A typical case was that of Commandant Chenu, an inspector who was withdrawn on Thomas's orders.

Several industrialists, Monsieur Renault, in Paris, and Monsieur Courville, the representative of Le Creusot in Le Havre, have informed me of the overly-critical and even slightly irregular attitude of Commandant Chenu towards the heads of the factories he visits; violent criticism of the industrialists in the presence of their workers; declarations that their products are defective, without giving proof; entering factories without letters of authorisation, etc. These methods are inadmissable, if the facts are correct. The School of Pyrotechnics would be well advised if in future it no longer entrusted this officer with any missions.[25]

Thus, for all the threat of severe penalties for manufacturers who produced defective shells, Thomas refused to back his inspectors when they unearthed the evidence which would have sustained these penalties. Under these conditions, penalty clauses remained largely inoperative.

The Buyer and Seller Relationship

Prices, insufficient production, loans, and penalty clauses: these were the chief subjects of discussion in the meetings held between representatives of France's leading shell producers and bureaucrats from the Under-Secretariat of State for Artillery and Munitions. A close examination of these meetings is instructive, for it reveals the nature and extent of some of the major struggles waged between bureaucrats and industrialists during the war. Unlike so many of the debates which accompanied the formulation of Clémentel's policy, the differences of opinion which emerged during these meetings were not based on theory or principle, but were related to eminently practical questions of bargaining. Each of the major issues discussed: prices, production, advances, and penalties, was bound by a common theme: money. In short, these meetings were bartering sessions between buyer and seller. The bureaucrats strove unceasingly to reduce to an acceptable level the extent to which the government was being exploited by industrialists. The industrialists were fighting for the best interests of their firms, continually aware that their great current prosperity could be instantly jeopardised by any one of the seemingly minor technical adjustments of contracts which bureaucrats constantly brought forward. On the outcome of these debates hinged the entire economic future of the companies concerned.

War Profits and War Scandals

As the war proceeded, the debate about prices spilled over the narrow confines of the conference room into the public forum. In the process, there was an important adjustment of terminology:

25. 94 AP 80: Note from Albert Thomas.

'price', a word essentially cool, technical, and rational in nature was abandoned in favour of its more emotive variant, 'profit'. The reader should be warned of several restrictions which hamper any discussion of French war profits during the 1914–18 period. For reasons which will become apparent, it is almost impossible to give fully documented and detailed examples of the profits of individual firms. The most one can do is to indicate the various ways in which large profits could be made during the war.

Why must any consideration of war profits be hedged with such qualifications? The reasons are varied. The first problem concerns the whole notion of the term 'profit'. What is a profit? In France, to this day there exists no standard, universally accepted definition of the word. If the term 'profit' is to have any useful, commonly understood meaning, that meaning can only be derived from standard bookkeeping procedures. For example, depreciation of capital equipment and the amortization of loans must be treated in some consistent, rational manner. In the case of family firms, there must be a sharp delineation between salaries paid to members of the family in their capacity as executives of the company, and profits. But such standard accounting methods simply did not exist in France during the First World War. As one American commentator has explained:

> It is not that French accounting ignored the concept of depreciation schedules and reserves; what matters rather than the *formal* accounting, is the *effective* accounting. The French attitude towards accounting is summarized as follows: the Frenchman has three sets of books: one for the tax collector, one for his wife, and the other for himself which he keeps in his head.[26]

As a result, since no one knew what a profit was in the first place, it was logically impossible to tell how large they were, in other than the most general fashion.

Furthermore, even if there had been a clear definition of 'profit' and exact figures were uncovered, there would still remain the vexed question: what constitutes a 'fair profit'? At what exact point does a reasonable profit become a 'war' (i.e. 'excessive') profit? Again, no simple standard exists.

Any approach, therefore, to the question of 'war profits' must be made with reservations. Hard information is notoriously difficult to obtain from the government, from public critics of the industrialists, and, *a fortiori*, from the industrialists themselves. In many

26. Pitts, 'Bourgeois Family', 400 (footnote).

cases, companies have no idea exactly how well they did during the war, and are in no rush to find out, but even in the case of those firms who publicly vowed during the war that they were producing military materials at cost-price, there is a marked reluctance to allow researchers access to the papers which might substantiate these claims. The area of war profits, then, is one in which the much-vaunted benefit of hindsight is of little, if any, advantage to the historian.

The Unreliability of French Accounting Methods

At an early stage in the war, the government became alert to the problem of war profiteers. Repeated attempts were made to legislate for war profits, but with little success, for the simple reason that there was no mechanism for determining the profits of a company. The state did not even enjoy the right to examine company records, such as they were. In any event, as has been suggested previously, accounting practices varied so widely from one firm to the next that it was impossible to say with certainty anything about the financial position of any firm. In a lengthy and admirable analysis of contracts signed by the government with two firms, Louis Loucheur's Eclairage Eléctrique, and Hervais, of Clermont-Ferrand, for the same model of shell detonator fuses, a government inspector exposed the weakness of the procedure currently used by the government for establishing prices. The chief element of confusion was the transfer of metal by the government to the industrialists, for which compensation was to be made in the final price of the shell:

> The confusion created by this question of pseudo-transfer of material and the complexity of accounting procedures would not be noticed during a cursory examination of the contract and could escape the attention of the industrialists themselves, if they did not perform an analysis in depth of their bookkeeping arrangements.[27]

So great was the confusion that there was a difference in the effective price paid for each shell of 78 per cent between the two companies, which only emerged from a complete study of the contract. Furthermore, it was possible that by using another accounting procedure, the difference between the two prices might emerge as 150 per cent, not 78 per cent. Clearly, the methods used by the Under-Secretariat were totally inadequate if their very complexity could mask such

27. 94 AP 74: *Rapport No.53 du Contrôleur de 1ere Classe de l'Administration de l'Armée Gache sur les marchés . . .*

differences not only from bureaucrats but apparently even from the industrialists themselves. Under such conditions of accounting, it is difficult to know whether industrialists like Loucheur should be credited with duplicity or merely a genuine unawareness of the true financial implications of the contract they were negotiating. As Emile Aimond, a senator, wrote in his report in March 1916 on a war profits tax bill:

Industrial and commercial accounting procedure bears no resemblance whatever to administrative accounting. For each industry there are rules consecrated by practice which must be respected at all costs. Besides, we can hardly force the great majority of tax-paying concerns to reconstitute their accounting procedure for several years on a fixed model.[28]

Thus, bills like this one, which became law on 1 July 1916, had little practical effect. In February 1917, Vincent Auriol reported on the results to date of this tax.[29] Although the war profits tax was retroactive, to date the state had collected only 400 million francs after one and a half years of war, which compared most unfavourably with the results achieved by the Excess Profit Duty in England. How could one explain this failure? Auriol placed part of the blame on the shoulders of the state administration.

Although this affirmation may seem paradoxical, we attribute the insufficiency of the yield of the tax to the insufficient devotion to their duty, in this regard, of the tax-gathering administration. It seems that not only has this administration not made every possible effort to prevent certain frauds which have become widespread and indeed are practically provoked by certain imperfections in the law; but . . . it has allowed and facilitated these frauds in violation of the law, to the detriment of the Treasury.

In other words there was complicity between bureaucrats and industrialists over tax-avoidance. Among the most favoured methods, said Auriol, was to use some fiction of accounting to diminish excess profits, either by claiming that normal profits were higher than they were, or simply by claiming a smaller profit than actually existed. Alternatively, profits could be reduced by deducting 'installations made with a view to creating war supplies', which, in practice, could mean buying land or investing money in other ventures. Then there were fictitious loans, falsified expenses, and

28. *Sénat, Annexe No.133.* 30 March 1916.
29. *Chambre des députés, Rapport Vincent Auriol, Annexe, No.3059,* 27 February 1917.

undervalued stock, all of which could be used to diminish profits. In stating their normal, pre-war profits, above which excess war profit tax was to be applied, industrialists and businessmen had three choices. Either they produced their books, or they took 6 per cent of the real capital invested in their plant, or they multiplied the value of their *patente* (tax of incorporation) by thirty. The most popular method of showing an inflated normal profit was to add the financial reserves of the company to the total capital for the purposes of calculation. Thus, if a firm had a capital of 10 million francs and reserves of 4 million francs to pay off debts, the normal profit was calculated as 6 per cent of 14 million. Not content with this, some industrialists calculated 6 per cent of war-time capital. Alternatively, there were ways of inflating the *patente*, and Auriol gave the example of a butcher whose peacetime *patente* was 200 francs, and who should, thereby, have declared a normal profit of 6,000 francs (200 × 30), but instead declared a normal profit of 750,000 francs. Finally, if an industrialist chose to have his books verified, this was not done by national government inspectors, but by local civil servants, who could be easily intimidated by a company.

Later Auriol discovered even more ways of increasing the figures for normal profits. The firm of Tréfileries du Havre, for example, increased its capital from 30 million to 45 million francs by distributing one new share for every two old ones, without receiving any payment for the new shares.[30]

Estimates of normal profits were important not only for excess profit tax, but for contract negotiations between manufacturers and bureaucrats of the Under-Secretariat. An industrialist could claim that he stood to lose money unless a certain price were paid for the article he manufactured, and there was no way of disproving his claim. In their estimates of what a fair price would be for a given item, bureaucrats had no real guidelines.

Profits and Swindles

Broadly speaking, one can discuss two categories of 'war profiteer' in France during the First World War: the established industrialist and the out and out swindler. Many profits were earned 'legitimately', that is, as a result of negotiations with representatives of the government, who, for reasons of inexperience or urgency, failed to defend the interests of the state as efficiently as they might have. But there are also numerous examples of contracts signed under the

---

30. *Chambre des députés. Rapport No.4053*, 11 November 1917.

most extraordinary conditions. Gaston Gros, in his celebrated book, *La République des Coquins*, which drew on reports by parliamentary commissions published after the war, gives several of the more spectacular instances of irregularities. A certain Lucien Kahn, an old gaol-bird who was wont to use an assumed title of nobility, won a contract worth 10 million francs. The bureaucrat who awarded him the contract immediately resigned his post and went into partnership with Kahn. In the end the state suffered a net loss of 6.5 million francs on the contract.[31] Fly-by-night operators with no industrial experience whatever applied for and were rewarded with armament contracts. One such was Madame Caron, a painter, who bid for contracts involving clothing, camping equipment, shoes, boots, barbed-wire, machine-guns, motorcycles, automobiles, lorries, 60 million litres of petrol, 50,000 horses, dried vegetables, cod, condensed milk, copper sulphate and railway cars. Her perseverance was rewarded, and she eventually won two contracts to furnish 60,000 snow-boots; she delivered 10,000.[32]

Non-delivery was a feature common to the operating procedures of many of these self-styled entrepreneurs. A typical case was that of a certain Monsieur Junot, who in March 1916 bid for a contract for shell casings, which he proposed to produce in two factories which he claimed to own in Paris. On 11 May, he signed a contract to produce 37,500 casings within three months at a price of 9 francs each, at a time when the average price being paid was only 6.5 francs. By 10 July, his company, the Industrielle Française, had delivered only 1,722 casings, and a check revealed that his Paris factories were closed and that he had moved to Montry. At Montry, there was no evidence that any casings were being manufactured. When the three months stipulated in the contract had elapsed, government officials attempted to locate Junot to tell him his contract had been annulled, but failed to do so, as he had no fixed address. In the meantime, another entrepreneur, Pamaron by name, essayed a further variation on the same swindle. Claiming to be a partner of Junot in the Industrelle Française, he applied to the Ironworks Administration (*Direction des Forges*) for permission to complete the contract. He maintained that he had several factories at his disposal, but it was soon discovered that, in reality, he had previously been involved in property rental and publicity, and that he owned no factories. This time the government refused to be taken in, and Pamaron's bid was dismissed.[33] The profit in this kind

31. G. Gros, *La République des Coquins* (Paris, 1934), 50.
32. Ibid., 65.
33. 94 AP 70: *Direction Générale des Fabrications de l'Artillerie, No. 1792.* 10.

of operation was made from the advances paid by the government in anticipation of the delivery of the finished products.

There were innumerable other cases of fraud, large and small, detected and undetected, by old established firms and by newcomers, which took place during the war. They ranged from the simplest of operations, such as changing a figure 1 to a figure 7 when requesting scarce material, practiced by the Grenoble firm of Gautier Frères et Chamoux,[34] to the highly sophisticated larceny of Frank Goldsoll, who embezzled $3.5 million by pretending to sell American lorries to the French government. The moral boundary between business acuity and criminal activity was constantly shifting, and a commercial operation which ultimately landed one man in gaol might land another a job in the government. The career of Louis-Dreyfus is instructive in this regard. Born in Zurich in 1867, trained as a lawyer in France, Louis-Dreyfus had been the deputy from La Lozère before 1914.[35] He also ran a family firm called Louis-Dreyfus et Cie, one of the largest importers of wheat into France before the war. During the war, the firm became responsible for importing wheat from Australia. At a meeting of the Budget Commission in 1915, Victor Boret, who was later to become Minister of Agriculture and Food, accused him of selling Australian wheat at excessive prices. He also accused him obliquely in the Chamber of Deputies of blackmailing the government into buying wheat at the price he set by threatening to sell it outside France. Louis-Dreyfus was also accused of selling wheat to neutral nations who resold it to the Germans, and even of selling goods directly to the Germans at the beginning of the war.[36] Nevertheless, these charges, which were never satisfactorily answered, in no way impaired his career; to the contrary: in 1917 Louis-Dreyfus became president of the importing section of the National Wheat Office.[37]

The Response of the Bureaucrats

Bureaucrats were poorly armed to deal with the great array of shady dealings and business malpractices which were perpetrated throughout the war. The chief problem was obtaining hard evidence against

November 1916.
34. F12 7670: *Importations et Répartitions: programmes, statistiques, fraudes.* 1917–18.
35. *Qui Etes-Vous? Annuaire des contemporains français et étrangers 1909–1910* (Paris 1910), 325.
36. 94 AP 73.
37. Beau de Loménie, *La Guerre*, 79.

businessmen and industrialists. Without the right to examine accounts, there was little a bureaucrat could do but accept the word of the industrialist about the nature of his operations and the size of his profits. But even if enormous profits or cases of palpable fraud were discovered, the need for productive capacity was so great that the government would only impose sanctions with the greatest reluctance.

The government was further compromised in its efforts to assert its authority over private enterprise by the fact that so many industrialists and businessmen also held part-time positions in the civil service. The phenomenon of the industrialist-bureaucrat was not a rare one during the war. Louis Loucheur, for example, was an armament manufacturer and an Under-Secretary of State simultaneously, before finally becoming Minister of Armament. Some companies capitalised on their allies within the government more blatantly than others. A cod-fishing company, the Morue Française, sold 5 million kilogrammes of cod, of which 600,000 were rotten, to the government at exorbitantly high prices, but fraud charges were held up by Joseph Thierry, the Under-Secretary of State for Food, who was a former director of the company.[38] Exbrayat, the trusted adviser of Albert Thomas, who was secretary of the Metals Commission, had been a director of the Banque Demachy, the bank of the *Comité des Forges*, before the war.[39]

Thus, bureaucrats could offer little resistance to the determined war profiteer. Profits may have been garnered by a process of open negotiation with bureaucrats, or by any number of deceitful means, simple or complicated, but they shared the common attribute as far as one can tell, of being large. From the government's point of view, the 'dishonest' industrialist was not the one who charged excessive prices — they all did — but the one who failed to deliver the goods. Monopolistic practices, blackmail by the threat of non-production, and large profits could all be countenanced on the sole condition that the army received the supplies.

The Post-War Outcry

Although the first scandal of war profits broke during the latter half of the war, it is a curious fact that the most revealing and sensational attacks on the 'merchants of death' did not get under way until 1933 in France, at a time when the effects of the depression were being

38. Ibid., 75.
39. *Le Crapouillot*, October 1933, 29.

most severely felt. The first article directly relating to French war profiteers in *La Crapouillot* was Jean Gaultier-Boissière's 'Les marchands de canons contre la Nation', which appeared in October 1933. Gaston Gros's *La République des coquins* was published in 1934. These attacks used information unearthed by various parliamentary commissions investigating war profits in the 1920s. In many cases, the findings of these commissions were inconclusive or never made public.[40] The most significant feature of the publicity given to war profiteers in the 1930s was the stress placed on the fact that it was not merely adventurers who had been guilty of the worst offences, but members of France's most respected industrial and commercial families, 'the Two Hundred Families', as they became labelled. During the war, attacks on war profiteers had concentrated on flashy parvenus who exhibited their newly gained wealth in an unseemly fashion. More traditional firms and the families that controlled them, companies like Saint-Gobain and Le Crousot, probably made far more money than all the *arrivistes* combined, but handled their earnings more discreetly and attracted less attention. During the war, it was the vulgarity and indecent ostentation at a time of national tragedy which offended, as much as the profits themselves. Again, one factor which may account for the time-lag in the attack on war profiteers was the lack, cited above, of a widely accepted definition of what constituted a just profit.

The criticism of war profiteers in the 1930s was in a sense a reflection of current social and economic hardship coupled with the development of new social criteria which judged the activities of wartime industrialists in a harsher light. It is essentially the exposures of the 1930s which have fashioned the views we hold today of industrialists and their activities during the Great War.

---

40. See for example, *Commission des marchés de guerre, Annales de la Chambre de députés. Tome 96. Annexe No. 1630.*

CHAPTER 8

The Comité des Forges

The *Comité des Forges* and the Wartime Bureaucracy

The 1914–18 war presented the *Comité des Forges* with an unparalleled opportunity to extend the sphere of its activities and to consolidate and strengthen the position of major metal producers. Completely unprepared for the logistical problems involved in supplying its armed forces with weapons at the beginning of the war, the French government cast about desperately for an organisation which could furnish war materials in as short a time as possible. The *Comité des Forges* was only too willing to oblige.

In essence, the chief function of the *Comité des Forges* during the war was to control the flow of all metal to French factories. Since so much of France's coal, cast iron, and steel resources had been located in the north-eastern corner of the country, which was lost to the Germans in the early days of the war, the *Comité des Forges* became chiefly an importing agency for foreign metal. At the same time, production in the centre of France, based on the great metallurgical concentration at Le Creusot, was intensified, and industrialists whose plants had been captured by the Germans were encouraged to re-establish factories at a safe remove from the front. The *Comité des Forges* co-ordinated and supervised all these developments. But an equally important function of the *Comité* was to divide armament contracts equitably among its members. In short, the *Comité des Forges* became a private consortium, free of state interference, a metals trust controlled by industrialists but financed by the state through loans and advances.

Initially the government placed complete faith in the ability of the *Comité des Forges* to supply its needs. As Albert Thomas told a meeting of manufacturers of 75 mm. shells in October 1915: 'The artillery section thought that French industrialists, having had

221

relations with the metallurgists of England and America in peacetime, could, in the present situation, serve a useful function by
searching for their own supplies abroad'.[1] But even by this date it
was clear that the *Comité* could not keep up with the demand for
metal and that the government would have to intervene. The great
clearing house of the *Comité des Forges* for both domestic and
imported metals was Le Creusot. An increasing number of industrialists who had been awarded contracts by the government on the
condition that they would supply their own metal, had applied to
Le Creusot instead, been refused, and returned to the government
complaining that they were unable to complete their contracts. It
was clear that a parallel structure would have to be created, whereby
some industrialists would be supplied with metal by Le Creusot,
while others would receive their metal from the government.[2] By
October 1915, there were two missions purchasing metal in America
on behalf of the French government, that of the Ministry of War and
that of the *Comité*. As the metal situation continued to deteriorate,
there was increasing pressure for even more direct state intervention.

One vital part of the wartime mechanism of the *Comité des
Forges* was the *comptoir*, a device carried over from the pre-war
period. The oldest of these, the *Comptoir de Longwy*, which was
founded to sell metal produced by the factories of Lorraine, became
the chief sales agency of the *Comité des Forges* during the war. It
was the *Comptoir de Longwy* which imported certain metals,
chiefly cast iron, from England and America on behalf of the
Comité des Forges. The *Comité* jealously guarded its control over
the *comptoirs*. In December 1915, for example, Pinot protested to
Thomas about the attempt of independent metal manufacturers who
were supplied by the various *comptoirs* to wield some influence over
their management.[3]

The Creation of a Sole Purchasing Agent for English Iron

As the war dragged on, the English insisted that France create a
single purchasing agent for all metals. The first metal to be affected
was iron. By January 1916, French metallurgists were placing
monthly orders for a total 115,000 tons of English iron, an amount
far greater than their real needs and well beyond the capacity of
English suppliers to export.[4] Thomas and Clémentel cast about for

1. 94 AP 72: 2 October 1915.
2. 94 AP 71: *Note 998*. 17 October 1915.
3. 94 AP 53: *Artillerie, Comptoirs du Comité des Forges*, 1 December 1915.
4. Pinot, *Le Comité des Forges*, 114.

an organism to centralise all demands for metal in France in order to distribute the 40,000 tons of metal which England could make available to France each month, and once again, the *Comité des Forges* was ready with a proposal. The *Comité* had always let it be known that it was prepared to undertake such an enterprise. In March 1916, a representative of the *Comité* wrote to the Ministry of Commerce volunteering to take over all purchasing operations of metal in England and America, both for armament manufacturers and private industry.

> The intervention of the *Comité des Forges* would be limited to the receipt of offers of material, the transmission of these offers to the industrialists, the confirmation of orders in the case of the acceptance by industrialists of the offers in question, and the assurance, as far as possible, of delivery, embarkation, and insurance. The intervention of the *Comité des Forges* would be free of charge to industrialists, except for a 1% levy to cover general expenses.[5]

Once again, the government seemed more willing to entrust import operations to an existing private body than to strengthen or create one of its own organisations. As he explained to an independent metallurgist who complained of the pre-eminence of the *Comité des Forges*:

> The British government has decided to grant permits to export cast iron to a single centralised organ nominated by me. The *Comité des Forges* has already created an organism with the help of the *Comptoir de Longwy*, and I extended its powers to include the totality of the quantity of cast iron which the British government wished to grant us each month.[6]

On 5 May 1916, Thomas officially charged the *Comité des Forges* with the task of importing all English iron.[7] It was the sheer availability of structures created by the *Comité des Forges* which led to so much power being concentrated in its hands.

The *Comptoir d'Exportation des Produits Métallurgiques*, also known as the *Comptoir de la rue Pillet-Will* (an affiliate of the *Comité des Forges* which had fallen into disuse during the war since France was no longer exporting metal, and then been reactivated and converted for the purpose of importing metal) was subsequently made the sole importing agency for foreign steel and tin into France; it continued, paradoxically, to be known as the *Comptoir d'Exportation*.

5. F12 7672: 23 March 1916.
6. 94 AP 110: *Albert Thomas to Gaston Prud'homme*, 19 March 1916.
7. Pinot, *Le Comité des Forges*, 117.

In July 1917, the government announced the new system for steel, and an interministerial decree was issued to this effect on 31 August 1917.[8] The *Comptoir d'Exportation* was to act as the agent of the Ministry of Armament and to distribute the 10,000 tons of steel the British government would make available to France each month. 90 per cent of the steel was to go to armament plants, the rest was to be divided among other domestic producers.[9] The government's interests were represented at the *Comptoir d'Exportation* by the presence of two army officers. Critics of the *Comité des Forges*, such as the deputy Edouard Barthe, were later to claim that the net effect of placing the *Comptoir d'Exportation* exclusively in charge of importing metals was to raise the price of steel from 60 francs a ton to a minimum of 95 francs, then 120 francs a ton. The *Comité des Forges* defended itself against such charges by pointing out that prices were established by interministerial decision, and consisted of a basic price with certain increases for different classes of metals, which were fixed by the Ministry of Armament on the recommendation of the Interministerial Commission for Metals.[10]

Bureaucrats and the Comité des Forges

This willingness of the government to abdicate its authority for supplying France with metals to the *Comité des Forges* was reflected by the gentlemanly tone of meetings held every two weeks of the Minister of War and his subordinates, private factory owners, and officials of the *Comité*. One reason for this harmony between bureaucrats and metallurgists was that several of the leading wartime civil servants in the Ministry of War and the Under-Secretariat of State for Artillery and Munitions had been associated with the *Comité des Forges* before the war. In his attack on the *Comité des Forges* in 1919, Barthe said that vital ministerial offices had been infiltrated by the 'creatures' of the *Comité*.

> One of them, Commandant X, in civilian life an executive of the bank of the *Comité des Forges*, in whose coffers are stowed away millions of francs paid in advance for contracts, as a soldier serves as the Secretary General of the Wood and Metals Services. In addition to these important functions, he had just been given the additional task of head of the Office

8. Ministerial decisions of 11 March, 17 March, & 4 May 1917 placed the task of importing tin in the hands of the *Comptoir d'Exportation*, while the Interministerial decision of 31 August 1917 dealt exclusively with steel.
9. 94 AP 73: Lettre 5896 du *Comité des Forges*, 21 July 1917.
10. *Chambre des députés*, 24 January 1919, 216.

of Import Exemptions at the Ministry of Commerce.[11]

'Commandant X' was Jules Exbrayat, formerly on the board of both the Banque Demachy and the Banque de l'Union parisienne, now secretary of the Metals Commission of the Under-Secretariat and one of Albert Thomas's chief advisers.[12] In London, the military attaché to the French Embassy, with special responsibility for controlling the provision of English metals for France, was General de La Panouse, who had married Sabine de Wendel, the daughter of France's leading metallurgist. The man who directed the French purchasing agency for metals under the supervision of General de La Panouse was his brother-in-law, Humbert de Wendel.[13] When a parliamentary commission was established to investigate the profits of war materials suppliers, the deputy charged with drawing up a report on the contracts of the metallurgical industry was Humbert's brother, François de Wendel.[14]

Slowly, however, the government began to create its own bureaucratic machinery. By 1916, there were two new state bureaucratic structures, the Consortium of Iron Merchants, and the Interministerial Commission for Wood and Metals.[15] The term 'consortium' in this context is misleading, since the Consortium of Iron Merchants was initially a collection of private producers rather than a closely-regulated government structure of the type Clémentel was to create in 1917. The Interministerial Commission was charged with centralising all purchases of metal and wood from abroad and distributing such materials, as well as those originating from sources within France, as equitably as possible. It was also given authority over relevant consortiums and comptoirs. In theory, it had direct control over the operations of the Comptoir de Longwy, the Comptoir d'Exportation, and the Machine Tool Consortium. As well, the Interministerial Commission held sway over ten related interministerial committees, such as those tin, zinc, and electrical construction.

At the same time, a Consortium of Iron Merchants in France was created, also supposedly under the jurisdiction of the Interministerial Commission, but in reality controlled by the Comité des Forges. Both the Consortium of Iron Merchants and the Comité de

11. Ibid., 207.
12. Beau de Loménie, La Guerre, 86.
13. Crapouillot, October 1933, 29.
14. Ibid., 30.
15. Journal Officiel, 16 June, 5294.

Forges had the same secretary, Goldberger.[16] The *Comité des Forges* sought to use the Consortium as a means of limiting the number of firms to whom it was responsible for supplying metal. By imposing price rules as a condition of membership in the Consortium, the *Comité des Forges* hoped to force all French metallurgists to adopt its general policy.[17] Through the Consortium, the *Comité* was able to use various decrees passed by the government as a means of imposing its will on independent metallurgists. On 11 May 1916, for example, the government issued a decree forbidding the unauthorised importation of metal into France. On 8 June, on behalf of both the *Comité des Forges* and the Consortium of Metal Producers, Robert Pinot wrote to Albert Thomas to complain that the decree had not yet been promulgated, and that as a result, independent metal producers had been charging much higher prices than those laid down in the decree and had been rushing to sign large contracts before the provisions of the decree came into effect.[18] The decree was eventually promulgated on 18 July 1916. The hand of the *Comité des Forges* was immeasurably strengthened by measures such as these, which banned the import of all metals except those authorised by the government after consultation with the relevant affiliated organisation of the *Comité*.

A year later, when the question of creating a sole purchasing agent for all foreign metals arose again, it seemed at one point that a government body, the Interministerial Commission itself, not the *Comptoir d'Exportation* or the *Comité des Forges*, might become such an agent. Gaillard, the president of the Interministerial commission, told a meeting in March 1917:

> In reality, the veritable sole purchasing agent would be the Interministerial Commission, or, more exactly, the sub-committees created by it, as we have done in the case of copper and tin, and as we shall do for steel.
> These committees would take charge of all purchases to be made in England and America and in other countries, and they would have a single representative in England, and in America, which would probably be the missions which are already there.[19]

In the end, the *Comité des Forges* won again, and its *Comptoir d'Exportation* became sole purchasing agent on behalf of the French government. Interestingly enough, the Consortium of Iron

16. F12 7672.
17. 94 AP 110: *Comité des Forges. Consortium des Fers. Procès-verbal de la séance du 10 août 1916.*
18. 94 AP 110: Robert Pinot to Thomas, 8 June 1916.
19. 94 AP 110: 12 March 1917.

Merchants, which the previous year had seemed to be the most likely instrument for the imposition of the policy of the Interministerial Commission was passed over completely in favour of the *Comptoir*.[20]

The Interministerial Commission did retain some control over the *Comptoir d'Exportation* with regard to the prices charged for re-selling imported metal to manufacturers and with regard to the method of distributing the metal. Each interministerial committee which was dependent on the Interministerial Commission submitted its request for metal to the Commission, which determined the proportion of metal to be distributed to each of the committees and ordered the *Comptoir d'Exportation* to act accordingly. A complicated line of command developed.

> In each committee, a civil servant manages the contingent allocated to it in the best interests of those who are to receive the metal. The purchase orders or vouchers, as the case may be, are established by the *Comptoir*, cleared by the controller of the committee, and transmitted to the Interministerial Commission, which sends them back to the *Comptoir* for execution.[21]

There seems to be something of the perpetual motion machine in this arrangement. Despite (or perhaps because of) the complexity of this process, the *Comité des Forges* was still able to use the *Comptoir* to serve the interests of its adherents. The *Comptoir* seems to be the key link in the chain, with the other organisms merely approving what had already been decided.

It will probably never be known why the decision of the Interministerial Commission in March 1917 to take over the responsibility for importing all foreign metal was subsequently reversed in August. Manteilhet suggests one possible explanation: Albert Thomas was less interested than Clémentel in the long-term uses of new bureaucratic structures.

> Since the Minister of Armament was not responsible for bringing about radical changes in the future in the economic field, he was satisfied with using the instruments of action which he found at hand, with having recourse to simple expedients. In this frame of mind, he gave the *Comité des Forges* the responsibility for supplying the industry of the nation with cast iron, steel, and sheet metal.[22]

20. *Comité des Forges, Rapport de la direction*, 18 May 1918, 14, 15.
21. Manteilhet, *Consortiums*, 19, 20.
22. Ibid., 24.

The Comité des Forges and the Ministry of Commerce

What initiative there was for the creation of governmental machinery to cope with problems of metal supply, and indeed, what opposition there was to the predominance of the *Comité des Forges*, came from the Ministry of Commerce, not the Ministry of Armament. Clémentel's view of the policy which should be applied to metals was radically different from that of Albert Thomas. For Clémentel, metals were a test case. If the government could find a solution to the problems of the metallurgical industry, this solution would be valid for other industries. Speaking in the Senate on 12 June 1917, Clémentel reviewed the wartime economic policy which he had attempted to implement thusfar.[23] He paid homage to the efforts which individual industrialists had made in supplying the needs of the country, but he underlined the necessity in the future for collective action by industrialists under the supervision of the government. The government's policy with regard to metals showed what could be done with scarce materials. Owing to the necessities of war, total control had been imposed by the government. The services of the Ministries of Armament and Commerce between them controlled all metal production and importation, and soon there would be a sole purchasing agent for metal abroad. Clémentel reminded the listeners that he had already found a system for distributing metal equitably among non-military domestic consumers. Throughout his speech, he stressed the fact that the government had created machinery for controlling metals, but he never once mentioned the vital role in the process played by the *Comité des Forges* and its subordinate organisations. It is plain, however, from his policy of establishing state-regulated consortia for other products that Clémentel would not allow the initiative to rest with the *Comité des Forges*. It was imperative that the government create a viable alternative.

Privately, the bureaucrats of the Ministry of Commerce had already engaged in light skirmishes with the *Comité des Forges* for more than a year. One of the most energetic leaders of the resistance movement within the Ministry of Commerce to the pretensions of the *Comité des Forges* was Henri Blazeix, one of Clémentel's closest associates and a leading civil servant. On 30 May 1916, he sent Clémentel a report on a meeting he held earlier in the month with Robert Pinot, the secretary general, and Cabaud, the president of the Consortium of Iron Merchants.[24] Pinot and Cabaud had re-

23. *Sénat*, 12 June 1917, 551–554.
24. F12 7661: *Note au sujet du Comité des Forges*, 30 May 1916.

quested total control by the Consortium of the entire monthly contingent of English metal which was reserved for non-military production in France. To this request Blazeix replied that the Technical Services of the Ministry of Commerce would make part of this contingent available to the Consortium to distribute among its members, but he expressly refused to consider granting the Consortium the *de facto* monopoly over metal which it desired, and he reserved the right for the Technical Service to make over to independent metal merchants and consumers as much material as it felt necessary. The government would not force all metal merchants to enter the Consortium, and material would always be made available for those who wished to remain outside, on the condition that the prices they charged for their products were no higher than those charged by members of the Consortium. Blazeix also indicated he was strongly opposed to the policy practised by Albert Thomas of giving the *Comité des Forges* and its organisations complete control over specific metals.

> As for the importation of steel, I decided nothing definite with Monsieur Pinot and have always said that as far as I was concerned, I was completely opposed to what has been done by the Under-Secretary of State for Artillery with regard to cast iron.

Finally, after Pinot had claimed that the *Comité des Forges* was volunteering its aid exclusively in the interests of the National Defence, absolutely free of charge, Blazeix pointed out that the iron merchants had done exceedingly well in the war by operating with the help of the services of the *Comité des Forges* and he specifically cited the case of two such metallurgists, Noyal and Plisson.

Nowhere is the divergence of the policies of the Ministry of Commerce and the Under-Secretariat of State for Artillery and Munitions more clearly illustrated than in this report. Despite all the pressure placed on the government to grant the *Comité des Forges* a monopoly over metals, Blazeix insisted on preserving the freedom of action of the bureaucrats of the Ministry of Commerce, and notably those of the Technical Services, whose head he was. One of the repercussions of this resistance to the *Comité des Forges* was that under the decree of 18 July 1916, which prohibited the importation of wood and metal, the authority to determine exemptions to the prohibition was given to the Interministerial Commission for Wood and Metals, not to the *Comité des Forges*, the *Comptoir d'Exportation*, or the Consortium of Iron Merchants.[25]

25. *Journal Officiel*, 21 July 1916, 6497.

Like a terrier, Blazeix kept his teeth dug firmly into the hide of the *Comité des Forges*. On 3 October 1916, for example, he sent a note to Guillet, the head of the First Technical Section of the Ministry, which dealt with metals, on the subject of the centralisation of the purchases of foreign metals.[26] The proposal of the *Comité des Forges* to act as sole purchasing agent could not be accepted under any conditions. Whatever its motives were, it was not possible to give a commercial enterprise, even one which made no direct profits, powers of the sort it requested. As for the Interministerial Commission, there could be no question of granting it powers which belonged exclusively to certain ministries. Blazeix appeared to suggest that the Interministerial Commission could not be trusted to defend with sufficient vigour the interests of the government against the incursions of the *Comité des Forges*, and that right-thinking individual ministries, particularly the Ministry of Commerce, should be given more authority to exert the will of the government over private industry.

Attacks and Counter-attacks

The Profits of the Comité des Forges

Ultimately, under pressure from Albert Thomas at the Ministry of Armament, the Ministry of Commerce had to give way over the question of the sole purchasing agent, and the *Comptoir d'Exportation* was designated, but at least some control was maintained over its activities by the Interministerial commission, as indecisive as that body may have been. But by now, as Blazeix had indicated in his reports, the damage had been done, and individual members of the *Comité des Forges* had already reaped enormous profits from the war. From 1915 on, there had been steadily growing public criticism of the excessive profits of metallurgists. In a session of the Senate Finance Committee in August 1915, Milliès-Lacroix presented a report on shell contracts passed by the government with private industrialists.[27] He maintained that the effective result of the collaboration of the *Comité des Forges* in the efforts of the National Defence had been 'to create a price-fixing consortium', and that the Ministry of War had capitulated without showing the least sign of resistance by asking manufacturers to produce shells 'at any price'.

26. F12 7672.
27. 94 AP 71.

Initially, the *Comité des Forges* replied to such attacks in a tone in which *hauteur* vied with tearful indignation. Robert Pinot replied to this particular criticism by writing to Peytral, the president of the Senate Finance Commission:

Allow me to express to you the painful emotion upon learning of such accusations felt by those who since the beginning of the war have had the responsibility and honour of placing the organisation of the *Comité des Forges* at the service of the National Defence.[28]

The two vice-presidents of the *Comité des Forges*, Pralon and de Wendel, had done their utmost, Pinot continued, to activate factories to supply metal to munitions manufacturers, some of whom were not even members of the *Comité* and had had no previous experience in this type of work. These two gentlemen, whose factories were now in occupied territory, asked nothing more, as did Pinot himself, in recompense for their labours than the satisfaction of accomplishing their duty. It would not be fitting to recall the services which the *Comité des Forges* had rendered and was rendering every day to the country, nor to point out that if the production of war materials and munitions had increased recently, it was only because of the efforts of the *Comité des Forges*. How could anyone make such base suggestions about the disinterested, non-commercial nature of the operations of the *Comité*? To protect the good name of the *Comité des Forges*, Pinot felt obliged to protest most strenuously against such allegations.

But replies such as these could not stem the growing criticism of the profits made by members of the *Comité des Forges*. Again, the attack within the public administration was spearheaded by the Technical Services of the Ministry of Commerce, led by the redoubtable Henri Blazeix, who peppered the *Comité des Forges* with questions about the nature of its operations. The answers given were vague in the extreme. A questionnaire sent by the Technical Services to the *Comité* included such questions as: What quantities of iron and steel had the *Comptoir d'Exportation* imported into France since its foundation? The reply came:

It is impossible to answer this question in the form it has been put . . . The *Comptoir* has imported in 1915 and 1916 and the first six months of 1917 about 30,000 tons of metal of all kinds, of English, American, and Canadian origin.[29]

28. 94 AP 71: Robert Pinot to Peytral, 27 August 1915.
29. F12 7672: 19 October 1917.

Another question was: What was the margin between the prices charged to French industrialists and those paid by the *Comptoir* in England and America?: 'In so far as the prices submitted for our examination by the Ministry of Commerce are concerned, it is extremely difficult to answer, since the questions put to us are so imprecise'. The question which Blazeix should have been asking, however, was not the amount of the profits of the *Comité des Forges* itself, but the amount of the profits of its individual members. It is quite probable that the *Comité des Forges* and its dependent organisations made very little profit. Like all consortia, the Consortium of Iron Merchants was limited to a profit of 6 per cent, and when this was exceeded, the excess was ostentatiously given to the war-orphans of post office workers.[30] Other profits were returned to the state. The official apologist for the *Comité des Forges* states quite truthfully:

> Of the 810,000,000 francs which passed through the hands of the *Comité des Forges* in the course of the operations for which it was responsible during the war, not one centime stayed in the till of the *Comité des Forges* or of the *comptoirs*.[31]

Where, then, did the money go? The answer is that the profits were going to individual metallurgists. As François-Poncet delicately phrased it: 'If the *Comité des Forges* was responsible for the management of the general interests of the corporation, it could hardly assume responsibility for the individual acts of its adherents, and, in particular, responsibility for their commercial acts'.[32]

The same strictures which were made about any discussion of war profits in the preceding chapter apply with equal force to the profits of members of the *Comité des Forges*. Any figures released officially are useless, since they give no indication of such factors as percentage return on capital, or the ratio of profit to turnover, or inflation. In short, there is no absolute incontrovertible proof of the true profits of any firm. All one has to go on are the token declarations of war profits made for purposes of paying the new war profits tax, and these figures give us but the faintest outline of the real financial situation of a firm. For what they are worth, a few examples of officially declared profits follow. Among members of the *Comité des Forges*, Les Forges et les Aciéries de Firminy increased its official earnings from 2.9 million francs in 1915 to 19.5 million in

30. Prompsat Archives T(2)5: *Les Précédents de la politique des contigents*.
31. François-Poncet, *Pinot*, 227.
32. Ibid., 228.

1918. The Aciéries du Saut-du-Tarn went from 745,000 francs in 1914 to 4.71 million in 1918, while the Tréfileries du Havre improved their profits from 3.95 million in 1914 to 9.12 million in 1918.[33]

The Comité des Forges Retaliates

Faced with such criticism, the *Comité des Forges* resorted to its own methods of retaliation. When they felt their efforts were too closely circumscribed by bureaucratic activity, representatives of the *Comité* did not hesitate to complain of excess paper work. At a meeting of shell manufacturers in January 1916, Léon-Lévy said that industrialists did not have the time to answer all the questionnaires and documents requesting information which were addressed to them.[34] If the *Comité des Forges* was being particularly hard pressed by bureaucrats for information, it did not hesitate to blackmail the government by threatening to cease operations forthwith if the bureaucrats persisted. On 29 October 1917, after replying to the questionnaire sent by the Technical Services of the Ministry of Commerce, Cabaud, the vice-president of the *Comptoir d'Exportation*, sent a letter to Clémentel which is a classic of its kind.[35] After reminding the minister, inaccurately, that the *Comptoir d'Exportation* had in no way solicited the tasks which had been entrusted to it by the Ministers of Commerce and Armament appealing to the patriotism and devotion of the *Comptoir* to the public interest, Cabaud said that those concerned had been only too pleased to serve and had expected no profit or gain for their labours. But now, a section of popular opinion, unaware of the motives which dictated governmental decisions in France and Great Britain, led astray by a malicious, partisan campaign, was beginning to complain. Not all the zeal and intelligence which the *Comptoir* had wielded in executing the decisions of the government had been enough to dissipate this feeling of unease. Certain people were thus inclined to make the *Comptoir* responsible for this feeling. Then came the threat.

> Let me add, in closing, that we shall not be able to continue to accomplish our mission under the present conditions. If, every time the government is questioned about the motives which dictated its decisions regarding metals and about the way in which it executed them, you are forced to come to ask us for information which only your own services and agents can supply, and if, to try to give you satisfaction, we must

33. *Crapouillot*, October 1933, 30.
34. 94 AP 72: 28 January 1916.
35. F12 7672.

draw up notes and statistics which will not tell anybody anything, we will be too distracted from our task to be able to continue to fulfil it.

Like other industries which were vitally involved with the war effort, under the menace of closer state intervention the *Comité des Forges* was able to play the ultimate trump card by threatening to bring operations to a complete halt unless the government called off its bureaucrats.

Confronted with such a challenge, the government could deliver no riposte. Occasionally, however, the challenge was met head-on. In January 1917, the vice-president of the *Comité des Forges* wrote to Albert Thomas in reply to a proposal by the government that the *Comité* should install a major steelworks in the Paris region.[36] The *Comité des Forges* refused to sign any agreement or to create a new company until the state paid a sum of money, to be fixed in advance rather than determined on a basis of actual construction costs. Back came a withering reply from Louis Loucheur, acting on Thomas's behalf. Invoking the note of outrage and indignation normally employed by representatives of the *Comité*, Loucheur said that he was surprised by the tone of the letter.[37] Perhaps he was mistaken, but he detected the implication that he and the government were unreliable, and of course he could not accept such an insinuation.

> If you embark with such pessimism on the programme which I have entrusted to you, there is every chance that we shall meet with failure.
> Without discussing the other points which your letter raises, I do not believe that agreement can be reached between us on the terms you propose.

As an industrialist who was acquainted with such manoeuvres himself, Loucheur realised that the only way to deal with threats of non-co-operation by the *Comité des Forges* was to call its bluff by counter-threatening to sign no more contracts. This was the only way to give the government any real negotiating strength, but it required a good deal of cool assurance and courage in the face of the constant danger of military defeat.

For all the bureaucratic machinery of the state by which it was theoretically bound and of which it complained so loudly, the *Comité des Forges* and its subordinate organisations continued to enjoy a large measure of independence in the running of their own affairs. Unlike Louis Loucheur, Albert Thomas lacked the con-

36. 94 AP 63: 21 January 1917.
37. 94 AP 63: 26 January 1917.

fidence to call the *Comité des Forges* to order. In every dispute, therefore, he was morally beaten from the outset. Nowhere can this be more clearly seen than in a note Thomas wrote to two of his advisers, Roques and Simiard, in August 1915.[38] Thomas wished to send a circular with some technical details about shell production to various industrialists.

Lastly, send it to the *Comité des Forges*. But we must not subordinate ourselves entirely to the *Comité des Forges* for the transmission of this circular. The *Comité* is quite capable of transmitting only that which it judges to be in accord with its intentions.

Thomas's observation is revealing. Knowing that his orders were likely to be deliberately misinterpreted, he still felt obliged to send a copy of the circular to the *Comité des Forges*, which would then send out its own version to its members. This, from the man responsible for supplying the French Army with munitions, seem a considerable admission of weakness. Little wonder it was that no real opposition to the ambitions of the *Comité des Forges* emerged while Thomas was in charge of armaments.

The Opposition of Independent Metallurgists

There was another potential source of opposition to the *Comité des Forges*, however: the independent metallurgists who refused to join the *Comité*, and their professional associations, such as the Consortium of Metal Producers (not to be confused with the *Comité's* own Consortium of Iron Merchants). These industrialists produced a meagre 2.5 per cent of all French metal products,[39] but the loudness of their protest was out of all proportion to their productive capacity. The methods used by the *Comité des Forges* to dispose of such spoilers could be crude in the extreme. The deputy Edouard Barthe cited the case of an independent metallurgist named Roty, who, at the beginning of the war, had made an arrangement with English metal producers to supply a number of French firms.[40] Although Roty had been mobilised as a soldier, he had obtained permission from his superiors to operate this organisation in his spare time. He received numerous orders, and he was able to supply French firms with metal at a cheaper price than the *Comité des*

38. 94 AP 72: *Note 360*, 22 August 1915.
39. Prompsat Archives T(2)5: Clémentel, *Les Précédents de la politique des contigents*.
40. *Chambre des députés*, 24 January 1919, 204, 205.

Forges. On 26 December 1917, Roty and two of his associates were arrested. They were held secretly for a month, detained in custody for another seven months, and were eventually acquitted on 9 December 1918. Charges had been laid by Garmond, an engineer and sometime journalist, who gave no evidence to the police commission to sustain his accusations. When Roty went to gaol, his organisation collapsed. At his trial it transpired that three of the bureaucrats of the Ministries of Armament and Commerce had been siding with the *Comité des Forges* by refusing to grant metal to independent metallurgists. It also emerged from the testimony of one of them, Henri Mathieu, of the Ministry of Armament, that the prices charged by Roty's organisation were lower than those charged by the *Comptoir d'Exportation*, not higher, as Garmond had maintained. Finally, under questioning Mathieu admitted that the operations of the *Comité des Forges* constituted a *de facto* monopoly.

Another metallurgist named Devaux, who was not a member of the *Comité's* Consortium of Iron Merchants, said that he had not received any steel in months. The Consortium favoured its friends to the exclusion of independent metal producers. Moreover, the Consortium had never abided by the price bases suggested by the government. It mattered not if the representatives of the government authorised the transfer of metal by the Consortium to independent producers: the Consortium refused to disgorge. A typical letter from the *Comité des Forges* to Crindal, the director of the Technical Section for Metals at the Ministry of Commerce, in reply to repeated authorisations by Crindal for two independent firms to receive metal, returned the authorisations with the comment: 'We cannot intervene on behalf of these demands, for the firms concerned are not members of the Consortium of Iron Merchants, nor of the Association of Iron Merchants of France'.[41] It should be remembered that at this point in the war Henri Blazeix, the head of Technical Services at the Ministry of Commerce, was asserting categorically that independent metal producers must be supplied. Nevertheless, the *Comité des Forges* felt itself sufficiently strong to run counter to official government policy and to take advantage of its position to undermine the activities of its enemies, the independent producers.

In 1915, this group of dissident metallurgists had broken away from the Union of Metallurgical and Mining Industries, another of the organisations of the *Comité des Forges*, to which most indus-

41. F12 7672: 25 August 1916.

trialists belonged. They created a rival association, the Mechanical Industries Association (*Le Syndicat des Mécanicians*). To give some idea of the strength of the *Comité des Forges* and the weakness of the independent metallurgists, it should be pointed out that of the fifty-seven specialised professional associations which grouped the totality of French metallurgists, the Mechanical Industries Association was the only one which did not belong to the Union of Metallurgical and Mining Industries.[42] The Association demanded that the *Comité des Forges* not be given monopoly privileges for importing metal, and that all metallurgists be given equal rights.[43] There were bitter complaints from the Association in 1916 when Thomas ordered the *Comité des Forges* to centralise all requests for English cast iron. These protests had little practical effect, however.

Dissident Members

There was one final group which could embarrass the *Comité des Forges*: discontented members within the *Comité* itself. In January 1917, there was a revolt within the Association of Iron Merchants of France, led by a new review, *La Métallurgie Française*, which summoned a meeting of all French metal merchants at the Café Cardinal on 25 January to criticise the operations of the Consortium of Iron Merchants and the *Comité des Forges*.[44] The *Comité des Forges* put pressure on the government to ignore the rebels,[45] several minor concessions were made to small metallurgists who complained of delays in supply, and the rebellion petered out. As we shall discover in a subsequent chapter, however, there were far more serious divisions than this within the *Comité des Forges*.

The End of the War

As was the case with many of the other industries which developed close, profitable ties with the government during the war, despite the obvious advantages of the relationship, the *Comité des Forges* repeatedly agitated for a return to the conditions of unrestricted competition of the pre-1914 period as soon as the war came to an end. In the annual report of the *Comité des Forges*, published in the middle of 1918, the executive officers restated the position which they had taken the previous year.

42. Pinot, *Le Comité des Forges*, 7.
43. 94 AP 110: 22 October 1916.
44. A full account of this dispute can be found in F12 7673.
45. F12 7673: *Comité des Forges* to Guillet, 14 January 1917.

If there has been a rapid development of these [wartime] services in view
of the situation, we have always believed and we believe today more than
ever that they must be an essentially temporary arrangement. More than
anyone else we wish, for the good of the country and ourselves, a return
to normal commercial practices and to the freedom of transactions.[46]

On 18 December 1918, shortly after the Armistice, Louis Loucheur re-established freedom of commerce for the metal industry.[47]
He also decreed that in view of the declining price of coal, iron and
steel prices should be reduced by 25 per cent. In an appendix to the
decree, published on 25 December 1918, however, the *Comité des
Forges* retained the exclusive right to import foreign metal, and as
domestic metal was still at a considerable premium, there was
substantial demand for imported metal. In retaliation for the lower
prices established by Loucheur, the *Comité des Forges* refused all
requests from industrialists for metal. Faced with a great outcry
from these industrialists, Loucheur reversed his decision, and on 12
January 1919, he ended the import monopoly of the *Comité des
Forges*. At this point, the *Comité* suddenly let it be known that it
had considerable stocks of metals and raw materials, and it became
apparent that the *Comité* had been stockpiling metals in the hope
that scarcity would drive prices up.

It is evident that the *Comité des Forges* enjoyed a unique position
of power and authority in France during the war. It overwhelmed
all attempts at opposition from the bureaucrats of the government,
from independent producers, and from its own members. The secret
of the success of the *Comité des Forges* was its willingness to take
the initiative in its dealings with the government to propose solutions, to volunteer to fill gaps. Rather than allowing itself to be
imposed upon by the government, by its policy of co-operation
from the outset of the war the *Comité* was able to create commercial
and industrial conditions highly favourable to itself and its members. By speaking with one voice, metallurgists avoided the dangers
of spoiling the market by competitive bidding for government
contracts.

Behind the facade of unity, however, there were bitter disputes
among members of the *Comité des Forges*, disputes in which bureaucrats were also deeply involved. One such conflict was the Caen
affair.

46. *Comité des Forges, Rapport de la Commission de direction*, 1918, 4.
47. For a full account of the developments of this period, see the speeches of
    Edouard Barthe, *Chambre des députés*, 24 January 1919, 219; 31 January 1919,
    345, 346.

CHAPTER 9

The Caen Affair

The confiscation of German factories located in France and the subsequent battles of competing groups of French industrialists to gain control of them constitute one of the most interesting developments in the relations between industrialists, bureaucrats and politicians during the war. The confiscation of factories created a situation in which the commercial position of an industrialist relative to his fellows could be substantially altered within a very short space of time by the acquisition of partially or fully built plants in exchange for very little capital outlay. In such a situation, bureaucrats were in a strong position as arbiters between the claims of rival industrialists. Just as the sequestration of German dye plants exposed the divisions within the French chemical industry, so the Caen affair revealed that the professional solidarity of members of the *Comité des Forges* took second place to their primordial sense of self-interest when they were confronted with the possibility of acquiring the rich prize of German-owned metallurgical works in France.

From about 1900 on, German industrialists had been investing heavily in French mining and metallurgical properties. In the east of France, in the area of Longwy and the Bassin de Briey, the Germans bought substantial interests in at least seven different properties between 1900 and 1907.[1] In all, eighteen properties in the east of France and ten in Normandy were linked to German interests before 1914.[2]

One of the biggest investors in France was the Thyssen firm, which owned a number of metallurgical establishments, the most

1. 94 AP 52: Ungeheurer, 'Des intérêts industriels de l'Allemagne en France avant la guerre', translated from *Technik und Wirthschaft*, May, July 1916.
2. *Crapouillot*, October 1933, 19.

extensive of which was in Calvados in Normandy.[3] In 1912, Thyssen laid a grandiose plan for the development of the region before the public authorities.[4] The mines of Soumont and Perrières would eventually produce 1 million tons of iron ore annually, 60 per cent of which was to be reserved for new blast furnaces to be built at Caen. These blast furnaces would have an initial productive capacity of 300,000 tons and would be linked to the mines by a special railway. A private port would also be built to service the complex. Three companies were created to undertake the various aspects of the project: a mining and railway company, with a capital of 12 million francs; a blast-furnace company, capitalised at 30 million francs; and a port company, with a capital of 3 million francs. On 3 April 1912, the government passed a decree authorising the creation of the railway. Construction began on the complex, but work was suspended when the war broke out. The Caen affair is essentially the story of two rival groups of French metallurgists attempting to capture control of the incomplete blast-furnaces of Caen.[5]

The tale is a complicated one, filled with Byzantine intrigues and a large cast of characters. As with longer nineteenth-century novels, it is perhaps best to draw up a table of the principal characters before the story unfolds. The dramatis personae can be divided into five groups: (1) the Schneider group, which controlled Le Creusot; (2) a rival alliance of industrialists, comprised of François de Wendel, the head of the de Wendel firm; Leopold Pralon, vice-president and member of the board of the Société des Haute-Fourneaux et Aciéries de Denain et Anzin; and Léon-Lévy, director of the Forges de Châtillon-Commentry et Neuves Maisons; (3) the bureaucrats of the Under-Secretariat of State for Artillery and Munitions, and in particular, those of the Contract Commission; (4) the French parliament, as personified principally by Senator Milliès-Lacroix, one of the most zealous guardians of its rights; (5) Albert Thomas. In addition, there were three minor characters: (1) the Thyssen firm, which owned the property; (2) a New York group, which also bid for Caen; (3) Paul Piketty, the owner of a construction company.

What made the blast-furnaces at Caen such a rich prize was not the intrinsic value of the plant itself, which was far from complete, but the fact that the government was prepared to pay large advances

3. *Chambre des députés*, 24 January 1919, 209.
4. 94 AP 62: Letter to *Ministère des Travaux Publics*. 4 March 1912.
5. Unless otherwise stipulated, material for the Caen affair is drawn from 94 AP 79.

to subsidise further construction costs. In March 1915, the government issued a decree outlining the conditions for granting advances
to cover the salaries and raw materials involved in construction.[6] In
July 1915, a further decree was issued, of which the first article read:

> For the duration of the hostilities ... in exceptional circumstances,
> suppliers of the Ministry of War may be granted advances necessary for
> the creation or development of productive capacity which is indispen-
> sable for the execution of contracts signed with the nation's industries.[7]

Empowered by these decrees, the government began spending
freely, and in the two months which followed their enactment,
between 50 million and 60 million francs was paid out in advances.[8]
The procedure for granting advances was further refined by the law
of 28 September 1915. Clearly the completion of the steel plant at
Caen could come under the category of factory specified by the
decree, since steel was an indispensable commodity for so many
armament factories.

The Initial Schneider Bid

The opening shot in the battle for the control of Caen came in a
letter from Schneider et Cie to Albert Thomas.[9] This letter was in
response to a general request by the government to metallurgists to
find ways for rapidly increasing the productive capacity of metals in
France. The Schneider firm proposed completing construction of
the Caen works and operating the plant once completed. A new
company would be formed for this purpose, composed of the
French shareholders of the old company, the Société des Hauts
Fourneaux et Aciéries de Caen, who had already indicated their
approval of the scheme, and Schneider et Cie, which would replace
the German shareholders. Schneider estimated that the cost of
paying off existing debts and completing construction would be
80 million francs (a remarkable figure, considering that the estimate
for the total cost of building the steel plant *and* the railway, mines,
and port in 1912 came to only 45 million francs). The state was
asked for an advance of 25 million francs in return for which it
would receive a first mortgage on the plant, an annual interest of

6. Decree of 27 March 1915.
7. Decree of 15 July 1915.
8. *Chambre des députés*, Métin, 24 September 1915, 1491.
9. 2 December 1915.

5.75 per cent, and a share in future profits.

Schneider's first bid was a strong one, particularly as the firm already controlled the votes of the French shareholders of the old Caen company. Confronted with this offer, Thomas sought the advice of the Minister of Finance, who counselled him to consider the bid seriously, but to consult with the financial commissions of both chambers of parliament before coming to any final decision.[10] The Minister of Finance also recommended that Thomas negotiate for a higher share of the profits. When consulted, the Budget Commission of the Chamber of Deputies informed Thomas that he was empowered to grant advances under the provisions of the law of 28 September 1915, and that the whole question was not within the competence of the Chamber.[11]

Armed with this information, Thomas gave his provisional consent to Schneider's offer and informed the firm of his decision on 3 January 1916. He agreed to advance 25 million francs, but stipulated that the money was to be spent on the first stage of construction, so that coke, cast iron, and steel would be produced by the end of 1916. He accepted the interest rate of 5.75 per cent and repayment over a thirty-year period starting in 1920, but he haggled over the government's percentage share of profits.

The Challenge of the de Wendel Group

In the meantime, however, a formidable challenger had entered the lists to defy Schneider et Cie. An opposition group, headed by François de Wendel, Léopold Pralon, and Léon-Lévy bombarded Thomas with three notes delivered in rapid succession.[12] The First Note asked whether the creation of a steel works at Caen would serve the national interest and answered its own question with a resounding no. If the government wanted more steel, the de Wendel group could find it elsewhere. It would take two years, not six months, to complete the Caen project, and even then, it would produce only 200,000 tons of steel annually: 'It seems evident that existing factories could easily produce this additional amount more rapidly, requiring fewer men from the army, and with less financial

10. 27 December 1915.
11. 27 December 1915.
12. The exact dates of these notes are uncertain, as they survive only in resumé form in Thomas's papers as the First, Second, and Third Notes, but they all appear to have been delivered between the end of December 1915 and the middle of January 1916.

help from the state.' There were thirty existing factories which could easily be expanded to produce the needed steel. The only possible advantage in completing the Caen project would be in the event of France losing the war, because if France won the war, a plant in Normandy would clearly be unable to compete with the metal which the reconquered province of Lorraine would produce.

The Second Note dealt with the specific point initially made by Schneider that the Caen plant would produce the rails which would be required to rebuild French railway lines after the war. The new Caen factory would be able only to provide 50,000 tons of rails, whereas existing factories could produce 310,000 tons, and this amount would be increased by the eventual addition of the production of plants in presently occupied zones.

The Third Note contained a graphic description of the actual extent of construction on the Caen site. Construction had hardly begun. Work had been started only on one of the four blast-furnaces, there were no visible signs of the steelworks and rolling-mills. Maintenance sheds, foundries, and housing for the workers were all incomplete. To date, some 45 million francs had been sunk into the project and another 60 million would be required to finish it. There followed a detailed analysis of existing factories in France which were currently underexploited, and the authors of the Note maintained that there was enough capacity to produce 1 million tons of cast iron a year without resorting to the new plant at Caen. The argument that it would take two years to complete construction was repeated, and the Note ended: 'The National Defence is not at stake in this project and there should be no question of rescuing individual firms and safeguarding regional interests.'

Other arguments were produced by the de Wendel group to counter the Schneider bid.[13] If the government confiscated German property in France, the Germans would do the same to French property in Germany and occupied French territory, and this would be manifestly unfair to industrialists with investments in these areas. It was also pointed out that by subsidising the Caen steelworks so heavily, the state was unfairly favouring one group of industrialists at the expense of another. Furthermore, it was maintained that the Caen project did not legally qualify for government help in the form of advances.

13. These arguments can be found in a note sent on 16 January 1916, but they must have been used earlier because the Schneider group rebutted them before this date.

Division within the *Comité des Forges*

Thus, by the middle of January 1916 the battle lines between the opposing members of the *Comité des Forges* had been clearly drawn. What was the nature of this split? The answer may be partially contained in a fascinating private report which reached Thomas on 4 January 1916, analysing the skirmishing which had already taken place behind the scenes and outlining the tactics which would be followed in the course of the next few days. The author of the report is unknown, but he was clearly someone sympathetic to and to some extent associated with the Schneider group. According to the report, the plot against Schneider was organised by de Wendel, Pralon, Léon-Lévy, and, astonishingly enough, Robert Pinot, secretary-general of the *Comité des Forges*. The organisers brought strong pressure to bear on Cavallier, of Pont-à-Mousson, and he in turn wrote to Théodore Laurent, one of the directors of the original Caen company, who had initially been sympathetic to the Schneider bid. Furthermore, the de Wendel group had begun a campaign to enlist the support of all firms with interests in Germany, including companies such as Saint-Gobain and Pathé, which were not involved in metallurgy.

Faced with this massive onslaught, the report continued, Schneider et Cie replied by planning a three-pronged attack, with the object of enlisting the support of leading members of the government. Théodore Laurent was won back to the fold, and a private meeting had been arranged for 7 January with Laurent, Schneider, and Briand, President of the Council of Ministers. Another director of Schneider, Fournier, had arranged a private meeting with Ribot, the Minister of Finance, for 5 January. Finally, the legal advisers of Schneider had prepared a report on the Caen project which was to be submitted to Albert Thomas on 6 January.

Thomas duly received this legal report, which dealt with most of the objections raised by the de Wendel group. In the first place, the Schneider project was in no way prejudicial to the interests of the German shareholders, who held only 24 per cent of the stock in the old company, and who would be treated in exactly the same way as their French counterparts. Since the company had been in danger of going bankrupt, all shareholders would be better off under the project proposed by Schneider. There was nothing which would be construed as vindicative in reorganising the Caen company. Negotiations for a similar arrangement had gone on even before the war, and an American group had made an offer in 1915. The Germans would have no pretext whatever for reprisals against French-owned factories in occupied territories, since the interests of German shareholders would be protected. As for the accusation that the Caen project could not be completed in under two years, this was untrue and made without sufficient research. Nor was it true to suggest that the state was unfairly subsidising one group of companies, or one area against another. The Caen project was far enough advanced that its completion was inevitable, whether the additional money required came from the government or from abroad. The Steel Corporation of America had already made a serious offer to finance the new company. The development of the Caen project could have a most beneficial effect in the immediate post-war situation by helping to diminish the amount of metal which would have to be imported into France while French factories liberated from the Germans were being restored to working condition. Since the installations at Caen represented only one-twelfth of France's total pre-war metal production, they could hardly be construed as a formidable competitor to existing industries. In the last place, there could be no doubt about the legality of the state advancing 25 million francs for construction costs, as this was clearly allowed by the law of 28 September 1915.

Rising to the challenge, the de Wendel group retaliated in a letter sent on 16 January 1916 not to Albert Thomas, but to Briand. Accompanying the letter was a delegation of metallurgists consisting of de Wendel, Pralon, Léon-Lévy, Delaye, and de Ribes, acting on behalf of twenty-three French companies with interests in Germany and Alsace-Lorraine. The letter reiterated the arguments in favour of using existing industrial capacity rather than building new plants. But by now, this argument had become almost secondary, and the main stress was placed on the possibility of German retaliation and the confiscation of a thousand million francs worth of French industrial property currently located in Germany or in the occupied zone.

Milliès-Lacroix and the Senate Finance Commission

On 22 January 1916, a new character appeared on the stage: Senator Milliès-Lacroix, the reporter of the Senate Finance Commission. On behalf of the Commission, he demanded full information from Thomas on the exact nature of the financial arrangement the government was planning with Schneider et Cie. He suggested that by his failure to consult with the Commission, Thomas had violated the constitutional rights of the Senate. On 23 January, Milliès-

Lacroix followed up his initial complaint with a letter to Thomas. The Senate Finance Commission could not approve of a contract it had not yet seen. If rumours regarding the size of the advance to be made to Schneider were correct, the sum was far greater than provided for by the law of 28 September 1915 and would unbalance the whole programme of military credits: 'The Finance Commission therefore unanimously expressed the opinion that such an operation cannot be undertaken without having first been submitted to the examination of the Finance Commissions of the two chambers.' Albert Thomas, quite naturally, was somewhat taken aback by this outburst, particularly in view of the fact that in the preceding month the Budget Commission of the Chamber of Deputies had clearly stated that advances of this kind made to private companies were of no concern to them. On 24 January he wrote back to Milliès-Lacroix explaining that since the lower house had declared the matter to be beyond its competence, he could hardly have expected a different decision from the Senate: 'Could I, indeed, consult the Finance Commission of the Upper House and thereby risk placing it in conflict with the Budget Commission of the Chamber, should it deliver a different decision?'

On the same day he sent this reply to Milliès-Lacroix, Thomas received yet another letter from the de Wendel group. The letter contained no new arguments, but produced more statistical information to sustain its previous criticism of the Schneider project. In the meantime the Schneider group kept pressing its case. It enlisted the services of Goutard, an appeal court lawyer, to prove that there was no danger of German reprisals. Thyssen owned only 7.5 million capital shares of the Caen firm, while French interests owned 22.5 million. The heart of the problem was that when the war started, Thyssen was no longer able to make capital investments in proportion to its share of the stock. The company was in danger of going under, and it was not only French interests in Germany which were at stake, but French interests in Caen as well. Did the rights of majority shareholders count for nothing? Could the government consent to the financial ruin of these shareholders because of the phantom threat of German retaliation?

The Bureaucrats Join the Fray

It was now the turn of the bureaucrats to make their entrance. Both groups of metallurgists had fully presented their cases, Thomas had given his provisional approval to Schneider, and parliament had been heard from. It was now the duty of the government offices concerned to give their opinion. On 25 January 1916, the legal and audit department (*Direction du Contrôle*) of the Under-Secretariat of State for Artillery and Munitions sent its report to Thomas. The legal department advised that if it could be assumed, which there was no way of proving, that the first deliveries of coke from the new plant could be made by 15 July 1916, the first cast iron by 15 October 1916, and the first steel by 15 November 1916, then the state should advance the necessary money. The 25 million francs concerned should only be used for the first stage of construction, which would cost a total 30 million francs. Thomas was advised that he should consult the finance commissions of both the Chamber of Deputies and the Senate, as Milliès-Lacroix requested, since certain technical aspects of the financing were not provided for by the law of 28 September 1915. Finally, Thomas should re-negotiate the section of the contract dealing with the share of the profit reserved for the government. It was theoretically possible that the board of management of the new company could vote not to give the state its fair share, and therefore, an arrangement should be made so that the state received its share automatically as soon as profits were made.

The most serious bureaucratic hurdle which the Schneider group had to clear was the Contract Commission. On 27 January 1916, Arthur Fontaine, the President of the Commission, delivered his verdict, which was favourable to the Schneider group. Fontaine began by listing the reasons for which the Caen project should be undertaken. It was absolutely vital that France increase its production of coke, cast iron, and steel in 1916. The new firm, the Société Métallurgique de Normandie, had offered sufficient guarantees both with regard to the quality of the future product and for the security of the state's loan. Fontaine then turned to consider the objections of the de Wendel group. He accepted the view put forward by Schneider that the foreign shareholders of the old company would be treated equally with French shareholders, that only 24 per cent of the capital was in foreign hands, that large sums of money were required to save the initial investment, and that the Germans had no pretext for reprisals. The Contract Commission had thoroughly investigated the possibilities of delays in production and had accepted the advice of Nadal, a mining engineer, which completely contradicted the ill-informed claim made by the de Wendel group that there would be a delay of two years before the plant went into production. As for the alternative proposed by the de Wendel group of reactivating or expanding existing facilities, Fontaine pointed out that in reality this proposal covered only cast iron, not coke and steel, and that the unexploited industrial capacity of these factories was far less than the group had claimed, since many of them were in the military zone near the front and were therefore subject to grave problems of transportation and supply. As for the accusation that the government was subsidising a region and a company which would compete unfairly with existing regions and companies, Fontaine replied that the mineralogical potential of Normandy was very great, that the *Comité des Forges* had always advocated the geographical diversification of the metallurgical industry, that more processed metal was needed in France, and that the west of France required development. Finally, Fontaine said that the advance of 25 million francs was legal under both the decree of 15 July 1915 and the law of 28 September 1915, and he approved the contract with Schneider.

A Desperation Bid by the de Wendel Group

The fight was far from finished, however. Despite the qualified approval of the bureaucrats, Thomas himself began to have second thoughts and refused to sign the contract. Schneider immediately prepared another offer, this time for coke and cast iron alone, requiring an advance of 7 million francs. The Contract Commission duly approved the new contract on 3 February, but once again, Thomas rejected the contract because of qualms about the advance. Meanwhile, the de Wendel group seized on the occasion to make a dramatic counter-proposal. On 3 February, the leaders of the group wrote to Briand to reiterate their fundamental opposition to the project, since it would not help the National Defence but rather lead to German reprisals. However, despite these objections, if the government had its heart set on a metallurgical complex at Caen, then they, the members of the de Wendel group, would undertake to build it:

> We have a great wish to avoid the slightest shadow of reproach of having put obstacles in the path of a creation which has been presented as useful for the National Defence, and at the same time, to save French firms situated in Germany, Alsace-Lorraine, and the occupied zone from the reprisals which the project proposed by Le Creusot [Schneider] could not have failed to provoke.

The de Wendel group would undertake that section of the project which might possibly yield useful results and contribute to the war effort. The group would require no financial assistance from the government; it would give the old company, Les Hauts-Fourneaux de Caen, a loan, without any financial or industrial profit for themselves. To show the utterly non-partisan spirit which animated this proposal, the group would invite all interested metallurgical firms in France to participate in this loan. Since the loan would go to the old Caen company as originally constituted, the Germans would have no pretext whatever for taking counter-measures, since the basic character of the company would remain unchanged, rather than being taken over by a firm like Schneider. The de Wendel group would limit construction to coke ovens, although blast furnaces would be built to produce cast iron if the government insisted, despite existing unused capacity which could be found elsewhere for this purpose. As for steel, some members of the group would build new furnaces adjacent to their old plants to supply the need:

> In conclusion, our project, whose patriotic and disinterested nature you will not fail to appreciate, has the advantage of freeing the state from all financial contribution and of allowing the old Caen company to carry on unchanged to the end of the war, so that it may investigate, in full freedom of choice, all possible combinations which might serve to assure its future.

In making this proposition, the de Wendel group was in the difficult position of remaining consistent with its previous opposition while presenting the government with a viable alternative. Cleverly exploiting the difficulties raised by the problem of the government loan, which had sabotaged the first contract with Schneider, the de Wendel group avoided the issue by asking for no loan. The de Wendel group resolved all the difficulties which they themselves had raised, which in itself was no mean feat. By the distinct lack of enthusiasm for their own counter-proposal, however, the group betrayed the fact that theirs was a wrecking measure, with the sole intention of frustrating the plans of Schneider, not providing the country with coke, cast iron and steel. The solution found to the problem of German retaliation seems as rhetorical as the problem itself. The issue of loans was merely seized on as a tactical device to embarrass Schneider. It is indeed doubtful whether the de Wendel group expected their bid to be taken seriously. They were less interested in taking over the Caen project then stopping it altogether.

Five days later, on 8 February 1916, the de Wendel group received some additional help from a new-found ally, the Senate Finance Commission. This time it was not the reporter, Milliès-Lacroix, but the president, Peytral, who wrote to the Minister of War on the subject of Schneider's proposed contract:

> I have the honour of informing you that the Finance Commission having consulted with the Under-Secretary of State for Artillery and Munitions on the question of the Caen affair and having deliberated upon the issue, has declared that the projected contract does not come under any of the paragraphs of Article Nine of the law of 28 September.[14]

The Final Decision

By now the tide seemed to be running strongly against the Schneider group. The legal department of the Under-Secretariat, which had given cautious approval to the first contract, now sent Albert Thomas a highly critical report of the second on 12 February. This report was important, for it explained for the first time the true motives of the Schneider group in promoting the Caen venture. The various factories of Schneider and its allies, the Aciéries de la Marine et d'Homécourt at Le Creusot, Saint-Chamond, Givors, and Bauron, were being extended, and by June 1917, they would need all 80,000 tons of cast iron and 50,000 tons of coke produced by the Caen works. The state, therefore, would only be allowed to distribute any excess material which might be produced, and all tangible advantages of the scheme would benefit only the Schneider group:

> This project to supply metal seems, in reality, to be only a means of justifying the financial participation of the state in the construction of the new installations at Caen. The loan requested this time is 7,000,000 francs of a total cost of 10,000,000 francs.

Furthermore, the guarantees offered by the group against the non-execution of the contract were minimal. The only guarantee proposed was the '*personal* guarantee' of the Schneider firm. For these reasons, the legal department took a dim view of the new contract.

The principal characters in the affair had now grouped themselves

14. Article Nine defined the conditions of eligibility for firms which wished to receive advances from the government for the construction or development of their factories.

into two unwieldy opposing camps. The Schneider group, led by Schneider et Cie and the Aciéries de la Marine et d'Homécourt, had now been deserted by most of its former sympathisers, except for one bureaucratic body, the Contract Commission, and its president, André Fontaine. Lined up on the other side was a formidable array consisting of de Wendel, Pralon, Léon-Lévy, twenty-three firms with interests in Germany, the Senate Finance Commission, the legal department of the Under-Secretariat, and Albert Thomas. From being odds-on favourite, the chances of the Schneider group winning the contract seemed greatly reduced.

If any work were to be done on the Caen project, it was imperative that a decision be reached quickly. The moment of truth came on 16 February 1916. On that day, de Wendel, Pralon, and Léon-Lévy addressed a final desperate appeal to Briand to allow them to take over Caen. But it was all to no avail. On the same day, the government signed a contract with the Schneider group,[15] granting a loan of 7 million francs to create a new company, the Société Normande de Métallurgie, with a minimum total capital of 25 million francs, for the purpose of building coke ovens and one blast-furnace at Caen. Under the arrangement, a contract was signed with the new company to produce initially 80,000 tons of cast iron. Separate contracts, ratified by the Contract Commission the following day, were signed with Schneider et Cie itself to produce 60,000 tons of steel for the government, and with the Aciéries de la Marine et d'Homécourt.

The Subsequent History of Caen

This swift, total, unexpected victory of the Schneider group is difficult to understand in the light of the developments of the fortnight which preceded it, but before considering the causes of this victory, it might be as well to allow the rest of the tale to unfold. On 22 February, a new participant briefly joined the fray. Ribot, the Minister of Finance, received a cable from New York informing him that the American International Corporation was prepared to supply money, machines, technical personnel, and even workers to complete the installation of blast-furnaces and a steelworks at Caen as quickly as possible. The Corporation was not interested in taking control of the firm, but merely in acting as bankers and advisers under conditions which could be left to subsequent negotiation.

15. 94 AP 80.

Périn, a well-known engineer, had already visited the Caen site on behalf of the Corporation and had conferred with Claveille, the director of the state railways, and the deputy Franklin-Bouillon. However, since the Caen contract had already been awarded, this proposal died a quiet death, and the American International Corporation was never heard from again.

Once the contract was safely within its grasp, the Schneider group seemed strangely lethargic in its attitude towards the Caen project, almost seeming determined to live up to the darkest aspersions which its rivals had cast on its ability to fulfil the contract within the required time. It was only on 5 June 1916, three and a half months after the contract was signed, that the new company got around to sending the Minister of Public Works a request for official permission to take over the obligations incurred by the former company in 1912 *vis-à-vis* the Ministry. Another letter from two of the directors of the new company, Théodore Laurent and Fournier, to the same minister of 29 August 1916 still refers to the future intentions of the company to operate the mines, complete the factories, and build the railway and port, with the implication that nothing, as yet, had been started. After another three months had elapsed, the government received a report on 29 November from Métivier, an engineer from Le Creusot, explaining why work on the project had still not advanced very far. The construction of the complex had been entrusted to the firm of Paul Piketty (a name to be encountered again in the affair of the Arsenal of Roanne). For some time, the work-site had been abandoned in the most deplorable state by this construction firm. Piketty was busy elsewhere carrying out surveys with a view to obtaining important building contracts with the Ministry of War. Since these contracts had practically been signed, Piketty had already withdrawn part of his equipment and workers from the Caen site and transferred them to the location of his new contract.

The situation hardly improved over the next few months, and it is unsurprising to find a letter in February 1917 from the vice-president of a parliamentary sub-commission for armaments to Albert Thomas requesting copies of all the letters which the de Wendel group had sent in late 1915 and early 1916 in opposition to the Caen project. But by now, as with most wartime miscalculations, it was far too late to undo the damage.

The Significance of the Caen Affair

What conclusions are to be drawn from the Caen affair? Undoubtedly, the most interesting aspect of the incident was the way in which it illustrated the sort of division which could exist within the *Comitè des Forges* behind the mask of professional solidarity. The myth of the indivisible monolith, if anyone had ever believed it, was now effectively laid to rest. The concern of individual firms to preserve their rights and power proved stronger than the desire to act in concert to extract greater riches from the government. Once again, the individualism of French industrialists triumphed over their sense of organisation and mutual self-interest. The affair proved that the contrariness and obstinacy which Clémentel encountered when he tried to force industrialists in other fields to participate in collective structures was not a reaction restricted to government intervention but rather an inherent characteristic of the general condition of French industrialists.

The episode raises a number of interesting, and in some cases unanswerable questions. What was the real issue at stake in the dispute? The initial bid of the Schneider group in December 1915 referred to the government's general request to the metallurgical industry to increase output in 1916, and the report of the legal department of the Under-Secretariat of State for Artillery and Munitions on 12 February 1916 confirmed the fact that by June 1917, the factories of Schneider and the Aciéries de la Marine et d'Homécourt would require all the cast iron and coke the new Caen complex could produce in order to fulfil contract obligations to the government. But if this were the case, if there was a genuine need for cast iron and coke which motivated the bid, why the inexplicable delays in proceeding with construction once the contract had been won? As it turned out, the Caen complex was hardly in a state to produce anything by June 1917.

One red herring in the case was the question of German retaliation. The spectre was first raised by the de Wendel group, and it was an argument which they, and they alone, sustained throughout the course of the dispute. The reply given by the Schneider group seemed eminently reasonable, and no one on the government side, either Thomas or his bureaucrats, ever appears to have given much serious credence to the issue. The plain fact was that the German shareholders were in the minority in the company, although Thyssen would appear to be the largest single shareholder. Apparently the Germans financed their takeovers of French companies with French money! The whole question of German retaliation never played any part in the decision of the government to reject the first two bids made by the Schneider group. The elaborate measures taken to ensure the protection of minority interests seemed to destroy the credibility of the de Wendel group's warning. And yet the fact that they were able to enlist the support of French firms with property in Germany or in occupied territory gives one reason to pause. In any event, there is little evidence to indicate that the Germans were in any way influenced by the decision to proceed with the Caen project. Alfons Horton, the head of the iron branch of the German government's Raw Materials Section (the K.R.A), did propose reactivating French and Belgian steelworks in the occupied zone, plants which German industrialists would far rather have seen destroyed, and annexing French and Belgian mines, but the German General Staff ordered his dismissal in early 1917.[16]

The real issue behind the Caen affair seems to have been the more prosaic problem of government advances. It was because of advances that Schneider's first two offers were rejected. In reality, the advances problem was made up of two separate components. In the first place, there was the constitutional and legal aspect: could the government grant such large sums under existing legislation? Need the finance commissions of the Senate and Chamber of Deputies be consulted? Were the rights of the state, particularly with regard to profit sharing, truly safeguarded? These questions may have seemed relatively unimportant, questions of procedure rather than substance, but they were, nevertheless, the reef upon which Schneider's initial, grandiose venture foundered. The second aspect of the advances problem was the more substantial: should the government give such tremendous financial advantages to one group of industrialists and not to another? The fact that Schneider et Cie and the Aciéries de la Marine et d'Homécourt were to receive the very large sum of 25 million francs at almost no cost, and in exchange for putting up only 5 million francs of their own money, was probably the real source of the opposition of the de Wendel group. The harmony and co-operative spirit of members of the *Comité des Forges* were dependent on the status quo, so that no firm advanced in the pre-ordained hierarchy at the expense of the others. But the Schneider group could not fail to improve their position relative to other metallurgical firms if they received such help from the government. Moreover, if Normandy were developed as a major metal-producing area in France, it would destroy all the existing balances and arrangements which had held the *Comité des Forges* together.

16. Feldman, *Germany*, 385.

The real significance of the question of French factories in occupied territory was that while they were being reconditioned after the war, the Caen complex, built during the war, would be in full production, ready to lure away traditional customers. The initial plan called for an installation which would produce only one-twelfth of the total amount of cast iron, coke, and steel produced annually in France, but given the great potential of the region, this would be but the first step. Had the project succeeded, there would have been an alliance of the metallurgical interests of Normandy and the centre of France against those of the north-east (Lorraine and the Bassin de Briey).

If such great issues were involved, why did Schneider not exploit its success after winning the contract in February 1916? One likely reason is that the third contract which was eventually signed was far less favourable to the Schneider group than the first. Instead of building a complex ultimately worth 80 million francs, with the government paying 25 million francs of the cost of the first stage in exchange for only 5 million of the group's money, the group was offered only 7 million francs at a cost of 3 million francs of their own money. Furthermore, there was no indication that the whole project would ever be worth more than 10 million francs, although it is interesting to observe that in their correspondence with the Ministry of Public Works in August 1916, Laurent and Fournier still indicated a desire to take up all the options offered under the original 1912 plan: mines, railroad, port, and plant. Since the government was not prepared to finance its grand schemes, the Schneider group lost interest in the Caen project.

The final question raised by the Caen affair concerns decision-making. Who blocked the first two contracts, and who decided that the third should be signed? What is odd about the three decisions is that each of them went in the opposite way one might have expected. The first two contracts appeared to enjoy the support, although qualified, of Albert Thomas and of the relevant bureaucratic bodies. Yet they failed, and not because of the efforts of the de Wendel group. Certainly, the political pressure put on Thomas by the Senate Finance Commission must have played a prominent part, and the final decision could only have been taken only by Thomas himself. What is even more astonishing, however, was the passage of the third contract. By now the opposition at all levels to the Schneider group seemed insurmountable. The Senate Finance Commission had declared its unalterable opposition to large advances, and the new contract still provided for an advance of 7 million francs. Thomas and the legal department of the Under-Secretariat had grave doubts about the scheme. The de Wendel group had redoubled its attacks. Who, then, did force the final decision? Possibly, pressure was brought to bear by other cabinet ministers. As the project required the formal recommendation of the Ministers of Finance and War to the President of the Republic, and as they had all been bombarded with letters from the rival groups, the ministers concerned may have decided to act themselves to resolve the deadlock. Thomas himself appears to have played no active part in the final decision, although in the absence of any concrete evidence, one can only speculate. Since the only bureaucratic support the victorious Schneider group received was from the Contract Commission, it is tempting to credit this body, and in particular, André Fontaine, with a large measure of responsibility for resolving the issue. But against this surmise can be cited another surprising feature of the decision: the speed with which it was reached despite all the obstacles thrown in its path. This rapidity suggests the hand of a minister rather than that of a bureaucrat. Bureaucrats were not only disinclined by temperament to proceed rapidly, they lacked the power to overrule all other voices in forcing a decision.

In the final analysis, no one emerged the victor in the Caen affair, except, ironically enough and by default, the de Wendel group, which had been opposed to the project from the start. The rights of parliament were hardly upheld, since the government signed a contract providing for an advance, despite the express prohibition of the Senate Finance Commission. Of the bureaucratic bodies concerned, only André Fontaine's Contract Commission was vindicated. The Schneider group failed to win the contract it wanted, the government failed to obtain the metal it needed, despite the expenditure of 7 million francs, and Albert Thomas seemingly failed to exert any control whatever over the situation. Above all, he failed to exploit the schism within the *Comité des Forges* to the advantage of the government: the high prices of armaments continued unabated.

As it turned out, the Caen affair was merely a warm-up exercise for Albert Thomas's last great battle with French metallurgists over the Arsenal of Roanne. Many of the leading characters from the Caen affair were to reappear to Roanne, but this time the stakes were greater: not the least of these was Albert Thomas's political career.

CHAPTER 10

The Arsenal of Roanne

It will be recalled that before 1914 the bulk of French armament production took place in government arsenals, which employed 38,000 workers, rather than in privately-owned armament factories, which employed only 12,500. The war led to a complete reversal of the traditional pattern of armament production in France. By 1918, of the 1.675 million workers engaged in war materials production, the state employed 295,000 in its arsenals, or 18 per cent of the total, to private industry's 1.38 million.[1] As we have seen, the *Comité des Forges* strove to meet the challenge of insufficient armament production, but there was a great deal of lost ground to be regained. France's largest metallurgical complex during the war was Le Creusot (owned by Schneider et Cie) whose capital worth was valued at 27 million francs in 1912. At the same date, the installations of Krupp in Germany were worth 225 million francs.[2] To compensate for the continuing shortage of munitions during the war, various schemes were considered. Of these, the most interesting was that of creating a National Steelworks, on the lines of the National Dyes Company, with private industrialists subscribing a portion of the capital. This scheme was originally proposed by Louis Loucheur. According to a confidential report sent to Albert Thomas in March 1917,[3] the principal reason that the project had failed was because of the unflagging opposition of François de Wendel, who was reported to have told a fellow member of the *Comité des Forges* that he would wreck the scheme even if he had to use his parliamentary authority as deputy to do so. De Wendel was a Republican deputy from the north-eastern metallurgical district of Briey who was

---

1. Oualid, *La Guerre*, 45.
2. Gignoux, *Roanne*, 13.
3. 94 AP 78.

elected for the first time in 1914.[4] De Wendel's opposition was comprehensible; his factories produced 220,000 tons of laminated steel, of which four-fifths was destined to be used in peacetime in Paris for construction. The creation of a steelworks close to Paris producing Martin steel, which was of a higher quality than the Thomas steel produced by de Wendel, would have spoiled the Paris market for laminated steel. To mask his opposition, de Wendel subscribed a small amount of stock in the new venture, while leading a resistance movement against it, aided by his *compagnons de route* from the Caen affair, Pralon and Léon-Lévy.

For lack of support, the National Steelworks scheme failed, and the government was still faced with a severe shortage of munitions. The existing national arsenals were one obvious source of new armament production, but none of them was built on a scale sufficient to make any serious contribution towards easing the chronic shortage of shells. There were, however, distinct administrative and legal advantages to be gained by using the old system of arsenals. They had enjoyed a legal existence for a considerable period of time, and well-established procedures existed for creating new ones.

Early in the war, a young engineer by the name of Hugoniot saw the possibility of putting the old institution of the state arsenal to new uses. Hugoniot was the protégé of one of Thomas's chief advisers, Eyrolles, of the *Ecole Normale*.[5] Hugoniot was to become the key figure in the affair of the Arsenal of Roanne; his was the initial idea, and it was he who almost single-handedly translated the idea into action. He was dynamic, a self-made man, the prototype of a 'captain of industry'.[6] Hugoniot had been greatly influenced by the success of the industrial techniques of Henry Ford in Detroit. He realised that mass-production would not only reduce the cost of manufactured items considerably, but lead to salary increases for workers. Ford had proved that with organisation it was possible to produce 3,000 automobiles a day, which could be sold at a low price; workers would enjoy an eight-hour day and earn larger salaries, while Ford would make considerable profits.[7] If the Ford technique were applied to armament production, more shells and cannons could be produced at lower cost and with fewer mobilised workers. These results, however, could be obtained only by making it in the industrialist's financial interest to increase the productivity

4. Archives de l'Assemblée Nationale, *Dictionnaire Parlementaire*.
5. Schaper, *Thomas*, 114.
6. Gignoux, *Roanne*, 40.
7. 94 AP 77: Hugoniot to Dulot, 28 January 1918.

of each worker. Hugoniot felt initially that a system of bonuses could be created whereby private industrialists would be rewarded for using fewer mobilised workers to produce more shells, and that this system would be sufficient to increase shell production without the further intervention of the state: 'It must be said that this system of bonuses will favour large industry to the detriment of small, but I believe, in all honesty, that this is the only practical way of achieving mass-production'.[8] A further refinement of the bonus system was profit-sharing. Profit-sharing between workers and management was an integral part of the success of Ford's mass-production and took the form of high wages. Hugoniot maintained that this canalisation of the profit motive into higher productivity on the part of the industrial workers and managers would be a leading characteristic of the post-war industrial world. Profit-sharing along the lines of the Ford experiment was the technique of the future.[9]

One of the ironies of the Roanne affair was that, to begin with, Hugoniot was a convinced partisan of private enterprise. In November 1915, Hugoniot was ordered to investigate the possibilities of building a plant capable of producing 100,000 75 mm. shells a day. He considered, then rejected the idea that the state itself should undertake such a project, and instead, he suggested asking André Citroën to build a plant within eight months, using 7,570 workers to produce 50,000 shells a day. The government did not exploit this possibility, but as late as August 1916, Hugoniot was still proposing that Citroën be given a contract to build a shell factory on the outskirts of Paris:

It may appear abnormal that the state itself should not undertake such a project directly, but it could only do so with a loss of several months; the organism of the state to which the execution of a project of this kind would be entrusted could never have the liberty and the means of action which are available to private industry.[10]

Subsequent events were to bear out the truth of this observation.

While extolling the virtues of private industry, Hugoniot had himself been proving that state factories, if properly managed, could also yield highly satisfactory results. In June 1915, Thomas decided to create an armament plant at Saint Pierre des Corps, on the outskirts of Tours, to produce components for 75 mm. shells. The state was to pay building costs, while a private group of industrialists

8. 94 AP 72: Hugoniot, *Rapport au Service industriel*, 28 August 1915.
9. 94 AP 77: Hugoniot to Thomas, 4 April 1917.
10. 94 AP 78: Hugoniot to Thomas, 28 August 1916.

would run the plant. In July, the private group renounced the project, but Thomas decided to press on with construction, which was completed by January 1916. Since private industry would not operate the plant, the crucial decision was made to revert to the old formula of declaring the establishment to be a state arsenal and to run it along traditional lines, using mobilised workers. At this point Hugoniot, who was serving as an artillery officer, was placed in charge (at his military salary of 22.5 francs a day). Within three months, he performed the phenomenal feat of increasing the production of partially completed shells from 2,700 to 30,000 a day, and this when the plant had been expected to produce only 20,000 a day at most. By economising on steel, each shell cost four francs less than anticipated. Rather than having different stages of shell production undertaken at great expense by little factories which were often widely separated, Hugoniot grouped the first four stages of production under one roof. The net result was that he saved the state some 3 million francs. The secret of his success was that he recruited talented civilian collaborators from private industry and promised them bonuses for greater productivity, bonuses which, incidentally, the Treasury never paid.[11]

In June 1916, Hugoniot wrote to the Under-Secretariat to report on his achievements and to request that his subordinates be given permanent contracts by the government in view of the splendid work they had done and the fact that they had given up lucrative positions in private industry. He also asked that his own contract be annulled, but that he be given an official function in the Under-Secretariat so that he could undertake new ventures of this kind. He concluded:

> I must stress the fact that an industrial organisation allowed me to obtain at Saint Pierre des Corps results which I could never have obtained with a traditional military organisation.
>   It is not possible to create intensely productive industries if one is hedged by peacetime procedures.[12]

In August 1916, Hugoniot underwent something of a conversion. While still believing in the superiority of the techniques of modern private industry, as evidenced by his letter urging the government to sign a contract with André Citroën to build a munitions plant, increasingly he was coming to the view that these techniques could also be applied successfully in a state establishment, and more

11. Gignoux, *Roanne*, 26–9.
12. 94 AP 77: Hugoniot to Under-Secretariat, 15 June 1916.

specifically, in a state arsenal. Saint Pierre des Corps was conclusive proof. On 25 August 1916, Hugoniot wrote a masterly letter to Thomas which effectively closed out all other options for increasing shell production but that of creating an enormous state arsenal.[13] The letter began in a circuitous fashion by referring to the offer of a French company to produce shells for Russia. It seemed unlikely that any group of private companies could produce the shells in the time required. Then Hugoniot came to the point. If the state could create an arsenal on an industrial basis similar to that of private companies, the best solution would be for the state to build its own plant to supply the Russians with shells at a much lower price than normal. Then he reverted to the current state of negotiations with Citroën, which, it seemed, were not advancing smoothly. Furthermore, he pointed out that unless something were done soon to rescue skilled workers from the army, they would be so dispersed that it would be impossible to trace them. The real question, said Hugoniot, was whether the state itself could undertake major industrial projects, or whether private enterprise alone was capable of such ventures. If the financial support of the state were assured, then it was simply a question of finding the right man. This man would have to be supported by a group of trained artillery officers who would be suitably rewarded for high productivity. Hugoniot ended his letter with a challenge to Thomas:

> This would be the best solution, but I do not believe it possible, because it is a principle of the state not to be able to trust anyone, and it is impossible to achieve a task of this scope without trusting those who are responsible for its execution; the state is more likely to paralyse their efforts by engulfing them in rules and regulations which are impossible to obey in current wartime industry.

In case Thomas missed the point, Hugoniot followed up his first letter with a second on 29 August 1916 with far more specific proposals to create several state munitions plants.[14] Furthermore, repeating a suggestion he had made in a note to Thomas on 5 June 1915, Hugoniot proposed that a complete study project be undertaken of the technical aspect of producing each kind of shell, and that inefficient industrialists who failed to manufacture according to certain norms be granted no more contracts.

Both of these notes left Albert Thomas to draw his own conclusions. There is every evidence to suggest that he received these

13. 94 AP 78: Hugoniot to Thomas, 25 August 1916.
14. 94 AP 78: Hugoniot to Thomas, 29 August 1916.

proposals with a great deal of interest. In May 1916, General Joffre had informed the government that after the experience of the Champaign campaign and the fighting on the Somme, he required far more artillery and a minimum of 200,000 75 mm. shells and 50,000 155 mm. shells a day. Like Hugoniot, Thomas had at first thought of private industry, and in July 1916, large numbers of contracts had been signed with various firms, but a great gap in shell production remained. Thomas had carefully considered Citroën's offer to produce 50,000 75 mm. shells a day, but rejected it for a variety of reasons. Other industrialists, notably the de Wendel group, fresh from their triumph of blocking the National Steel-works project, were distinctly hostile to building any new factories, as they believed the war would be over by the end of 1916, and they wished to invest no more in armament production.[15] Thomas was therefore receptive to suggestions from any quarter. It is clear that Hugoniot's ideas had impressed him generally before any specific project had actually been proposed. In June 1916, Thomas sent out an order to all his staff to launch an investigation of the industrial processes involved in producing each piece of war material.[16] This note was a verbatim copy of the letter which Hugoniot had sent to him nearly a year earlier, in June 1915, and to which Hugoniot was to refer in his letter of 29 August 1916.[17]

Thomas drew the conclusions which Hugoniot hoped he would and acted with great, indeed almost excessive, rapidity. On 3 September 1916, within five days of receiving Hugoniot's last letter, Thomas decided that the state would build a huge arsenal at Roanne, in the centre of France almost halfway between Vichy and Lyon. The selection of this location dated back to September 1915, when Thomas had asked Hugoniot to investigate the possibilities of creating an artillery plant at Roanne. The site was in many ways ideal. It was away from the fighting, well serviced by existing railways and waterways, in an industrial region with ready supplies of coal, steel, electricity, and labour.[18]

It is surprising that Thomas should have been quite so hasty in making this decision, because there is no indication that any precise plans for the proposed complex had been drawn up beforehand. Nor did Thomas consult the Ministry of Finance, the financial section of the Ministry of War, or either of the parliamentary finance commissions.

15. Gignoux, *Roanne*, 35–7.
16. Ibid., 23, 24.
17. 94 AP 78.
18. Gignoux, *Roanne*, 44.

Naturally, Thomas placed Hugoniot in charge of the project. Hugoniot also moved with incredible speed. Three days after receiving his commission, on 6 September 1916, he went to Roanne and contacted a local *notaire* through whom, on 11 September, he purchased a property of 405 hectares at a cost of 2 million francs. In doing so, he undoubtedly obtained a good price, since the 0.55 francs per square metre he paid was well below the current market value, and a château and park was thrown into the bargain, but he also incurred the first of the great string of administrative and procedural errors which were to litter his trail through the months ahead. To begin with, legally Hugoniot was only allowed to make purchases under a limit of 50,000 francs without the approval of the parliamentary finance commissions. By dividing up the price paid for the land into slices of 50,000 francs, and by borrowing money personally, he evaded this proviso. Secondly, it was against official bureaucratic procedure to use a *notaire* for government transactions. Thirdly, he had bought the land by the metre and not the hectare. Lastly, he had failed to take the wartime moratorium on mortgages into account, under which the state was to make no firm purchases of land during the war, but was to regularise all transactions afterwards.[19] These may have seemed petty transgressions, but the fault lay in their accumulation.

Hugoniot's unorthodox tactics threw the bureaucrats of the Under-Secretariat of State for Artillery and Munitions into confusion. On 21 September, for example, General Ronneaux, the head of the Artillery section, received a request from Hugoniot for official permission to import machinery which he had purchased abroad. This was the first that Ronneaux had heard of the Arsenal of Roanne, and he wrote to Thomas requesting further information. On 23 September, Thomas replied and explained the reasons which lay behind the creation of an arsenal at Roanne.[20] In the first place, qualified workers, particularly those who had been taken from the army, had to be placed in larger, more efficient groupings to increase productivity. Then, there was the immediate need of the army for shells, and most especially for 50,000 155 mm. shells a day, as well as cannons and other artillery equipment. Finally, the state needed a guaranteed production of war materials after the war. For these reasons he had decided to create a new arsenal at Roanne under the direction of Hugoniot, who would receive a contract to construct and operate the establishment. Thomas asked Ronneaux

19. Ibid., 50.
20. 94 AP 78: Thomas to Ronneaux, 23 September 1916, *Note 386.*

to do everything he could to help Hugoniot, particularly with regard to the financing of the operation, even if only on a provisional basis.

By October 1916, plans for the Roanne complex had become more precise.[21] The scale of the project was grandiose. Eventually the site would cover some 1300 hectares. Four enormous workshops would be built, each measuring 300 metres by 200, each with its own stores building 250 metres by 30.[22] At one end of the site would be a warehouse for finished shells with a floor-space of 5,000 square metres. There would be 13 hangars, each measuring 100 metres by 15 metres; there would be an electrical plant 1,200 metres long capable of producing 15,000 kilowatts; there would be 14 steam generators; there would be three enormous foundries for iron, steel, and bronze. The total floor-space of the project covered 35 hectares. 20 kilometres of tramway and 40 kilometres of rail would be built, and at the end of the canal there would be a port 300 metres long. There would be 3,000 new machine tools and 2,000 electrical motors. There would be a workers' city with housing for 1,000 families and 1,500 single men, with camps for 3,500 more, as well as schools, co-operative stores, a hospital, and a post office.

The cost of the project would be on a similarly lavish scale. Land, railway, port, and roads would cost 10 million francs. Buildings: 40 million francs; installations to produce 155 mm. shells: 25 million francs; installations to produce 75 mm. shells: 20 million francs; tooling for other calibre shells, and cannon: 20 million francs; electrical energy: 20 million francs; unforeseen expenditure: 15 million francs; total cost: 150 million francs.[23] In return for this huge investment, Hugoniot calculated that the arsenal would produce daily 12,000 155 mm. shells at 75 francs each instead of the 95 francs currently paid, 40,000 75 mm. shells at 4.25 francs instead of 7.5 francs, and four heavy cannons. If production were begun quickly, the state would save 4 million francs a month on the 75 mm. shells alone. If everything went according to plan, the entire complex would thus be paid for in 315 days. The project was enormous but not unprecedented. In 1916, Krupp had started work on a complex of the same size outside Munich. Moreover, the success of the Saint Pierre des Corps experience had shown that Hugoniot's techniques did work in practice.

The success of the project hinged entirely on the speed of its execution. The slightest delay would diminish the financial advan-

21. 94 AP 78: Hugoniot to Thomas, 1 October 1916.
22. 94 AP 77: *Rapport du maire de Roanne*, 26 March 1919.
23. Gignoux, *Roanne*, 40–2.

tages of the scheme considerably. To achieve the required speed, Hugoniot had to break a number of rules and procedures, as he had always warned Thomas he would. But while these administrative short-cuts were essential, he made himself vulnerable to the danger of being challenged by those responsible for maintaining the rules. If the opposition grew too strong, the project would be delayed and the advantages frittered away. Thomas was faced with an irreconcilable problem: either he was to allow Hugoniot to cut corners and save time but expose the project to attack from several quarters, or he was to proceed according to the rules and gain nothing.

On 13 October 1916, Thomas officially announced the creation of an arsenal at Roanne by a ministerial decision. No details about the organisation or the financing of the complex were revealed. Immediately there was trouble. On behalf of the Senate Finance Commission, Milliès-Lacroix wrote to Thomas requesting copies of the plans, the reasons for embarking on such an enterprise, an estimate of the expenses, and an explanation of the proposed administration of the arsenal.[24] At the beginning of November, Thomas replied.[25] He recalled the request of Joffre for more shells, he cited the success of the Saint Pierre des Corps project, and he referred to the need for the state to preserve war materials plants after the war. He also added a new argument: the notion of price control, and the need to force private industry to lower its prices by subsidising a serious competitor.

> I think that it is very necessary to present private industry, whose strength has greatly increased, with state factories which will prevent the creation of a veritable monopoly whose consequences would be harmful, as much from the point of view of price as of the quality of production.

This motive was laudable, but it gave a hint for further opposition, which was to come this time from private industry.

Thomas's letter left Milliès-Lacroix dissatisfied because it failed to provide much of the information he had requested. There was a simple reason for this: in many cases, the information did not exist. In particular, Thomas was unable to send a detailed copy of the plans because they had not yet been drafted. In the meantime, Hugoniot was working with great energy, accumulating errors as he went. The problem of finance continued to preoccupy him. He employed a number of legal fictions to pay off suppliers, but he was forced to take more drastic measures to pay his personnel. On 28

24. *Sénat*, 28 March 1917, 320.
25. 94 AP 78: Thomas to Milliès-Lacroix, 3 November 1916.

November, he told Thomas that he had borrowed personally first 60,000 then 120,000 francs from André Citroën to pay his workers. He said that if he had waited for three months until the proper credits could be voted, the state would lose 27 million francs which it might otherwise have gained. He asked for a clarification of his own personal contract. He was ready to take full responsibility for the operations of the new factory, but he could not continue to incur personal debts to save the state millions of francs. If he had been hired only to construct the plant, he would not bother seeking out collaborators from private industry to run it. If he ran it, he demanded a share of the profits in the case of increased productivity for his collaborators and himself, with a maximum bonus of 1,000 francs per man per month. He said that it was only fair that if he asked top men to give up lucrative jobs in private industry he should be able to pay them 50,000 francs a year. If Thomas gave his authorisation, he would immediately hire the 150 engineers and plant managers he required.[26]

Hugoniot now began to pay the price for moving too quickly. In December, while contracts for the new buildings were still being bid for, the first machinery from England began to arrive at Roanne. Since 30 million francs worth of machinery could hardly be left out in the snow and cold, Hugoniot was forced to build temporary buildings to house them, at a total cost of 700,000 francs, paid, as usual, in slices of 50,000 francs to avoid having to seek the approval of higher authorities.[27]

By now, the higher authorities in question, notably the Senate Finance Commission, were becoming somewhat impatient with the persistent refusal of the Under-Secretariat of State for Artillery and Munitions to advise them of what was happening. In January 1917, Senator Milliès-Lacroix had an interview with Thomas during which he pointed out that the Minister of Finance had insisted that the Finance Commission of the Senate be consulted on a particular contract for 200,000 francs, but that as yet there had been no similar request for an official authorisation by the Commission for an expenditure of 150 million francs for the Arsenal of Roanne.[28] In haste, the Under-Secretariat began to repair its defences. On 21 January, General Ronneaux sent a personal note to Albert Thomas summarising the legal position of the state with regard to the new arsenal.[29] After reviewing developments to date and reminding

26. 94 AP 77: Hugoniot to Thomas, 28 November 1916.
27. Gignoux, *Roanne*, 51.
28. 94 AP 77: Thomas, *Note 5354*, 23 January 1917.
29. 94 AP 78: Ronneaux to Thomas, 21 January 1917.

Thomas that he had warned him previously of the various errors Hugoniot had committed, he outlined the laws governing arsenals, beginning with the law of 16 March 1882 and working forward. He then discussed the creation of various arsenals since the war. The critical question was that of credits. When the creation of Roanne was decided upon in September 1916, the budget for the fourth quarter of 1916 had long since been prepared. The first expenses were placed under Chapter 20 of the budget, a contingency fund, because of the urgency of the situation. When the military budget for the first quarter of 1917 was being prepared in October 1916, specific provision was made for the Arsenal of Roanne. While this procedure flouted peacetime rules governing military expenditure, it was entirely in accordance with current wartime practice. From the beginning of the war, the procedure had been, except in the case of purchases made abroad, to spend the money first and receive official approbation from the Treasury afterwards. Ronneaux concluded:

> The expenses incurred at the time of the creation of the Arsenal of Roanne were treated in exactly the same way as all other expenses incurred in France. There was no reason to treat these particular expenses differently.

Although this answer may have been technically correct, it in no way satisfied Milliex-Lacrois. For one thing, there was a legal difference between spending money on ordinary military contracts and creating an entirely new establishment. By the decree of 8 November 1911 governing public administration, no new establishment could be created without a decree of the *Conseil d'Etat*, after a vote on the credits by both chambers of parliament.[30] Previous exceptions to the rule during the war were merely for improvements to existing establishments, and nothing approaching the size of Roanne had ever been built without passing through the correct channels. Accordingly, Milliès-Lacroix launched a full-scale attack against the arsenal. On 18 January 1917, he telephoned the Ministry of Armament, as it had just become, and demanded a complete list of arsenals created since the outbreak of the war, the date of their creation, the amount spent on them, and their production figures.[31] On 30 January, Milliès-Lacroix sent a further list of questions to Thomas. A copy of Hugoniot's suggested answers to the questions exists.[32] Milliès-Lacroix began by asking for a copy of

30. Gignoux, *Roanne*, 46, 47.
31. 94 AP 78: *Message téléphoné*, 18 January 1917.
32. 94 AP 78: Milliès-Lacroix to Thomas, 30 January 1917.

all documents relating to Roanne written before October 1916. None existed, replied Hugoniot. Next, Milliès-Lacroix wished to know who had authorised the expenditure of money on the project, and under which regulation. He also wanted to find out whether a certain number of credits had been made over to Hugoniot to spend on Roanne. Hugoniot answered that he had spent the money first and asked for the authorisation afterwards. Thirdly, Milliès-Lacroix asked about Hugoniot's personal loans from Citroën and about his general procedure for dealing with suppliers. Hugoniot said that he paid the suppliers first, they then delivered their material to the Arsenal and were paid again, whereupon they immediately reimbursed Hugoniot. Fourthly, Milliès-Lacroix wanted to know whether detailed plans had existed for the administrative and financial organisation of the establishment, both for its construction and operation, at the time its creation was announced on 13 October 1916. Hugoniot replied that no detailed plans had been drawn up, since the normal administrative regime of artillery establishments would apply. (This was less than the truth, in view of the fact that Hugoniot intended to create a profit-sharing arrangement for the personnel of the new plant.) Finally, Milliès-Lacroix asked whether a contract had been drawn up for Hugoniot (it had not), and for lists of the personnel and board of directors of Roanne, which were supplied.

The board of directors was presided over by Louis Loucheur, who had just been made Under-Secretary of State for War Production under Thomas at the Ministry of Armament. In addition to wartime bureaucrats like General Ronneaux, Colonel Payeur, and Hugoniot himself, the board contained two industrialists, Louis Renault and Lazare Lévy. An explanation of the minutes of their meetings from January to March 1917 reveals a curious lack of concern for the mounting problems of the Arsenal, and in particular, delays in construction.[33] Instead, there were lengthy discussions on such topics as a bakery for the workers' town. The presence of Louis Loucheur on the board, as we shall see later, may not be altogether unconnected with this lassitude. One cause of the relative inactivity of the board may have been the fact that its functions were very loosely defined. It was ordered to examine all useful questions, but in theory, Hugoniot was not obliged to consult the board.

In February, there was a further difficulty. André Matter, the chief legal expert of the Ministry of Armament, sent a note to Thomas to explain that a contract with Hugoniot to provide for

33. 94 AP 77.

profit-sharing was impossible.[34] Neither the public authorities, nor, for that matter, public opinion, would readily accept the principle that employees of a state arsenal should make exceptional profits without taking exceptional personal risks of a financial nature. The only real solution would be for Hugoniot and his associates to form a private company by putting up a portion of their own money, and the state then signing a contract with this company.

In March 1917, the crisis of the Arsenal of Roanne became public knowledge, and the *Affaire de Roanne* began in earnest. On 8 March Milliès-Lacroix delivered a highly critical report to the Senate on the state of affairs at Roanne.[35] He outlined the administrative and financial errors that had occurred thusfar, he criticised the proposed profit-sharing arrangements and pointed to the large number of engineers and managers who were already employed in state establishments receiving nothing more than a meagre military stipend, he criticised the creation of a powerless board of directors who could only give advice when requested by Hugoniot. Then Milliès-Lacroix turned to the actual state of construction at Roanne. The project had been so badly conceived that two of the four plants, those producing steel and cannons, had already been abandoned. Although the first production of shells had been announced for April 1917, no building as yet had a roof, and many buildings had not yet been begun. The administrative structure of the complex was still uncertain, it had yet to be proved that production would be as rapid as Hugoniot had predicted, and it was unclear what would become of Roanne after the war. Men, material, transportation, and money had all been wasted copiously on the project. In conclusion, Milliès-Lacroix prepared the following resolution: 'The Senate, disapproving of the errors which the creation of a new military arsenal at Roanne has given rise to, invites the government to put an end to the scheme'.

This public exposure of the situation at Roanne led to a nasty press campaign against Thomas and his collaborators, which was only exacerbated by a second report which Milliès-Lacroix delivered to the Senate on 28 March.[36] Again, he recalled the sequence of events in the autumn of 1916, laying particular stress on the fact that Thomas had been unable to supply him with the plans of the project since none existed, and since no technical, administrative, or financial studies had been undertaken before the project had been

---

34. 94 AP 77: A. Matter, *Organisation de l'Arsenal de Roanne*, 9 February 1917.
35. *Documents parlementaires – Sénat*, 1917, 99–105. *Annexe No. 75, Rapport Spécial de M. Milliès-Lacroix sur l'Arsenal de Roanne*, 8 March 1917.
36. *Sénat*, 28 March 1917, 320–30.

Albert Thomas gave a vigorous defence of his policy before the senators. He reviewed the motives which had led to the creation of Roanne: the need to conserve labour, the necessity of increasing production, the reluctance of private industry to build new productive capacity, and the need for military factories in the post-war period. He admitted that administrative errors had occurred in implementing the plan, but he stressed the importance of striking quickly if the full advantages of the project were to be realised. Each day saved represented a profit for the state. As for the financing of the Arsenal, this had been calculated on a basis of the price of shells in August 1916. The 150 million francs investment would be amortised by a saving of 150 million francs on shell prices, and at the end of it all, the state would own outright a magnificent factory. Thomas then moved on to the controversial topic of profit-sharing. Milliès-Lacroix had misrepresented the entire issue. The profits were to be shared by all the top personnel of the Arsenal, not merely given to Hugoniot alone. Thomas subscribed wholeheartedly to what he felt was a radically new concept in labour relations.

launched. All that was known was the total cost: 150 million francs. Milliès-Lacroix then dwelt lovingly on the subject of the controversial profit-sharing contract which Hugoniot had requested at the end of November. Hugoniot wanted half the profits of Roanne after the capital had been amortised. By his own calculations, this meant that he would be earning 4,000 francs a day, 120,000 francs a month, 1.44 million francs a year on the daily production of 50,000 75 mm. shells alone. Other shells would be worth as much again. He was also to receive an emolument of 0.1 per cent of total construction costs, or 150,000 francs. Finally, Milliès-Lacroix reminded the Senate again of the fact that two of the four original plants had been abandoned and written off as a pure loss.

> Hugoniot has constantly advocated one idea, which seems to me a new one that the state would be well-advised to consider in the future, the idea of interesting the personnel of our factories in productivity . . . of instituting a share in the profits when economies are achieved on the cost-price of shells.

These sentiments were vigorously applauded by the senators on the left. Thomas reminded the Senate that all of the unorthodox procedures which had accompanied the creation of Roanne had been employed for the sole purpose of saving the state money. As for delays, severe weather and import problems had been major contributing factors. Despite all evidence to the contrary, Thomas insisted that the project was well in hand, that no part of it had been abandoned, and that it would be finished by July 1917. He defended the administration of the Arsenal, and in particular, the board of directors, which was not a board of directors in the traditional sense, but represented, a new formula. What, exactly, this formula was, he failed to say.

Thomas came in for some sharp criticism from the senators, but he was firmly upheld by Ribot, the Minister of Finance, and in the end, the support for the government, indicated by a show of hands, was almost unanimous. Some sections of the press, however, were considerably less impressed by Thomas's defence.[37] In the days following the debate in the Senate, his policy was approved by *Le Temps*, *L'Intransigent*, *La France*, and *L'Humanité*, which published the stirring headline: 'The Arsenal will live'. But against Thomas were massed *L'Action Française*, *Le Radical*, *Libre Parole*, *Bataille*, *Liberté*, *Journal du peuple*, and *Echo de Paris*. The theme which united the opposition was that the Arsenal of Roanne was part of a sinister plot on the part of the socialists. An article appeared in *Echo de Paris* claiming,

> In the minds of our socialist leaders the Roanne enterprise and the war are two different things. Is the Roanne enterprise an arsenal? Yes, in a sense, but above all, it is an experiment in state socialism, and an experiment which, instead of helping the war effort, is destined to help socialism . . . . The socialist leaders carry through their ideas; they use the war period and the pretext of the war to promote their ideas. The socialist group is the only one within the National Defence to act constantly in the interest of their own party.[38]

Further Opposition to Roanne:
Bureaucrats and Industrialists

It is time to pause to consider the activity which was going on behind the scenes while the parliamentary and press campaigns against Roanne were in full cry. If Hugoniot was the moving force behind the Arsenal of Roanne, Milliès-Lacroix was its chief critic. What were his fundamental objections to the project? According to a confidential report prepared for Thomas by his advisers,[39] it was

37. A full collection of press clippings can be found in 94 AP 78.
38. 31 March 1917.
39. 94 AP 78: *Roanne, Note confidentialle sur ce que seraient, au fond, les dispositions de M. Milliès-Lacroix*.

not the financial aspect of the question which most offended
Milliès-Lacroix, it was the lack of administrative organisation, for
which he blamed not Hugoniot, interestingly enough, but Thomas's
bureaucrats,

> who, since the beginning, have viewed this creation with deep-seated
> hostility and not only displayed bad faith in assuring administratively its
> realisation, but passively allowed administrative irregularities to accu-
> mulate, or in any case, did nothing to give this new institution the
> administrative structure which was indispensable.

According to the report, Milliès-Lacroix drew a distinction between
bureaucrats of the Artillery section of the Ministry of Armaments
and bureaucrats of the Powder section. Both broke administrative
rules in implementing their plans, both placed bright young men in
charge of huge state establishments, but only the Powder section
gave these men the necessary support by creating a sound administration. Associates of Milliès-Lacroix maintained that he was quite
prepared to see Hugoniot remain in charge, as long as the administrative situation was regularised, possibly by giving Hugoniot and
his associates higher military rank and salaries.

This report raises two interesting points. In the first place, it
shows Milliès-Lacroix in a more constructive light than might have
been expected for a man who advocated cancelling the entire
Roanne project. Undoubtedly he was also driven by a strong
feeling that the rights of parliament in financial matters ought to be
respected, but his opposition seems less partisan and more reasonable than his uncompromising public attitude indicated, although he
was not above deliberately distorting the nature of the profit-
sharing arrangement proposed by Hugoniot, in order to make his
point more dramatically. Secondly, his alleged criticism of the
bureaucrats of the Artillery section of the Ministry of Armament
was diametrically opposite to that made by newspapers like *Echo de
Paris* and *Liberté*. 'Monsieur Lebureau' was not criticised by
Milliès-Lacroix for being too rapacious but for being too timid, for
resisting innovation, for being unwilling to create new structures to
support new forms of state institutions, for failing to support
Hugoniot and Thomas.

Were Milliès-Lacroix's allegations valid? It is difficult to see why
bureaucrats should have chosen to adopt such a policy of malevol-
ent neglect. Possibly, they were irked because they had not originally been consulted about the project and were resentful of the
rapid ascension of a man who was, strictly speaking, not one of

them. Certainly, there is little documentary evidence of any actual acts of sabotage committed by bureaucrats against the Arsenal of Roanne, but, as we shall see later, the legend of the bad faith of bureaucrats as a contributing factor to the Roanne fiasco was a most persistent one.

If the role of the bureaucracy is curiously ambivalent throughout the Roanne affair, there can be less doubt about that of private industry, which was generally hostile. What is curious about this opposition is that at least one section of private industry was doing extremely well by supplying Roanne with new machinery and equipment. A list of contracts submitted to Milliès-Lacroix in March 1917 by Thomas revealed that a wide range of companies had signed contracts to supply Roanne, including Piketty, the construction firm which had reneged on its obligations at Caen in order to bid for Roanne and now received a contract for 3.37 million francs as a reward for its misdoings. Other French companies included Boussipon (9.2806 million francs), Champigneul (8.165 million francs), and the Société Alsacienne (412,900 francs).[40] Other advances paid to industrialists to provide new tooling machinery included France's leading automobile manufacturers: 6 million francs to André Citroën, who had been so helpful in lending money to Hugoniot; 4.8 million francs to Delauney-Belleville; 2.4 million francs to Panhard; and 7.2 million francs to Louis Renault. A further 7 million francs went to Louis Loucheur's company, Eclairage Eléctrique,[41] despite (or because of?) the fact that he was a deputy minister at the Ministry of Armament. It is difficult to see what could give these particular industrialists, at least, cause to complain.

But Thomas became convinced that business interests were actively working against him and said so publicly in later years. Looking back at the Roanne affair in 1919, he said that the massive press campaign against the Arsenal had been sponsored by private industry.[42] In March 1917, Thomas received a private report which attempted an explanation of the opposition of various groups of industrialists.[43] The main opponents of the scheme were the metallurgists. Although Thomas had solicited their help for the project, they objected to the choice of Hugoniot as director, since he was an engineer, not a metallurgist, by profession. They also objected to the fact that a man like Paul Piketty, whose honorability was as dubious as his technical and financial competence, was placed in

40. 94 AP 78: *Etats des marchés principaux*, 12 March 1917.
41. 94 AP 77.
42. 94 AP 77: *Conférence de Roanne*, 28 February 1919.
43. 94 AP 78: *Affaire de Roanne*, March 1917.

charge of construction. Although the anonymous author of the report had no definite proof, it seemed that the metallurgists had declined to participate in the project because of pressure placed on them by the de Wendel group. This group wished to undermine the Arsenal of Roanne for the same reason it had worked against the National Steelworks: it did not want any competition in the munitions market from state-supported factories.

The opposition of the big metal interests to Roanne, as described in this report, seems comprehensible enough. Unlike automotive firms such as Citroën and Panhard, they had received no share in outfitting the new arsenal. Instead, they were faced with the threat of a formidable competitor producing shells at far lower prices than they themselves currently charged. The link between the metallurgists and the newspaper campaign was natural, indeed, traditional. Whether it is possible to go further and ask if there was not also some connection between the metallurgists and Milliès-Lacroix is another matter. Certainly, his opposition served their interests most admirably, whatever its motivation.

The Role of Louis Loucheur

The most subversive element working against the Arsenal of Roanne appears to have been Louis Loucheur, chairman of the board of directors of the Arsenal and Under-Secretary of State for War Production. It should be stressed that the evidence for this supposition is circumstantial, and that the argument which follows is therefore speculative rather than conclusive. Loucheur was not only one of the chief administrators of the Roanne project, he was also directly one of the chief private suppliers of material to the Arsenal through his company the Eclairage Eléctrique, although he claimed to have given up all his business interests when he became deputy minister. Despite his involvement with the project, both public and private, there is evidence to suggest that Loucheur was secretly working against the Arsenal. His ambition was unmistakable: he wished to become Minister of Armament. Thomas himself was fully aware of the possible treachery of his deputy minister. In March 1917, he received a letter from a friend in St Etienne describing a visit of Loucheur to the town the previous week.[44] Loucheur had unveiled his plans to certain industrial friends, notably the mayor of St Etienne, Jean Neyret, president of the board of the

---

44. 94 AP 77: Georges Gandrille to Thomas, 12 March 1917.

Aciéries de Firminy, and director and major shareholder of several coal mines, hydroelectric complexes, and chemical companies. Loucheur informed Neyret that the Arsenal would be abandoned as a factory and used as a warehouse, with possibly one workshop preserved to repair artillery equipment. Obviously, these declarations were completely counter to Thomas's policy. It will be recalled that this was also the period during which Loucheur was pursuing his campaign against Thomas in private conversations with other ministers.[45]

In May 1917, Thomas received another report on Loucheur's activities as a double-agent, this time from Jules Uhry, a friend in Roanne.[46] Uhry reproached Thomas for not coming more often to visit Roanne in person. Loucheur and Munich, his executive assistant, made frequent trips to see the Arsenal, sometimes alone, other times with Hugoniot. Loucheur's chief method of creating confusion apparently was to spread false rumours. Loucheur let it be known that Thomas, who had recently been on a mission to Russia, would remain there as French ambassador. Those in charge of construction at Roanne complained that they felt the presence and authority of Loucheur too strongly, and the influence of Thomas not enough. Uhry also warned Thomas that he was in danger of losing local support in the area, and that he must try to cultivate the sympathy of the local socialists, the Workers' Exchange (Bourse du Travail), and the co-operative movement. In June, Uhry sent Thomas another note from Roanne.[47] 'In my opinion it is imperative at the present time that you and your team control the management of your project, and not Loucheur and Munich.'

Despite the warnings of his friends and associates, however, Thomas left Loucheur where he was. It seems difficult to believe that he could have entertained any doubts about Loucheur's intentions. Rather, it is more likely that by this time Loucheur had insinuated himself so firmly into the mechanism of armament production and was supported by so many powerful allies in the government that it would have been a hopeless task to dislodge him. Thomas must have realised that Loucheur was after his job, for there could have been no other motive for his waging such a persistent underground campaign against Roanne.

45. See above, Chapters 2 and 6.
46. 94 AP 77: Jules Uhry to Thomas, 14 May 1917.
47. 94 AP 77: Jules Uhry to Thomas, 25 June 1917.

The End of the Affair

Thus, by March 1917, Thomas and Hugoniot were faced with the opposition of the Senate Finance Commission, much of the press, the metallurgists, Louis Loucheur, and possibly a section of the bureaucrats of the Ministry of Armament. On 4 April 1917, Hugoniot wrote a bitter letter to Thomas.[48] His industrial technique of profit-sharing had been condemned out of hand by the Senate Finance Commission in March. 'This is an accepted decision, and in my opinion there is no way of reversing it for the moment.' The post-war industrial struggle would demonstrate the error of the Senate's ways, for profit-sharing was the technique of the future. Hugoniot had warned Thomas at the time he first took on the project that he could only take full responsibility on the clear understanding that modern industrial methods would prevail. 'I considered the creation of Roanne as my absolute domain. I had nothing in mind but the achievement of this creation, and I put aside administrative methods because they were too slow to prove satisfactory.' Hugoniot frankly admitted that for the past three months, since the beginning of the political campaign against the Arsenal, he had achieved nothing useful. Had he been left alone, he could have produced shells by May, but as it was, he felt the project needed a new director. He could not now ask men in private industry to give up lucrative positions in order to work for the state for nothing. He reminded Thomas that he himself had received nothing other than his salary as a sub-lieutenant, despite all the personal financial risks he had taken. He had not been recalled from the front to serve in the Ministry, he had already been serving in private industry, and if he had been interested in private gain, he could just as easily have stayed there. Now all he asked was to be allowed to retire, or failing that, to undertake some small project not directly connected with military production (this was underlined), such as electricity.

In view of what had happened, Hugoniot's desire to retire was understandable, but Loucheur, in his capacity as chairman of the board, made him Director-General of the Roanne Arsenal, a duty which entailed Hugoniot's remaining at the Ministry in Paris, out of harm's way. An engineer from the highways department (*Ponts et Chaussées*) was placed in charge of directing work on the site. With Hugoniot's removal to Paris and the appointment of a second director, all of the creative impulse went out of the project.

What was to become of the Roanne Arsenal? So much money had

48. 94 AP 77: Hugoniot to Thomas, 4 April 1917.

been spent on it thus far that there was no going back. Thomas had staked his political career on the Arsenal and his career and the Arsenal disintegrated together. Construction dragged on in a lacklustre fashion through the summer of 1917. Thomas came down to inspect the Arsenal in August, but before he arrived, he received an urgent letter from Jules Uhry warning him that he would find the site camouflaged to give the impression of greater progress being made than there had been in reality.[49] A number of workers had come to Uhry with the report that they had been ordered to build the facades of various buildings, which they were to remove as soon as Thomas had completed his tour. Photographs taken of the Arsenal in September 1917 revealed that the pumping station, electrical plant, workshops, and blast-furnaces were still being built. It was at this point that Thomas resigned, to be replaced by Louis Loucheur as Minister of Armament.

Once installed at the Ministry Loucheur seemed content to allow the Arsenal to slide into even greater abandon. Thomas's name was linked for eternity in the press with the project, he had become known as the 'duc de Roanne', and it served Loucheur's purposes to maintain the Arsenal as a perpetual memorial to his predecessor's incompetence. The main buildings of the complex were only completed in the spring of 1918, and even then, they were used inefficiently.[50] Albert Thomas was to claim in later years that the Arsenal had proved useful from April to June 1918 during the last German offensive. 'Roanne, at this moment, became in a certain way the industrial plant and the arsenal which would save the world!'[51] But the facts hardly bear out this contention. In April 1918, workers in the plant were assigned the task of reconditioning infantry rifles. In May they repaired artillery wagons, in June they made optical instruments. By October, they were making wooden handles for revolvers. In June 1918, some twenty months after the announcement of the creation of a new arsenal which would produce 50,000 75 mm. shells a day, the Arsenal of Roanne produced only 1,170 shells during the entire month,[52] a small number indeed with which to save the world. At this point, during the Second Battle of the Marne, Loucheur asked André Citroën to take over the Roanne project, in collaboration with a director who would be appointed by the state. Citroën replied that he would be able to produce 40,000 shell casings a day within three months, although

49. 94 AP 77: Jules Uhry to Thomas, 7 August 1917.
50. Gignoux, *Roanne*, 75.
51. 94 AP 77: *Conférence de Roanne*, 28 February 1919.
52. Gignoux, *Roanne*, 56.

the other components for the shell would still have to be produced elsewhere.

By September 1918, it was calculated that the Arsenal of Roanne had cost the country a total of 203 million francs and had produced in exchange materials worth only 15 million francs.[53] In November 1918, the Armistice put an end to any plan to salvage Roanne, although on 15 November Loucheur told a meeting of the Commission of the Army of the Chamber of Deputies that Roanne could be used to repair and build railway wagons and locomotives, as well as weapons and telephone equipment.[54] The Arsenal suffered a further indignity on 7 December 1918 when the Chamber of Commerce of Roanne passed a resolution deploring the fact that the establishment of the Arsenal had endangered the traditional industries of the area, paper, dye works, and weaving, by drying up local supplies of labour.[55] The Chamber of Commerce roundly condemned the government for its failure to take a proper general view of the project and for the irresponsible actions of bureaucrats. Since there was no logical connection between the sort of work performed by labourers at the Arsenal and the salaries they received, local wages had been driven up astronomically, as had the prices in the local shops. The salaries of textile workers had increased 250 per cent in this area, as compared with only 60 per cent in the rest of France. In response to this resolution, Loucheur announced his future plans for the Arsenal.[56] The plant would be used to repair the rolling-stock of the state railways. This task would require no more than 1,200 men, and the rest would be dismissed immediately. The Arsenal would become an ordinary factory, somewhat bigger than most, but not so big as to crush the traditional industries of the area, which must be favoured at all costs.

At the end of December 1918, on behalf of the Finance Commission of the Senate, Milliès-Lacroix gave another report on the state of affairs at Roanne.[57] It was decided to reduce the budget of the Ministry of Armament by 150 million francs, as a prelude to the eventual reintegration of artillery establishments with the Ministry of War. At the same time, the principle was established that the state would undertake no work which could be performed by private

53. Ibid., 77.
54. *Documents parlementaires — Chambre des députés*, 1919, 1274–80. *Annexe No. 6045, Proposition de loi tendant a l'autonomie financière et industrielle des établissements de l'Etat*, 19 April 1919.
55. Albert Thomas, 'Le Dossier de Roanne', *L'Information Ouvrière et Sociale*, 19 January 1919, 3.
56. Ibid., 4.
57. *Sénat*, 30 December 1918, 921–4.

industry. It was also revealed that the total expenses involved in building Roanne now stood at 248,129,874 francs.

The revelations of the Chamber of Commerce of Roanne and the Finance Commission of the Senate led to a second press campaign against the Arsenal, more bitter than that of March 1917. Typical headlines read: 'The Colony of Parasites', The Paradise of Shirkers', and 'Roanne a New Sodom'. Thomas was attacked personally and accused simultaneously (and contradictorily) of using the Arsenal as a means both of creating a personal fortune and advancing the cause of state socialism. *Le Temps*, originally a supporter of the project in March 1917, now attacked Roanne as the very symbol of state interference:

> Are we ever to be delivered of this policy of state socialism? Or rather, to the contrary, will France continue to humiliate her liberating genius before the eyes of the defeated enemy? Will the state abstain from playing the role of armament manufacturer, transporter, constructor, factory owner, and distributor of contracts? . . . The country is tired of this policy of state socialism. It was tolerable during the war, but now we must be delivered. For the country, it is a question of life and death.[58]

Le Démocratie Nouvelle went much further, and under the headline 'The Scandal of Roanne. The Affair was Dishonest from its Birth', announced that Albert Thomas would be brought to trial for his part in the stealing and corruption which had accompanied the creation of the Arsenal.[59] Stung by this criticism, Thomas wrote to Loucheur a few days later to say that although he had no objection to polemics being addressed against him, such as the report of the municipal council of Roanne, the latest series of articles contained serious misstatements of fact, and he requested an official inquiry into the Roanne affair to clear his name. 'You will certainly appreciate, as I do, that we can not allow public opinion, parliamentary, and working-class opinion to entertain any doubts on this matter.'[60] Loucheur replied evasively and promised nothing.[61]

By now, public interest in the Arsenal was rapidly diminishing, and there seemed little point in holding an inquiry. The municipal council of Roanne was also having second thoughts about the wisdom of its attack on the Arsenal in December, and on 26 March 1919, Bonnaud, the mayor of Roanne, produced a report which

58. *Le Temps*, 8 January 1919. Copies of this and other articles can be found in 94 AP 77.
59. *La Démocratie Nouvelle*, 10 January 1919.
60. 94 AP 77: Thomas to Loucheur, 18 January 1919.
61. 94 AP 77: Loucheur to Thomas, 31 January 1919.

seemed the polar opposite of the first.[62] Instead of asking for the Arsenal to be shut down, he now requested that the plant be fully exploited. Evidently the Roanne area was suffering from a post-war slump. He proposed that a 'consortium' be created to administer the Arsenal; by this he meant a triple alliance of the state, private industry, and the workers, who would share in the management of the enterprise. He outlined in detail the magnificent facilities which had been created and which were now lying idle. The number of workers at the Arsenal had fallen from 6,538 to 1,500, and their sole task was to repair one railway wagon a day. The arsenal could be used to produce rolling-stock for the railways, or ships (presumably very small ships, since the only place they could be launched was in the canal). The mayor still maintained that state socialism had been the downfall of the original project and that the collaboration of private industry was required, but he admitted that only the state had the necessary resources to support a project of this scope.

Albert Thomas considered this report a vindication of his policy, and encouraged by this apparent return to public favour, on 19 April 1919 he proposed a bill which would have had the effect of making state arsenals financially autonomous, as Hugoniot had always advocated, so that they could be operated with the benefit of modern industrial techniques. Specifically, he said that state arsenals should be maintained in peacetime to supply the army with material and munitions so that France would retain its military supremacy over the vanquished enemy. But there was another great task which state establishments could perform: they could take part in the industrial and economic revival of France which Loucheur, now Minister of Reconstruction, so fervently desired. Why should the resources of private industry be developed while those of state establishments were wasted? Arsenals could produce all manner of mechanical devices: they could build railway wagons, agricultural machinery, mining equipment, machine tools, precision instruments, sewing-machines, automobiles, and many other items. State arsenals could also be used to control the price of consumer goods by producing them in competition with private industry. Like the mayor of Roanne, Thomas advocated the tripartite management of arsenals, with the collaboration of the state, private industry, and workers.[63]

But Loucheur would have none of this, and in the same month, he gave orders that all work on Roanne was to be stopped. Some of

62. Albert Thomas, "Le Dossier de Roanne", *L'Information Ouvrière et Sociale*, 13 April 1919.
63. *Documents parlementaires — Chambre des députés. 1919. Annexe No. 6045.*

the equipment and fixtures of the complex were subsequently auctioned off. The sale included such unexpected items as 6 children's cradles, 78 pillows, 85 bed pans for women, 196 glass urinals, 2,800 mattresses, and 98 bidets.[64]

Still, the Arsenal was not quite dead. In September 1919, the hawk-eyed deputy Emmanuel Brousse noticed two unobtrusive items in the budget of the Ministry of War and immediately brought them to the attention of the Chamber.[65] The deputies were being asked to approve the expenditure of a further 128,000 francs to install warehouses for war chemical materials at Roanne. Brousse felt that this was asking too much and that the Arsenal should be liquidated completely, not enlarged. He also noticed a further sum of 600,000 francs which was to be spent to maintain the Arsenal. The Arsenal still employed 1500 workers and 700 office staff (despite the flight of bidets and bed-pans) who were engaged in repairing four railway wagons a day. 'It is time we put an end to the scandal of Arsenal of Roanne. It has gone on far too long.' This sentiment was received with loud cheers from the deputies, and indeed, from this time forth, little was ever heard of the Arsenal of Roanne again.

The Anatomy of a Failure

When we come to analyse the reasons for the Roanne *débâcle*, to start with it is clear that the project was launched with too great haste and too little planning. The initial error may have been one of statistical miscalculation. Hugoniot's calculations about the economic viability of the enterprise were based on shell prices in mid-1916, when private industry was making a 50 per cent profit on each 75 mm. shell sold to the government and a 75 per cent profit on each 155 mm. shell. Within the next few months, these calculations were rendered obsolete by major changes in the price of raw materials, as well as by the fact that the state was able to obtain more favourable contracts from private industry. New calculations in 1917 revealed that even if the project had gone ahead on schedule, it would have taken a great deal longer than the 315 days originally predicted to amortise the cost of the Arsenal. If the cost had remained steady at 150 million francs, it would now have taken 1,500 days to pay for the plant once it was in full operation.[66] Thus, even if the plan

64. *France du Sud Ouest*, 21 August 1919.
65. *Chambre des députés*, 24 September 1919, 4522.
66. Gignoux, *Roanne*, 42–43.

had succeeded perfectly, the Arsenal was built too late in the war to have been economically viable, although of course Thomas and Hugoniot had no way of knowing this in 1917.

Thomas and Hugoniot were, however, guilty of making a number of mistakes which might have been avoided. It was not the opposition of the Senate which caused the machinery from England to arrive in the middle of December 1917 before there were buildings to house it, but disorganisation. The same could be said of many of the delays which prolonged the construction of the Arsenal. The repeated complaint of Milliès-Lacroix that no master plan had been drawn before the project was announced was entirely correct, although, as one commentator pointed out, in a sense Saint Pierre des Corps, Hugoniot's first arsenal, was the model for Roanne.[67] Again, the fact that a complete study for the project would have involved a loss of four months was a mitigating factor in Hugoniot's favour, since the whole rationale of Roanne lay in the rapidity of its completion.

Another mistake was the failure of Thomas to draw up a firm contract with Hugoniot before the project had begun. Thomas's defence was that he had enough confidence in Hugoniot to let him proceed without one, but the issue was not one of confidence in Hugoniot. Rather, by leaving the agreement vague and undefined, Thomas left himself open to misinterpretation and attack, since those who were opposed to the project could circulate the most fantastic rumours about the profit-sharing arrangements of the Arsenal and there was no firm document with which to refute them. The whole issue of profit-sharing was badly presented. It was not made clear from the outset that the lump sum which Hugoniot was to receive (a minimum of 80,000 francs, a maximum of 150,000, or one one-thousandth of the total cost) was not to be kept by Hugoniot for himself but divided among all the top managers which he would lure away from private industry. Another part of the agreement was that if the price per 75 mm. shell dipped below 4.25 francs, any profits were to be split equally between the executive of the Arsenal and the state. Milliès-Lacroix immediately claimed that Hugoniot would earn one million francs in this fashion, although again, the profits were to be shared by all the plant managers.

Quite aside from the presentation of the issue, there was a serious case to be made against profit-sharing in state establishments. If Milliès-Lacroix tended to exaggerate and misinterpret deliberately the profit-sharing proposals, he also made the sound observation

67. Ibid., 34.

that it was unjust to single out the managers of the Arsenal of Roanne for special financial consideration when all the officers working in other state arsenals were receiving minimal remuneration. As André Matter of the legal department of the Ministry of Armament commented, these men should not receive exceptional rewards unless they were prepared to take exceptional personal financial risks.

But of all the errors of judgement committed by Thomas and Hugoniot, the worst was undoubtedly the way in which they arranged the financing of the Arsenal. It was this issue which gave the Senate Finance Commission the pretext for launching its attack. It was a tactical blunder not to make some gesture at least of consulting the Minister of Finance and the parliamentary finance commissions about the Arsenal rather than presenting them with a *fait accompli*. The budget for the fourth quarter of 1916 was not voted until three weeks after the decision on 3 September to go ahead with the Arsenal. As Gignoux remarks, it seems incredible that at least some reference could not have been made in the budget to the Roanne project.[68] Faced with such apparently high-handed tactics, Milliès-Lacroix's reaction was comprehensible. Once again, Thomas and Hugoniot had made themselves unnecessarily vulnerable to criticism.

But the Roanne affair was more than a tragedy of errors. It was above all a series of power struggles: private industry against the state, the Senate Finance Commission against the Ministry of Armament, one section of the bureaucracy against another, Thomas against Loucheur. Often there was little correlation between the publicly-stated issues and the real issues. The motive common to all parties was self-interest. The question of the general good or the fate of France in the conflict with Germany seemed to interest none of the participants except Thomas and Hugoniot.

What did each of these participants want and what part did each play in the ultimate failure of Roanne? To what extent did Thomas's own bureaucrats undermine the success of the scheme? It will be recalled that there was some evidence to suggest that Milliès-Lacroix apportioned a considerable part of the blame for the mishandling of the administration and financing of the Arsenal to bureaucrats within the Ministry of Armament. This view is supported in a long report on the causes for the failure of Roanne.[69]

68. Ibid., 48.
69. 94 AP 77: Although this report is undated and its author unknown, it appears to have been drafted as the basis of a possible future official defence of the Roanne scheme.

The main contention of the report was that the bureaucrats effectively foiled the project:

> As we shall see, it is not too much to say that the scheme has been, to use the correct term, sabotaged, first of all by a bureaucracy which was hostile, or at the very least, uncomprehending; and then, it must be said, by administrative controls which were justifiable in principle, but hasty and sterile in execution.

The report went on to point out that Thomas had informed the leading civil servants of his department in September 1916 that the Arsenal would be built and would require the creation of a suitable administration to run it; the bureaucrats had done nothing until December. All the bureaucrats had done was raise objections and insist on the correct papers being filled out, with the result that at least a month was lost at the very beginning of the project. This petty concern for correct procedures had nearly resulted in the loss of the option which Hugoniot had obtained on the land through the *notaire*, a loss which would have necessitated rebuying the land at a much higher price. It is difficult to determine whether the bureaucrats concerned were being deliberately unhelpful, or merely incompetent. As had been suggested before, the bureaucrats may have felt piqued at not being consulted about Roanne in the initial stages of planning.

But for Thomas the bureaucrats were merely minor villains. In 1919 he stated that the greatest part of the blame for the failure should be placed squarely on the shoulders of the Senate.

> It is now a question of discovering the responsibility of this senatorial assembly which, undoubtedly, had nothing against me personally . . . but which, at the same time, by its campaigns, by its reports, demoralized the man who could have directed the establishment, annihilated his genius, broke his career, and tried to sully his reputation. If there is a primary responsibility to be borne, it is there.[70]

One might go further and credit Milliès-Lacroix himself with a certain amount of bad faith, as evidenced by his deliberate misrepresentation of the profit-sharing arrangements with Hugoniot. But the clash between Milliès-Lacroix and Thomas must also be seen in the wider context of the continuing dispute between parliament and the government about the responsibility for directing the course of the war. To recapitulate, until December 1914, the government had

70. 94 AP 77: *Conférence de Roanne*, 28 February 1919.

ruled by executive decree, but in 1915 both chambers of parliament began using their commissions, such as those for finance, to reassert their authority. With the implementation of secret committees in 1916, parliament's control over the army and ministries increased. In 1917, the arrival of Clemenceau heralded the end of secret committees, and there was a revival of strong executive government operating through decrees.[71] The Roanne affair falls into the period during which parliamentary control was at its height. Roanne was only one of a series of clashes between Albert Thomas and parliament. In September 1915, for example, the president of the Budget Commission of the Chamber of Deputies wrote a strongly-worded protest to Thomas about the lack of information emanating from the Under-Secretariat of State for Artillery and Munitions.[72] In particular, he complained of the ill will of the Powder section (the same Powder section later praised by Milliès-Lacroix!), which refused to answer inquiries from the Commission at all, or did so in an evasive, unhelpful manner. Two paragraphs of the letter deserve to be quoted at length, for they summarise perfectly the issues which were to be involved in the Roanne dispute the following year.

> Finally, it seems to us that we are always coming up against this deliberate policy, against which we shall not cease to protest, of presenting the major commissions of parliament with a *fait accompli*. It is always the same policy of control after the fact, which only offers us a choice between silence and criticism, both perfectly useless from the point of view of achieving anything.
>
> We see our role differently, and we believe you agree with us. It would be intolerable if our activity should be rendered impossible by the resistance of bureaucrats of your administration, and we shall not hesitate, if the present situation continues, to ask you to take the necessary measures to bring it to an end.

In the light of this letter, the opposition of the Senate Finance Commission to the Arsenal of Roanne takes on a totally different meaning. Roanne was no isolated incident, but the culmination of a series of quarrels. The failure of the project was the price Thomas had to pay not only for his mishandling of Senate sensibilities in this one particular instance but for a general lack of diplomacy with regard to parliament over a much longer period of time.

If Thomas blamed the Senate for spearheading the opposition to Roanne, he also blamed private industry for its role in working against the Arsenal. As was indicated earlier, he later came to believe

71. Renouvin, *Formes*, 143–50.
72. 94 AP 103: President of the Budget Commission to Thomas, 18 September 1915.

that the attack of the newspapers on the Arsenal had been inspired by the industrialists. Thomas always believed that the nature of this opposition was essentially ideological, that the arguments in the press against the menace of state socialism reflected the opinions of the industrialists. It seems more likely, however, that the industrialists, and in particular the metallurgists, opposed the Arsenal on more practical grounds as a rival to their own factories, which, indeed, it was intended to be. Roanne had to be sabotaged to protect their own economic interests.

But if the industrialists were successful in opposing the project, Thomas believed that this was in part due to the intervention of Louis Loucheur on their behalf. Publicly, Thomas never ascribed to Loucheur the baser motive of aspiring to take over the Ministry of Armament, but he did accuse him of negligence in the management of state arsenals and of exhibiting too great a concern for the welfare of industrialists.

> I am entitled to say that the Minister of Industrial Reconstruction [Loucheur], despite the friendly obligations he owed me, neither defended nor developed the Arsenal of Roanne as he ought to have.
> I am aware of the rumours circulating about Monsieur Loucheur: my accusation is not of this nature. But I must say that, frequenting industrial circles as he does, preserving despite everything his previous attitude in his heart of hearts, he is not disposed to develop state establishments, and consciously or unconsciously, he allows their development to lag, he thinks of them only when he might have need of them, as in June 1918.[73]

Privately, he was less reserved in his criticism of Loucheur. In January 1919, he was amused to receive an allegorical poem, penned by an unknown hand, about the Arsenal of Roanne called 'A Little Tale of the Great War'. The action of the poem was set in 200 BC at the time of the Punic Wars. Albertus, the famous tribune, decrees that a great forge is to be built to produce javelins, swords, and catapults. He is aided by the Consul Strabo; 'strabo' in Latin means 'cross-eyed', as does 'louche', by a curious coincidence, in French. But Strabo is also an ironmaster and has extracted many talents from the Latin Treasury. His business menaced by the nasty tribune Albertus, he decides to overthrow him: 'Et Strabon dit, louchant un peu/Au Tribun candide et farouche/"Je vois la paille en ton oeil bleu/Mon ami, ton affaire est louche"'.[74]

Undoubtedly, Loucheur appears to have been the greatest winner

73. 94 AP 77: *Conférence de Roanne*, 28 February 1919.
74. 94 AP 77.

in the Roanne affair. Again, any definitive judgement of his role in the affair must be qualified by the incomplete nature of the evidence, but what evidence there is all points in the same direction. Loucheur was chairman of the board of directors of the Arsenal, but this apparently in no way interfered with his other interests. Far from losing business, his old firm, the Eclairage Eléctrique, made a fortune from supplying equipment for the new arsenal. At the same time, since the project failed, the position of the firm as a shell manufacturer was never menaced by state competition. Finally, his double-dealings were rewarded by his being made Minister of Armament. Performing an incredible three-ring circus act as successful bureaucrat, industrialist, and politician, Loucheur established a record which can have few competitors in the annals of opportunism.

If the Arsenal of Roanne made Loucheur's career, it broke that of Hugoniot, at least temporarily. Not only his reputation but his self-confidence was tarnished by the failure of the Roanne venture. Understandably, he became bitter. On 24 February 1918, he wrote to one of Thomas's closest associates:

> As far as Roanne is concerned, the Hugoniot affair must no longer be considered, because the Hugoniot affair no longer exists.
> I will not resume the effective management of either the construction or the operation. I have released the collaborators I had reserved for the scheme. I will restrict my activities to those of an unpaid consulting engineer. I do not wish to talk about it any more.
> I still have absolute confidence in the Boss [Thomas], but none in the state.[75]

And how did the 'Boss' himself react to the Roanne fiasco? Despite the heavy, often unjust, criticism levelled against him, no hint of resentment can be detected in Thomas's speeches and letters. Despite the apparent machinations of Loucheur, he bore him no grudge. In supporting the Roanne project, Thomas had intended only to help the war effort by producing more shells at cheaper prices. He was being perfectly sincere when he denied the charge that Roanne was an implement with which he planned to extend state socialism. The idea of industrial competition, he said, was not necessarily a socialist one. Furthermore, he was convinced that the military strength of France after the war could be maintained only through the preservation of arsenals like Roanne.

Looking back at the Roanne project, Thomas recognised the

75. 94 AP 78: Hugoniot to Simiard, 24 February 1918.

errors which had been committed, but he remained convinced that the original conception was good. He never allowed the Roanne affair to become his albatross, and the derisory title of 'duc de Roanne' was to fade quickly enough. After losing his ministry, he wasted no time lamenting his fate, but continued to offer his help and advice to the government and to his successor. The final irony of the story may be that while Roanne contributed to the closing of Albert Thomas's political career, it thereby launched him on the international path which was ultimately to establish his lasting reputation.

Conclusion

The particular form which the extension of state control over industry took in France during the First World War was the product of the interactions and clashes of bureaucrats, industrialists, and politicians in a situation of crisis.

The general crisis of the war produced two specific industrial problems: supply and production. To satisfy both civilian and military needs, the French government was obliged not only to provide factories with raw materials, despite shortages which became increasingly acute as the war progressed, but also to direct production, to initiate industrial programmes to meet the strategic demands of the army, and to furnish the civilian population with basic consumer goods which would otherwise have been quite unobtainable.

The rhythm of the changing relations between bureaucrats, industrialists, and politicians was set by military developments and British pressure. By an inexorable process resulting from the loss of the industrial north-east in 1914 and the subsequent growing shortage of maritime transport and almost all essential raw materials as the war continued, the French government became the sole importer and distributor of raw materials to industry. Eventually, the government created consortia and omnia to supply the raw materials which industry required, and these bodies, closely supervised by the Ministry of Commerce, monopolised transport, arranged foreign payment, requisitioned supplies, determined industrial priorities, fixed prices, and limited profits. This policy was imposed in part by Great Britain, which felt that in return for benefits bestowed on France by the creation of interallied shipping and supply organisations, it was reasonable to insist that French businessmen be subject to the same kind of bureaucratic control as their British counterparts. In the words of one commentator:

The *rapprochement* of the two economic systems was thus as inevitable as economic co-operation between the two allies was indispensable. At the beginning of the war these truths were apparent to no one, but they became increasingly self-evident as the war progressed.[1]

Military events also forced the hand of the French government in other ways: Joffre's insistence on greatly increased shell production in May 1916, for example, obliged Albert Thomas to create the Arsenal of Roanne. Private industry did not have the resources necessary to initiate this kind of production programme on its own in the time required. Military needs were the final argument in any discussion between bureaucrats and industrialists. The argument could be used by the government to justify the obligatory co-ordination of private industry or the establishment of state industry, but it could also be effectively invoked by industrialists who could threaten to boycott an essential programme unless their demands were met.

Of the three groups called upon to respond to the twin crises of industrial supply and production in wartime, French bureaucrats seemed initially the least well-equipped to deal with the situation. The production of Gobelins tapestries and matches were of little value in running a wartime industrial economy. Two ministries ultimately became responsible for establishing industrial policy during the war: Commerce and Industry, and Armament. Before the war, the Ministry of Commerce had been chiefly concerned with the expansion of trade abroad, the protection of domestic industries from foreign competition, and such minor chores as the supervision of weights and measures, chambers of commerce, and technical colleges. Its twenty-three bureaucrats had no direct industrial experience. The Ministry of War in 1914 had ten bureaucrats with some knowledge of industrial matters, chiefly through their contact with the inefficiently administered network of state arsenals. It is hardly surprising that faced with this small handful of inexperienced civil servants, industrialists won easy victories in their negotiations with the state in 1914. It would take bureaucrats several years to recover the initiative.

The mobilisation of a wartime administration to deal with industrial problems in France can be understood only by reference to the careers of two ministers, Etienne Clémentel and Albert Thomas, because each was personally responsible for recruiting, organising, and directing the new bureaucrats of the two ministries which made the critical industrial decisions.

1. Hinds, 'Coopération', 22.

Etienne Clémentel ultimately controlled all non-military industry in France. The Ministry he inherited from Gaston Thomson in October 1915 was disorganised and lacked direction, though it had already developed several *ad hoc* bureaucratic organisms to deal with specific problems such as wheat and chemicals. For the first year and a half of his administration, there were few major changes in the organisation of the Ministry as Clémentel struggled to deal with immediate problems. As he became settled in his office, however, relatively free from political pressure, Clémentel came to realise that a far greater industrial effort was required not only for France to supply the needs of the civilian population and to win the war, but to prepare for the post-war world, and that only the state could direct such an effort. British pressure on France to restrict her imports gave Clémentel in March 1917 the first major weapon he needed to coerce industrialists. It was from this date that the growth in numbers of bureaucrats and bureaucratic structures in the Ministry of Commerce occurred. Clémentel created the 'Extraordinary War Services' of the Ministry of Commerce, a completely new wartime bureaucracy entirely independent from the rest of the Ministry. The power and the attributes of the Ministry grew rapidly, initially because the British forced France to take ever greater control of her economy, later as Clémentel profited from the protection of Clemenceau's authoritarian rule. It was the control of the distribution of raw materials to private industry which gave Clémentel and his bureaucrats their principal hold over the industrialists. The control of raw materials, helped by the threat of requisition, led to the creation of technical committees within the Ministry, the consortium system, and eventually to the establishment of the National Dyes Company and the National Shoe.

It was only in the last two years of the war that Clémentel and his bureaucrats possessed the means of controlling French industry, and it was only in the last year of the war that the controls began to work. The essential problem was endeavouring to create bureaucratic structures for industry faster than industrialists could wriggle out of them. In the face of the determined opposition of the industrialists, there was a constant devaluation of bureaucratic machinery until bureaucrats found the measure of their opponents: the restriction of imports and the evolution of the consortium system are cases in point. Often loopholes were plugged too late to prevent costly and damaging abuses by industrialists.

Albert Thomas and the bureaucrats of the Minister of War's Under-Secretariat of State for Artillery and Munitions (later the Ministry of Armament) were responsible for organising all French war industries. Thomas created the new Under-Secretariat in May 1915 and staffed it with his own men. The power of Thomas and his bureaucrats stemmed from the fact that they were the country's biggest purchasing agents. The buyer and seller relationship with industrialists created a special set of problems for these bureaucrats. From the outset, they were forced to haggle with the more experienced industrialists over prices, production, advances, and penalties. The bureaucrats in charge of war production were also more exposed to potential public and political criticism, as was their minister, than Clémentel and his men. Because of his greater vulnerability, and because he was less interested in long-term reforms than solving immediate problems, Thomas initially moved less boldly than Clémentel against the industrialists, and when he did decide to act forcefully to defend the interests of the state by creating the Arsenal of Roanne, his efforts were crowned with failure. His successor at the Ministry of Armament, Louis Loucheur, was more successful in dealing with military industrialists because he himself was one.

The fact that there were two ministries responsible for controlling industry in France during the war, even if there was a line of demarcation between military and non-military production, inevitably led to rivalries. These rivalries were in part between the ministers themselves over their respective authorities, in part between competing groups of bureaucrats reflecting their ministers' differing philosophies of state control (as, for example, regarding the treatment of the *Comité des Forges*), and in part between the client industrialists of each ministry: should metal be used exclusively for munitions, or could some be spared for Pleyel pianos?

But there were also great similarities between the two ministries. By 1918, in both ministries, bureaucratic hierarchies and structures had been regularised, and the technical services of both had become increasingly co-ordinated through interministerial committees. Even more important was the fact that both ministries were staffed by the same kind of unbureaucratic bureaucrats. These wartime bureaucrats were former teachers and professors, or freshly graduated students, scientists, engineers, or industrialists. It is paradoxical that such a fierce controversy should have arisen during the war about the rapacious advances of Monsieur Lebureau when so few of the men against whom the attacks were directed were, by training, inclination, or method, bureaucratic. Released from the traditional concern of the civil servant for a steady climb up the well-trodden ladder of the bureaucratic hierarchy by the display of unadventurous efficiency, these wartime bureaucrats brought bold and unfamiliar techniques to bear on the formidable problems of supply and production posed by the war.

Moreover, the bureaucrats of the Ministries of Commerce and Armament were given the power by their respective ministers to implement ideas, power which often went unchallenged by more traditional bodies in authority such as the Chamber of Deputies or the Senate. Decisions of such major importance as the creation and elaboration of the system of consortia were the consequence of a series of administrative rather than legislative initiatives. At their best, particularly towards the end of the war as their authority, experience, and self-confidence grew, wartime bureaucrats were capable of exhibiting extreme efficiency in their dealings with industry. The preparation which preceded the establishment of a National Dyes Company deserves to be singled out as an example of first-rate planning, with the steady evolution of structures from an office to a commission to a *syndicat* to a company, accompanied by a gradual intensification of psychological pressure on the chemical industry. At their worst, even wartime bureaucrats with all the authority at their command could not be forced to act and think like industrialists beyond a certain point. The affair of the Arsenal of Roanne showed the limits of the ability of the state to create its own successful industrial enterprises. In this case, the state failed as an industrial power not merely because of the external opposition of private enterprise, but because of competing elements contained within itself: bureaucrats, parliament, and ministerial ambition.

If wartime bureaucrats were not true bureaucrats, were wartime industrialists true industrialists? In the most straightforward sense they were; with a few notable exceptions, most of the industrialists who were prominent in France from 1914 to 1918 were industrialists before the war. Furthermore, on a basis of the five representative industries studied in this book — metals, chemicals, petroleum, vegetable oil, and shoes — it could be said that during the war French industrialists deployed their traditional methods in an untraditional situation. The arena for indulging their most heartfelt inclinations had suddenly become much greater, and they did not hesitate to act.

As with the wartime bureaucracy, wartime industrialists are best understood by being considered in two separate categories: non-military and military. All of the industries under consideration fell to some extent under both categories, but it is a corollary of the division of administrative responsibility for industrial policy between the Ministry of Commerce and the Ministry of Armament that French industrialists, in mirror image fashion, had two basic forms of contact with the state during the war.

In the case of the industries which dealt with the Ministry of Commerce, the industrialists concerned enjoyed a comparatively long period of relatively free and highly profitable commercial activity; it was not until 1917 that the state began to apply the clamps. Since the principal instrument of the Ministry for regulating the activities of the industrialists was the distribution of raw materials, and since the machinery for administering this distribution was highly complex and required much refining, it was only in 1918 that these industrialists were brought under various degrees of state control, ranging from consortia to national companies.

The ironmasters escaped more or less scot-free from the clutches of the Ministry of Commerce. They and the other military industrialists found themselves selling their wares to Albert Thomas and his bureaucrats. Here, negotiations were not chiefly over raw materials, but over prices, delivery dates, and the quality of the product. Military industrialists were in constant contact with the state at a much earlier date than their non-military brethren, but paradoxically enjoyed a greater degree of freedom from state interference throughout the war. This was in part because of the initiative taken early in the war by the *Comité des Forges* to substitute itself for the state bureaucracy, and in part because the desperate nature of the military situation did not allow the Ministry of Armament the luxury of experimenting as freely with state-administered alternatives as the Ministry of Commerce. The failure of the National Steelworks and the Arsenal of Roanne vividly demonstrates the difference between the power of military and non-military industrialists in forestalling state control.

Industrialists, however, also displayed certain individual characteristics during the war which can be comprehended only in the light of the pre-1914 situation of the specific industries involved.

The ironmasters had developed an organisation for dealing with the state before the war, the *Comité des Forges*, and it continued to do so most efficiently during the war. Whether they came from traditional families or had risen through the ranks as engineers, the ironmasters were a tough and talented group of men, able to recover from the loss of their ore and factories, to convert themselves into importing agencies for foreign metals by adapting pre-war institutions such as the *Comptoir de Longwy*, and to finance the construction of new productive capacity by *auto-financement* with government money, under the system of wartime advances. French ironmasters saw the war as an occasion for continuing their drive for greater efficiency and corporate integration, and accordingly, attempted to eliminate small metal producers, as they had before the war. Finally, when the pre-war geographic balance of power among the ironmasters threatened to be upset by one group from the centre of France acquiring a German-owned metallurgical complex in Normandy at the expense of another group from the north-east, the *Comité des Forges* found itself no more capable of resolving this dispute than it had similar disputes in the nineteenth century. When fundamental questions of individual self-interest were at stake, the group solidarity of the ironmasters collapsed, but the collapse was too temporary to allow bureaucrats to reap any advantages.

Chemical industrialists had been as successful as the ironmasters before the war, and they, too, quickly recovered from their initial losses of productive capacity, besting bureaucrats in the first critical bargaining sessions over prices and advances, and building new plants away from the front. Pre-war rivalries within the industry continued unabated during the war: Saint-Gobain *versus* Kuhlmann for the control of the sulphuric acid market, for example; or the attempt of Saint-Denis to purge France of German-owned dye factories. Ultimately these rivalries and the lack of a chemical trade association with authority comparable to that of the *Comité des Forges* enabled the state to intervene to form the Consortium of Chemical Products and the National Dyes Company.

The success of the state in taking control of the French petroleum industry during the war is explicable partly in terms of its pre-war organisation: it was a virtual consortium by 1914; partly because of the grave military consequences of a petrol shortage: there was a clear case of *force majeure*; and partly because of pre-war political agitation for the state to take over the industry, agitation which continued to grow during the war. Alternatively, the success of the French Vegetable Oil industry in manipulating the French Vegetable Oil Consortium to its own profitable purposes can also be attributed to the existence of a pre-war monopoly of producers which merely transformed itself into the Consortium, as well as to the inherent technical complexity of the industry which made any form of state supervision troublesome. The thousands of French shoemakers who composed the French shoe industry had no such pre-war advantages of organisation; their very diversity made administrative control through the National Shoe scheme time-consuming but not difficult.

As for the impact of wartime politics on the intervention of the state in industry, it is clear that the impact was less great during than before the war. Ministers and bureaucrats had greater authority and were more independent from parliamentary pressure in the running of their ministries during the war. The revival of pre-war ministerial instability and political partisanship in 1916 and 1917 brought Albert Thomas's career as Minister of Armament to an end, but it had little effect on the policies of Etienne Clémentel and Louis Loucheur. Traditional methods of French parliamentary control, such as debate, procedural sabotage, and the work of commissions, had very little influence on the course of state industrial intervention. Though many of Clémentel's and Thomas's policies gave rise to intense parliamentary debates and much public criticism, only the Arsenal of Roanne offers the example of a government industrial project being brought to a halt by the determined opposition of the Senate Finance Commission and its reporter. There is also little evidence, except possibly in the case of the National Steelworks, that industrialists were very successful in lobbying with politicians for favours. Finally, as before the war, ideology and party doctrine had little discernable influence on industrial policy. Doctrinal considerations were invoked in debate for display purposes only, and in the end, practical considerations prevailed and parliamentarians generally supported the government's efforts to solve each industrial problem as it emerged. The supreme importance of the war effort overrode all other considerations.

This book began with a quotation: 'The World War of 1914–18 and its economic aftermath gave to this emerging *étatisme* a tremendous impetus which it has not ceased to feel to this present day'.[2] It must end by asking how true in the final analysis this observation is for one particular aspect of *étatisme*: the intervention of the state in industry. What *was* the end result of the wartime interactions and clashes of bureaucrats, industrialists, and politicians?

It is true that in a general way the authority of the French state over many aspects of national life increased considerably after the 1914–18 war. The bureaucracy grew in numbers from 800,000 in 1914 to 1.25 million in 1926.[3] The state enacted significant measures of social legislation: the protection of workers, the introduction of paid holidays, pensions, the extension of state pawnshops and state deposit banks.

But in the specific area of industrial intervention, however, the legacy of wartime *étatisme* was less marked. The end of the war brought an abrupt halt to interallied economic co-operation, despite the continuing shortages of raw materials, transportation facilities, and financial credit after the Armistice. With the disappearance of

2. W. Sharp, *The Government of the Third Republic* (New York, 1938), 207.
3. A. Ferrat, *La République à refaire* (Paris, 1945), 207.

interallied economic structures, it was inevitable that parallel mechanisms of economic control within each state would also soon disappear. Without the two-fold justification of the wartime crisis and British pressure, post-war French governments could offer no convincing rationale for maintaining such useful devices as the consortium or the National Shoe. The official date for the cessation of hostilities was 24 October 1919, at which time all laws and decrees which were to last 'for the duration of the war' came to an end. Post-war relations between the state and industry soon came to resemble those of the pre-war period.

By 1921, the Ministry of Commerce and Industry had returned to the peaceful and modest pattern of its pre-war existence. After an uninterrupted stint of five years as Minister, Etienne Clémentel had departed after his defeat in the autumn elections of 1919. The power of the Ministry of Commerce had stemmed from its control of raw materials. When that power disappeared, everything disappeared. The elaborate structures which had administered French industry were dismantled one by one, with the first materials and services to be controlled — wheat, coal, and shipping — the last to be de-controlled.[4] Imports and exports became free once more, subject only to normal customs regulations. The wartime bureaucrats returned to their classrooms or to private industry. It should also be pointed out, however, that as Clémentel had advocated, there was closer consultation between industrialists and bureaucrats in the 1920s, with a greater representation of *syndicats* and trade associations in government councils, commissions, and offices. As well, there was a move towards more economic planning; in 1925, the National Economic Council was founded, with representatives of both the state and private interest groups.[5]

The authority of the Ministry of Armament, based as it was on the immense financial resources placed at its disposal for the purchase of armaments, evaporated after the Armistice. The Ministry itself disappeared, and a new Ministry of Industrial Reconstruction re-emerged, still administered by Louis Loucheur. All controls over metals soon were lifted, and the Ministry served chiefly as a financial sponsor for reconstruction projects in war-damaged French departments in the north.

As in the pre-1914 period, power reverted to the politicians, who once again controlled the course of state industrial intervention. Measures of state interference were dependent once more upon the

4. A. Delemer, *Le Bilan de l'étatisme* (Paris, 1922), 53–61.
5. B. Chenot, *Organisation économique de l'état* (Paris, 1951), 52–3.

mechanics of the parliamentary process. Politicians continued to take a more practical than ideological view of industrial problems in the 1920s, favouring compromises and half-measures as before. Thus, when the industrial resources of Alsace-Lorraine reverted to France after the Treaty of Versailles, coal mines were transferred to private French iron and steel companies, potash mines and nitrogen plants were administered by a government agency, and government and private interests jointly participated in two 'mixed enterprises', the Compagnie de Navigation du Rhin and the Chantiers et Ateliers du Rhin. The agency administering the new state industries was attached to the Ministry of Public Works.[6]

The 1930s present a more complicated picture. In the first place, there was a continuation of the pre-war and wartime political inclination to find practical and compromise solutions to the new industrial problems of the decade. Thus, in return for its financial support, the state participated in further mixed enterprises, such as the Compagnie Française des Pétroles, the steamship company the Compagnie Générale Transatlantique, and the Compagnie Nationale du Rhône, a hydroelectric firm, though the state had relatively little control over the direction of these companies. In the second place, in an attempt to solve the growing economic crisis, politicians passed a number of measures in the 1930s which were directly inspired by the wartime economic system. From 1931 to 1935, all imports were controlled by licence. There was also a regulation of prices for certain staples, such as wheat, and the control of certain industries, such as shoes, to curb overproduction. Finally, with the accession to power of the Popular Front in 1936, there was a genuine break with the political past. The issue of industrial nationalisation had been widely debated in the electoral campaign which led to the formation of the Popular Front Government. One could at last speak of an ideology of state interference dominating political action. The nationalisation of part of the munitions and aircraft industries in 1936, the nationalisation of the railways in 1937, and the acquisition of a controlling interest in the Bank of France were measures inspired as much by motives of political doctrine as practicality. A new Ministry of the National Economy was created as an administrative expression of the special interest of the Popular Front in economic questions.[7]

Perhaps the most graphic means of measuring the legacy of

6. M. Ventenat, *L'Expérience des nationalisations. Premier bilan* (Paris, 1947), 68–83.
7. W. Baum, *The French Economy and the State* (Princeton, 1948), Chapter Seven. Chenot, *Organisation*, 53–63, 150–1.

wartime industrial policy to the inter-war period is by returning to the five basic industries as they stood in 1939. One of them, the vegetable oil industry, had no more contact with the state between the wars than it had before 1914. Another, the iron and steel industry, continued to thrive as it had before and during the war, virtually untouched by the state, except for the nationalisation in 1936 of two small torpedo plants and ten small and specialised munitions factories. One found its production in the early 1930s temporarily regulated as closely as it had been during the war: the shoe industry. As for petroleum, the government's 25 per cent share in the Compagnie Française des Pétroles was the fulfilment of the pre-war proposal made by various deputies to create a *régie intéressée*, or mixed enterprise, for the industry. Finally, one section of the French chemical industry, the dyes industry, benefited hugely from the government's insistence at Versailles that the Germans turn over 50 per cent of their stocks of dyes to the Allies, as well as a sizeable proportion of their dyes production for five years, and their chemical patents. Another branch, involved with fertiliser production, faced a new competitor in the form of a state-owned company in Alsace. On the whole, however, the chemical giants like Saint-Gobain were as free from government interference as they had been before the war, and prospered mightily.[8] Thus, the degree of state industrial intervention between the wars varied considerably from industry to industry, and was far from overwhelming.[9]

State industrial policy in the First World War had a notable influence on French industrial mobilisation in the Second, chiefly as a result of the law of 11 July 1938. The law was a plan for the general organisation of the state in wartime; its economic sections were a coherent summary of the experience of the state with economic and industrial controls during the First World War. The law provided for the complete control of the production, circulation, and sale of goods by a group of war ministers, each given unlimited power over a specific economic sector: transport, food, imports, labour, and production. Technical committees and consortia were to be revived. The state was given the authority to expand its own industries and to requisition private industries if need be. The Minister of Commerce would be responsible for centralising 'the production and distribution of finished industrial products intended to satisfy the needs of the economic life of the country'. There was provision for the re-creation of the Ministry of Armament. Finally, the rights of

8. Choffel, *Saint-Gobain*, 85.
9. H. Laufenburger, *L'Intervention de l'état en matière économique* (Paris, 1939).

parliament and its commissions to monitor the actions of ministers in war was firmly reasserted, but the law also recognised the need for greater executive control than in peacetime.[10]

The law of 11 July 1938 was duly activated when war broke out in 1939. The war ministers took their posts according to plan, and a complete state-controlled wartime economic system was created. After the fall of France, the Vichy regime took over and strengthened these economic structures. A Ministry of Industrial Production was established to allocate raw materials and control prices and production, with the help of Organisation Committees which administered every branch of commerce and industry. These committees were made up of businessmen and bureaucrats and operated in the same manner as the consortia of the First World War. Government Allocation Committees performed the same functions as the old technical committees of the Ministry of Commerce and made final decisions on the allocation of raw materials. With its stress on industrial concentration and productivity, on state economic planning and management, and on the necessity of preparing for the post-war economic world, Vichy had the power and ruthlessness to force through economic measures that Clémentel only dreamt of.[11]

The real growth of state control of industry came only after the Second World War, with the nationalisation of Renault, Gnôme et Rhône, mines, air, transport, gas, electricity, coal, and various banks, petroleum, and insurance companies.[12] It has been suggested that this modern state industrial system in France owes much to the law of 11 July 1938, essentially the rationalisation of the industrial experience of the state in the 1914–18 war, as transmitted to post-war France via Vichy:

> in certain respects the most interventionist measures which France has experienced subsequently are in themselves nothing but variations on the themes of the law of 1938, which spelled out a complete system of institutions and regulations to deal with the economic necessities of war.[13]

Happily, however, the further investigation of the validity of this proposition will be undertaken by some future historian; it goes well beyond the scope and ambitions of this present one, whose task is now ended.

10. *Journal Officiel*, 13 July 1938, 8330–7.
11. R. Paxton, *Vichy France. Old Guard and New Order* (New York, 1972), 193–4, 216–20, 355–6.
12. P. Naville, *L'Etat entrepreneur. Le cas de Renault* (Paris, 1971), 13–14.
13. Chenot, *Organisation*, 60.

Bibliography

Manuscript Sources

Archives nationales, Paris

Series F 7 (Police):

12,842   Reports from police informers on relations between private companies, politicians, and newspapers from 1895 to 1925. Contains information on the *Comité des Forges*, Albert Thomas, and Louis Loucheur

Series F 12 (Commerce and Industry):

7657–8133   These 400 boxes of documents deal with the services of the Ministry of Commerce and Industry created specifically for the 1914–18 war

7657–7661   The general wartime organisation of the Ministry

7662–7759   The archives of the ten sections of the Technical Services of the Ministry, each of which dealt with certain raw materials. 7663–7683, for example, are the papers of the First Section, Metal and Wood

7762–7795   The Executive Committee for Imports

7796–7819   French commercial services, abroad

7837–7839   Sequestered German property

7999–8028   The Economic Action Services created by the Ministry of War in each of France's military districts. These boxes contain some information about industrialists and local Consultative Committees for Economic Action

8029–8044   Preparations for the post-war period and the reorganisation of the French economy

Series 94 AP (the Albert Thomas Papers):

1–424   This large collection of documents deals with Thomas's administration first as Under-Secretary of State for Artillery and Munitions, then as Minister of Armament, and finally with the

Prompsat Archives, Prompsat (Puy-de-Dôme)

Etienne Clémentel's private papers were discovered through the kind assistance of his widow, Mme Clémentel, and his daughter, Mme Arizzoli-Clémentel, in a large cupboard in the painting studio of the country house where he spent the last years of his life. As the papers were arranged in no particular order, I have used the following system of classification. The first letter of a dossier number refers to the shelf (T = top, M = middle, B = bottom); the next number in brackets refers to the number of the pile on the shelf, numbered from left to right; the final number refers to the number of the dossier within the pile, numbered from top to bottom. Thus M(1)5, for example.

The range of the material in the archives is extensive and covers the entire span of Clémentel's political career from 1900 to 1925. For the purposes of this thesis, the most useful parts of the archives were the collections of speeches, press clippings, and special reports from his collaborators. Clémentel's views on regionalism, his plans for the reorganisation of the French economy after the war, his contribution to interallied policy during the war and at the Versailles Peace Conference, and his financial policy from 1924 to 1925 when he was Minister of Finance during the *Cartel des Gauches* are particularly well documented. In addition, there is abundant material relating to Clémentel's artistic, literary, philosophical, and historical interests. The papers are now housed in the Archives departementales du Puy-de-Dôme (Clemont-Ferrand).

Public Record Office, London

Series CAB 23, volumes 1–8. (War Cabinet Papers):
These daily minutes of British War Cabinet meetings were begun in December 1916, when Lloyd George came to power, and continued uninterrupted for the remainder of the war. They are essentially the records of decisions taken rather than opinions expressed, but they are a useful guide in determining the exact chronology of policy making. Much valuable information is also contained in the reports frequently appended to the minutes by individual members of the War Cabinet.

Series MT 23 (Ministry of Transport):
These papers cover shipping questions in the first half of the war, when they were the responsibility of the Ministry of Transport. There were only two dossiers of interest in this series:

578/T47943/1916   French tonnage questions. Letters from the French Ambassador
581/T480503/1916   Acceptance by the French government of requisitioned vessels for transport of steel

Series MT 25 (Ministry of Shipping):
These are the documents of the Ministry of Shipping, created in December 1916. Of relevance were:

6/7114/1917   International Shipping Committee. Minutes of Meetings held in March 1917
10/21068/1918   Allied Maritime Transport Council. Minutes of Meetings and various Memoranda
11/23971/1918   Tonnage Committee (Allied Maritime Transport Council) Minutes
15/42709/1918   Allied Shipping Situation June 1918
22/61067/1918   Inter Allied Control Bureau in London to be Constituted by the Governments of Great Britain, France, Italy, Japan, and the United States
22/61738/1918   Utilisation of tonnage
22/61759/1918   Tonnage Policy and Position 1917 and 1918
44/37639/1920   Survey of Transport Department work in the year 1st August 1914 to 31st July 1915
45/45611/1920   War Cabinet Reports on Work of Ministry of Shipping 1917–18
67/29597/1922   Historical notes

Printed Sources

Primary Sources

Almanach national (Paris 1910, 1913)

d'Avenel, G., 'Fonctionnaires de l'Etat et des administrations privées', *La Revue des Deux Mondes*, 15 July 1906

Barthélemy, J., 'Du renforcement du Pouvoir Exécutif en temps de guerre' — 'Le contrôle parlementaire en temps de guerre' in G. Jeze (ed.) *Problèmes de politique et finances de guerre* (Paris, 1916)

Buisson, F., *La Politique radicale* (Paris, 1908)

Chardon, H., *L'Administration de la France. Les Fonctionnaires* (Paris, 1908)

Clémentel, E., *L'Ame celtique, Michelet* (Clermont-Ferrand, 1898)

——, 'Discours de M. Clementel', *Le Musée social* (Paris, 1 May 1918)

——, *La France et la politique économique interalliée* (Paris, 1931)

Comité des Forges de France. Assemblée générale ordinaire du 16 Mai 1918. Rapport de la commission de direction (Paris, 1918)

'Les Consortiums', *Le Temps*, 12 September 1918

En écoutant Etienne Clémentel (Riom, 1964)

'Ententes ou Consortiums? M. Lémery donne la parole aux producteurs et nous dit son plan de réforme', *Information*, 29 June 1918

L'Illustration (Paris, 1914–18)

Jaurés, J., *Oeuvres*, vi, *Etudes socialistes, 1897–1901* (Paris, 1933)

Jolly, J., *Dictionnaire des parlementaires Français*, 7 vols., (Paris, 1960–72)

Journal officiel (Paris, 1906–20)

Justin, *La Responsabilité du parlement sous le régime parlementaire* (Paris, 1918)

Loucheur, L., *Carnets secrets 1908–1932* (Brussels, 1962)

Manteilhet, J., *Vers une économie nationale. Le Régime des consortiums* (Paris, 1918, privately printed)

Ministère du Commerce et de l'Industrie, *Bulletin Consulaire Français*, volume XI, 1886 (Paris, 1886)

Ministère du Commerce, *Rapport général sur l'industrie Française, sa situation, son avenir*, 3 vols., (Paris, 1919)

'La Mise en réquisition générale', *Le Temps*, 25 June 1917

L'Oeuvre artistique d'Etienne Clémentel (Paris, 1926)

L'Oeuvre d'un ministre du Gouvernement de Défense Nationale, 1915–1919 (Paris, 1919)

Pinot, R., *Le Comité des Forges au service de la nation (Août 1914–Novembre 1918)* (Paris, 1919)

——, *Les Industries métallurgiques et la guerre* (Paris, 1916)

Poincaré, R., *Au service de la France*, 10 vols., (Paris, 1926–33)

Projet de réorganisation des services du Ministère du Commerce et de l'Industrie (Paris, 1917)

'La Question des consortiums devant le comité parlementaire français du commerce', *Le Temps*, 25 June 1918

Qui Etes-Vous? Annuaire des contemporains français et étrangers 1909–1910 (Paris, 1910)

Ribot, A., *Journal d'Alexandre Ribot et correspondances inédites 1914–1922* (Paris, 1936)
——, *Letters to a Friend* (London, 1925)
Romains, J., *Les Hommes de bonne volonté*, xvi, *Verdun* (Paris, 1938)
Romier, M., *Rapport sur les consortiums* (Paris, 1918)
Samuel, R. and G. Bonét-Maury, *Les Parlementaires français 1900–1914* (Paris, 1914)
Tout-Paris. Annuaire de la société parisienne (Paris, 1914, 1922, 1927)

Secondary Sources

Aftalion, A., *The Effect of the War upon French Commercial Policy* (Oxford, 1923)
——, *L'Industrie textile en France pendant la guerre* (Paris, 1925)
Albert Thomas 1878–1932 (Annemasse, 1932)
Albert Thomas vivant (Geneva, 1957)
Annuaire-Adresses des sociétés anonymes (Paris, 1919)
Annuaire-Chaix. Les principales sociétés par actions (Paris, 1913, 1922, 1927)
Arnaud, R., 'Etienne Clémentel, président-fondateur de la Chambre de Commerce Internationale, 1864–1936' (unpublished article, Paris, 1969)
Augé-Laribé, M., *L'Agriculture pendant la guerre* (Paris, 1925)
Barthélemy, J., *Essai sur le travail parlementaire et le système des commissions* (Paris, 1934)
——, *Le Gouvernement de la France* (Paris, 1924)
Baum, W., *The French Economy and the State* (Princeton, 1958)
Beau de Loménie, E., *Les Responsabilités des dynasties bourgeoises* (Paris, 1943–1963), 4 vols.
Bell, P., 'The Direction of Entrepreneurial Explorations. A Review Article' *Explorations in Entrepreneurial History/Second Series*, vol. 5, no. 1, Fall 1967
Bloch, C., *Bibliographie méthodique de l'histoire économique et sociale de la France pendant la guerre* (Paris, 1925)
Bloch, R., *Histoire du Parti Radical-Socialiste* (Paris, 1968)
Bonnefous, G., *Histoire Politique de la Troisième République* (2nd edn., Paris, 1965, 1967), 2 vols.
Boswell, J., B. Johns, 'Patriots or Profiteers? British Businessmen and the First World War' *The Journal of European Economic History*, vol. 11, no. 2, Spring 1982
Boudet, J. (ed.), *Le Monde des affaires en France de 1830 à nos jours* (Paris, 1952)
Bruun, G., *Clemenceau* (Hamden, Connecticut, 1968)
Burke, K. (ed.), *War and the State: The Transformation of British Government, 1914–1919* (London, 1982)
Cameron, R., 'L'économie francais: passé, présent, avenir', *Annales*, September–October 1970
——, 'Profit croissance et stagnation en France au xixe Siècle', *Economie appliquée*, no. 1, 1957
Carnot, R., *L'Etatisme industriel* (Paris, 1920)

Chastenet, J., *Histoire de la Troisième République* (Paris, 1955)
Chenot, B., *Les Entreprises nationalisées* (Paris, 1956)
——, *Organisation économique de l'état* (Paris, 1951)
Choffel, J., *Saint-Gobain. Du miroir à l'atome* (Paris, 1960)
Clapham, J., *The Economic Development of France and Germany 1815–1914* (4th edn., Cambridge, 1951)
'Etienne Clémentel', *Le Temps*, 26 December 1936
Etienne Clémentel, préface d'Edmond Haraucourt (Paris, 1932)
1665–1965, Compagnie de Saint-Gobain (Paris, 1965)
Coston, H., *Le Retour des "200 Familles"* (Paris, 1960)
Courthéoux, J.-P., 'Les pouvoirs économiques et sociaux dans un secteur industriel: la sidérugie,' *Revue d'Histoire Economique et Sociale*, no. 3, 1960
Le Crapouillot (Paris, 1916–35)
Crouzet, F., 'Essai de construction d'un indice annuel de la production industrielle française au xixe siecle', *Annales*, 1970, 56–99
Crozier, M., *Le Phénomène bureaucratique* (Paris, 1963)
Dearle, N., *Dictionary of Official War-Time Organizations* (London, 1928)
Delemer, A., *Le Bilan de l'Etatisme* (Paris, 1922)
Doukas, K., *The French Railroads and the State* (New York, 1945)
Ducasse, A., J. Meyer, G. Perreux, *Vie et mort des Français 1914–1918* (Paris, 1959)
Fairlie, J., *British War Administration* (New York, 1919)
Farrar, M., 'Politics vs Patriotism: Alexandre Millerand as French Minister of War', *French Historical Studies*, vol. XI, no. 4, Fall 1980
Fayle, C., *Seaborne Trade*, 2 vols. (London, 1920)
Feldman, G., *Army, Industry, and Labour in Germany 1914–1918* (Princeton, 1966)
——, *Iron and Steel in the German Inflation, 1916–1923* (Princeton, 1977)
Ferrat, A., *La République à refaire* (Paris, 1945)
Ferry, A., *Les Carnets secrets, 1914–1918* (Paris, 1957)
Fontaine, A., *L'Industrie française pendant la guerre* (Paris, 1924)
François-Poncet, A., *La Vie et l'oeuvre de Robert Pinot* (Paris, 1927)
Gerschenkron, A., *Continuity in History and Other Essays* (Cambridge, Mass., 1968)
——, *Economic Backwardness in Historical Perspective* (Cambridge, Mass., 1962)
Gide, C. (ed.), *Effects of the War on French Economic Life* (Oxford, 1923)
Gignoux, C.-J., *L'Arsenal de Roanne et l'Etat industriel de Guerre* (Roanne, 1920)
——, *L'Economie française entre les deux guerres 1919–1939* (Paris, 1942)
Gille, B., *La sidérugie française au xixe siècle* (Geneva, 1968)
Girault, R., 'Pour un portrait nouveau de l'homme d'affaires français vers 1914', *Revue d'Histoire Moderne et Contemporaine*, T.xvi, July–September 1969
Goguel, F., *La Politique des partis sous la IIIe République* (3rd edn., Paris, 1958)
Gooch, R., *The French Parliamentary Committee System* (New York, 1935)

Gournay, B., *Introduction à la science administrative* (Paris, 1966)
Grabau, T., 'Industrial Reconstruction in French World War I' (Indiana University Ph.D. thesis, 1976)
Grandin, A., *Bibliographie générale des sciences juridiques, politiques, économiques et sociales de 1800 à 1925–1926*, 3 vols. (Paris, 1926)
Grégoire, R., *The French Civil Service* (Brussels, 1964)
Gros, G., *La République des coquins* (Paris, 1934)
Halévy, D., *La République des comités* (Paris, 1934)
Hamon, A., *Les Maîtres de la France*, 2 vols. (Paris, 1936–7)
Hardach, G., *The First World War, 1914–1918* (Berkeley, 1977)
Hartry, G., *Renault, usine de guerre, 1914–1918* (Paris, 1978)
_____, *Louis Renault, Patron absolu* (Paris, 1982)
Hauser, H., *Le Problème du régionalisme. L'organisation gouvernementale pendant la guerre* (Paris, 1924)
Hinds, L., 'La Coopération économique entre la France et la Grande Bretagne pendant la Première Guerre Mondiale' (Paris thèse de doctorat de troisième cycle, n. d.)
History of the Ministry of Munitions, 6 vols. (London, 1922)
Hohenberg, P., *Chemicals in Western Europe 1850–1914* (Chicago, 1967)
Huber, M., *La Population de France pendant la guerre* (Paris, 1931)
Hurwitz, S., *State Intervention in Great Britain* (London, 1968)
Jeanneney, J.-N., *François de Wendel en république: l'argent et le pouvoir, 1914–1940* (Paris, 1976)
de Jouvenal, R., *La République des Camarades* (Paris, 1914)
Kaiser, J., *Les grandes batailles du radicalisme 1820–1901* (Paris, 1962)
Kemp, T., *Economic Forces in French History* (London, 1971)
_____, *The French Economy 1913–1939* (London, 1972)
Kindleberger, C., *Economic Growth in France and Britain 1851–1950* (Cambridge, Mass., 1964)
King, J., *Generals and Politicians. Conflict between France's High Command, Parliament, and Government, 1914–1918* (Berkeley, 1951)
Kuisel, R., *Ernest Mercier, French Technocrat* (Berkeley, 1967)
_____, *Capitalism and the State in Modern France* (Cambridge, 1981)
Lalumière, P., *L'Inspection des Finances* (Paris, 1959)
Landes, D., 'French Entrepreneurship and Industrial Growth in the Nineteenth Century', *The Journal of Economic History*, ix, no. 1 (New York, 1949)
_____, 'Observations on France: Economy, Society, and Polity', *World Politics*, ix (Princeton, 1957)
_____, 'French Business and the Businessman: A Social and Cultural Analysis' in E.M. Earle (ed.) *Modern France* (New York, 1964)
Larigaldie, P., *Les Organismes interalliés de contrôle économique* (Paris, 1925)
Laufenburger, H., *L'Intervention de l'état en matière économique* (Paris, 1939)
Lefranc, G., *Le Mouvement socialiste sous la Troisième République* (Paris, 1963)
Legendre, P., *L'Administration du XVIII Siècle à nos jours* (Paris, 1969)
Lévy-Leboyer, M., 'La Croissance économique en France au xixe Siècle',

Annales, 1968, 788–807
Lloyd, E., *Experiments in State Control at the War Office and the Ministry of Food* (Oxford, 1924)
Lloyd George, D., *War Memoirs*, 6 vols. (London, 1934)
Maier, C., *Recasting Bourgeois Europe* (Princeton, 1975)
Marcellin, L., *Politique et Politiciens pendant la guerre* (Paris, 1923)
Marche, L., *Le Mouvement des prix et des salaires pendant la guerre* (Paris, 1925)
Markovitch, T., 'L'Industrie française de 1789 à 1964', *Cahiers de l'Institut de Science économique appliquée*, AF 4, no. 163, (July, 1965)
Marwick, A., *The Deluge. British Society and the First World War* (London, 1967)
Mauro, F., 'La Pensée économique de Jean Jaurès', *Jean Jaurès*, présenté par Vincent Auriol (Paris, 1962)
Mayer, A., *The Persistence of the Old Regime: Europe to the Great War* (New York, 1981)
McNeill, W., *The Pursuit of Power. Technology, Armed Force and Society since A.D.1000* (Chicago, 1982)
Miguel, P., *Poincaré* (Paris, 1961)
Monnet, J., *Mémoires* (Paris, 1976)
Naville, P., *L'Etat entrepreneur. Le cas de la régie Renault* (Paris, 1971)
Nicolet, C., *Le Radicalisme* (Paris, 1967)
Olphe-Galliard, G., *Histoire économique et financier de la guerre* (Paris, 1925)
Osgoode, S., *French Royalism since 1870* (The Hague, 1970)
Oualid, W., C. Picquenard, *La Guerre et le travail. Salaires et tarifs* (Paris, 1928)
Paxton, R., *Vichy France. Old Guard and New Order* (New York, 1972)
Palmade, G., *French Capitalism in the Nineteenth Century* (Newton Abbot, 1972)
Peiter, H., 'Institutions and Attitudes: The Consolidation of the Business Community in Bourgeois France, 1880–1914', *Journal of Social History*, vol. 9, no. 4, June 1976
———, 'Men of Goodwill: French Businessmen and the First World War' (University of Michigan Ph.D. thesis 1973)
Perreux, G., *La Guerre de 1914–1918* (Paris, 1964)
———, *La Vie quotidienne des civils en France pendant la Grande Guerre* (Paris, 1966)
Piatier, A., *L'Economie de guerre* (Paris, 1939)
Piettre, A., *Economie dirigée d'hier et d'aujourd'hui du colbertisme à notre temps* (Paris, 1947)
Pinot, P., *Le Contrôle du ravitaillement de la population civile* (Paris, 1925)
Pipkin, C., *Social Politics and Modern Democracies*, 2 vols. (New York, 1931)
Pitts, J., 'The Bourgeois Family and French Economic Retardation' (Harvard University Ph.D. thesis 1957)
———, 'Continuity and Change in Bourgeois France' in S. Hoffman (ed.), *France: Change and Tradition* (London, 1963).
Poidevin, R., *Les Relations économiques et financières entre la France et*

l'Allemagne de 1898 à 1914 (Paris, 1969)
Priouret, R., *Origines du patronat français* (Paris, 1963)
Puget, H., *Bibliographie de la fonction publique et du personnel civil des administrations publiques* (Paris, 1948)
Reclus, M., *Grandeur de 'La Troisième'* (Paris, 1948)
Rèmond, R., *La Droite en France*, vol. 1 (3rd edn., Paris, 1968)
Renouvin, P., *La Crise Européene et la Première Guerre Mondiale* (5th edn., Paris, 1969)
_____, *Les Formes du gouvernement de guerre* (Paris, 1925)
Ridley, F., J. Blondel, *Public Administration in France* (London, 1964)
Rist, C., *L'Evolution de l'économie française 1910–1937. Tableaux statistiques* (Paris, 1937)
Sait, E., *Government and Politics of France* (London, 1920)
Salter, J., *Allied Shipping Control* (Oxford, 1921)
Sauvy, A., *Histoire économique de la France entre les deux guerres*, 3 vols. (Paris, 1965–72)
Sawyer, J., 'The Entrepreneur and the Social Order. France and the United States' in W. Miller (ed.), *Men in Business* (Cambridge, Mass., 1952)
Schaper, B., *Albert Thomas, trente ans de réformisme social* (Assen, 1959)
Scott, J., *Republican Ideas and the Liberal Tradition in France 1870–1914* (New York, 1966)
Sharp, W., *The French Civil Service: Bureaucracy in Transition* (New York, 1931)
_____, *The Government of the French Republic* (New York, 1938)
Siegfried, A., *Tableau des partis politiques en France* (Paris, 1930)
Soltau, R., *French Parties and Politics 1870–1921* (New York, 1965)
Soulié, M., *La Vie politique d'Edouard Herriot* (Paris, 1962)
Soulier, A., *L'Instabilité ministérielle sous la Troisième République* (Paris, 1939)
Suarez, G., *Briand*, 5 vols. (Paris, 1938)
Thibaudet, A., *Les Idées politiques de la France* (Paris, 1932)
Trachtenberg, M., "'A New Economic Order': Etienne Clémentel and French Economic Diplomacy during the First World War", *French Historical Studies*, vol. X, no. 2, Fall 1977
_____, *Reparation in World Politics: France and European Economic Diplomacy, 1916–1923* (New York, 1980)
Ventenat, M., *L'Expérience des nationalisations* (Paris, 1947)
Viallate, A., *L'Activité économique en France de la fin du xviiie siècle à nos jours* (Paris, 1937)
Vic, J., *La Littérature de guerre*, 5 vols. (Paris, 1923)
Who's Who in France (9th edn., Paris, 1969)
Willard, C., *Les Guesdistes* (Paris, 1965)
Winckler, H. (ed.), *Organisierter Kapitalismus: Veraussetzunger und Anfänge* (Gottingen, 1974)
Wormser, G., *La République de Clemenceau* (Paris, 1961)
Zeldin, T., *France 1848–1945*, vol. 1, (Oxford, 1973)
Zévaès, A., *Jean Jaurès* (Paris, 1941)

Index